CASSELL LANGUAGE GUIDES

GERMAN

Other titles in the Cassell Language Guides series are:

FRENCH Valerie Worth-Stylianou
ITALIAN Noemi Messora
SPANISH Anthony Gooch

CASSELL LANGUAGE GUIDES

GERMAN

A handbook of grammar, current usage and word power

Revised paperback edition
with exercises by Geran Jones

Christine Eckhard-Black
Ruth Whittle

CASSELL

May this book contribute to the mutual understanding of English and German speakers.

Cassell
Wellington House
125 Strand, London WC2R 0BB, England

215 Park Avenue South
New York, NY 10003 USA

Hardback edition first published 1992
This paperback edition with exercises first published 1995

British Library Cataloguing-in-Publication Data
Eckhard-Black, Christine
Cassell language guides: German. A handbook of grammar, current usage and word power.
I.Title II. Whittle, Ruth III. Series
438.2

ISBN 0–304–33471–5

Typeset by Litho Link Ltd, Welshpool, Powys, Wales
Printed and bound in Great Britain by Redwood Books Limited, Trowbridge, Wiltshire

Contents

Introduction

Cassell is launching this completely new series of Language Guides to meet the needs of English-speaking students and users of German. We are assuming that you, the reader, have some grasp of the basics of German, and want to improve your command of the spoken and written language. You may be studying German as part of your education, or it may be that in your professional capacity you have dealings with German-speaking colleagues or customers, or you simply enjoy using your German when on holiday abroad. We believe that the unique three-part structure of our series is equipped to meet your needs.

Part 1 provides a concise reference grammar. We include all the main areas treated in full-length reference grammars, with a particular focus on those areas which cause problems to the English-speaking learner. Explanations are always followed by examples from contemporary usage. The index to the book enables you to locate sections on specific points easily.

Part 2 demonstrates how to use the contemporary language in specific contexts. There are forty sections on key functions of language, such as giving advice, expressing agreement, making apologies. These sections aim to make you aware of the importance of the sociolinguistic context, i.e. that we adapt the way we express ourselves according to the situation we are in and the person to whom we are speaking. If you were asking for advice in English, you would be likely to express yourself differently when talking to a friend as opposed to an official whom you had never met before. Of course, similar nuances exist in German, and for the foreign speaker it is important to develop sensitivity to the right expression for a particular context. So the 'register' or degree of formality of expressions is indicated. The last twenty-two sections of Part 2 look at the language required for specific tasks: telephoning, writing letters, essays and CVs. Generous illustrations are given, again with attention to the context in which you are speaking or writing.

Part 3 concentrates on building up your word power in German. It offers a convenient bank of important idioms based on verbs, nouns, adjectives and adverbs. Other sections focus on particularly rich areas of vocabulary (synonyms, slang, *faux amis*, proverbs), or deal with key thematic areas relevant to various groups of readers (e.g. travel, finance, literature). Part 3 can be used for reference, if you come across a particular expression and want to track down its meaning, or as a basis from which to build up your own active vocabulary.

Since the series is aimed at English-speaking learners of German, one essential feature is the bilingual nature of the Language Guide. All examples, from short phrases to whole letters, are translated into English. So you can see at a glance what is being illustrated.

Finally, all our examples are drawn from authentic contemporary situations. This is the 'real' German that is spoken and written in German-speaking countries. To remind you of this, we include a number of illustrations which show German in action.

We hope you enjoy using this book: *Viel Spaß*!

VALERIE WORTH-STYLIANOU
Series Editor

Note to revised and extended edition

This revised edition of *Cassell Language Guides: German* contains a new section, Part 4, which gives exercises for you to practise the main points covered in Part 1, the concise reference grammar. The reader could either work through all the exercises systematically to achieve a complete revision of grammatical usage, or just concentrate on those that relate to areas found problematic. Each section of Part 4 corresponds to one or more of the sections of Part 1, and the cross-reference is given at the start of the section. We suggest you read through the relevant section or sections in Part 1 before doing the exercises.

In keeping with the bilingual and authentic focus of the rest of the book, Part 4 uses two types of exercise. Those labelled **A** require translation of individual sentences from English to German, and are designed to test a basic grasp of the grammatical point. Those labelled **B** require you to complete gaps or rewrite parts of authentic German texts, taken from a range of sources. As far as possible, we have indicated the author and title for books, and the titles of magazines and periodicals used. At the end of the book you will find a key with suggested answers for the exercises, but remember that these provide only *one* correct, idiomatic version. In some cases there may be another slightly different but correct answer.

CHRISTINE ECKHARD-BLACK
RUTH WHITTLE
January 1995

Acknowledgements

The authors would like to thank all those who have supported them in their aim, especially their families at home and abroad, past and present.

We are also grateful to Dr Valerie Worth-Stylianou and to Steve Cook, our editor, for initiating the project, as well as to friends and colleagues for help with proof-reading and for their valuable suggestions.

CHRISTINE ECKHARD-BLACK
RUTH WHITTLE
1992

Note to the reader

If you want to find out more about German pronunciation in general, or to check the pronunciation of a given word in one of our examples, we suggest you consult *Cassell's German–English Dictionary*, which offers a key to the pronunciation and gives the transcription of words according to the symbols of the International Phonetic Association.

The material presented in all three parts provides you with illustrations of key aspects of grammar, current usage and word power. If you would like to find out more about a particular topic, the list of books in the Bibliography (p. 584) will be useful.

Abbreviations and symbols

acc. / A	accusative
coll.	colloquial
dat. / D	dative
f.	feminine
[FA]	*faux amis* (see section 138)
gen. / G	genitive
m.	masculine
n.	neuter
nom. / N	nominative
pl.	plural
sg.	singular
< >	indicates the register of language, e.g. < formal >
*	irregular verbs (see the list at the end of the book)
◊	separable prefix (see section 34)
♦	inseparable prefix (see section 34)
! or !!	vulgar word or expression
★	potential confusion: beware!
≈	approximate equivalent

PART 1

A concise reference grammar

Ruth Whittle

Introduction to the parts of speech

The structure of every language consists of a number of building blocks. The rules according to which these blocks can be arranged make up the character of a particular language. The fundamental building block of any utterance is a **word**, e.g.:

a **noun**	*Haus*	house
often preceded by an **article**, which can be		
a **definite** article	*das Haus*	the house
or an **indefinite** article	*ein Haus*	a house
or a **demonstrative article**	*dieses / jenes Haus*	this / that house

Normally, a one-word sentence will not be sufficient to communicate a message. To express an action or a state of being the sentence requires a **verb**:

Das Haus ist schön.
The house is nice.

schön describes the noun and is called an **adjective**. The sentence above expresses a complimentary opinion about the noun. The sentence below describes an action:

Familie Schmitt kauft das schöne Haus.
The Schmitt family buys / is buying the nice house.

We can further differentiate this action by inserting a **modal verb**:

Familie Schmitt will das schöne Haus kaufen.
The Schmitt family wants to buy the nice house.

In these examples we can see that the verb is the foundation stone of the German language: verbs can bind a variable number of elements, relating different nouns to each other. In the example above, *kaufen* binds *Familie Schmitt* – the **subject** – and *das Haus* – the **object**.

Kaufen can in fact bind more than one object:

Familie Schmitt kauft ihrer Tochter ein schönes Haus.
The Schmitt family buys / is buying their daughter a nice house.

The role of each object is clear because in German each is in a different **case** (see section 5).

It is not always necessary to use a noun if it is clear who or what is being referred to. Then it is possible to replace the noun with a **pronoun**:

> *Sie kaufen es ihr.*
> They buy it for her.

In German there are numerous little words – used more often in the spoken than in the written language – which add flavour to an utterance without making it much longer. Their precise meaning in a given context depends to some extent on the way the word is stressed. Some examples of these **modal particles** are given below.

> *Er wollte das Haus doch kaufen.*
> But (I thought) he wanted to buy the house.

You might say this to express surprise at the news that your friend did not buy the house he had intended to buy.

> *Eigentlich wollte er nicht heiraten.*
> Originally (from all we knew) he did not want to get married.

Here, your friend did in fact marry, contrary to all expectations. An explanation of this change of heart might be phrased as:

> *Aber er fühlte sich doch zu allein.*
> But he felt too lonely after all.

The previous two examples are independent sentences, but as in English we could easily string them together:

> *Eigentlich wollte er nicht heiraten, aber er fühlte sich doch zu allein.*

Aber provides the link between the two sentences: it coordinates them and is therefore called a **coordinating conjunction**. Let us change the sentence slightly:

> *Er heiratete, weil er sich allein fühlte.*
> He married because he felt lonely.

Weil connects the main clause (*Er heiratete*) to the subordinate clause. The latter cannot stand on its own. Hence, *weil* is a **subordinating conjunction**. Note that *weil* sends the verb of the **subordinate clause** to the end of the clause. This is a specific feature of German word order and may well cause problems for the learner (cf. section 56). In spoken German you will frequently hear the 'wrong' word order from natives (especially with *weil*), but this should not encourage you to do the same. As a foreigner, you may well be corrected if you make 'mistakes' such as choosing the colloquial word order, even though this would be overlooked in a native speaker. One of the aims of the book is therefore to provide you with useful ideas about spoken German and point out possible pitfalls.

A further source of difficulties are German **prepositions**, especially in verbal constructions:

Er wartet eine Stunde am Bahnhof auf sie.
He waits for her at the station for an hour.

The construction *warten auf* has to be learnt just as 'to wait for' must be learnt. There are relatively few logical combinations of verbs and prepositions.

NOUNS

1 Gender

German has three genders: masculine, feminine and neuter. The grammatical gender rarely reflects the natural gender and hence needs to be learnt.

(a) Natural and grammatical gender are identical

Family relationships

die Mutter mother	*der Onkel* uncle
der Vater father	*die Enkelin* grand-daughter
die Tochter daughter	*der Enkel* grandson
der Sohn son	*die Kusine / Cousine* cousin (f.)
die Tante aunt	*der Cousin* cousin (m.)

Professions

For women the ending *-in* is added to the masculine term, e.g.:

der Lehrer / die Lehrerin teacher

Occasionally the choice of ending for the female title contains an all-important distinction between one job function and another. For example, a hairdresser is *der Friseur* and his female counterpart is *die Friseuse*, whereas *die Masseurin* is the feminine equivalent of *der Masseur* (a qualification recognized by the Chamber of Commerce). *Die Masseuse*, on the other hand, can mean prostitute.

In the age of equal opportunities for men and women there are linguistic areas of doubt and confusion. Thus, whilst you may mention that *eine Professorin* now has a certain chair, you write to her as *Sehr geehrte Frau Professor*.

Progressive journalists employ the term *Diplom-Kauffrau* as the female equivalent for *Diplom-Kaufmann* (a person with a university degree in economics) and a further alternative is *Diplom-Kaufmännin*. However, neither term has been officially adopted in German universities yet. When in doubt, you need to find out about the exact job title.

(b) Grammatical gender contradicts natural gender

These cases are not very frequent and can be learnt easily:

das Kind child
das Mädchen girl
das Mannequin mannequin
das Fräulein miss
das Opfer victim (m. / f.)

When these words are replaced by a pronoun, this will often reflect the natural rather than the grammatical gender.

Fräulein, the diminutive of *Frau* and grammatically neuter, has caused protest not only among feminists (there is no *Herrlein* for bachelors!). Unlike *Mademoiselle* in France and 'Miss' in Anglo-Saxon countries, this term is now officially outcast. Thus, all girls will be called *Frau* (+ name) as soon as they are no longer addressed by their first name – probably from around the age of eighteen, though it depends on the work environment.

N.B. Diminutives ending in *-chen* or *-lein* are always neuter, whatever the natural gender (see below).

Animal terms that are used when talking about the species rather than about the gender of a particular animal are also neuter.

das Eichhörnchen squirrel
das Huhn chicken
das Kalb calf
das Kaninchen rabbit
das Krokodil crocodile
das Meerschweinchen guinea pig
das Nashorn rhinoceros
das Pferd horse
das Rind cattle

(c) Rules for the grammatical gender

Do not despair! It is not necessary to learn the gender of every noun individually. Certain groups of nouns can be classed together:

Masculine nouns: *der*

- Seasons of the year, months, days of the week, points of the compass:

der Frühling spring
der Mai May
der Montag Monday
der Norden north
(EXCEPTION: *das Frühjahr* spring)

- Names of mountains:

  der Montblanc, der Großglockner
  (EXCEPTION: *das Matterhorn*)

- Most nouns derived from strong verbs:

  der Zug draught, train   *der Tritt* kick

- Nouns ending in *-ig, -ling, -ant, -er, -ismus, -or*:

  der Pfennig penny
  der Lehrling apprentice
  der Protestant Lutheran
  der Sprecher speaker
  der Marxismus marxism
  der Tutor tutor
  (EXCEPTION: *das Restaurant* restaurant)

Feminine nouns: *die*

- Nouns with derived (i.e. Latinate) endings: *-ion, -anz, -enz, -ie, -ik, -ur, -age, -ette*

  die Information information
  die Vakanz vacancy (for a job, especially in Austria)
  die Lizenz licence
  die Kopie copy
  die Chronik chronicle
  die Figur figure
  die Garage garage (in Austria and Switzerland also petrol station)
  die Diskette floppy disk

- Nouns ending in *-heit, -keit, -ei, -schaft, -ung, -tät, -nis*:

  die Krankheit illness
  die Wirklichkeit reality
  die Malerei painting
  die Freundschaft friendship
  die Nahrung food
  die Fakultät faculty
  die Kenntnis knowledge

- Cardinal numbers used as a noun (cf. section 140), e.g. in a game:

  Ich habe eine Eins gewürfelt.
  I have thrown a one.

- Names of aeroplanes and ships:

  die Boeing 747, die Alte Liebe

Neuter nouns: *das*

- Names of continents, countries, islands and place names, which are used without an article when not accompanied by an adjective:

  Europa
  Deutschland

Helgoland
Bonn, Berlin, London

- Names of hotels, cinemas, and cafés:

  das Hilton, das Savoy, das Vier Jahreszeiten
  das Metropol
  das Kempinski

- Chemicals ending in *-in* and *-ol*:

  das Dioxin dioxine
  das Benzol benzene, benzole

- Letters of the alphabet:

  das Ypsilon y

- Diminutives ending in *-lein* and *-chen*:

  der Baum → *das Bäumchen* (small) tree
  die Maus → *das Mäuschen* (small) mouse
  der Mann → *das Männlein* (small) man
  also: *das Männchen*

- Nouns derived directly from infinitives:

  Rauchen ist hier verboten. No smoking.

- Nouns ending in *-um*, *-ment*, *-ett*, and *-icht*

  das Wachstum growth
  das Siechtum long illness, probably without recovery
  das Fundament foundation
  das Argument argument/reason
  das Lazarett military hospital
  das Gewicht weight
  (EXCEPTIONS: *der Reichtum* wealth
  der Irrtum error)

(d) Gender of compound nouns

In compound nouns, it is always the second (or last) part of the word that determines the gender (and also the plural form):

die Ware + *der Handel* → *der Warenhandel*
die Matter (river) + *das Horn* → *das Matterhorn*
das Auto + *die Fahrt* → *die Autofahrt*

(e) Gender and semantic distinction

The gender of some nouns varies. In some instances there is no difference in meaning, e.g.:

der/das Meter metre
der/das Liter litre
der/das Kristall crystal (referring to the raw material)

But there are other nouns where a change in gender results in a change in meaning, e.g.:

der Alp ghost (as in *Alptraum*, nightmare)
die Alp pasture up on the mountain

der Band volume
das Band ribbon/ligament/ (conveyor) belt/bond

der Bulle bull
die Bulle papal bull

der Laster truck/lorry
das Laster vice

die Mark currency
das Mark marrow

der Mast ship mast
die Mast intensive feeding of animals

der Otter otter
die Otter viper

der See lake
die See sea

To complicate matters further, the gender (and meaning) of some nouns varies from country to country. In some instances this is because of a difference in ideology.

der Militär soldier (former GDR)
das Militär armed forces (generally used term)

das Kaffee café (former GDR), now spelt *Café* if neuter
der Kaffee coffee (generally used term)

2 The article

German differentiates between the **definite** article ('the') and the **indefinite** article ('a'), just as English does. However, since the structure of the German language is synthetic rather than analytic (i.e. the function of each part of a sentence is determined by word endings rather than position and prepositions), relations must be made clear by the use of different cases (see section 5). The article together with the noun (and possibly the adjective that goes with a particular noun) must therefore be put into the appropriate case, i.e. it needs to be declined.

(a) The definite article

	SINGULAR			PLURAL
	m.	f.	n.	(m. / f. / n.)
N	*der*	*die*	*das*	*die*
A	*den*	*die*	*das*	*die*
G	*des*	*der*	*des*	*der*
D	*dem*	*der*	*dem*	*den*

(b) The indefinite article

As in English, there is **no plural** for the indefinite article. This phenomenon is also known as 'zero article'.

	m.	f.	n.
N	*ein*	*eine*	*ein*
A	*einen*	*eine*	*ein*
G	*eines*	*einer*	*eines*
D	*einem*	*einer*	*einem*

There is however a plural form for other article words such as *kein* (see section 11):

N	*keine*
A	*keine*
G	*keiner*
D	*keinen*

The declensions of the indefinite and definite articles must be memorized, but this is not as difficult as it seems since both sets of endings change in the same way. Therefore you only need to learn the nominative of each set and the other inflections of one set only.

Both definite and indefinite articles can be replaced by pronouns. Pronouns that follow the declension of the definite article will be referred to as ***der*-words**, those which follow the indefinite article as ***ein*-words.**

(c) *der*-words

Below, only the masculine, feminine and neuter nominative forms are given.

Demonstrative pronouns (see also section 9)

dieser, diese, dieses this
jener, jene, jenes that
derjenige, diejenige, dasjenige that (one)
derselbe, dieselbe, dasselbe the same (one)

Ich begrüße all diejenigen, die trotz des schlechten Wetters gekommen sind.
I welcome all (those) who have come despite the bad weather.

Er mußte immer wieder dasselbe machen.
He had to do the same (thing) again and again.

★ N.B. Both parts of the compound pronouns need to be declined, but the endings of *-jenige* and *-selbe* follow the *ein*-words (cf. section 9).

Indefinite pronouns (see also section 11)

irgendeiner, irgendeine, irgendeines some/any
mancher, manche, manches (pl. *manche*) some
welcher, welche, welches (pl. *welche*) which
keiner, keine, keins (pl. *keine*) no one

Manche Kinder konnten schon mit fünf Jahren lesen.
Some children could already read when they were five.

Keiner hatte an diese Möglichkeit gedacht.
No one had thought of this possibility.

Plural indefinite pronouns

beide both
sämtliche all, each
irgendwelche some / any

Er mochte beide. He liked both (of them).

Possessive pronouns (see also section 7)

meiner, meine, meins (etc.) mine (etc.)

Das ist mein Buch. Ist dies hier deins?
This is my book. Is this one yours?

(d) *ein*-words

- The possessive adjective (*mein*, *dein*, *sein*, etc.)

- Indefinite pronouns used as adjective or article (masculine, feminine and neuter nominative forms listed):

kein, keine, kein no / not any
irgendein, irgendeine, irgendein some / any

(e) Use of the article

The use of the article in German is very similar to its use in English. However, differences exist in four main areas.

- There is **no notional plural**, i.e. if a noun has a singular ending then the article and the verb ending will be singular, even if you think of the noun as plural:

Die Polizei beobachtet (sg.) *den Verkehr.*
The police **are** (pl.) monitoring the traffic.

- **Professions** take no article in German:

Er ist Lehrer. He is **a** teacher.

However:

Er ist der Lehrer meiner Tochter.
He is my daughter's teacher.

Here, *Lehrer* is referring to a particular person rather than to the profession as such.

- The same holds true for the playing of **instruments**:

Sie spielt Klavier. She plays **the** piano.

If you add a qualifying adverbial phrase, you can say:

Sie spielt sehr schön Klavier.
She plays the piano very well.

But in nineteenth-century German literature you may well find sentences such as:

Sie spielt die Violine sehrschön.
She plays the violin very beautifully.

• References to countries, continents and regions often cause problems as far as gender and number are concerned.

No article is required before names of towns and before the following countries, continents and areas, but you need to know the gender if you wish to replace the name of the country, continent etc. with a pronoun. (All towns are neuter and so are replaced by **es** if you want to use a pronoun rather than a noun. *Den Haag* is used with an article.)

	MASCULINE	NEUTER
Countries	*Irak*	*Belgien* Belgium
	Iran	*Bulgarien* Bulgaria
		Deutschland Germany
		Frankreich France
		Großbritannien GB
		Ireland
		Japan
		Korea
		Luxemburg
		Polen Poland
		Rumänien Romania
		Rußland Russia
		Thailand
		Ungarn Hungary
Continents		*Afrika*
		Amerika
		Asien
		Australien
Areas		*Bayern* Bavaria
		Burgund Burgundy
		Galizien Galicia

Certain areas or countries are used **with** the article, for example:

	MASCULINE	FEMININE	NEUTER
Countries	*der Libanon* Lebanon	*die Mongolei* Mongolia *die Schweiz* Switzerland *die Tschechische Republik* Czech Republic *die Türkei* Turkey	
Areas	*der Balkan* the Balkans *der Bodensee* (and all other lakes) *der Ferne Osten* Far East *der Mittlere Osten* S.W. Asia (incl. Nepal and Afghanistan) *der Nahe Osten* Middle East *der Schwarzwald* Black Forest	*die Antarktis* Antarctic *die Arktis* Arctic *die Europäische Gemeinschaft* EC *die Sowjetunion* (former) Soviet Union	*das Baltikum* Baltic States
Some French regions	*der Jura*	*die Dordogne*	*das Languedoc*

The following countries are **plurals** and are **preceded by the article:**

die Benelux-Länder Benelux countries
die Niederlande Netherlands
die Philippinen Philippines
die Vereinigten Staaten (or *die USA*) United States

also:

die Golfstaaten Gulf States
die Vereinten Nationen United Nations

3 Formation of the plural

In English and French, the plural form is often simply indicated by adding an *-s* to the singular form. Unfortunately, matters are not quite so easy in German. There are basically five ways to form the plural:

(i) No change or only change to umlaut (ä, ö, ü)

der Lehrer / die Lehrer teacher / teachers

This pattern is valid for nouns ending in *-er*, if they derive from verbs, e.g. *der Lehrer* (from *lehren*), *der Arbeiter* (from *arbeiten*), etc.

All diminutives ending in *-chen* and *-lein* are identical in singular and plural:

das Mädchen / die Mädchen girl / girls
das Kindlein / die Kindlein little child / little children

Where the stem vowel of a masculine noun is *a* or *o* and the noun ends in *-el* or *-en*, there is also no plural ending, but in many cases a change from vowel to corresponding vowel + umlaut.

der Bogen / die Bögen bow / bows
der Apfel / die Äpfel apple / apples

(ii) Plural -e or umlaut + -e

Many masculine and neuter monosyllabic and compound nouns with a monosyllable at the end fall into this category, but it is not possible to give a hard and fast rule:

der Brief / die Briefe letter / letters
der Arzt / die Ärzte doctor / doctors
der Bahnhof / die Bahnhöfe railway station / stations

Nouns ending in -är, *-eur*(m.), *-ent*:

der Millionär / die Millionäre millionaire / millionaires
der Friseur / die Friseure hairdresser / hairdressers
das Argument / die Argumente argument / arguments

★ N.B. The *ß* at the end of a noun changes to *ss* in the plural when it is preceded by a short vowel:

der Fluß / die Flüsse river / rivers

Also, nouns ending in *-nis* will change to *-nisse*:

das Zeugnis / die Zeugnisse (school) report / reports

(iii) Plural *-(e)n*

It is particularly helpful to learn this pattern since it is the most common one.

All feminine nouns ending in *-e* take an *-n* in the plural:

die Dame / die Damen lady / ladies

All nouns ending in *-ung*, *-heit*, *-keit*, *-schaft* and *-ei* take *-en*:

die Entschuldigung / die Entschuldigungen excuse / excuses
die Bosheit / die Bosheiten wickedness
die Freundlichkeit / die Freundlichkeiten friendliness
die Gemeinschaft / die Gemeinschaften community / communities
die Partei / die Parteien party / parties

In job titles for women *-in* becomes *-innen*:

die Journalistin / die Journalistinnen
(woman) journalist / journalists

Nouns ending in *-ent*, *-oge*, *-ist*, *-ant*, *-enz*, *-ie*, *-ik*, *-ion*, *-tät*, *-um*:

der Referent / die Referenten speaker / speakers (at a conference)
der Pädagoge / die Pädagogen educationalist / educationalists
der Komponist / die Komponisten composer / composers
der Lieferant / die Lieferanten distributor / distributors
die Referenz / die Referenzen reference / references
die Kompanie / die Kompanien company / companies
die Chronik / die Chroniken chronicle / chronicles
die Aktion / die Aktionen action / actions
die Universität / die Universitäten university / universities
das Museum / die Museen‡ museum / museums

‡ The *-um* in the singular becomes *-en* in the plural.

(iv) Plural *-er* or umlaut + *-er*

The majority of nouns in this category are neuter monosyllables, e.g.:

das Bild / die Bilder picture / pictures
das Buch / die Bücher book / books

(v) Plural *-s*

There is no general rule to say which words take an *-s* for their plural form, but they tend to be nouns derived from English, French and Italian which have come into the German language in the twentieth century.

das Büro office
der Chef boss
das Detail detail
das Kino cinema
das Musical musical
der Park park
die Pipeline pipeline
das Radio (Swiss German: *der Radio*) radio
der Refrain chorus / refrain
das Repertoire repertoire
der Rowdy hooligan, vandal
die Show show
die Single single (record)
der Slogan slogan
das Spray spray
das Studio studio
der Teddy teddy-bear
der Teeny teenager < slang >
das Ticket ticket
das Photo photo

Endings derived from Latin or Greek

Apart from nouns which belong to one of these patterns, some words still have endings which derive directly from Latin or Greek. Only a few examples are given here and it should be stressed that the notion of a 'correct' plural in these cases may vary from country to country.

Plural *-a*

das Genus / die Genera gender / genders
das Lexikon / die Lexika dictionary / dictionaries
das Tempus / die Tempora tense / tenses

Plural *-i*

der Modus / die Modi mode / modes

4 Compound nouns

German is the language of compound words. These cause difficulties to the foreign speaker. The following rules will help you to understand existing compounds but are not always reliable when inventing new ones.

(a) Meaning

The first part of the compound noun always defines the second part:

> *der Berufsmusiker* a musician who plays music professionally, as opposed to *der Amateurmusiker*

(b) Gender

The gender is always determined by the last part of the compound noun (see p. 9):

> *das Auto + der Fahrer → der Autofahrer* car driver

(c) Formation

The main groups of compound nouns can consist of:

ADJECTIVE + NOUN	*die Warmluft* warm air
	das Kleinkind toddler
NOUN + VERB	*das Autofahren*‡ car driving

‡ *Fahren* is used as a noun here: infinitives used as nouns are always neuter (see above, p. 9).

NOUN + NOUN	*das Modehaus* fashion store
	die Autofahrt outing by car

Nouns can be linked in three different ways.

(i) Two nouns are simply combined as in the previous example:

Mode + Haus = Modehaus (also: *Modenhaus*)
Zug + Reise = Zugreise
Schiff + Fahrt = Schiffahrt‡

‡ There can never be more than a double consonant. If there should logically be a third one, as here, it is omitted.

(ii) Combination with the help of a linking *-s* or *-es*:

Beruf + Musiker = Berufsmusiker
Verkehr + Amt = Verkehrsamt
Bund + Tag = Bundestag (German Parliament)

(iii) Combination with the help of a linking *-n*:

Schokolade + Torte = Schokoladentorte
Straße + Fest = Straßenfest

In a compound noun the linking consonants *-(e)s* and *-n* represent the last letter of the first word, so the above examples are hyphenated as follows if they occur at the end of a line:

Berufs – musiker
Verkehrs – amt
Bundes – tag
Schokoladen – torte
Straßen – fest

5 Declension of nouns in the singular and plural

Most of the features of the German case system derive from Latin. But there are only four (not six) cases: the subject case or **nominative**, and three object cases, i.e. the **accusative**, the **dative**, and the **genitive**.

The following examples show how the cases correspond to the structure of the English language.

NOMINATIVE:	*Das ist Herr Kluge.* (subject) This is Mr Kluge.
ACCUSATIVE:	*Er schenkt Blumen.* (direct object) He gives flowers.
GENITIVE:	*Das sind Herrn Kluges Blumen.* (possessive) Those are Mr Kluge's flowers.
DATIVE:	*Er gibt sie ihr.* (indirect object) He gives them to her.

Note that whereas the rules for applying the nominative and the genitive are virtually identical in the two languages, those for the accusative and dative are often not.

There are five different patterns according to which nouns are declined. Knowing the plural form will give you a clue as to which pattern a particular noun follows.

(a) Pattern 1: nominative plural -e

der Fisch fish

	SINGULAR	PLURAL
N	*der Fisch*	*die Fische*
A	*den Fisch*	*die Fische*
G	*des Fisch<u>es</u>*	*der Fische*
D	*dem Fisch*	*den Fisch<u>en</u>*

Note the *-es* in the genitive singular and the *-n* in the dative plural.

Whether the genitive takes the full ending *-es* or the shortened ending *-s* is largely a matter of convention and taste. What sounds better, *des Buches* or *des Buchs*? There is a tendency nowadays to omit the linking *-e-*, but if the noun ends in *-s*, *-ß*, *-x*, *-t*, *-tsch* or *-z*, the ending should definitely be *-es*, e.g.

das Versäumnis / des Versäumnisses absence / omission
Gott / Gottes God

(b) Pattern 2: -n in all plural forms; -n in accusative, genitive and dative singular (so-called weak nouns)

der Affe monkey

	SINGULAR	PLURAL
N	*der Affe*	*die Affen*
A	*den Aff<u>en</u>*	*die Affen*
G	*des Aff<u>en</u>*	*der Affen*
D	*dem Aff<u>en</u>*	*den Affen*

There are eight exceptions to this pattern. Here the genitive singular ends in *-ens*:

der Buchstabe letter	*der Glaube* belief
der Friede peace	*der Name* name
der Funke spark	*der Same* seed (also *der Samen* semen)
der Gedanke thought	*der Wille* (no pl.) will

(c) Pattern 3: -n in all plural forms; no endings in the singular

All feminine nouns follow this pattern.

die Biene bee

	SINGULAR	PLURAL
N	*die Biene*	*die Bienen*
A	*die Biene*	*die Bienen*
G	*der Biene*	*der Bienen*
D	*der Biene*	*den Bienen*

(d) Pattern 4: *-s* in all plural forms; gen. *-s* in the singular

das Musical musical

	SINGULAR	PLURAL
N	*das Musical*	*die Musicals*
A	*das Musical*	*die Musicals*
G	*des Musicals*	*der Musicals*
D	*dem Musical*	*den Musicals*

As you can see, this is the most modern pattern as it virtually does away with declension endings. It applies to many loan-words which have come into German since the Second World War.

(e) Pattern 5: adjectival nouns

Many adjectives can be used as nouns. They are then spelt with a capital letter and declined according to the usual adjective patterns (see pages 42–5). For example:

deutsch	sg.	*der Deutsche* the German	*ein Deutscher* a German
	pl.	*die Deutschen* the Germans	*Deutsche* Germans
angestellt	sg.	*der Angestellte* the employee	*ein Angestellter* an employee
	pl.	*die Angestellten* the employees	*Angestellte* employees
grün	sg.	*der Grüne / ein Grüner* the / a member of the Green party	
	pl.	*die Grünen / Grüne* the members / members of the Green party	

For the use of participles as adjectives and nouns, see pages 55–6.

Special rules for the genitive

Note that some words derived from Greek or Latin and ending in *-us* or *-os* do not take a genitive ending.

das mittelalterliche Bild des Kosmos
the medieval image of the cosmos

im Zeitalter des Feudalismus in the feudal period

Also, if a name ends in *-s*, e.g. *Familie Schmidts*, then the contemporary form of the genitive is simply an apostrophe:

Familie Schmidts' neues Auto
the Schmidts family's new car

In your reading of German literature you may come across more elaborate (obsolete) forms such as *Familie Schmidtsens neues Auto* or *Klausens Frau* (Claus's wife).

However, there is a tendency to avoid the *s'* genitive and use instead *von* + dative:

das neue Auto von Familie Schmidts
die Frau von Klaus

With names only the last part shows the genitive:

die Werke Johann Wolfgang von Goethes
the works of Johann Wolfgang von Goethe

but:

am Hofe Karls des Großen
at the court of Charlemagne

die Schlachten Karls V. (read: *Karls des Fünften*)
the battles of Charles V

Geographical names with no article take the genitive *-s*. However, if the name ends in *-s*, use *von*:

die Museen Münchens the museums of Munich

but:

die Museen von Paris the museums of Paris

Both these constructions are often avoided by substituting an adjective for the genitive:

die Münchner Museen the museums of Munich
die Pariser Museen the museums of Paris

This variation works with most towns except the ones which already end in *-er* :

die Busse von Manchester the Manchester buses

N.B. There is a difference between ***das Berliner Abkommen*** and ***das Berlin-Abkommen*** even though both terms could be translated into English as 'the Berlin agreement'. ***Das Berliner Abkommen*** refers to any agreement that was negotiated or signed in Berlin and ***das Berlin-Abkommen*** is the Allied agreement on the status of West Berlin after the Second World War, which was valid between 1971 and 1990.

PRONOUNS

6 Personal pronouns

(a) Function and forms

Personal pronouns normally replace a noun, and, like nouns, they must be declined. As in English, there are three 'persons' in German, in both the singular and the plural, but in addition German differentiates between a formal and an informal form in the second person.

SINGULAR

	N	A	G	D	
1st	*ich*	*mich*	*meiner*	*mir*	
2nd	*du*	*dich*	*deiner*	*dir*	informal
	Sie	*Sie*	*Ihrer*	*Ihnen*	formal
3rd	*er*	*ihn*	*seiner*	*ihm*	
	sie	*sie*	*ihrer*	*ihr*	
	es	*es*	*seiner*	*ihm*	

PLURAL

	N	A	G	D	
1st	*wir*	*uns*	*unser*	*uns*	
2nd	*ihr*	*euch*	*euer*	*euch*	informal
	Sie	*Sie*	*Ihrer*	*Ihnen*	formal
3rd	*sie*	*sie*	*ihrer*	*ihnen*	

(b) Use

Genitive

Genitive pronouns are rarely used and can nearly always be replaced by a preposition + dative or accusative. They occur in biblical or church texts and older literature.

An Allerseelen wird der Toten gedacht. →
An Allerseelen wird ihrer (gen.) *gedacht.*

or:

An Allerseelen denkt man an die Toten.
An Allerseelen denkt man an sie. (acc.)

On All Souls we commemorate the dead.
On All Souls we commemorate them.

du* and *Sie (cf. section 71)

In a business context you always expect to be on *Sie*-terms with your opposite numbers, even if the relationship is very good and has lasted a long time. Germans who travel a lot usually know about the Anglo-Saxon tendency to use the first name right from the start and they may do this with you, thinking it will make you feel more at home. At the same time, they will naturally address their longest-standing colleague in their own work environment as *Herr Müller* or *Frau Winter*.

If the *du* is introduced, it is done according to the following rules:

- The older and / or more senior person offers it to the younger / junior person. (This takes precedence over other considerations.)

- A woman offers it to a man. The fact that this rule is often not obeyed even in Germany and by Germans is one of the consequences of radical emancipation, but there is some confusion about the borderline between courteous behaviour and staid or openly discriminating behaviour.

- *Du* may have been introduced during a pub crawl. This does not necessarily mean you are still on *du*-terms the next morning!

- Especially among men there is a rite called *Bruderschaftstrinken*. This is a particular kind of drinking ceremony where the person who offers you the *du* makes a toast. You then have to drink from your glass with your arm twisted around the arm of your new *Duzbruder*. It is often a serious ceremony and meant for keeps.

When you address somebody with *du*, *Sie* or *ihr* in a letter, these pronouns start with a capital (see p. 244). This applies to transcripts of dialogue as well.

es

- *Es* can stand for all neuter nouns. However, occasionally the notion of natural gender supersedes grammatical gender:

Das Mädchen hat blonde Haare. Sie gefällt mir.
The girl has blond hair. I like her.

- *Es* can also introduce a sentence. However, if it does, the verb agrees with the following noun, not with *es* (but cf. section 132, *geben*):

  Es werden viele Besucher erwartet.

or:

  Viele Besucher werden erwartet.
  Many visitors are expected to come.

- *Es* can anticipate a dependent clause. The verb in the introduction is always in the singular:

  Es scheint sicher, daß die Messe ein Erfolg wird.
  It seems certain that the trade fair will be a success.

- As in English, there are a number of expressions and phrases that start with the impersonal pronoun:

  Es regnet / schneit . . . It is raining / snowing . . .
  (all expressions concerning the weather)

  Es handelt sich um . . . It is about . . .

However, it is also used in the following expressions:

  Es geht ihm gut. He is fine.
  Es gefällt ihr gut hier. She likes it here.

(c) Word order in sentences with pronouns

- **noun + noun**: dative precedes accusative:

  Ich gebe unserem Partner den Auftrag.
  I give the order to our partner.

- **pronoun + noun**: the pronoun precedes the noun:

  Ich gebe ihn unserem Partner. I give it to our partner.

- **noun + preposition + noun**: noun precedes the preposition + noun:

  Ich habe die Frage an meinen Partner weitergegeben.
  I have passed the question on to my partner.

- **pronoun + preposition + pronoun**: the simple pronoun precedes the preposition + pronoun:

  Ich habe sie an ihn weitergegeben.
  I have passed it on to him.

- **pronoun + pronoun**: an accusative pronoun precedes a dative pronoun:

  Ich gebe es ihm. I give it to him.

7 Possessives

Possessives can either perform the function of the article (possessive adjective) or they can replace a noun (possessive pronoun). As pointed out in section 2, the declension of the possessive adjective follows the pattern of *ein*-words whereas the declension of the possessive pronoun follows the pattern of *der*-words.

Note also that the gender of the possessive depends on the noun to which it refers or which it replaces; the case depends on the function of the expression.

	PERSONAL PRONOUN	POSSESSIVE PRONOUN (nom. sg. m.)	POSSESSIVE ADJECTIVE (nom. sg. m.)
SINGULAR	*ich*	*meiner*	*mein*
	du	*deiner*	*dein*
	Sie	*Ihrer*	*Ihr*
	er	*seiner*	*sein*
	sie	*ihrer*	*ihr*
	es	*seiner*	*sein*
PLURAL	*wir*	*unserer*	*unser*
	ihr	*euer*	*euer*
	Sie	*Ihrer*	*Ihr*
	sie	*ihrer*	*ihr*

For declensions see also section 13.

Consider the following examples:

Heute habe ich den ganzen Tag ein Auto.
Es gehört dem Mann, mit dem ich verheiratet bin.
Today I have a car for the whole day.
It belongs to the man to whom I am married.

This could be expressed more elegantly and briefly by using a possessive adjective:

Heute habe ich den ganzen Tag das Auto meines Mannes.
Today I have my husband's car for the whole day.

Your friend might ask you:

Wessen Auto hast du heute?
Whose car have you got today?

Das Auto meines Mannes.
(but: *Das Auto meiner Mutter.*)

You could indicate to your friend that a particular car belongs to your husband (your husband already having been mentioned in the conversation) by using a possessive pronoun:

Das ist seines. That's his.

Similarly:

Das Mädchen hat einen Hund. Der Hund gehört ihr.
The girl has a dog. It belongs to her.

Das ist der Hund des Mädchens.
That is the girl's dog.

Es ist ihr Hund. That's her dog.

With a possessive pronoun:

Es ist ihrer. It's hers.

In the third person singular *sein* serves both masculine and neuter, *ihr* is for feminine owners.

8 Reflexive and reciprocal pronouns

(a) Reflexive pronouns

Consider the following sentences:

1 *Er wäscht das Auto.* He washes the car.
2 *Er wäscht sich.* He washes himself.
3 *Er wäscht ihr die Hände.* He washes her hands.
4 *Er wäscht sich die Hände.* He washes his hands.

Sentence 1 shows the use of *waschen* with an accusative object; sentence 3 shows its use with a dative object. In contrast to that, *waschen* in sentences 2 and 4 takes a reflexive pronoun. In fact, *waschen* can combine an accusative and a dative reflexive pronoun, as shown in sentences 3 and 4.

The verb *waschen* is extremely versatile. It can be used:

- with an **accusative object** (*das Auto*)
- with an **accusative reflexive pronoun**:

  Wen wäscht er? Whom is he washing?
  Sich. Himself.
- with a **dative reflexive pronoun** and an **accusative object**:

  Wem wäscht er die Hände? Whose hands is he washing?
  Sich. His own.
- with a **dative** (non-reflexive) pronoun and an accusative object.

  Wem wäscht er die Hände? Whose hands is he washing?
  Ihr. Hers.

When you learn a new verb, it is therefore extremely important that you memorize the different ways in which it can be used. For example, with *waschen* you would learn:

sich waschen
(jemandem) etwas waschen
sich etwas waschen

As you can see, the dative object is optional, but if you have one, you must also have an accusative object. As for the reflexive option, you need to learn whether the reflexive pronoun must be dative or accusative. One of the general guidelines for getting things right here is that in one single sentence you can only have one object of each sort unless the object is governed by a preposition.

Similarly:

sich ansehen to look at oneself
jemandem etwas ansehen to recognize something in someone
sich etwas ansehen to go and look at something

Also:

sich kämmen, sich rasieren (see section 33).

PERSONAL PRONOUN	ACCUSATIVE REFLEXIVE PRONOUN	DATIVE REFLEXIVE PRONOUN
ich	*mich*	*mir*
du	*dich*	*dir*
er / *sie* / *es*	*sich*	*sich*

PERSONAL PRONOUN	ACCUSATIVE REFLEXIVE PRONOUN	DATIVE REFLEXIVE PRONOUN
wir	*uns*	*uns*
ihr	*euch*	*euch*
Sie	*sich*	*sich*
sie	*sich*	*sich*

As you can see, the reflexive pronouns in the accusative and dative case are identical in all persons in the plural, and in the third person singular.

(b) Reciprocal pronouns

In the plural, the meaning of the reflexive pronoun could be either reflexive or reciprocal. To emphasize that an action is reciprocal, *gegenseitig* (each other) can be inserted:

Sie liebten sich. (ambiguous) They loved themselves / each other.

Sie liebten sich gegenseitig. (unambiguous) They loved each other.

Another way of indicating that the action is reciprocal is to insert *einander* (each other); this makes *sich* superfluous:

Sie liebten einander. They loved one another.

9 Demonstratives

Like possessives, demonstratives can perform the function of an article (demonstrative adjective) or they can replace a noun (demonstrative pronoun).

As the term implies, **demonstratives** help to put stress on the position of something or someone in relation to something or someone else.

In the spoken language this can be done without the use of a demonstrative by emphasizing **the article**.

Ich meine die Frau mit dem großen Koffer. (nicht die mit der Handtasche)
I am talking about the woman with the big suitcase. (not the one with the handbag)

Alternatively, the demonstrative can be employed. Both the demonstrative adjective and the demonstrative pronoun are declined as *der*-words (see section 2).

(a) *dieser* and *jener*

dieser, diese, dieses this
jener, jene, jenes that

Dieser refers to the object or person close at hand, or 'the latter'; *jener* to the object or person further away, or 'the former'. For the declension of *dieser* and *jener* see section 2.

(b) *derjenige*

A combination of the two patterns described above is used for additional stress when singling out an individual from a crowd:

derjenige, diejenige, dasjenige that one

Ich möchte denjenigen sehen, der bei diesem Wetter schwimmt.
I would like to see the person who would go swimming in this weather.

	MASCULINE	FEMININE	NEUTER
N	*derjenige*	*diejenige*	*dasjenige*
A	*denjenigen*	*diejenige*	*dasjenige*
G	*desjenigen*	*derjenigen*	*desjenigen*
D	*demjenigen*	*derjenigen*	*demjenigen*

★ N.B. *der-, die-, das-* are declined as the article (i.e. as a *der*-word), whereas *-jenige* is declined as an *ein*-word. Both parts of the compound must be declined (see section 2).

(c) *hier-* or *da- / dort-* + preposition

All combinations of *hier-* + preposition and *da- / dort-* + preposition can serve as demonstratives:

Wohin soll ich kommen?
Hierhin! (Nicht dahin / dorthin.)
Where should I go?
Here! (Not there.)

Hier- is used for the object closer to the speaker, *da-* is used for the object further away. *Dort-* is only used in a geographical sense, and can therefore not be combined with prepositions as generally as *da-*.

10 Relative pronouns

(a) Function

A relative pronoun links a dependent clause to the main clause. It refers to a noun or a pronoun in the main clause. Its gender and number must agree with the preceding noun whereas the case is dependent on the following verb or verb + preposition, i.e. on the function of the relative pronoun in the dependent clause:

Das ist der Mitarbeiter, den ich Ihnen vorstellen wollte.
This is the colleague whom I wanted to introduce to you.

Relative clauses, both defining and non-defining, must always be separated off by a comma.

Das ist die Frau, die ich liebe.
This is the woman (whom) I love.

Heute morgen löste sie das schwierige Problem, an dem sie schon lange gearbeitet hatte.
This morning she solved the difficult problem, at which she had been working for a long time.

The forms of the relative pronoun are the same as the forms of the definite article except for three instances:

dessen: masculine and neuter genitive singular
deren: feminine genitive singular; feminine and neuter genitive plural
denen: dative plural (all genders)

The following table will help you to identify the various possible combinations:

Masculine singular

CASE	FORM	EXAMPLE
N	der	*Der Herr, der dort steht, ist noch jung.* The man who is standing there is still young.
A	*den*	*Der Herr, den Sie dort sehen, ist noch jung.* The man whom you see there is still young.
G	*dessen*	*Der Herr, dessen Krawatte rot ist, ist noch jung.* The man whose bow tie is red is still young.
D	*dem*	*Der Herr, dem Sie heute morgen einen Auftrag gegeben haben, ist jetzt hier.* The man to whom you gave an order this morning is here now.

Feminine singular

CASE	FORM	EXAMPLE
N	*die*	*Das ist die Besprechung, die wichtig ist.* This is the meeting which is important.
A	*die*	*Das ist die Besprechung, die wir alle wichtig finden.* This is the meeting (which) we all find important.
G	*deren*	*Das ist die Besprechung, deren Wichtigkeit wir alle schätzen.* This is the meeting whose importance we all appreciate.
D	*der*	*Das ist die Besprechung, der wir alle solche Wichtigkeit beimessen.* This is the meeting to which we all accord such importance.

Neuter singular

N	*das*	*Hier sehen Sie das Büro, das sehr dünne Wände hat.* Here you see the office which has very thin walls.
A	*das*	*Hier ist das Büro, das Sie alle kennen.* Here is the office (which) you all know.
G	*dessen*	*Hier ist das Büro, dessen Wände sehr dünn sind.* Here is the office whose walls are very thin.
D	*dem*	*Hier ist das Büro, dem Sie ein neues Image geben sollen.* Here is the office to which you are supposed to give a new image.

Plural (all genders)

N	*die*	*Hier sind die Banknoten, die gefälscht sind.* Here are the banknotes which are forged.
A	*die*	*Das sind die Banknoten, die wir gefunden haben.* These are the banknotes (which) we found.
G	*deren*	*Das sind die Banknoten, deren Echtheit die Polizei überprüfen will.* These are the banknotes whose authenticity the police want to check.
D	*denen*	*Das sind die Fälscher, denen wir auf die Spur gekommen sind.* These are the forgers (whom) we tracked down.

(b) Relative pronouns + preposition

The case of the relative pronoun is decided by the preposition, which immediately precedes the relative pronoun:

sich auf (+ acc.) *verlassen* to rely on someone

Die Angestellten, auf die wir uns verlassen können, bekommen eine Gehaltserhöhung.
The employees on whom we can rely will get a salary rise.

über (+ acc.) *lachen* to laugh about someone / something

Der Witz, über den wir lachen, ist schon uralt.
The joke which we are laughing about is really very old.

(See also sections 33 and 45.)

(c) Syntax and style

★ Usually the relative clause is inserted after the noun or pronoun to which it refers, as can be seen from the table above. However, the word order is considered clumsy if the relative clause is much longer than the part of the main clause which follows the relative clause:

Ich habe die Schlüssel, die ich so lange gesucht habe, schließlich gefunden.
I finally found the keys for which I had been looking for such a long time.

A better structure would be:

Ich habe die Schlüssel schließlich gefunden, die ich so lange gesucht habe.

As in English, it is best not to make the relative clause too long or too complicated, otherwise the sentence will be hard to follow. Note that in German the relative clause can only refer to the noun in the main clause and not to the whole phrase. Compare the following examples:

My wife invited all my former colleagues for my birthday, which was a lovely idea.
Es war ein wunderbarer Gedanke meiner Frau, alle meine früheren Kollegen zu meinem Geburtstag einzuladen.

The first sentence is fairly typical of spoken English and the second shows how an alternative construction would be chosen in German.

(d) Relative pronoun after an indefinite pronoun

As the term suggests, an indefinite pronoun refers to an unidentified or unspecified subject or object. However, the relative pronoun which follows an indefinite pronoun is determined in the same way as with nouns or pronouns:

Hier ist niemand, der mich kennt.
Wer kennt mich?
Niemand.
There is nobody here who knows me.
Who knows me?
Nobody.

In the case of neuter indefinite pronouns (*alles*, *etwas*, *nichts*) you can use either of the relative pronouns *das* or *was*.

Das ist etwas, das / was ich schon lange tun wollte.
Was ist es?
Das.
This is something (that) I have wanted to do for a long time.
What is it?
That.

Was refers to the whole idea of the sentence (*Ich wollte es schon lange tun. Was?*) and hence works as it would in an indirect question.

Der Chef hat mir gesagt, er wäre um 15.00 Uhr wieder da. Das ist alles, was ich weiß.
The boss told me he would be back at 3 p.m. That's all I know.

(e) Relative pronoun after a superlative

The relative pronoun used to refer to a superlative is usually *was*:

Das ist das Interessanteste, was ich je gehört habe.
This is the most interesting (story) I have ever heard.

However, in some instances the declined relative pronoun is used:

Das ist eines der besten Bücher, die ich je gelesen habe.
Das ist eines der besten Bücher, das ich je gelesen habe.
This is one of the best books I have ever read.

In the first sentence, the relative pronoun depends on *Bücher*, and thus has to take the plural form; in the second, *eines der besten Bücher* is thought of as a unit, with the stress on *eines*, hence the singular relative pronoun is being used.

11 Indefinites

In terms of meaning, the position of this group is between that of the demonstrative and the personal pronoun. Indefinites are used when an unidentified group of people or things is either referred to collectively or singled out. As with possessives and demonstratives (see sections 7 and 9), an indefinite can replace a noun (indefinite pronoun) or determine a noun (article word).

These words need to be declined. As has been explained in section 2, indefinite pronouns follow the declension of *der*-words, whereas the article words follow the declension of *ein*-words. However, not all indefinites exist in all forms.

(a) Collective meaning

alles / alle all

	PRONOUN		ARTICLE WORD	
	SINGULAR	PLURAL	SINGULAR	PLURAL
N	*alles*	*alle*	*alle(s)*	*alle*
A	*alles*	*allen*	*alle(s)*	*alle*
G	*von allem*	*von allen*	*von allem*	*aller*
D	*allem*	*allen*	*allem*	*allen*

Alles can only be used in the singular when referring to materials or abtract nouns:

Alles Vergängliche
Ist nur ein Gleichnis. (Goethe, *Faust*)

Everything mortal
is but a shadow.

Alle Welt wußte davon.
Everybody knew about it.

keiner nobody / ***kein*** not a, not any, no

PRONOUN

	SINGULAR			PLURAL
	MASCULINE	FEMININE	NEUTER	
N	*keiner*	*keine*	*kein(e)s*	*keine*
A	*keinen*	*keine*	*kein(e)s*	*keine*
G	–	–	–	–
D	*keinem*	*keiner*	*keinem*	*keinen*

ARTICLE WORD

	SINGULAR			PLURAL
	MASCULINE	FEMININE	NEUTER	
N	*kein*	*keine*	*kein*	*keine*
A	*keinen*	*keine*	*kein*	*keine*
G	*keines*	*keiner*	*keines*	*keiner*
D	*keinem*	*keiner*	*keinem*	*keinen*

Keiner hatte ihn gewarnt. No one had warned him.

Kein Mensch wollte helfen. Not a soul wanted to help.

★ N.B. In the genitive, *kein* can only be used as an article word.

niemand no one

Niemand exists only as a pronoun and in the singular.

N *niemand*
A *niemand(en)*
G *niemandes*
D *niemand(em)*

Niemand hatte ihn gewarnt. No one had warned him.

★ N.B. The accusative and dative endings for *niemand* and *jemand* are frequently dropped in spoken German.

Today the genitive is often replaced by the dative.

With the genitive:

Ich kenne niemandes Adresse hier.

With the dative:

Ich kenne die Adresse von niemandem hier.
I know no one's address here.

With the accusative ending:

Ich kenne niemanden hier.

With the zero ending:

Ich kenne niemand hier.
I don't know anyone here.

sämtliches all

Sämtliches is declined as a *der*-word both when it is used as a pronoun and when it is an article word.

Er hat sämtliches Material verloren.
He lost all the material.

(b) Selective meaning

jeder each

Jeder is declined as a *der*-word, both when it is used as a pronoun and when it is used as an article word.

Jeder in der Stadt wußte von dem Skandal.
Everyone in town knew about the scandal.

mancher some

Mancher is declined as a *der*-word, both when it is used as a pronoun and when it is used as an article word.

Er dachte so manches Mal an seine Kindheit zurück.
Every now and again he thought back to his childhood.

In a literary context, *manch-* is often used with the singular. The meaning can differ slightly from the plural. Compare these two examples:

Er hatte manche Schwierigkeit, bevor er zum Ziel kam.
He had no few difficulties before he reached the target.

Er hatte manche Schwierigkeiten, bevor er zum Ziel kam.
He had a number of difficulties before he reached the target.

mehreres several

Mehreres implies more than *manche*.

	PRONOUN		ARTICLE WORD
	SINGULAR	PLURAL	PLURAL
N	*mehreres*	*mehrere*	*mehrere*
A	*mehreres*	*mehrere*	*mehrere*
G	–	*mehrerer*	*mehrerer*
D	*mehrerem*	*mehreren*	*mehreren*

Es gibt mehreres, was ich dir sagen muß.
There are a number of things I need to tell you.

Hat er eine Frau? Nein, mehrere.
Has he got a (= one) wife? No, several.

einiges some

Einiges (sg.) is declined as a neuter *der*-word:

Auf ihrer Reise hatte sie einiges durchgemacht.
On her journey she went through quite a bit.

The plural *einige* is declined like a *der*-word, too:

Einige wußten noch nichts darüber.
Some didn't know about it yet.

irgendeiner / irgendein any

The indefinite pronoun *irgendeiner* is declined as a *der*-word. The indefinite article word *irgendein* is declined as an *ein*-word.

irgendwelche any(body / thing)

Irgendwelche is the plural of *irgendeiner / irgendein*. It is declined as an *ein*-word. *Irgend-* stresses the fact that the selection is at random.

Gibt es irgendwelche Fragen? Are there any questions?

(irgend-)jemand someone

Singular only:

N	*jemand*
A	*jemand(en)*
G	*jemandes*
D	*jemand(em)*

Used for persons and only as a pronoun (for an explanation of the declension, see *niemand*).

man impersonal you / one

Singular only:

N	*man*
A	*einen*
G	–
D	*einem*

Used only for persons and only as a pronoun:

Man ist nicht sicher, ob alle Verletzten gefunden worden sind.
It has not been established whether all casualties have been accounted for.

Einem wird ganz anders zumute, wenn man bedenkt, daß noch nicht alle Verletzten gefunden worden sind.
It is rather worrying that not all casualties have been accounted for yet.

If you use *man*, be consistent and don't change between *man* and a personal pronoun. A genitive form does not exist.

wer somebody

N	*wer*
A	*wen*
G	*wessen*
D	*wem*

Davon kenne ich keinen. Kennst du wen?
I do not know anyone among them. Do you know somebody?

Used only for persons and as a pronoun; also as a question word.

The indefinites listed above can also be shown as pairs of opposites:

jemand / niemand someone / no one
alle / keiner all / none
mehrere / einige several / a few
alles / mehreres, manches all / some

12 Interrogatives

The interrogative pronoun replaces a noun in a question; the interrogative adjective takes over the function of the article. *Wer* and *was* are only used as singular pronouns:

	PERSON	OBJECT
N	*wer* who	*was* what
A	*wen*	*was*
G	*wessen*	*wessen*
D	*wem*	–

The singular forms are used whether the noun in the answer is singular or plural:

Wen suchst Du? Whom are you looking for?
Den Mann mit der Zeitung. The man with the newspaper.
Die kleinen Kinder. The little children.

The genitive forms sound awkward and are heard less and less frequently.

The dative for objects is often supplied by the dative form of *welcher*, i.e. *welchem* (sg.) and *welchen* (pl.).

In welchem Buch haben Sie die Lösung gefunden?
In which book did you find the solution?

Welcher (a regular *der*-word) can also be used as an interrogative adjective:

Welches Datum haben wir heute? What is the date today?

Welch- is often found undeclined in an exclamation if it stands in front of *ein*:

Welch ein Unglück! / Welches Unglück!
What a disaster!

Welch ein Held! / Welcher Held!
What a hero!

Instead of asking a question with *welch-*, you can alternatively use *was für ein*. This is slightly more informal (see section 57):

Welches Auto fährst du jetzt?
Mit was für einem Auto fährst du jetzt?
What / Which car do you drive now?

In was für eine Wohnung will er ziehen?
In welche Wohnung will er ziehen?
Which / What flat does he want to move into?

Ein is declined as the **indefinite article** here. The case of *ein* as indefinite article in these examples does not depend on *für* but rather on the prepositions *mit* and *in*.

For interrogative pronoun + preposition, see section 53.

ADJECTIVES

13 Declension of a single adjective

Cf. section 140, ordinal numbers.

(a) Before a noun

In German, an adjective always has to be declined when it stands **immediately before the noun**:

> *Externe Faktoren bestimmen das Kaufverhalten.*
> External factors determine consumer behaviour.

but:

> *Die Faktoren für das Kaufverhalten sind extern.*
> The factors for consumer behaviour are external.

In the first example, *extern* comes before the noun *Faktor*; in the second example the adjective comes after the noun and is therefore not declined.

A simple noun group can appear in four variations:

1 = article + noun
2 = definite article + adjective + noun
3 = indefinite article + adjective + noun
4 = zero article + adjective + noun

1	*das*		*Brot*	the		bread
2	*das*	*frische*	*Brot*	the	fresh	bread
3	*ein*	*frisches*	*Brot*	a	fresh	loaf of bread
4		*frisches*	*Brot*		fresh	bread

This is an example for a neuter noun. With neuter nouns a final *-s* occurs once in each combination, i.e. either in the article or in the adjective, and so is called the signal consonant. Where the article carries the signal, the adjective often ends in *-n*. In the following tables, the signal consonant is underlined.

Masculine singular: *der Tee*

N	*der*		*Tee*
	der	*starke*	*Tee*
	ein	*starker*	*Tee*
		starker	*Tee*
A	*den*		*Tee*
	den	*starken*	*Tee*
	einen	*starken*	*Tee*
		starken	*Tee*
G	*des*		*Tees*
	des	*starken*	*Tees*
	eines	*starken*	*Tees*
		starken	*Tees*
D	*dem*		*Tee*
	dem	*starken*	*Tee*
	einem	*starken*	*Tee*
		starkem	*Tee*

Feminine singular: *die Limonade*

N/A	*die*		*Limonade*
	die	*süße*	*Limonade*
	eine	*süße*	*Limonade*
		süße	*Limonade*
G/D	*der*		*Limonade*
	der	*süßen*	*Limonade*
	einer	*süßen*	*Limonade*
		süßer	*Limonade*

Neuter singular: *das Bier*

N/A	*das*		*Bier*
	das	*leckere*	*Bier*
	ein	*leckeres*	*Bier*
		leckeres	*Bier*
G	*des*		*Bieres*
	des	*leckeren*	*Bieres*
	eines	*leckeren*	*Bieres*
		leckeren	*Bieres*
D	*dem*		*Bier*
	dem	*leckeren*	*Bier*
	einem	*leckeren*	*Bier*
		leckerem	*Bier*

Plural (all genders): *die Säfte*

N/A	*die*		*Säfte*
	die	*gesunden*	*Säfte*
	keine	*gesunden*	*Säfte*
		gesunde	*Säfte*
G	*der*		*Säfte*
	der	*gesunden*	*Säfte*
	keiner	*gesunden*	*Säfte*
		gesunder	*Säfte*
D	*den*		*Säften*
	den	*gesunden*	*Säften*
	keinen	*gesunden*	*Säften*
		gesunden	*Säften*

Dieser, *jener*, *jeder*, *welcher* and *mancher* are *der*-words and the following adjective is declined accordingly.

Kein, *mein / dein / sein* (etc.), *irgendein* are all *ein*-words, and so the following adjective is again declined accordingly.

Adjectives after *viele*, *einige*, *mehrere*, *wenige*, *ein paar* and *zwei*, *drei*, etc. are declined as adjectives after the zero article.

(b) Adjectives treated as nouns

After the indefinite pronouns *etwas*, *mehr*, *nichts*, *viel*, *wenig* the adjective is treated as a noun, i.e. it must be declined and capitalized; the **gender** of such a noun is always **neuter**:

Wir erwarten nichts Gutes.
We expect nothing good.

Das Geschäft hatte wenig Brauchbares.
The shop had little that was useful.

(c) Adjectives used in apposition

In a similar way, adjectives can be used in apposition to a noun; again, they then function as nouns. The gender is determined by the noun which the adjective refers to. Very often this construction cannot be literally translated into English:

Meine Mutter, die Gute, schickte mir einen Geburtstagskuchen.
My dear mother sent me a birthday cake.

Note that the appositional phrase must be separated off by commas.

(d) Adjectives which cannot be declined

There are a number of adjectives which cannot be declined at all. Most of them are used only in spoken German. The adjective is conceived as an extension of the noun and both are understood as a unit.

Das ist eine klasse Fête.
This is a great party.

Du hast wirklich eine super Frau.
You have really got a super wife.

Herr Mayer war schon immer ein prima Chef.
Mr Mayer has always been an excellent boss.

(e) Morphological changes

- Adjectives ending in *-el* drop the final vowel when declined:

  dunkel dark → *das dunkle Haus* the dark house

- Adjectives ending in *-en* and *-er* drop the *-e* in the spoken language:

  munter lively → *die munt(e)ren Kinder* the lively children

- The adjective *hoch* changes to *hoh-* when declined:

  die hohen Bäume the high trees

14 Declension of two or more adjectives

Normally, when you have a string of adjectives that precede a noun, all must be declined in parallel:

Dies ist ein großer moderner Betrieb.
This is a big modern factory.

The exceptions to this rule are listed below:

- After *beide* the second adjective in the dative singular masculine and neuter is usually declined as after *der*-words:

  beide geschäftlichen Partner both business partners

- After *folgend-*, the second adjective is often declined as after *der*-words, especially in the singular:

  folgendes wichtige(s) Detail the following important detail

- After *sämtlich-*, the second adjective is usually declined as after *der*-words in the singular and in the plural:

Singular:
mit sämtlichem neuen Datenmaterial
with all the new data material
rather than:
mit sämtlichem neuem Datenmaterial

Plural:
sämtliche starken Männer
all strong men
rather than:
sämtliche starke Männer

- If *viel* is declined, the adjective that follows is declined as after *der*-words in the neuter nominative and accusative and the dative singular masculine and neuter, and sometimes in the genitive plural:

  mit vielem anderen Material with a lot of other material

- If *wenig-* is declined, the second adjective is declined as after a *der*-word in the dative singular masculine and neuter, otherwise as after the zero article:

  aus wenigem billigen Material from a small quantity of cheap material

- If *viel* and *wenig* are not declined, the following adjective is declined as after the zero article.

★ N.B. There is a difference in meaning between declined and undeclined *viel / wenig*:

aus wenig billigem Material
out of material that was expensive (= hardly cheap!)

mit viel gutem Willen with a lot of good will

Here, *billig* and *gut* are modified by *wenig* and *viel*. *Wenig* and *viel* are therefore adverbs and remain undeclined.

In the declined version of the sentence, *billig* and *wenig* are two characteristics of the material which are not connected as such:

Das Material ist billig und wir haben nur wenig.
The material is cheap and we only have a little of it.

- *Ein wenig* remains undeclined and means 'a little':

Trinken Sie doch noch ein wenig Wein.
Have another drop of wine.

Ich spreche nur ein wenig Deutsch. I only speak a little German.

- If two or more adjectives are connected by a hyphen or occur as a compound, only the last one is declined:

die deutsch-deutschen Beziehungen
the relationship between West and East Germany

die blau-weiß-rote Fahne the French or British flag

die blaugestreifte Hose the trousers with the blue stripes

15 Comparative and superlative adjectives

The English language has two ways of grading an adjective – the **synthetic** form:

nice, nicer, the nicest

and the **analytical** form:

beautiful, more beautiful, most beautiful

German only has the synthetic form; the endings are in fact quite close to the corresponding forms in English:

schön, schöner, am schönsten nice, nicer, the nicest

★ N.B. An adjective ending in *-er* could either be a declined basic form or the comparative:

Das ist ein wunderbarer Mann. This is a wonderful man.

Die Landschaft war wunderbarer als alles, was sie vorher gesehen hatten.
The landscape was more wonderful than anything they had ever seen before.

A declined comparative would then have two endings:

Hans ist ein größerer Mann als Uli. Hans is a taller man than Uli.

If the comparative or superlative is placed before a noun, it must be declined:

> *Das ist die schönste Blume von allen.*
> This is the most beautiful flower of all.

It is not declined if it stands after a noun:

> *Diese Blume ist am schönsten.*
> This flower is the most beautiful.

(a) Morphological changes

Most adjectives do not only add the endings *-er* and *-est(en)* but also **change the vowel to the corresponding vowel + umlaut:**

a* becomes *ä

alt	*älter*	*am ältesten*	old
kalt	*kälter*	*am kältesten*	cold
lang	*länger*	*am längsten*	long
nahe	*näher*	*am nächsten*	close

o* becomes *ö

groß	*größer*	*am größten*	big
hoch	*höher*	*am höchsten*	high

u* becomes *ü

jung	*jünger*	*am jüngsten*	young
klug	*klüger*	*am klügsten*	intelligent

(b) Exceptions

There are, as usual, exceptions to the rule: some adjectives have substitute forms for the comparative and superlative:

gut	*besser*	*am besten*	good
viel	*mehr*	*am meisten*	much

(c) Adjectives consisting of two parts

In adjectives which consist of two parts, only one part is graded; this is usually the second part:

> *die altmodischsten Kleider* the most old-fashioned clothes

In instances where the first part has retained some independence, this can be graded instead:

das dichtestbevölkerte Bundesland

also:

das am dichtesten bevölkerte Bundesland
the most densely populated federal state

★ but not:

das dichtestbevölkertste Bundesland

In spoken language, you occasionally hear both parts graded. In the age of the superlative, creativity is occasionally overcreative and produces hypercorrect forms.

16 Expressing similarity and dissimilarity

(a) Similarity

This is expressed by using (*nicht*) *so* + adjective + *wie*:

Deutschland ist so groß wie Großbritannien.
Germany is as big as Great Britain.

Großbritannien exportiert nicht so viele Produkte wie Deutschland.
Great Britain does not export as many products as Germany.

Similarity can be emphasized by adding *genau*, *eben* or *gerade* in front of *so*:

Benzin ist fast genauso teuer wie Diesel.
Petrol is nearly as expensive as diesel.

(b) Dissimilarity

This is expressed by using the comparative + *als*:

London hat mehr Einwohner als Berlin.
London has more inhabitants than Berlin.

★ N.B. You will hear *wie* instead of *als* in certain regions. Grammatically speaking, this is incorrect and derives from a false parallelism.

There are other ways of expressing dissimilarity:

Das Land litt nicht so sehr unter der Inflation, als vielmehr unter dem hohen Zinssatz.
The country did not suffer so much from inflation but rather from high interest rates.

The dissimilarity can be emphasized by adding ***weitaus***, ***bedeutend***, ***wesentlich***, ***noch***, ***viel***, etc. in front of the comparative:

> *In den sechziger Jahren war der Dollar weitaus mehr wert als heute.*
> In the sixties the dollar was worth a lot more than it is today.

17 Alternatives to the superlative form

The superlative can be expressed by using the corresponding form of the adjective:

> *Das ist das spannendste Buch, das ich kenne.*
> This is the most exciting book I know.

- You can add emphasis by inserting *aller-*:

> *Das ist nur für unsere allerbesten Kunden.*
> This is only for our very best clients.

- At the same time, you often find a more implicit 'superlative':

> *schön:* *die bildschöne Frau* (literally: as pretty as a picture)
> *neu:* *das nagelneue Haus* (literally: as new as a nail)
> *modern:* *die hochmoderne Fitnessanlage*
> (literally: highly modern)

These compound adjectives are understood as entities in themselves rather than as superlatives of a basic adjective.

- The prefixed *hyper-*, *super-* or *über-* can often add a negative connotation to the adjective:

  sensibel: *das hypersensible Kind* (hypersensitive)
  klug: *die superkluge Schülerin* (literally: super-intelligent)
  lang: *das überlange Kleid* (literally: over-long)

- An implicit superlative can also be expressed by adding an adverb:

  Er war äußerst zuvorkommend. He was highly obliging.

  ein besonders profitables Projekt
  a particularly profitable project

  ein höchst interessantes Gespräch
  a most interesting conversation

  ein überaus / übermäßig großzügiger Chef
  a more than generous boss

★ N.B. *Übermäßig* ('beyond measure') can have a negative connotation ('he is too generous'), whereas *überaus* is neutral in this respect.

(See also section 135, on adverbial nuance.)

18 Formation of adjectives

Some adjectives (e.g. colours) must be learnt as straightforward vocabulary items (see section 134). In other instances the way the adjective is formed may well help you to work out its meaning. It is therefore important to recognize recurrent patterns.

Adjectives derived from nouns by adding *-isch*, *-(l)ich*, or *-ig*

das Kind child	*kindisch* childish
die Kunst art	*künstlich* artificial
die Gunst favour	*günstig* favourable
but: *die Trauer* grief	*traurig* sad

Unfortunately, it is difficult to predict these patterns and they are rather more useful for your passive understanding than for your own invention of adjectives.

-lich can add a nuance to an adjective (e.g. all colours):

Die Tasche ist braünlich. The bag is brownish.

Das Haus ist ärmlich. The house is humble. (literally: poorish)

Adjectives derived from nouns by adding *-ant* (foreign ending)

das Risiko risk	*riskant* risky
der Charme charm	*charmant* charming

Again, this is a pattern that is useful to recognize but it should be applied with caution.

Adjectives derived from nouns by adding *-bar*

das Wunder miracle	*wunderbar* wonderful
das Mittel means	*mittelbar* indirect(ly)

As you can see from these examples, the suffix *-bar* can give the adjective a meaning which is not obviously connected with the meaning of the noun. So it may be worth checking in a dictionary.

Adjectives derived from verbs by adding *-bar* to the stem

Das ist machbar. It can be done / accomplished. (i.e. it is feasible)
Das ist fühlbar. It can be felt.
Das ist brennbar. It can be burnt. (i.e. it is combustible)

Adjectives derived from verbs by adding *-end* to the stem

The *-end* suffix makes a **present participle** out of a verb. Some participles have, however, become so independent of the original verb that they are not thought of as derived forms any more:

entsprechend respective(ly)
vielsagend telling / significant
entdeckendes Lernen discovery learning

This pattern is especially productive for the foreign speaker because all *-end* forms are legitimate as participles and can therefore be used as adjectives.

Adjectives derived from past participles

As in English, past participles can be used as adjectives:

ein gelungener Witz	a successful joke
gebratener Fisch	fried fish
das verbotene Buch	the forbidden book

THE VERB AND ITS TENSES

19 Personal endings

In English, the only marked person ending is the *-s* in the third person singular (e.g. 'he says'). German has marked endings for all persons and they are identical for most verbs; German has no separate continuous form ('he is saying', etc.).

(a) Present tense

ich	*gehe*	I	go, am going
du	*gehst*	you	go, are going
er / sie / es	*geht*	he / she / it	goes, is going
wir	*gehen*	we	go, are going
ihr	*geht*	you (plural)	go, are going
Sie	*gehen*	you (formal)	go, are going
sie	*gehen*	they	go, are going

A number of endings are identical:

wir	*gehen*	*er / sie / es*	*geht*
Sie	*gehen*	*ihr*	*geht*
sie	*gehen*		

The forms ending in *-en* are identical with the infinitive.

EXCEPTIONS

If the stem ends in *-d* or *-t*, or consonant + *m* or *n*, you need to insert *-e-* between the stem and the ending in the *du*, *er / sie / es* and *ihr* forms.

reden to talk
du redest er redet ihr redet

arbeiten to work
du arbeitest er arbeitet ihr arbeitet

atmen to breathe
du atmest er atmet ihr atmet

rechnen to calculate
du rechnest er rechnet ihr rechnet

On the other hand, if the stem ends in *-s*, *-ss* or *ß*, no further *s* is added in the *du* form.

reisen to make a trip *heißen* to be called
du reist er reist ihr reist *du heißt er heißt ihr heißt*

If the infinitive ends in *-eln* or *-ern*, the *-e-* of the ending is dropped in the first and third person plural and second person formal:

hämmern to hammer
wir hämmern sie hämmern Sie hämmern

Wissen and all the modal verbs have no *-t* in the third person singular. At the same time, the stem vowel changes in some instances:

wissen to know	*er weiß*
müssen to have to	*er muß*
dürfen to be allowed / permitted	*er darf*
können to be able to	*er kann*
wollen to want to	*er will*
mögen to like	*er mag*
but: *sollen* to ought to	*er soll*

(b) Imperfect tense

ich holte	I fetched
du holtest	you fetched
er / sie / es holte	he / she / it fetched
wir holten	we fetched
ihr holtet	you (plural) fetched
Sie holten	you (formal) fetched
sie holten	they fetched

Again, some forms are identical:

wir holten	*ich holte*
Sie holten	*er / sie / es holte*
sie holten	

(c) Participles

Formation

The **present participle** is formed by adding *-end* to the stem:

kommen → kommend *kommende Woche*
come → coming in the coming week

The **past participle** is identical with the form of the main verb in the perfect tense:

braten → gebraten	*gebratener Fisch*
fry → fried	fried fish

Functions

Participles are difficult to classify as they have neither a clear time aspect nor can their ending be called a personal ending. Present and past participles are used frequently in English – mainly as gerunds. This is not so in German, where the English gerund is replaced by alternative constructions. In the first example, the gerund is translated by using a subordinate clause:

Having heard that his friend was ill, he went to visit him immediately.
Nachdem / als er gehört hatte, daß sein Freund krank war, besuchte er ihn sofort.

The participle in German can have the function of an adjective, an adverb or a noun.

The participle functions as an **adjective** in:

Sie hatte nicht mit diesem überraschenden Besuch gerechnet.
She had not expected this surprising visit.

Ich hätte gerne ein weichgekochtes Ei.
I would like a soft-boiled egg.

The participle functions as an **adverb** in:

Die Dame trug eine auffallend große Tasche.
The lady carried a conspicuously big handbag.

Man konnte nur gebeugt durch das Tor gehen.
One could only get through the gate by bending down.

The participle functions as a **noun** in:

Niemand hörte die Rufenden.
Nobody heard the shouting people.

Die Zahl der Ermordeten ging in die Hunderte.
There were hundreds of people killed. (literally: murdered ones)

If used as a noun or adjective, the participle must be declined. Participles used as nouns are also referred to as **adjectival nouns** because the form of such participles is identical with those of adjectives (see section 5(e)).

20 Tenses

German has the same set of tenses as English and they are formed in virtually the same way. As in English, we differentiate between **weak** and **strong** verbs.

Weak verbs are those whose imperfect tense and perfect tense are indicated by the addition of prefixes and suffixes according to a predictable pattern:

holen	*holte*	*hat geholt*
to fetch	fetched	has fetched

The past participle can be recognized by the prefix *ge-* and the *-t* ending.

Strong verbs are those where the stem vowel changes in the imperfect tense and in the past participle. The past participle takes the prefix *ge-* and the suffix *-en*. In the following example the stem vowel changes from *e* to *a* to *o*:

nehmen	*nahm*	*hat genommen*
take	took	has taken

Furthermore, there are **irregular verbs**. In a table of verbs, these are normally listed together with the strong verbs. Irregular means that the verb is conjugated partly like a strong verb and partly like a weak verb (hence the term **mixed verbs**) and / or that the basic tenses do not all have the same stem. Both the English verb 'to be' and the German *sein* are irregular. A number of others are discussed in sections 25–32.

In the table of irregular verbs on pp. 581–3, the following parts of the verb are listed: the infinitive, the third person singular of the present tense, the first and third person singular of the imperfect tense and the past participle. A second table (pp. 571–80) helps you to identify infinitives of irregular verbs.

21 Present tense and imperfect tense

(a) Formation of the present and imperfect of weak verbs

In weak verbs the present and imperfect tenses are formed by adding to the stem of the verb the set of personal endings given below for *holen*, 'to fetch'. The personal endings of the imperfect are identical to those of the present tense except for the third person singular, with a *-t(e)* between the stem and the ending.

holen to fetch

	PRESENT	IMPERFECT
ich	*hole*	*holte*
du	*holst*	*holtest*
er / sie / es	*holt*	*holte*
wir	*holen*	*holten*
ihr	*holt*	*holtet*
Sie	*holen*	*holten*
sie	*holen*	*holten*

(b) Formation of present and imperfect of strong verbs

The set of personal endings remains the same as with the weak verbs but the imperfect tense is indicated by a change of the stem vowel and there is no personal ending in the first and third person singular, as shown below for *kommen*, 'to come'.

kommen to come

	PRESENT	IMPERFECT
ich	*komme*	*kam*
du	*kommst*	*kamst*
er / sie / es	*kommt*	*kam*
wir	*kommen*	*kamen*
ihr	*kommt*	*kamt*
Sie	*kommen*	*kamen*
sie	*kommen*	*kamen*

★ N.B. The consonant following the stem vowel sometimes changes from a double to a single one.

Strong verbs must be learned individually as the change of vowel cannot be guessed. It is easier to learn them if those that make the same change are grouped together. Here are some examples from the major groups:

a / ä	***u***	***a***	
fahren (fährt)	*fuhr*	*gefahren*	to drive
a / ä	***ie***	***a***	
lassen (läßt)	*ließ*	*gelassen*	to let
raten (rät)	*riet*	*geraten*	to advise
i	***a***	***u***	
binden	*band*	*gebunden*	to bind
finden	*fand*	*gefunden*	to find
ie	***o***	***o***	
fliegen	*flog*	*geflogen*	to fly
fliehen	*floh*	*geflohen*	to escape
ei	***ie***	***ie***	
beweisen	*bewies*	*bewiesen*	to prove
schreiben	*schrieb*	*geschrieben*	to write
e	***a***	***o***	
helfen	*half*	*geholfen*	to help
treffen	*traf*	*getroffen*	to hit / meet
e	***a***	***a***	
brennen	*brannte*	*gebrannt*	to burn
rennen	*rannte*	*gerannt*	to run
e / i	***a***	***e***	
essen (ißt)	*aß*	*gegessen*	to eat
messen (mißt)	*maß*	*gemessen*	to measure

★ N.B. *-ss-* becomes *-ß* at the end of a word (see section 68).

22 Perfect tense and pluperfect tense

(a) Formation of the perfect

The perfect and pluperfect are known as compound tenses because they are formed by an auxiliary verb + a main verb (also called 'full verb'). Just as in English, the perfect comprises an auxiliary used in the present tense + the past participle. In German, the auxiliary can be either *haben* (to have) or *sein* (to be).

There are no foolproof rules to tell you when to use *sein* and when to use *haben*, but there are some helpful guidelines. When the verb implies a change from one place to another or from one state to another, *sein* is more likely. In all other cases *haben* is probably right. Some examples are given below.

Weak verbs

with *haben*	with *sein*
holen holte habe geholt	*reisen reiste bin gereist*
to fetch	to make a trip
ich habe geholt	*ich bin gereist*
du hast geholt	*du bist gereist*
er/sie/es hat geholt	*er/sie/es ist gereist*
wir haben geholt	*wir sind gereist*
ihr habt geholt	*ihr seid gereist*
Sie haben geholt	*Sie sind gereist*
sie haben geholt	*sie sind gereist*

Strong verbs

with *haben*	with *sein*
verlieren verlor hat verloren	*kommen kam bin gekommen*
to lose	to come
ich habe verloren	*ich bin gekommen*
du hast verloren	*du bist gekommen*
er/sie/es hat verloren	*er/sie/es ist gekommen*
wir haben verloren	*wir sind gekommen*
ihr habt verloren	*ihr seid gekommen*
Sie haben verloren	*Sie sind gekommen*
sie haben verloren	*sie sind gekommen*

With regard to the perfect, strong and weak verbs differ only in so far as the participle of **weak verbs** consists of *ge-* + stem + *-t* whereas the participle of **strong verbs** consists of *ge-* + stem with vowel change + *-en*. There are a number of **mixed verbs** (partially weak and partially strong), in which the stem vowel changes but the past participle ends in *-t*, e.g.:

bringen	*brachte*	*gebracht*	to bring
denken	*dachte*	*gedacht*	to think
brennen	*brannte*	*gebrannt*	to burn

(b) Formation of the pluperfect

The pluperfect comprises the appropriate form of *sein* and *haben* in the imperfect tense + the past participle.

with ***sein:*** *war gekommen* had come
with ***haben:*** *hatte geholt* had fetched

ich war	*gekommen*	*ich hatte*	*geholt*
du warst	*gekommen*	*du hattest*	*geholt*
er / sie / es war	*gekommen*	*er / sie / es hatte*	*geholt*
wir waren	*gekommen*	*wir hatten*	*geholt*
ihr wart	*gekommen*	*ihr hattet*	*geholt*
Sie waren	*gekommen*	*Sie hatten*	*geholt*
sie waren	*gekommen*	*sie hatten*	*geholt*

23 Use of the present and past tenses

(a) Present

The use of the **present tense** is virtually identical with its use in English. However, in instances where the action started in the past but continues in the present, the present tense is used in German rather than the perfect.

Ich wohne schon seit zwei Jahren in England.
I have already lived in England for two years.

The present tense can be used to refer to the immediate future (see p. 62).

(b) Imperfect or perfect?

The imperfect is used to narrate events which happened in the past. In English the rules for using the imperfect and the perfect are based on a sensitivity to tense (i.e. relevance of the narrated event to present moment). In German, however, the choice of imperfect or perfect is based on style.

According to *Grundgrammatik Deutsch*, the use of the imperfect is predominant in Northern Germany, whereas the perfect is more common in Southern Germany. In a formal context and certainly in written German, e.g. in minutes or in longer narratives, the predominant tense should be the imperfect. In personal letters you would expect a mixture of the perfect and the imperfect.

When people are narrating events that are still very vivid in their minds, or they wish to convey a sense of immediacy in telling a story, sentences are often linked with *und dann* and the perfect is employed:

> *Und dann ist Rotkäppchen in den Wald gelaufen und hat den Wolf getroffen. Der hat sie dann gefragt . . . und schließlich hat Rotkäppchen ihn zum Haus der Großmutter geführt.*
> And then Little Red Riding Hood ran into the woods and there she met the wolf. He asked her . . . and in the end Little Red Riding Hood led him to her grandmother's house.

When modal or other auxiliary verbs refer to a past event, they are generally in the imperfect tense as it is felt that the perfect sounds clumsy or more complicated, especially in spoken German:

> *Ich durfte gestern abend in die Disco gehen.*
> *Ich habe gestern abend in die Disco gehen dürfen.* (more difficult)
> Last night I was allowed to go to the disco.

> *Ich hatte die ganze Woche eine Erkältung.*
> *Ich habe die ganze Woche eine Erkältung gehabt.* (clumsier)
> I had a cold all week long.

Similar rules dictate the use of the pluperfect of *sein*:

> *Vor meinem letzten Urlaub war ich in Köln zum Einkaufen.* (preferred)
> *Vor meinem letzten Urlaub bin ich in Köln zum Einkaufen gewesen.* (clumsy)
> Before my last holiday I went to Cologne to go shopping.

(c) Pluperfect

The pluperfect is used to express anteriority (i.e. an event or action which happened before another past event or action referred to) but the rules – e.g. in reported speech – are not as strict as in English or French.

Er hatte noch nicht einen Satz gesagt, als man ihn unterbrach.
He had not said one single sentence when he was interrupted.

24 Tenses of the future

As in English, the future and the future in the past (also called the future perfect) are compound tenses. The auxiliary is *werden*. The auxiliary takes the personal endings and the main verb remains in the infinitive:

(a) Formation of the future

ich	*werde*	*kommen*
du	*wirst*	*kommen*
er / sie / es	*wird*	*kommen*
wir	*werden*	*kommen*
ihr	*werdet*	*kommen*
Sie	*werden*	*kommen*
sie	*werden*	*kommen*

You can see that the only difficulty about the future tense is due to the irregular forms of *werden*.

(b) Use of the future tense

The future tense is obviously used for future events, but the rules are flexible to some degree. When the speaker adds an expression of time (in the future), he or she will often use the present tense. For example, someone planning their holidays six months in advance might say:

Im Sommer fahre ich wieder in die Alpen.
In the summer I will go the Alps again.

The future tense could also be replaced by a modal verb, e.g. *wollen* (to want to). *Wollen* both expresses an intention and points to the future:

Im Sommer will ich wieder in die Alpen fahren.
In the summer I want to go to the Alps again.

On the other hand, the future tense can be used to convey decisiveness relating to future action:

Wir werden nicht zulassen, daß unsere Produktion durch Streiks gefährdet wird.
We will not allow our production to be jeopardized by strikes.

(c) Future in the past

As the term suggests, the future in the past is at the same time a future and a past tense. The speaker is commenting on a change of situation which he or she cannot check at the time of speaking or writing. Imagine the following scenario:

A salesman tells his secretary at 2 p.m. that she must cancel an appointment with a client at 5 p.m. because he needs to go and see someone else. At 2 p.m. he might therefore tell a colleague that his secretary will cancel the appointment:

Sie wird den Termin absagen. (future tense)

or:

Sie sagt den Termin ab. (present tense)

At 6 p.m. he is slightly worried whether his secretary managed to ring this client but he will assume:

Sie wird den Termin abgesagt haben. (future in the past)
She will have cancelled the appointment.

Even if he is still worried he cannot call her to find out because she will have gone home by now:

Sie wird nach Hause gegangen sein. (future in the past)

(d) Word order with compound tenses

The auxiliary verb – *haben*, *sein* or *werden* – takes the position of the conjugated verb (i.e. the one that takes the personal endings). In a statement, this will always be the second position (IIa). The remainder of the verb goes to the end of the sentence (IIb):

I	IIa			IIb
Ich	*habe*	*dich*	*heute*	*besucht.*
Ich	*hatte*	*dich*	*heute*	*besucht.*
Ich	*werde*	*dich*	*heute*	*besuchen.*
Ich	*werde*	*dich*	*heute vor 4 Uhr*	*besucht haben.*‡
Ich	*werde*	*dich*	*heute*	*besuchen dürfen.*‡

I visited you today.
I had visited you today.
I will visit you today.
I will have visited you today before 4 o'clock.
I will be allowed to visit you today.

All the complements are arranged between IIa and IIb (see section 55).

‡ N.B. Where there are more than two parts to the verb, the order is:

- the auxiliary (with the personal endings)
- complements (if there are any)
- full verb
- infinitive of *haben / sein* or of a modal verb

MODAL VERBS

Modal verbs are auxiliary verbs, i.e. they modify the action described by the full verb. In conjunction with a modal verb, the full verb always appears in the infinitive.

In the present and imperfect the modal verb takes the personal ending:

Ich konnte nicht schlafen.
I couldn't sleep.

In the other tenses the auxiliaries (*haben* for the perfect and pluperfect and *werden* for the future) take the personal endings, whereas both the modal verb and the full verb appear as infinitives.

Wir haben den Arzt fragen müssen.
We had to ask the doctor.

Wir werden den Arzt fragen müssen.
We will have to ask the doctor.

Word order with modals

When the present or imperfect tense is used, the full verb goes to the end of the sentence; with other tenses, the infinitive of the modal verb goes to the end and is immediately preceded by the infinitive of the full verb.

25 *dürfen*

If *dürfen* is used in a positive clause, *können* can be substituted for it.

However, in the negative *dürfen* expresses prohibition:

Hier dürfen Sie nicht parken.
You must not park here.

Hier können Sie nicht parken might suggest that there is a physical obstacle (you are not able to park here).

Verb pattern

dürfen durfte hat . . .dürfen

	PRESENT	IMPERFECT	PERFECT
ich	*darf*	*durfte*	*habe . . . dürfen*
du	*darfst*	*durftest*	*hast . . . dürfen*
er / sie / es	*darf*	*durfte*	*hat . . . dürfen*
wir	*dürfen*	*durften*	*haben . . . dürfen*
ihr	*dürft*	*durftet*	*habt . . . dürfen*
Sie	*dürfen*	*durften*	*haben . . . dürfen*
sie	*dürfen*	*durften*	*haben . . . dürfen*

26 *können*

Können has three partially interrelated meanings:

(i) *Ich kann skifahren.*
I can ski.

Here, *können* describes **an ability**.

(ii) *In Deutschland kann man gut essen.*
In Germany you can eat well.

In this context, *können* means 'to have the opportunity or possibility to do something'.

(iii) *Sie können hier parken.*
You can park here.

The emphasis, in this case, is on the fact that something is **permitted**. *Dürfen* is also used for this purpose. The distinction between *können* and *dürfen* is similar to that between the English verbs *can* and *may*.

Sie dürfen hier parken.
You may / are allowed to park here.

Verb pattern

können konnte hat. . . können

	PRESENT	IMPERFECT	PERFECT
ich	*kann*	*konnte*	*habe . . . können*
du	*kannst*	*konntest*	*hast . . . können*
er / sie / es	*kann*	*konnte*	*hat . . . können*

	PRESENT	IMPERFECT	PERFECT
wir	*können*	*konnten*	*haben . . . können*
ihr	*könnt*	*konntet*	*habt . . . können*
Sie	*können*	*konnten*	*haben . . . können*
sie	*können*	*konnten*	*haben . . . können*

27 *mögen*

Mögen is a complicated modal verb because in some ways it behaves like a defective (i.e. incomplete) verb. Unlike a typical English defective verb (e.g. 'must') it can be conjugated through all the tenses; however, it changes its meaning, so that the tense structure is supported by other verbs.

(a) To express preference

Ich mag die deutsche Küche. I like German cooking.

Here, *mögen* refers to a preference of a more permanent nature. To express a preference in the past you would say:

Als Kind mochte ich die deutsche Küche.
When I was a child I liked German cooking.

In the perfect tense:

Als Kind habe ich die deutsche Küche gemocht

(b) To express a wish

Ich möchte bitte ein großes Bier. I'd like a large beer.

Möchte is the subjunctive of *mögen* but it has taken on a meaning which is independent of its mood. In this instance it expresses a wish for something at the present point in time.

In the past, *wollen* would be used instead of *möchte*:

Bitte, was haben Sie bestellt? (waiter asks customer)
What did you order, please?

Ich wollte ein großes Bier. (customer replies)
I wanted a large beer.

In the perfect this would be:

Ich habe ein großes Bier gewollt.

Verb pattern

	PRESENT	IMPERFECT	PRESENT	IMPERFECT
ich	*mag*	*mochte*	*möchte*	*wollte*
du	*magst*	*mochtest*	*möchtest*	*wolltest*
er / sie / es	*mag*	*mochte*	*möchte*	*wollte*
wir	*mögen*	*mochten*	*möchten*	*wollten*
ihr	*mögt*	*mochtet*	*möchtet*	*wolltet*
Sie	*mögen*	*mochten*	*möchten*	*wollten*
sie	*mögen*	*mochten*	*möchten*	*wollten*

Perfect: *ich habe gemocht, ich habe gewollt.*

28 *müssen*

Müssen always expresses a necessity in the sense of constraint:

Ich muß jetzt wirklich gehen. I must go now.

Ich muß die Rechnung zahlen. I must pay the bill.

The demand is inherent in the subject matter. There is an imperative obligation to pay the bill. If negated, *müssen* means 'need not'. This meaning is contrary to the English 'must not'.

Ich muß heute nicht ins Büro fahren.
I needn't go to the office today.

Instead of *nicht müssen*, we can use *nicht brauchen*, which takes *zu* before the main verb.

Ich brauche heute nicht ins Büro zu fahren.

Also:

Ich brauche heute nur ins Büro zu fahren.
I only need to go to the office today.

★ N.B. *Brauchen* can only be used as a modal verb with *nicht* or *nur*. *Brauchen* would otherwise be a full verb which is followed by an object.

Ich brauche eine neue Jacke.
I need a new jacket.

★ N.B. You will find that many Germans use *nicht brauchen* without *zu*. This is partly a feature of dialect, but is also because many people confuse the rules, assuming that if there is no *zu* with *nicht müssen*, then it must be left out with *nicht brauchen*. This is incorrect.

Verb pattern

müssen mußte hat . . . müssen

	PRESENT	IMPERFECT	PERFECT
ich	*muß*	*mußte*	*habe . . . müssen*
du	*mußt*	*mußtest*	*hast . . . müssen*
er / sie / es	*muß*	*mußte*	*hat . . . müssen*
wir	*müssen*	*mußten*	*haben . . . müssen*
ihr	*müßt*	*mußtet*	*habt . . . müssen*
Sie	*müssen*	*mußten*	*haben . . . müssen*
sie	*müssen*	*mußten*	*haben . . . müssen*

29 *sollen*

Sollen is related in meaning to *müssen*. It is the only regular modal verb.

(i) *Der Arzt sagt, ich soll zwei Tage zu Hause bleiben.*
The doctor says I should stay at home for two days.

Here, there is also a certain **constraint**, but it is imposed by a third person; also, **there is scope for taking a different course of action**. Thus *sollen* is more appropriate than *müssen*.

(ii) *Du sollst nicht töten.*
Thou shalt not kill. (as in the Ten Commandments)

Sollen is used to express a moral imperative.

Verb pattern

sollen sollte hat . . . sollen

30 *wollen*

Wollen expresses an intention:

Er will noch heute die Arbeit fertigmachen.
He wants to finish the work today.

When it is used to demand something, *ich will* is stronger and less polite than *ich möchte:*

Ich will noch einen Kaffee.
I want another coffee.

Ich möchte noch einen Kaffee. (more polite)
I would like another coffee.

Verb pattern

wollen wollte hat... wollen

	PRESENT	IMPERFECT	PERFECT
ich	*will*	*wollte*	*habe... wollen*
du	*willst*	*wolltest*	*hast... wollen*
er / sie / es	*will*	*wollte*	*hat... wollen*
wir	*wollen*	*wollten*	*haben... wollen*
ihr	*wollt*	*wolltet*	*habt... wollen*
Sie	*wollen*	*wollten*	*haben... wollen*
sie	*wollen*	*wollten*	*haben... wollen*

The English 'I will' is normally rendered by *ja* (e.g. in the marriage vows), and more casually by *ja, das mache ich.*

31 Modal verbs used as full verbs

You will **hear** modal verbs being used as full verbs. When that is the case, the forms of the perfect are changed to the regular perfect:

ich habe gedurft
ich habe gekonnt
ich habe gemocht
ich habe gemußt
ich habe gesollt
ich habe gewollt

This perfect of modal verbs is used instead of the usual perfect (*ich habe . . . dürfen*) in certain dialect areas, especially in Southern Germany. Its use is quite idiomatic.

Modal verbs employed as full verbs acquire a meaning of their own, which is independent of the tense of the verb:

Darf ich? May I?

You might say this when offering to do something for someone, e.g. helping someone into his or her coat, offering to carry someone's luggage, or pouring your guest another glass of wine.

When making an appointment you would say:

> *Können Sie um 14 Uhr?* Can you come at 2 p.m.?

When someone is asked why she did not make it to an appointment, she might reply:

> *Ich habe nicht gekonnt.*
> (Instead of *Ich habe nicht kommen können.*)
> I was not / have not been able to.

A child might say to its mother:

> *Ich muß ganz dringend.* I must go to the loo now.

In the last three examples, the main verb is simply left out for reasons of economy.

If a wife finds her husband smoking, although the doctor has forbidden it, she might angrily say:

> *Du sollst doch nicht!* But you shouldn't!

Again, the main verb (this time *rauchen*) is left out.

OTHER GROUPS OF VERBS

32 Special verbs

There are a number of other verbs which are not conventionally classed as modal verbs. However, these verbs do modify a given expression and, more importantly, their meaning as a modal differs from their meaning as a full verb.

werden

Werden is irregular.

Verb pattern

werden wurde geworden

	PRESENT	IMPERFECT	PERFECT	PLUPERFECT
ich	*werde*	*wurde*	*bin geworden*	*war geworden*
du	*wirst*	*wurdest*	*bist geworden*	*warst geworden*
er / sie / es	*wird*	*wurde*	*ist geworden*	*war geworden*
wir	*werden*	*wurden*	*sind geworden*	*waren geworden*
ihr	*werdet*	*wurdet*	*seid geworden*	*wart geworden*
Sie	*werden*	*wurden*	*sind geworden*	*waren geworden*
sie	*werden*	*wurden*	*sind geworden*	*waren geworden*

The perfect given here is that of the full verb. When *werden* is used as an auxiliary, the past participle is *worden*.

Use

(i) *Werden* can be used as a full verb:

Ich werde am Sonntag fünfzehn.
I will be fifteen years old on Sunday.

Ich bin fünfzehn. I am fifteen years old.

As you can see, *Ich werde fünfzehn* is not the future tense but the present tense used with a future meaning. *Werden* is, so to speak, the **dynamic** counterpart of the **static** *sein*.

(ii) *Werden* can be used as a modal verb. Then it means 'I suppose':

Sie wird krank sein. I suppose she is ill.

Although it looks as if this sentence refers to the future, this is not so.

Future tense would be:

Sie wird krank werden. She will be(come) ill.

The following sentence is ambiguous:

Er wird ins Büro gehen.
He will go to the office. / I suppose he is on his way to the office.

Fortunately, if we want to refer to the **past**, this can be done unambiguously by using the future in the past:

Er wird ins Büro gegangen sein.
I suppose he will have gone to the office.

(iii) *Werden* as an **auxiliary** is used for the **passive voice**. Here again it contrasts with *sein*. Compare the following sentences in the present tense:

Das Büro wird verkauft. The office is being sold.

Das Büro ist verkauft. The office is sold.

Compare the following sentences in the perfect:

Das Büro ist verkauft worden. The office has been sold.

Das Büro ist verkauft gewesen. The office was sold.

Whereas *werden* expresses an action (**actional passive**), *sein* conveys a result (**resultative passive**).

lassen

(i) The construction *lassen* + a full verb is used to refer to something that happens without the subject's active involvement. In the examples given below, the speaker gets someone else to do something for him or her:

Ich lasse meine Frau anrufen.
I am having my wife called.

Ich lasse meine Haare schneiden.
I have my hair cut.

(ii) *Lassen* + object functions in the same way and with the same meaning as the English 'to leave (behind)':

Ich lasse meinen Schirm heute zu Hause.
I am leaving my umbrella at home today.

(iii) *Lassen* can mean 'to allow someone to do something':

Ich lasse die Kinder im Garten spielen.
I allow the children to play in the garden.

There are a number of **compound verbs** with *lassen*.

liegen◊lassen	*stehen◊lassen*
sitzen◊lassen	*ruhen◊lassen*

All of these verbs mean 'to leave behind'. *Liegenlassen* works for anything that has been put on something (e.g. on a table):

Ich habe mein Portemonnaie auf dem Schreibtisch liegen(ge)lassen.
I have left (or forgotten) my purse on the desk.

N.B. When a *-lassen* compound is used in the perfect tense, both the infinitive (*liegenlassen*) and the past participle (*liegengelassen*) are correct.

Sitzenlassen spelt as one word has a number of idiomatic meanings:

Diesen Vorwurf lasse ich nicht auf mir sitzen.
I will clear myself from this reproach.

Er hat seine Braut sitzen(ge)lassen.
He jilted his bride.

Der Lehrer hat meinen Sohn sitzen(ge)lassen.
The teacher had my son repeat a year.

Stehenlassen, too, has various idiomatic meanings:

Er ließ das Essen stehen und ging.
He left the table and went.

(*Das Essen, den Kaffee* etc.) *stehenlassen*
not to touch (one's food, coffee, etc.)

Er ließ ihn stehen, ohne ein Wort zu sagen.
He left him standing without a word.

Er ließ ihn im Regen stehen. < coll. >
He left him in the lurch.

Ruhenlassen:

Weißwein sollte man ein paar Tage im Keller ruhenlassen, bevor man ihn trinkt.
You should let white wine rest in the cellar for a few days before you drink it.

33 Reflexive verbs

This section deals with verbs which take a reflexive pronoun. This pronoun may be in the accusative or in the dative case. An attempt has been made to group the verbs semantically.

No distinction is made here between verbs which can **only** be used with a reflexive pronoun and those that can be used with either a normal object **or** a reflexive pronoun.

German often uses reflexives where English does not, and the meaning of the expression does not necessarily derive from the literal meaning of the verb.

The following lists are not comprehensive, but they include the most frequently used constructions.

(a) Everyday verbs

With accusative reflexive pronoun

sich waschen to wash (oneself)
sich kämmen to comb one's hair
sich frisieren to do one's hair
sich schminken to put on make-up
sich an◊sehen to look at oneself
sich rasieren to shave
sich an◊ziehen to get dressed
sich aus◊ziehen to get undressed
sich um◊ziehen to get changed
sich erkälten to catch cold

Er ist erst zwölf Jahre alt. Er rasiert <u>sich</u> noch nicht.
He is only twelve. He doesn't shave yet.

With dative reflexive pronoun

sich die Zähne putzen to brush one's teeth
sich die Nase putzen to blow one's nose
sich die Hände waschen to wash one's hands

Note that whereas English always uses a possessive pronoun with parts of the body, German, in many instances, prescribes the use of a reflexive pronoun:

Vor dem Essen mußt du <u>dir</u> die Hände waschen.
Before dinner you have to wash your hands.

(b) Verbs of communication

With accusative reflexive pronoun

sich (um etwas) bewerben to apply (for something)
sich (an etwas) erinnern to remember (something)
sich (nach etwas) erkundigen to inquire (about something)
sich (bei jemandem für etwas) entschuldigen to apologize (to someone for something)
sich irren to err
sich (bei jemandem) vor◊stellen to introduce oneself (to someone)
sich (mit jemandem) unterhalten to converse (with someone)
sich (mit jemandem) verabreden to make an appointment (with someone)
sich fragen (+ indirect question) to wonder (+ indirect question)

Darf ich mich vorstellen? May I introduce myself?

Ich frage mich, ob wir das Problem heute lösen konnen.
I wonder whether we can solve the problem today.

With dative reflexive pronoun

sich (etwas) ein◊bilden to imagine (something)
sich (etwas) vorstellen to imagine
sich (über etwas) klar sein to be clear (on something)
sich (etwas) vor◊nehmen to make plans (for something)
sich (etwas) überlegen to think about something
sich (etwas) denken to think (about something) to oneself
sich (über etwas) einig sein to agree (on something)
sich (mit jemandem) be- / an◊freunden to become friends (with someone)

Für nächstes Wochenende habe ich mir einen richtigen Hausputz vorgenommen.
I intend to do a real spring-clean next weekend.

(c) Verbs of emotion

With accusative reflexive pronoun

sich (über etwas /jemanden) ärgern to be / get annoyed (at something / someone)
sich (über etwas) freuen to enjoy something
sich (auf etwas / jemanden) freuen to look forward to (something / someone)
sich (vor etwas / jemandem) fürchten to be afraid (of something / someone)

sich (in jemanden) verlieben to fall in love (with someone)
sich (mit jemandem) vertragen to get on (with someone)

Über Ihren freundlichen Brief habe ich mich sehr gefreut.
I very much enjoyed your friendly letter. (opening formula in a letter)

(d) Reflexives with impersonal verbs

With accusative reflexive pronoun

es dreht sich um it is about
es handelt sich um ‡ it is about
es fragt sich (+ indirect question) the question is (+ indirect question)
es stellt sich heraus, daß it turns out that
es versteht sich von selbst, daß it goes without saying that

Es versteht sich von selbst, daß wir alle Kosten tragen.
It goes without saying that we will carry all the costs.

‡ Contrast *es handelt von*, which is followed by the dative.

With dative reflexive pronoun

es fehlt mir an (+ dative) I lack
es ist mir eine Freude it is a pleasure for me
es ist mir (un)möglich it is (not) possible for me
es ist mir peinlich I am embarrassed
es ist mir recht it's OK with me
es macht mir Spaß / Freude (+ *zu* + infinitive) it gives me pleasure
es scheint mir, daß it seems (to me) that

Im Moment ist es mir unmöglich, Ihnen den Liefertermin zu geben.
It is impossible for me to give you the delivery date at this point.

34 Verbs with separable and inseparable prefixes

Many verbs can take a prefix. In morphological terms, two categories of prefixed verbs are distinguished: those with separable and those with inseparable prefixes.

(a) Inseparable prefixes

(i) The prefixes *be-*, *emp-*, *ent-*, *er-*, *ge-*, *miß-*, *ver-*, *wider-* and *zer-*, as well as the latinate prefixes *de(s)-*, *dis-*, *in-* and *re-* are inseparable. These prefixes are unstressed.

Verbs with these prefixes never take *ge-* in the past participle, even if they are weak. Compare:

deuten hat gedeutet to interpret
bedeuten hat bedeutet to mean

Most inseparable prefixes of German origin have no meaning of their own. Exceptions include *zer-*, which always refers to a destructive action, and *miß-*, which negates the usual meaning of the verb:

reißen to tear
zerreißen to tear apart

verstehen to understand
mißverstehen to misunderstand

The meaning of the prefixed word is not necessarily perceptibly close to the meaning of the original verb.

(ii) If a verb is prefixed by a preposition, it is normally inseparable if the meaning of the preposition is not literal.

suchen to look for

etwas / jemanden versuchen to try
etwas / jemanden besuchen to visit
jemanden um etwas ersuchen to beseech / implore someone for something
etwas / jemanden untersuchen to examine something / someone

But the following two verbs are separable:

jemanden um etwas an◊suchen to submit a request to someone
sich etwas aus◊suchen to choose something

(iii) Verbs ending in *-ieren* are also inseparable:

etwas probieren to try something (out)

(b) Separable prefixes

Separable means:
- that the past participle has a *-ge-* inserted between the prefix and the verb
- that the verb splits into prefix and verb in the present and imperfect.

If the prefixes *durch-*, *hinter-*, *über-*, *um-*, *unter-*, *voll-* and *wieder-* have a concrete meaning, then they are separable:

durch◊kommen to get / pull through
ich komme durch ich kam durch ich bin durch gekommen

All compound verbs behave like verbs with separable prefixes, e.g. *kennen◊lernen*:

Wir lernten sie erst gestern abend kennen.
We only got to know them last night.

(c) Special cases and exceptions

There are a number of verbs where the same prefix may be either separable or inseparable, but depending on the stress the verb has a different meaning and a different past participle. Verbs with the prefix *durch-*, *hinter-*, *über*, *um-* and *unter-* are in this category.

Where the stress is on the prefix, the prefix is separable and the past participle takes *-ge-*. If the stress is on the verb itself the prefix cannot be separated from it, and the *-ge-* is dropped from the past participle. Here are some examples of these pairs:

durch◊schauen to look through (e.g. binoculars)

Ich habe durchgeschaut, aber trotzdem nichts gesehen.
I looked through but I still didn't see anything.

durchschauen to see through someone / something

Ich habe dich durchschaut. Das ist ein ganz übler Trick.
I've seen through you. That's a very dirty trick.

durch◊suchen to search

Ich habe den Schrank von oben bis unten durchgesucht, aber ich kann kein Paar passender Socken finden.
I have searched the wardrobe from top to bottom but I cannot find a matching pair of socks.

durchsuchen to search

Gestern abend durchsuchte die Polizei das Haus des Verdächtigten.
Last night the police searched the suspect's house.

um◊reißen to pull down / uproot
Der Sturm hat Hunderte von Bäumen umgerissen.
The storm uprooted hundreds of trees.

umreißen to sketch out

Zu Beginn der Sitzung hat er seine Pläne kurz umrissen.
At the beginning of the meeting he briefly sketched out his plans.

When a verb is prefixed by two components, the prefix is normally separable. The two parts of the prefix stay together:

herausfinden to find out

Wir haben alles über deine Pläne herausgefunden.
We have found out all about your plans.

dahinterstehen to back / stand behind

Der Chef stand voll dahinter.
The boss backed it fully.

35 The infinitive and *zu*

Consider the following sentences:

Ich möchte ihm helfen. I'd like to help him.

Ich biete ihm an, ihm zu helfen. I am offering to help him.

In the first sentence there is a modal verb, and it needs an infinitive to go with it. In the second example the verb *an◊bieten* introduces a dependent clause. If the subject in the main clause is identical with that in the dependent clause, use the ***zu* + infinitive** construction. Otherwise you need to use a relative clause:

Ich hoffe, daß er heute kommt. I hope he is coming today.

The following tables list the most frequently used verbs which take *zu* + infinitive.

Verbs expressing a personal attitude

- Positive attitudes:

bitten to ask
ein◊laden to invite
empfehlen to recommend
erwarten to expect
glauben to believe
hoffen to hope
scheinen to appear
vermuten to assume
vor◊haben to intend
vor◊schlagen to suggest
wünschen to wish

- Negative attitudes:

ab◊lehnen to refuse
erlauben to permit
fürchten to fear
nicht / nur brauchen to need not / only (cf. section 28)
verbieten to prohibit

Verbs expressing an action

- Positive actions:

an◊bieten to offer
an◊fangen to start
auf◊hören to finish
beginnen to begin
raten to advise
versprechen to promise
wagen to dare

- Negative actions:

vergessen to forget
versäumen to miss

Examples

Ich rate Ihnen, diese Stelle anzunehmen.
I advise you to accept this job.

Wir beginnen heute, Sie in das Bankrecht einzuführen.
Today we start to introduce you to banking law.

N.B. If the verb has a separable prefix, *zu* is inserted between the separable part and the main verb.

★ N.B. The infinitive + *zu* is also compulsory with the following expressions:

(i) After expressions starting with *es ist* (+ adjective):

Es ist schwierig, neue Märkte in der industrialisierten Welt zu gewinnen.
It is difficult to win new markets in the industrialized world.

(ii) After expressions with *ich habe* (+ object):

Ich habe die Absicht, ihm das persönlich zu sagen.
I intend to tell him about it personally.

Zu always goes as close as possible in front of the infinitive.

Ich hatte vor, gestern mittag zurückzukommen, aber dann war es doch wichtig, noch bei der Konferenz zu bleiben, und so habe ich ganz vergessen, für unseren Besuch heute abend einzukaufen.
I had intended to come back yesterday at lunchtime but then it was important to stay at the conference and so I quite forgot to go shopping for our visitors tonight.

MOOD

When we analyse the mood in which a verb is used, we are interested in the degree of certainty with which a statement is made. The indicative and the imperative are the moods in which certainty is expressed; the subjunctive conveys some degree of doubt and hypothesis.

36 The indicative

The indicative is the **mood of certainty**. A varying degree of uncertainty can be communicated by inserting a modal particle (see section 47) or an adverb.

Grammatically speaking, the forms of the moods of uncertainty – the conditional and the subjunctive – can be derived from the indicative.

37 The subjunctive

(a) Use

The subjunctive mood is used in four different situations:

(i) When you make a hypothesis:

> *Er könnte schon nach Hause gegangen sein.*
> He may already have gone home.

Here, the hypothetical character of the sentence may also be expressed in the indicative: you would then add a modal particle to mark the 'mood':

> *Vielleicht ist er schon nach Hause gegangen.*
> Perhaps he has already gone home.

(ii) When you express a hypothetical condition:

Wenn Sie früher zu mir gekommen wären, hätten wir den Bankrott verhindern können. (bank manager to client)
If you had come to me earlier, we could have prevented your bankruptcy.

This, too, is a hypothetical sentence: at the time of speaking, the condition can no longer be fulfilled.

(iii) When you report what someone else has said (cf. section 123):

In der Anklage heißt es, Frau X sei am Raubüberfall in Trier beteiligt gewesen. (a journalist reporting on a court case)
Mrs X is accused of having been involved in the hold-up in Trier.

(iv) When you want to utter a request or question politely:

Könnten Sie mir sagen, wie spät es ist.
Could you please tell me the time.

As you can see from these examples, the subjunctive mood is used in **formal situations**. In the first example the subjunctive would quite often be avoided in spoken language (*Vielleicht ist er schon nach Hause gegangen* would be more common). Alternative structures for expressing the conditional are discussed in section 38. Situation (iii) obviously occurs most frequently in written German, and of course in news reporting. An appreciation of the usage in situation (iv) is vitally important for the successful businessman or politician – and for the tourist.

The subjunctive mood implies a certain degree of doubt. In a report about court procedures, it is a legal requirement to give the accused the **benefit of the doubt** and hence to state allegations in the subjunctive. In a polite request, the use of the subjunctive is more elegant. It gives the person you are talking to some 'breathing space', although you may expect compliance with your request just as much as if you had asked in the indicative or the imperative!

In German (unlike English), the forms of the subjunctive and the imperfect indicative can be distinguished readily:

Könntest du die Tür zumachen?
Would you be kind enough to close the door?

Konntest du die Tür zumachen?
Were you able to close the door?'

(b) Polite requests and questions

Requests and questions can be uttered with totally different degrees of firmness and politeness. Situation (iv) above shows the use of the subjunctive to make a polite request, but there are other ways of making requests, as listed below.

In the imperative:

Schreiben Sie den Bericht bis morgen.
Finish the report by tomorrow.

There is no doubt that you want the report by tomorrow and there is no room for discussion.

With a modal verb:

Sie müssen den Bericht bis morgen fertigschreiben.
You must finish the report by tomorrow.

This, too, precludes any discussion.

With a question:

Können Sie den Bericht bitte bis morgen fertigschreiben?
Can you finish the report by tomorrow, please?

This variation, especially if a full stop is used at the end rather than a question mark, is firmly polite. The tone of voice used indicates to what extent the hearer is expected to comply with the request.

With the imperfect subjunctive (also called **Konjunktiv II** – see below):

Könnten Sie den Bericht bitte bis morgen fertigschreiben.

Despite the fact that the subjunctive is usually associated with a degree of uncertainty, the following requests anticipate a positive reaction:

Hätten Sie ein wenig Zeit heute nachmittag?
Would you have some time in the afternoon?

Würden Sie mir meine Tasche bringen?
Would you bring me my bag?

Möchten Sie eine Tasse Kaffee?
Would you like a cup of coffee?

Indirect questions in the subjunctive mood **oblige** the person addressed to do something.

Könnten Sie mir sagen, wo der Bahnhof ist?
Could you tell me where the station is?

Dürfte ich fragen, ob Sie heute abend schon eine Verabredung haben ?
May I ask you whether you already have an engagement tonight?

(c) Grammatical and morphological aspects of the subjunctive

The examples showing the use of the subjunctive in polite requests are all instances of the imperfect subjunctive. This form is used more often than the present subjunctive, and the latter can always be replaced by the imperfect subjunctive. Details of the two forms are given below.

It is important to note that whether present or imperfect, the subjunctive is not a tense, even if it looks like it.

(d) The present subjunctive (Konjunktiv I)

For all verb classes, the present subjunctive is formed by inserting an -e- between the stem of the verb and the present tense ending wherever possible, except for the third person singular, which ends in -e instead of *-t*.

	INDICATIVE		SUBJUNCTIVE
ich	*gehe*	*ich*	*gehe*
du	*gehst*	*du*	*gehest*
er / sie / es	*geht*	*er / sie / es*	*gehe*
wir	*gehen*	*wir*	*gehen*
ihr	*geht*	*ihr*	*gehet*
Sie	*gehen*	*Sie*	*gehen*
sie	*gehen*	*sie*	*gehen*

The stem vowel in strong verbs does not change to an umlaut:

	INDICATIVE		SUBJUNCTIVE
ich	*fahre*	*ich*	*fahre*
du	*fährst*	*du*	*fahrest*
er / sie / es	*fährt*	*er / sie / es*	*fahre*
wir	*fahren*	*wir*	*fahren*
ihr	*fahrt*	*ihr*	*fahret*
Sie	*fahren*	*Sie*	*fahren*
sie	*fahren*	*sie*	*fahren*

It is clear that the subjunctive may often be identical to the indicative. In these instances, the present subjunctive is always replaced by the imperfect subjunctive (see below).

The subjunctive forms of *sein* or *werden* occur frequently in reports about an event that has happened in the past. These two sentences describe an event in the past:

Die Firma hat Erfolg gehabt.
Die Firma hatte Erfolg.
The firm was successful.

In the subjunctive mood, these sentences become:

Die Lokalzeitung berichtet, die Firma habe im vergangenen Jahr Erfolg gehabt.
The local newspaper reports that the company was successful in the past year.

In the subjunctive, **no difference between the perfect and the imperfect can be made.**

The following table will help you identify the subjunctive when it is used in a statement referring to the **past**. Where the present subjunctive is identical to the indicative, it is replaced by the imperfect subjunctive. (The present forms are underlined.)

	with *haben*		with *sein*
	schreiben to write		*reisen* to travel
ich	*hätte geschrieben*	*ich*	*sei gereist*
du	*habest geschrieben*	*du*	*seist gereist*
er / sie / es	*habe geschrieben*	*er / sie / es*	*sei gereist*
wir	*hätten geschrieben*	*wir*	*seien gereist*
ihr	*habet geschrieben*	*ihr*	*seiet gereist*
Sie	*hätten geschrieben*	*Sie*	*seien gereist*
sie	*hätten geschrieben*	*sie*	*seien gereist*

Sein, this most irregular of all verbs, is unambiguous in the subjunctive, whereas the *ich*, *wir*, *Sie* and *sie* forms of *haben* are identical to the indicative. In these instances, use the imperfect subjunctive.

(e) The imperfect subjunctive (Konjunktiv II)

The imperfect subjunctive is morphologically related to the imperfect tense: the personal endings of weak verbs are in fact identical in the imperfect and the imperfect subjunctive. Strong verbs have an -*e*- between the stem and the personal ending where possible, and their (single) stem vowel has an umlaut. If the verb has a diphthong (as in *brauchen*), no change is made:

	IMPERFECT INDICATIVE		IMPERFECT SUBJUNCTIVE
ich	*ging*	*ich*	*ginge*
du	*gingst*	*du*	*ging(e)st*
er / sie / es	*ging*	*er / sie / es*	*ginge*
wir	*gingen*	*wir*	*gingen*
ihr	*gingt*	*ihr*	*ging(e)t*
Sie	*gingen*	*Sie*	*gingen*
sie	*gingen*	*sie*	*gingen*

The stem vowel in strong verbs is modified with an umlaut:

	IMPERFECT INDICATIVE		IMPERFECT SUBJUNCTIVE
ich	*fuhr*	*ich*	*führe*
du	*fuhrst*	*du*	*führest*
er / sie / es	*fuhr*	*er / sie / es*	*führe*
wir	*fuhren*	*wir*	*führen*
ihr	*fuhrt*	*ihr*	*führet*
Sie	*fuhren*	*Sie*	*führen*
sie	*fuhren*	*sie*	*führen*

Even where the imperfect subjunctive forms of weak verbs are identical to the indicative, this does not create ambiguity because this form of the subjunctive is used either to replace a present subjunctive, e.g. in reported speech, in which case it is clearly marked:

Er sagte, er wolle / wollte morgen kommen.
He said he wanted to come tomorrow.

or in hypotheses or polite requests, where it cannot be mistaken for a past tense form:

Wenn du nach Oxford reistest, könntest du dein Englisch verbessern.
If you went to Oxford you could improve your English.

Wenn Sie mir bitte einen Platz freihielten.
If you would be so kind as to keep a seat for me.

Replacing the imperfect subjunctive

Both in grammar books and among German native speakers there are discussions about when to use a subjunctive form (rather than the indicative) and also about when the imperfect subjunctive can be replaced by a *würde*-form + infinitive (English 'would' + infinitive). Here again, it is a question of taste and style rather than a matter of grammatical rules.

However, it can be safely said that where a subjunctive form sounds 'odd', or obsolete, the *würde*-form (imperfect subjunctive of *werden*) comes into play. However, *würde* should not be over-used in one sentence, and never in connection with *sein.*

Sie wäre froh, wenn er die Blumen gösse. (obsolete)
Sie wäre froh, wenn er die Blumen gießen würde. (preferred)
She would be glad if he could water the flowers.

★ Avoid:

Sie würde froh sein, wenn er die Blumen gießen würde.

Also, in most contexts it sounds less than elegant if the subjunctive of modal verbs is replaced by the *würde*-form.

Ich würde das nicht tun können. (avoid)
Ich könnte das nicht tun. (preferred)
I would not be able to do that.

Having said this, matters become really intricate if a reported statement refers to the past:

	IMPERFECT SUBJUNCTIVE	*WÜRDE*-FORM
PRESENT	*ich schriebe*	*ich würde schreiben*
PAST	*ich hätte geschrieben*	*ich würde geschrieben haben*

- With a modal verb:

PRESENT	*ich könnte schreiben*	*ich würde schreiben können*
PAST	*ich hätte können schreiben*	*ich würde geschrieben haben können*

In all persons, *würde* takes the regular personal endings of the subjunctive.

38 The conditional

Some grammarians treat the conditional as a tense rather than as a mood. Generally speaking, this represents a rather theoretical approach because the meaning of the conditional as a tense has been lost.

The conditional is used to express a condition the fulfilment of which is doubtful, or which cannot be fulfilled (any more).

(i) *Die Firma profitiert, wenn der Ölpreis steigt.*
The company benefits if / when the oil price increases.

In sentence (i), a **real condition** is being reported: if a, then b. There is no doubt about the fulfilment of this condition and the statement expresses neither hope nor any other emotion. Therefore, the **indicative** is used.

(ii) *Die Firma profitierte / würde profitieren, wenn der Ölpreis stiege.*
The company would benefit if the oil price increased.

The situation in sentence (ii) is one of hope. A **hypothesis** is being made, and there is an expectation that the oil price will in fact increase. Therefore the **subjunctive** is used, **both in the main clause and in the dependent clause**. In the main clause, the imperfect subjunctive can be replaced by a *würde*-form. Just as 'would' must not be used in the 'if'-clause in English, *würde* should not be used in the *wenn*-clause. Note that in German the two clauses must be separated by a comma.

★ N.B. Sometimes a conditional clause is used without an actual condition. In German, as indeed in English, this construction is used for polite suggestions:

Es wäre vielleicht ratsam, wenn wir die Polizei informierten.
It might be advisable to inform the police.

Sentence (iii) involves a **contrary-to-fact condition** – the company has not benefited, the oil price did not increase:

(iii) *Die Firma hätte profitiert, wenn der Ölpreis gestiegen wäre.*
The company would have benefited if the oil price had increased.

In both the dependent and the main clause, the imperfect subjunctive must be used. *Hätte profitiert* is an example of a verb which takes *haben*; *wäre gestiegen* is an example of a verb which takes *sein*.

Word order in the conditional

Note that in all three possibilities listed above (sentences (i)-(iii)), there is a main clause and a dependent clause. Therefore the verb in the dependent clause goes to the end. If there is more than one verb (as in (iii)), then the auxiliary verb comes last, preceded by the main verb.

The conjunction *wenn* may be omitted if the sentence starts with the verb of the dependent clause which carries the personal endings. A linking *so* is inserted between the two clauses, after the comma:

(i) *Steigt der Ölpreis, so profitiert die Firma.*
(ii) *Stiege der Ölpreis, so profitierte die Firma / würde die Firma profitieren.*
(iii) *Wäre der Ölpreis gestiegen, so hätte die Firma profitiert / würde die Firma profitiert haben.*

With modal verbs

(i) *Wir rufen Sie an, wenn wir liefern können.*
We'll call you when / if we can deliver.

(ii) *Wir riefen Sie an, wenn wir liefern könnten.*

or:

Wir würden Sie anrufen, wenn wir liefern könnten.
We would call you if we could deliver. (But we can't yet, so we are not calling you at this point!)

(iii) *Wir hätten Sie angerufen, wenn wir hätten liefern können.*
We would have called you if we had been able to deliver.

The word order in the dependent clauses of the three sentences does not change. **The modal verb always goes to the end.**

The difference between sentence (iii) with the modal verb and the earlier sentence (iii) is that where there is a modal, the auxiliary verb precedes the main verb. In this way the main verb is framed by the auxiliary and the modal.

Again, *wenn* can be avoided by starting with the subjunctive of the dependent clause:

(i) *Können wir liefern, so rufen wir Sie an.*
(ii) *Könnten wir liefern / Würden wir liefern können, so riefen wir Sie an.*
(iii) *Hätten wir liefern können, so hätten wir Sie angerufen / würden wir Sie angerufen haben.*

39 The imperative

The imperative is used for giving commands. Whereas in English the imperative always looks like the infinitive (e.g. 'Go!'), in German it is derived from the second person of the present tense.

These are the forms:

INDICATIVE	IMPERATIVE
Hilfst du?	*Hilf!*
Helfen Sie? (sg. / pl.)	*Helfen Sie!*
Helft ihr?	*Helft!*

In the *du*-form the *-st* is dropped; all the other forms are identical to the indicative.

Irregular verbs which take an umlaut in the *du*-form of the indicative lose it in the imperative:

Läufst du?	*Lauf!*
Hältst du?	*Halt!*

Some forms of the verbs *haben* and *sein* are, as usual, irregular:

Hast du?	*Hab!*
Bist du?	*Sei!*
Sind Sie?	*Seien Sie!*

All other forms of *sein* and *haben* are regular.

You will find that some imperatives in the *du*-form end in *-e*:

Sage mir, was du liest und ich sage dir, wer du bist.
Tell me what you read and I will tell you who you are.

The -*e* is used in older and / or literary texts. However, the -*e* is always compulsory if the stem of the verb ends in -*ig* or in a combination of consonants:

> *Entschuldige bitte!* I am sorry.
> *Antworte mir!* Answer my question!
> *Rechne das nochmal durch!* Do these figures again!

Alternatives to the imperative

It is not only in the English-speaking world that you find 'commands' in public places. The imperative is not normally used to express such commands. Instead, you will see an infinitive construction which is similar to the English gerund, although the gerund may not occur in the English version of the 'command' (see section 91).

> *Rauchen verboten!* No smoking / Smoking prohibited.

If you were to make this request to a friend or colleague, you would use either the **imperative**:

> *Rauchen Sie bitte nicht!*

or **a modal verb**:

> *Sie dürfen hier nicht rauchen!* You must not smoke here.

Of course you can make such a command sound much more polite if you use the **subjunctive**:

Würden Sie hier bitte nicht rauchen.
Wenn Sie hier bitte nicht rauchen würden.
Would you not smoke here, please.

Similarly, compare the use of the infinitive construction, the imperative, and a modal verb to express a command:

Radfahren verboten! No cycling.

Fahren Sie hier nicht Rad! Do not cycle here.

Sie dürfen hier nicht radfahren! You must not cycle here.

40 Active and passive voice

Semantically the main difference between the active and the passive voice is the emphasis on the 'initiator of the action' in the active voice:

Der Chef berät die Kunden.
but: *Die Kunden werden (vom / durch den Chef) beraten.*

The boss advises the clients.
The clients are advised (by the boss).

As in English, the object (*vom / durch den Chef*) is normally left out in the passive voice unless the emphasis is placed directly on it.

The passive voice is formed with the auxiliary *werden* + past participle:

PRESENT :	*Die Kunden werden beraten.*
IMPERFECT :	*Die Kunden wurden beraten.*
PERFECT :	*Die Kunden sind beraten worden.*
PLUPERFECT :	*Die Kunden waren beraten worden.*
FUTURE :	*Die Kunden werden beraten werden.*
FUTURE IN THE PAST :	*Die Kunden werden beraten worden sein.*

When a sentence is transformed from the active to the passive voice, subject and object swap functions, just as in English. The new object is linked to the verb by ***durch*** **+ accusative** (emphasis on process) or ***von*** **+ dative** (emphasis on agent).

Language learners frequently run into problems when they need to transform a sentence with more than one object. Compare the following active / passive pair:

Die Universität verlieh Herrn Müller den Preis. (active voice)
The university conferred the prize on Mr Müller.

Der Preis wurde Herrn Müller (von der Universität) verliehen. (passive voice)
Herrn Müller wurde der Preis verliehen. (passive voice)
The prize was conferred on Mr Müller (by the university).

Herrn Müller retains the function of a dative object in both the active and the passive voice.

Herrn Müller could be replaced by a pronoun:

Die Universität verlieh ihm den Preis. (active voice)

When *Herrn Müller* is replaced by a pronoun with the passive, either the subject or the dative object may go at the start of the sentence:

Der Preis wurde ihm (von der Universität) verliehen.
Ihm wurde der Preis (von der Universität) verliehen.

Use of the passive

In a well-planned German text or speech the passive voice would be far less frequent than in English. It is felt to be clumsy when used repeatedly and, because of the tendency to avoid the initiator of the action, can become inaccurate; a loss of impact and authenticity may result. There are alternatives to the passive voice which make your style easier to grasp and more interesting.

41 Different ways of conveying the passive sense

(a) *man*

Active constructions using the pronoun *man* are frequently used instead of the passive. In terms of personal endings, *man* functions like the third person singular:

> *Man weiß doch, daß diese Firma letztes Jahr hohe Profite gemacht hat.*
> It is well known that this company made high profits last year.

Man-sentences function well in contexts where a personal view is presented as the general view. Quite often English would have 'It is (known, necessary etc.)' or 'You . . .'

(b) *ist zu*

This construction is very similar to its equivalent in English. Compare the first sentence, which uses the passive voice, with the second, which shows the construction with *ist zu*:

> *Ein deutlicher Aufwärtstrend kann gesehen werden.* (passive voice)
> A clear upward trend can be seen.
>
> *Ein deutlicher Aufwärtstrend ist zu sehen.*
> A clear upward trend is to be seen.

(c) The participle

The use of the participle is a device often found in academic writing. Some participial constructions are so intricate that you will have the impression you are in a Latin class, but it is generally not very difficult to recognize them.

> *Wir müssen die auf der Messe neugewonnenen Geschäftskontakte gut pflegen.*
> We have to nurture those contacts which were recently acquired at the trade fair.

Here, we are not told **who** acquired those contacts although it would be possible to make this explicit by means of a dative object, e.g. *von unseren Mitarbeitern* (by our employees).

(d) Reflexive + participle

Das sich verteuernde Rohöl spielt für die Wirtschaft eine wichtige Rolle.
Crude oil, which is getting more and more expensive, plays a key role in the economy.

Again, we have skilfully avoided saying **who** initiated the increase in price.

(e) *Läßt sich* + infinitive

Das läßt sich machen.
That can be done.

Dieser Schaden läßt sich sicher reparieren.
This damage can surely be repaired.

Läßt sich + infinitive can only be used in the third person singular. The initiator of the action does not have any space in this grammatical construction.

(f) Verb + *bar*

This construction functions much like option (e).

Das ist mach bar.
That is do-able.

Dieser schaden ist sicher reparierbar.
This damage is surely repairable.

When you have to choose between different stylistic options, i.e. active or passive voice, *man*, or participle, you should first consider that variation always makes things more interesting and more readable. Secondly, it is generally true that German uses the passive voice rather less than English. Common introductions such as 'It is felt that . . .' should not be rendered word for word. You either specify who thinks what or you say something like *Allgemein denkt man* . . . but certainly not *Es wird gedacht* . . .

PARTICLES

Particles are to a language what nails or screws are to a building: they are rather small and insignificant in relation to the size of the whole edifice, but they hold everything else together.

The term 'particle' is used here in a broad sense: it includes conjunctions, prepositions, modal particles and dialogue particles. All particles are invariable – i.e. they cannot be declined or conjugated. Adverbs are sometimes included in this grouping but in this book they are dealt with separately (see sections 50-4). At the end of this chapter on particles, there is also a note on non-verbal communication.

Compare the following sentences:

Er liebte das Geld, weil er keines hatte.
He loved money because he did not have any.

Er liebte das Geld, obwohl er keines hatte.
He loved money although he did not have any.

Er liebte das Geld, aber er hatte keines.
He loved money but he did not have any.

The relationship between this man's love for money and his actual financial situation is different in each sentence; yet this difference is indicated by only three little words. In these examples those little words are particles called conjunctions.

42 Conjunctions

A conjunction stands between two words, phrases or clauses and links them.

There are two groups of conjunctions: **coordinating conjunctions** link two main clauses or two subordinate clauses; **subordinating conjunctions** link a main clause and a subordinate clause. This distinction is important in so far as it determines the word order of the clause which follows the link.

Two clauses or phrases are always separated by a comma, except in the uses of *und* and *oder* explained below.

und

If the subject in the second part of the sentence is identical with the one in the first part, there is no comma. If the subject changes, a comma is required:

Ich bin froh und glücklich.
Ich bin froh, und er ist glücklich.

I am joyful and happy.
I am joyful and he is happy.

oder

If the options are not mutually exclusive, there is no comma:

Was möchtest du? Honig oder Marmelade?
What would you like. Honey or jam?

But if both options cannot be chosen at the same time, a comma is required:

Entweder du heiratest mich, oder ich sterbe.
Either you marry me or I die.

43 Coordinating conjunctions

In a complex sentence linked by a coordinating conjunction, the word order remains the same as if the two clauses were independent sentences:

Heute ist es heiß. Wir gehen ins Schwimmbad.
Today it is hot. We are going to the swimming pool.
Heute ist es heiß, und wir gehen ins Schwimmbad.

As you can see, the position of *wir* (the subject) and *gehen* (the verb) does not change.

There are four groups of coordinating conjunctions:

(i) Conjunctions which add thoughts or pieces of information

und and
sowie as well as
sowohl . . . als auch not only . . . but also

Für die Immatrikulation im Universitätssekretariat bringen Sie bitte Ihre Zeugnisse, den Personalausweis, sowie drei Lichtbilder mit.
For matriculation in the university office, please bring your certificates, your identity card, as well as three passport photos.

Das ist sowohl richtig als auch wichtig.
This is correct as well as important.

(ii) Conjunctions which give a reason

denn as, for

(iii) Conjunctions which express opposition

aber but
doch however
jedoch but
sondern but
d.h. (das heißt) i.e. (that is)
teils . . . teils . . . partly . . . partly . . . / some . . . others . . .

Der Flug war teils angenehm, teils (war er) aber ziemlich unruhig.
The flight was partly pleasant but (it was) partly quite rough.

If the verb as well as the subject is identical in both parts of the sentence, it can be omitted in the second part. Compare the example given above, where they are identical, with the following sentence, where the verb changes:

Teils unterhielten sich die Leute, teils rauchten sie.
Some of the people were chatting, others were smoking.

For the use of *aber* and *sondern*, compare the following two sentences:

Ich bin müde, aber glücklich.
I am tired but happy.

Ich bin nicht traurig, sondern glücklich.
I am not sad but happy.

In the first sentence, A and B are contrasted. In the second sentence, however, 'not A' and B are contrasted. Hence, when you want to express **not A but B** you must use *sondern*.

(iv) Conjunctions expressing an alternative

oder or
entweder. . . oder either . . . or
nicht nur . . . sondern auch not only . . . but also
weder. . . noch neither . . . nor
bzw. (beziehungsweise) that is / respectively

Beziehungsweise is always abbreviated to *bzw.*

Its function is similar to *das heißt* but it places a stronger emphasis on the alternative:

Er konnte bzw. wollte nicht kommen.
He could not, or rather did not want to, come.

44

Subordinating conjunctions

(For an explanation of word order with subordinating conjunctions, see section 56.)

There are several groups of subordinating conjunctions:

(i) Conjunctions suggesting an explanation

da, weil because
zumal especially as
um so mehr als all the more as
um so weniger als all the less as

Man muß ihm helfen, zumal er doch krank ist
We must help him, especially as he is ill.

Man muß ihm helfen, um so mehr als er krank ist.
We must help him, all the more as he is ill.

(ii) Concessive conjunctions

obgleich, obwohl, obschon although

Er ging zur Arbeit, obwohl / obgleich er krank war.
He went to work although he was ill.

Obschon is rarely used today but may be found in some literary texts.

(iii) Conjunctions suggesting a time aspect

- Simultaneity:

  als when *wenn* when *während* while

- Non-simultaneity:

  bevor / ehe before
  nachdem after
  sobald as soon as

- Length of time:

  bis until
  seit / seitdem since
  solange as long as

  Ich kenne die Dame, seit / seitdem sie hier wohnt.
  I've known the lady since she moved here.

  Wir sind mit der Familie befreundet, solange wir denken können.
  We've been friends with the family for as long as we can remember.

(iv) Conjunctions expressing a consequence

so daß so that
damit so that, in order to

N.B. An infinitive clause *(um ... zu)* should be used if the subject in the main clause is identical with that of the subordinate clause:

Die Gesellschaft muß einen Kredit aufnehmen, um wettbewerbsfähig zu bleiben.
The company has to take out a loan in order to remain competitive.

If there are two different subjects, use *damit* or *so daß*:

Die Bundesrepublik muß die Steuern erhöhen, damit die neuen Bundesländer wirtschaftliches Wachstum finanzieren können.
The Federal Republic must increase tax so that the new *Länder* can finance economic growth.

N.B. An infinitive clause (*ohne ... zu*) should be used if the subject in both clauses is identical; *ohne ... daß* must be used if there are two different subjects:

Er war die ganze Nacht gefahren, ohne eine Pause zu machen.
He had driven all night long without taking a break.

Sie veranlaßte die Änderungen, ohne daß ihre Kollegen davon wußten.
She initiated the changes without her colleagues knowing about it.

(v) Conjunctions expressing a condition

wenn if
falls in case
soviel / soweit in as far as

(vi) Conjunctions linking two clauses in comparison

als ob as if
je (+ comparative) . . . *um so* (+ comparative) the (+ comparative) . . . the (+ comparative)
je (+ comparative) . . . *desto* (+ comparative) the (+ comparative) . . . the (+ comparative)

Sie tat, als ob sie nichts gehört hätte.
She pretended not to have heard anything.

Je weniger Öl wir haben, um so / desto höher steigt der Preis.
The less oil we have, the higher the price climbs.

(vii) Conjunctions conveying the idea of exchange

statt daß / anstatt daß
statt . . . zu / anstatt . . . zu } instead of + gerund

(viii) *daß* and *ob*

These are two important conjunctions.

daß that
ob whether

Daß is used when something is certain:

Ich weiß sicher, daß er heute kommt.
I am certain that he is coming today.

Ob is used when something is uncertain, and in indirect questions:

Ich weiß nicht, ob er heute noch kommt.
I am not sure whether he is still coming today.

Ich möchte wissen, ob noch ein Zimmer frei ist.
I would like to know whether you still have a room.

45 Prepositions

(See also sections 8, 10 and 33.)

Prepositions are a set group of words. They generally describe a geographical relationship between objects.

Prepositions take a particular case (see p. 20), i.e. they determine the case of the article + noun that follows. Some prepositions take more than one case, and the change in case usually signifies a change in meaning.

Some prepositions are combined with the article unless the article is in a position of particular stress, as in:

Ich habe das Brot bei dem Bäcker gekauft, der nur Bio-Produkte führt.
I bought the bread at the baker's that stocks only organic products.

They are combined as follows:

an + dem = am
zu + dem = zum
bei + dem = beim
in + dem = im
von + dem = vom

an + das = ans
zu + der = zur
in + das = ins

Prepositions also occur in set combinations with either a verb, adjective or noun. The original meaning of the preposition may have been lost, or it may be hard to discern, so the meaning and use of these set combinations must be learned individually. A selection of useful combinations can be found in section 46.

The prepositions are grouped according to which case(s) they take.

(a) Prepositions which take the accusative

bis until / up to

Place

Ich begleite Sie bis Hamburg.
I'm accompanying you as far as Hamburg.

Time

Bis nächsten Sonntag. See you next Sunday.

durch through, with the help of, by means of

Way

Wir sind durch die Schweiz nach Italien gefahren.
We went to Italy via Switzerland.

Duration

Wir fuhren den ganzen Tag durch.
We travelled all day long.

N.B. As the verb is *durch◊fahren, durch* must go at the end of the sentence.

Method

Die Öffentlichkeit hat davon durch die Presse erfahren.
The public knew about it through the press.

entlang along

N.B. *entlang* takes the accusative if it follows a noun / pronoun (see below, p. 108).

Wir machten eine Bootsfahrt den Rhein entlang.
We went on a boat trip along the Rhine.

für for (purpose)

Wir brauchen Mitarbeiter für unsere neue Filiale.
We need new employees for our new branch.

Das Geschenk ist für ihn.
The present is for him.

gegen against / around

Opposition

Das kommunistische Manifest ist gegen / wider den Kapitalismus.
The Communist Manifesto is against capitalism.

Er fuhr gegen die Mauer.
He drove into the wall.

N.B. Unlike *gegen*, *wider* (a less common preposition but one which also takes the accusative) can only be used in an abstract sense.

Time

Wir sind gegen den frühen Nachmittag bei Ihnen.
We will be with you sometime in the early afternoon.

ohne without

Viele Leute möchten den Winter ohne weißen Schnee.
Many people prefer winter without the white snow.

um at / around

Place

Der Wagen biegt um die Ecke.
The car is coming round the corner.

Number / time

Dieses Kleid kostet um die 200 DM.
This dress costs about 200 DM.

Der Zug fährt um 14.31 Uhr.
The train leaves at 14.31.

(b) Prepositions which take the dative

ab from

Place

Diese Flüge gehen ab Frankfurt.
These flights depart from Frankfurt.

Time

Ab Mitte der Woche haben wir neue Waren.
From the middle of the week onwards we will have new stock.

aus from / out of / for

Ich komme aus dem Osten von England.
I come from the East of England.

Aus diesem Grunde bin ich für den Kandidaten.
I support the candidate for this reason.

außer except for

Alle sind da außer dem jüngsten Schüler.
All are there except for the youngest pupil.

bei at / with

Place

Herr Mayer arbeitet bei einer Bank.
Mr Mayer works at a bank.

Ich habe ein Zimmer bei der netten Familie nebenan.
I have rented a room with the pleasant family next door.

Time

Das Kleid habe ich beim letzten Sommerschlußverkauf bekommen.
I got this dress in the last summer sales.

Condition

Bei dem Schnee fahre ich nicht nach London.
In this snow I will not go to London.

entgegen against / contrary to

Entgegen allen Voraussagen wurde das Wetter besser.
Contrary to all predictions the weather improved.

gegenüber opposite / as opposed to / in relation to

Place

Der Reichstag in Berlin liegt gegenüber dem Brandenburger Tor.
The Reichstag in Berlin is opposite the Brandenburg Gate.

Comparison

Gegenüber der Muttersprache bleibt die Fremdsprache immer schwierig.

or:

Der Muttersprache gegenüber bleibt die Fremdsprache immer schwierig.
Compared with one's mother tongue, a foreign language always remains difficult.

Attitude

Seinen Mitarbeitern gegenüber ist er fair.
He is fair with his employees.

mit with

Ich komme mit meiner Freundin.
I am coming with my girlfriend.

Mit diesem Werkzeug können Sie nichts ausrichten.
With this tool you cannot possibly do anything.

nach to / after / according to

Direction

Fährt dieser Zug nach Hamburg?
Does this train go to Hamburg?

N.B. In this sense *nach* is used in connection with towns and countries without an article; *in* is used with countries which are preceded by an article or an adjective + article (cf. section 2).

Fährst du diesen Sommer wieder in die Schweiz?
Are you going to Switzerland again this year?

Time

Wir besuchen Sie nach 16.00 Uhr.
We will visit you after 4 o'clock.

According to

Den Zeitungen nach / Nach den Zeitungen werden die Steuern dieses Jahr steigen.
According to the newspapers, taxes are going to rise this year.

N.B. *Meiner Meinung nach* in my opinion

entlang along

N.B. *entlang* takes the dative if it **precedes** a noun / pronoun (cf. above, p. 104).

Entlang der Landstraße standen viele große Bäume.
Along the country road there were a lot of big trees.

seit since / for (time aspect only)

Familie Wegener lebt seit drei Jahren in der Schweiz.
The Wegeners have been living in Switzerland for three years.

Seit 1990 ist er Direktor unserer Firma.
He has been company director since 1990.

If the event reaches to the present moment, use the present tense (see section 23).

von from / by

Place

Der Wagen kam von rechts.
The car came from the right.

Time

Von heute an rauche ich nicht mehr.
From today onwards I will not smoke any more.

Agent

Diese Entscheidungen werden vom Chef selbst getroffen.
These decisions are made by the boss himself.

As a substitute for a genitive (cf. section 5):

ein Kollege von mir (instead of *einer meiner Kollegen)*
a colleague of mine

zu to

Place

Gehst du schon zur Schule?
Do you already go to school?

Zu is used for particular places. It implies a strong sense of direction and can often be replaced by *in*: the use of *in* specifies that your business is **inside** the building.

Time

Zum 18. Geburtstag bekam er ein Auto.
He was given a car for his 18th birthday.

(c) Prepositions which take either the dative or the accusative

Consider the following pair of sentences:

Darf ich Ihnen noch Wein in Ihr Glas gießen?
Haben Sie noch Wein in Ihrem Glas?

In the first sentence, *in* takes the **accusative**; in the second, *in* takes the **dative**. The choice between the accusative and the dative with *in* is determined by the following semantic distinction:

If there is an action involving a sense of direction, use the **accusative**. If there is no action or motion, use the **dative**.

Note that this guideline applies only to the prepositions *an, auf, hinter, in, neben, über, unter, vor* and *zwischen*.

The following sets of examples contrast the choice of **accusative** or **dative** for each of these prepositions.

With the accusative

Er stellt den Schirm an die Wand.
He puts the umbrella against the wall.

Er stellt den Schirm hinter die Tür.
He puts the umbrella behind the door.

Er stellt den Schirm in die Badewanne.
He puts the umbrella into the bath.

Sie setzt sich zwischen ihre Eltern.
She sits down between her parents.

Sie setzt sich unter den Baum.
She sits down under the tree.

Sie setzt sich vor das Haus.
She sits down in front of the house.

Völlige Stille legte sich über die Zuhörer.
Complete silence came over the audience.

Der Hund legte sich auf den Teppich.
The dog went to lie on the carpet.

Der Hund legte sich neben den Sessel.
The dog went to lie next to the armchair.

With the dative

Der Schirm steht an der Wand.
The umbrella is leaning against the wall.

Der Schirm steht hinter der Tür.
The umbrella is behind the door.

Der Schirm steht in der Badewanne.
The umbrella is in the bath.

Sie sitzt zwischen ihren Eltern.
She is sitting between her parents.

Sie sitzt unter dem Baum.
She is sitting beneath the tree.

Sie sitzt vor dem Haus.
She is sitting in front of the house.

Völlige Stille lag über den Zuhörern.
Complete silence was over the audience.

Der Hund lag auf dem Teppich.
The dog lay on the carpet.

Der Hund lag neben dem Sessel.
The dog lay next to the armchair.

(d) Prepositions which take the genitive

Place	*außerhalb*	*außerhalb des Gartens* outside the garden
	innerhalb	*innerhalb der gebildeten Gesellschaft* within the educated society
	oberhalb	*oberhalb der Schneegrenze* above the snow line
	unterhalb	*unterhalb der Kirche* below the church

Time	*während*	*während des Tages* during the day
Reason	*wegen*	*wegen des Regens* because of the rain
	with pronouns:	*meinetwegen, deinetwegen . . .* because of me, because of you . . .
Exchange	*statt* *anstatt* *an Stelle*	*Ich kam statt / anstatt / an Stelle meines Vaters.* I came instead of my father.
Concessive	*trotz*	*Er kam trotz seiner Erkältung.* He came despite his cold.

In spoken German, the genitive is nowadays often replaced by the dative. Signs like the one below show to what extent the genitive (here: *unseretwegen*) has been forgotten even in an official context.

46 Verbs and adjectives with prepositions

This list contains frequently used combinations of verbs or adjectives with prepositions which are particularly useful for communicating information, views and feelings. They are grouped according to preposition and case. In many instances the literal meaning of the preposition has been lost, and the preposition used in the equivalent English expression does not normally give a clear guide as to which German preposition should be used. For a list of the reflexive verbs which take specific prepositions, see section 33.

an + accusative

an◊knüpfen an to refer to
appellieren an to appeal to
denken an to think of
glauben an to believe in
(sich) hängen an to be attached to
schreiben an to write to

an + dative

arbeiten an to work at
leiden an (einer Krankheit) to suffer from (an illness)
sterben an (einer Krankheit) to die of (an illness)
erkranken an (einer Krankheit) to fall ill with (an illness)
es fehlt an‡ is lacking
interessiert sein an to be interested in
gewinnen an to gain
verlieren an to lose
hängen an to depend on
liegen an‡ to depend on
teil◊haben an (etwas) to share (something)
teil◊nehmen an to participate in
zweifeln an to doubt

‡ *Es fehlt ihm an Feingefühl.* He lacks sensitivity.
Es liegt nur an dir. It is entirely down to you.

auf + accusative

achten auf to pay attention to
an◊spielen auf to allude to

antworten auf to answer
gespannt sein auf to be excited about
hoffen auf to hope for
pochen auf to insist upon
reagieren auf to react to
stolz sein auf to be proud of
trinken auf to drink to
vertrauen auf to rely on
warten auf to wait for

auf + dative

basieren auf to be founded on
beharren auf, bestehen auf to insist on
beruhen auf, fußen auf‡ to rely on

‡ *Unsere Annahmen beruhen auf der These, daß . . .*
Our assumptions rely / are based on the thesis that . . .

für + accusative

dankbar sein für to be grateful for
sorgen für to take care of
sich für etwas entschuldigen to apologize for something
stimmen für to vote for
verantwortlich sein für to be responsible for

mit + dative

bekannt sein mit to be acquainted with
diskutieren mit (jemandem) to discuss with (someone)
einverstanden sein mit (etwas) to agree on (something)
rechnen mit to expect
reden mit, sprechen mit (jemandem) to talk to (someone)
verheiratet sein mit to be married to
verwandt sein mit to be related to
zufrieden sein mit to be satisfied with

über + accusative

berichten über to report about
diskutieren über to discuss
froh sein über to be glad about
klagen über to complain about
lachen über to laugh about
meditieren über to meditate on

nach◊denken über to think about
philosophieren über to philosophize about
sprechen über to talk about

um + accusative

klagen um, trauern um to grieve for
bangen um to fear for / worry about
sich sorgen um to worry about

47 Modal particles

(a) Use

Modal particles add a 'flavour' to what people say, just as herbs and spices add flavour to food. The particular effect achieved has much to do with the dexterity and individual preferences of the speaker.

The meaning of a particular modal particle often depends on its place in the sentence and on the stress it is given. Hence, modal particles are more frequent in – but by no means exclusive to – the spoken language. Modal particles are **never declined.**

The meaning of the following sentence can be changed by the way the words are stressed (as indicated by the underlining):

Ich wollte ihm doch helfen.
Ich wollte ihm doch helfen.

Stress on *doch*:
I wanted to help him (although I had said earlier that I would not); here, *doch* means 'contrary to expectations'.

Stress on *helfen*:
But I wanted to help him (i.e. I did not mean to hurt him but I wanted to be of help); here, *doch* could be substituted by *aber*.

It is difficult for non-native speakers to get a firm grasp on modal particles. Start by using the more common ones and ask native speakers whether the desired effect has been achieved. Gradually you will find out your own preferences and enjoy the use of these linguistic 'herbs and spices'.

Some modal particles may also act as a completely different part of speech. These alternative uses are indicated in the list that follows. It is essential to be aware of these double functions, especially for understanding written texts.

(b) The most common modal particles

aber expresses insistence or surprise

Ich will aber keinen Spinat.
But I do not want any spinach.

Das ist aber teuer.
This is really expensive.

N.B. *aber* can also be used as a coordinating conjunction (see section 43):

Paul ist nicht reich, aber glücklich.
Paul is not rich but he is happy.

also summarizes a train of thought

Also, ich mache das gerne.
OK, I'd like to do that.

Also is often used to introduce a (potentially emotional) conclusion.

denn expresses interest

Bist du denn von allen guten Geistern verlassen?
Have you gone completely mad? (good humoured)

N.B. *denn* can also be used as a coordinating conjunction (see section 43):

Du brauchst ihm kein Geld zu geben, denn er ist reich.
You do not need to give him any money as he is rich.

doch reinforces something already stated and understood

Sei leise, du weißt doch, daß ich jetzt arbeiten muß.
Be quiet. You do know that I must work now.

N.B. *doch* can also function as a dialogue particle (see section 48).

ja similar to *doch* but less aggressive

Du weißt ja, daß ich nächste Woche in Urlaub fahre.
Incidentally, you know that I am going on holiday next week.

N.B. *ja* is also used as a dialogue particle (see section 48).

(c) Less frequently used modal particles

bloß / nur simply / only

Sie brauchen bloß / nur auf diesen Knopf zu drücken. (in a commercial)
You simply need to press this button.

N.B. *bloß* can of course be used as an adjective:

Von hier können Sie das Matterhorn mit bloßem Auge erkennen.
From here you can see the Matterhorn with the naked eye.

eben / halt used in sentences with a logical conclusion, often suggests resignation

The cleaner is off sick for the week and the manager tells her colleague:

Dann müssen wir diese Woche eben / halt ohne Putzhilfe auskommen.
Then we'll just have to make do without the cleaner for this week.

N.B. ***eben*** can also be used as an adjective meaning 'level / flat':

Unser Garten ist ganz eben. Our garden is completely flat.

It is also an adverb of time (see section 50) and of manner (see section 51):

Er ist eben zur Tür hereingekommen.
He has just come through the door.

eigentlich really / actually / by the way
(implies a request to look at something more closely)

Weißt du eigentlich, wie spät es ist?
By the way, do you know how late it is?

Heidegger, still one of the most widely read German linguistic philosophers even in the English-speaking world, tells us that *eigentlich* really means 'authentically' and should not be used to communicate vagueness.

N.B. *eigentlich* is also used as an adjective, in which case it is declined:

Er arbeitet hier als Kellner. Das ist aber nicht sein eigentlicher Beruf.
He works here as a waiter. However, that is not his real job.

★ N.B. English speakers tend to translate the much-loved English modal particle 'really' by *wirklich*. This is usually wrong; you should simply leave it out or try either *eigentlich* or – on a rather informal level – *echt*. Incidentally, 'Not really!' translates as *Eigentlich nicht!*

(ein)mal makes a question sound less formal

Kann ich mal telephonieren?
May I use your telephone?

In sentences which express a demand, *(ein)mal* weakens the demand so that it sounds more like an offer:

Dann kommen Sie (ein)mal heute nachmittag in meinem Büro vorbei.
Why don't you come by my office in the afternoon.

N.B. There is a very fine line between *(ein)mal* used as a modal particle and *(ein)mal* used as an adverb of time (see section 50):

Ich möchte gerne (ein)mal nach Indien fahren.
I would like to go to India (once).

Er sagte mir einmal, daß er Dichter sei.
He told me once that he was a poet.

nämlich refers back to an explanation given earlier

Ich kann nicht kommen. Ich bin nämlich krank.
I cannot come. I am sick (you see).

Nämlich is difficult to translate exactly into English.

schon emphasizes certainty

Mother to son after he has eaten several packets of chocolate biscuits:

Du wirst schon sehen, später hast du dann Bauchschmerzen.
You'll see, you'll have a stomach-ache later.

N.B. As an adverb *schon* means 'early / already' (see section 50):

Ihr seid schon da? You are already here?

wirklich

Es geht mir wirklich (nicht) gut.
I am really (not) well.

wohl (a) synonym of *bitte*; (b) indicates supposition

(a) *Könnte ich wohl mal telephonieren?*
Could I use the telephone please?

(b) *Er wird wohl später kommen.*
He will probably come later.

(d) Modal particles and sentence structure

It is not possible to give straightforward rules for the position of modal particles, as has been explained at the beginning of this section. However, the majority of the modal particles can be inserted in the 'inner field' (see section 55). Once you have distributed all the other parts of the sentence, i.e. pronouns, all adverbs and *nicht*, the modal particle goes in front of the object and / or in front of the negation. Only *aber*, *also*, *dann* and *eigentlich* can also be the first element in a sentence, as shown in the alternative versions of the first two examples given below. If the modal particle is the first element, it is stressed; in the case of *aber*, both the first element and the subject are stressed. The following examples show the position of modal particles and the way they inflect meaning.

Er wollte die Rechnung eigentlich (nicht) bezahlen.
Eigentlich wollte er die Rechnung (nicht) bezahlen.
He did (not) really want to pay the bill.

Weißt du eigentlich, wie spät es ist?
By the way, do you know how late it is?

Ich will aber keinen Spinat.
Aber ich will keinen Spinat.
But I don't want any spinach.

Ich wollte ihm doch (nicht) helfen.
But I did (not) want to help him.

Weißt du denn gar nicht, daß er reich ist?
Do you really not know that he is rich?

Du weißt doch, daß ich jetzt arbeiten muß.
You know I must work now.

Sie brauchen nur auf diesen Knopf zu drücken.
You simply need to press this button.

Wir müssen dann eben ohne Putzhilfe auskommen.
Then we'll just have to make do without the cleaner.

(e) Accumulation of modal particles

As a rule the stressed particle carries the meaning whereas the accompanying particles add flavour to this meaning. They can, for example, make the statement more or less casual, more or less emotional, more or less demanding, etc.

> *Ich wollte ihm doch eigentlich helfen.*
> I had intended to help him (and not hurt him).
>
> *Ich wollte ihm eigentlich doch bloß helfen.*
> *Ich wollte ihm doch eigentlich bloß helfen.*
> I had really only intended to help him (and now he asks me for something completely different).
>
> *Du könntest ihm wohl eigentlich helfen.*
> I suppose you could really help him.

It is very hard to translate the emotional content of modal particles as their meaning is highly idiomatic. This is all the more true when non-verbal signals enter into the process of communication. A sentence which includes many particles may therefore be difficult to interpret, even for native speakers.

8 Dialogue particles

Dialogue particles occur whenever a speaker makes a decision or reacts to one. German dialogue particles often stand for a whole sentence:

> *Rauchen Sie? –Ja (, ich rauche).*
> Do you smoke? –Yes (, I do).

German has three particles for saying 'yes' or 'no': *ja*, *nein* and *doch* (cf. French *si*). *Doch* is used to supply an affirmative response to a negative question.

> – *Interessieren Sie sich für Computer?*
> – *Ja!* / *Nein!*
> – Are you interested in computers?
> – Yes! / No!
>
> – *Interessieren Sie sich nicht für Computer?*
> – *Doch!* (affirmative) / *Nein!* (as in English)
> – Aren't you interested in computers?
> – Yes (, I am). / No (, I am not).

A second set of dialogue particles is just as essential when it comes to good relationships: to express gratitude and to ask for something. Even though you may get the impression from the German younger generation that *bitte* and *danke* have lost their importance, most well-travelled Germans seem to appreciate Anglo-Saxon courtesy. So do not hesitate to use these particles whenever appropriate. However, the use of these two little words can be a little confusing to the speaker of English.

In some situations, for example, if someone you do not know well offers you coffee, it is both more polite and clearer if you always use the full form: *Ja, bitte!* or *Nein, danke!* However, the shorter forms are more common.

– *Möchten Sie einen Kaffee?*
– *Bitte (= Ja, bitte). / Danke (= Nein, danke).*

– Would you like a coffee?
– Thank you (= Yes, thank you). / No, thank you.

Bitte translates a wealth of English expressions; the most common contexts are listed here.

- Requests:

Bitte, darf ich heute ins Kino gehen?
Darf ich bitte heute ins Kino gehen?
Darf ich heute bitte ins Kino gehen?
May I go to the cinema today, please?

When in doubt, add another *bitte* to your request!

- Affirmative answer to an offer: *Ja, bitte.*

- Waiter serving your meal or shop assistant giving you your shopping:

Hier, bitte (schön). Here you are.

You would respond by saying *Danke!*, but note that if you want to reply in a complete sentence, *danke* (unlike *bitte*) can only stand at the beginning or end of the sentence:

Danke, das ist sehr nett von Ihnen.
Das ist sehr nett von Ihnen, danke.
Thank you, that is very kind of you.

- Man letting a woman pass through the door first:

Bitte (schön)! (accompanied by a gesture) After you!

Occasionally you might say:

Nach Ihnen! (accompanied by a gesture) After you!

- For 'you are welcome':

  – *Danke für den schönen Abend.*
  – *Bitte, gern geschehen.*
  – Thank you for the enjoyable evening.
  – You are welcome.

- If you have not understood something properly and would like the speaker to repeat it:

  Bitte? / Wie bitte?

This is an abbreviated form of:

Bitte, können Sie das noch einmal wiederholen?
Pardon, would you please be so kind as to repeat that?

- To receive an apology:

Whenever someone apologizes to you, you should react by saying *bitte* as a sign that you have accepted the apology. Apologies themselves can also be categorized as dialogue particles:

Entschuldigung! / Verzeihung! Excuse me.

Entschuldigen Sie! < formal >
Entschuldige! < informal >
Excuse me.

Das tut mir leid! I am sorry.

Pardon! (with the accent on the second syllable, as in French)
Sorry.

9 Non-verbal communication

Gestures are another essential part of the process of communication (see also section 73). When you make a phone call in a foreign language it becomes particularly obvious how much you would rather say in sign-language than with words.

The meaning of most gestures, e.g. for saying 'slowly please', 'please listen carefully', 'no', 'thank you', etc., is the same in German and in (British) English. Some people are more hesitant to use them alone for fear of appearing too aggressive, especially the ones for 'slowly please' and 'No, thank you, I won't have this'. As long as you smile, such gestures do not seem aggressive in a German context, unless

Ja!

Yes!

Nein.

No! (It cannot be true.)

Sehr gute Qualität!

Excellent quality!

Bitte noch einmal, ich habe
Sie nicht verstanden.

Could you repeat this, please.
I didn't quite get it.

Nein.

Certainly not!

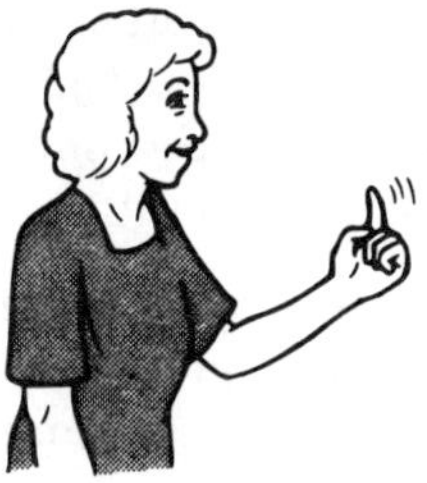

Kommen Sie!

Come here! / Come with me!

you use some of the ruder ones, e.g. for saying that somebody is stupid.

It should be noted in this context that Germans do not often make fun of themselves. They would not be likely to make a negative comment about themselves and expect the person they were speaking to to find it funny or modest. Putting two (straight) fingers to one's temple (meaning 'I could shoot myself for this, I have been so stupid') could be misunderstood by Germans – they might think it means the exact opposite: 'Are **you** stupid!'; although Germans normally only use one (bent) finger to show that they think someone else is stupid (or mad). This particular gesture is described as *jemandem ein Vögelchen zeigen* (literally: to show someone a little bird).

Ich bitte um Ruhe.
Bitte langsam!

Please be silent. /
Easy now!

Nein danke, ich nehme es nicht! /
ich tue es nicht!

No, thank you. I won't do it! /
I won't take it.

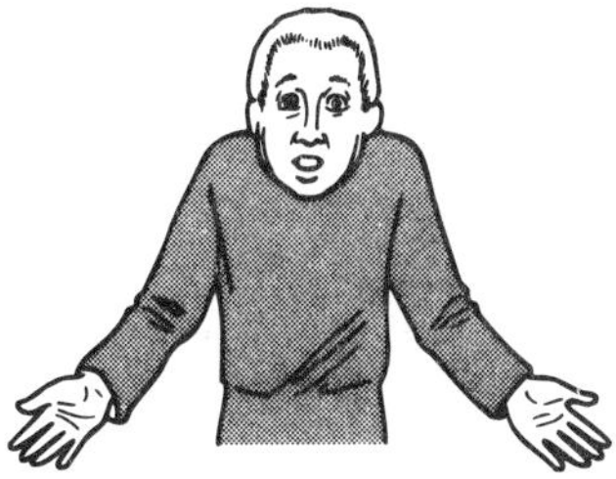

Ich weiß es nicht.

Don't know.

Bitte hören Sie gut zu!

Now listen!

ADVERBS AND ADVERBIAL PHRASES

Adverbs and adverbial phrases (e.g. *heute nachmittag*) specify the verb (as opposed to adjectives, which specify the noun). They are thus not essential for the basic message of a sentence, but they convey valuable background information.

> *Heute nachmittag will ich gern gegenüber in das Geschäft gehen. Dort gibt es nämlich meine Lieblingsschallplatte.*
> This afternoon I would like to go to the shop opposite. There, I can buy my favourite record.

In this example, the adverbs are *heute nachmittag, gern, gegenüber* and *dort.*

(a) Form

In English, adverbs can often be recognized by their ending *-ly*.

> It suddenly occurred to me that . . .
> *Plötzlich fiel mir ein, daß . . .*

An important group of adverbs are formed by suffixing other parts of speech (e.g. *neulich* recently) and there are a number of monosyllabic adverbs (e.g. *bald* soon, *erst* first).

In German, adverbs cannot be declined, but they can be graded.

(b) Comparative and superlative of adverbs

When adjectives are used as adverbs, they are graded in the usual way:

> *Die neue Maschine arbeitet besser als die alte.*
> The new machine works better than the old one.

The following adverbs have irregular forms when graded:

bald	*eher*	*am ehesten*	soon
gern	*lieber*	*am liebsten*	
oft	*öfter*	*am häufigsten*	often
häufig	*häufiger*	*am häufigsten*	often / frequently

Gern(e) is used to indicate preferences:

Er trinkt gerne Kaffee. He likes coffee.
Er trinkt lieber Wein. He prefers wine.
Er trinkt am liebsten Sekt. His favourite drink is champagne.

Some adverbs have a further superlative form:

Er begrüßte sie aufs freundlichste. < literary >
He welcomed her in a very friendly way.

Der Brief muß schnellstens abgeschickt werden.
The letter has to be sent off as soon as possible.

The usual comparative is occasionally replaced by a construction with *des*:

Früher habe ich ihn des öfteren im Konzert getroffen.
In former times I used to meet him rather frequently at concerts.

(c) Position

The adverb can occupy different positions in a sentence:

Er entdeckte plötzlich das Gespenst.
He suddenly caught sight of the ghost.

Plötzlich entdeckte er das Gespenst.
Suddenly, he caught sight of the ghost.

Er entdeckte das Gespenst plötzlich.
He caught sight of the ghost all of a sudden.

When the adverb is at the beginning of a sentence it counts as the first element and must be followed by the (main part of the) verb (see section 55).

(d) Order of adverbs within a sentence

There are three semantic categories of adverbs and adverbial phrases:

(i) Adverbs of **place**:
da there *dort* there *hier* here

(ii) Adverbs of **time**:
heute today *gestern* yesterday *nächstes Jahr* next year

(iii) Adverbs of **manner**:
gerne willingly *sicherlich* certainly
normalerweise normally

It is important to recognize the meaning of the adverb you want to use as the order of adverbs is fixed in German:

time – manner – place.

Der Chef möchte den Bewerber um 15.00 Uhr gerne in seinem Büro treffen.
The boss would like to meet the applicant in his office at 3 o'clock.

As you can see, the borderline between adverbs and adverbial phrases can be blurred, but it is generally not difficult to distinguish the three semantic categories.

If two adverbs of the same category occur in the same sentence, the more general one takes precedence:

Er sieht die neuen Bewerber immer nachmittags.
He always sees the new applicants in the afternoon. (i.e. he never arrranges to see them in the morning)

If the order of the adverbs is reversed, there is a change in meaning:

Er sieht die neuen Bewerber nachmittags immer.
He always sees the new applicants in the afternoon. (i.e. he may not be prepared to do so in the morning)

50 Adverbs of time

An adverb of time can convey three different kinds of information:

- a point in time
- duration
- repetition

(a) A point in time

(i) In relation to the present moment

We can imagine these adverbs lying on two converging lines which meet at the present point in time. One line has its point of origin in the distant past, the other one in the distant future. We can thus identify pairs:

PAST	FUTURE
einst, einmal once	*einst, einmal* one / some day
damals at the time	*(zu)künftig* in future
früher earlier	*später* later
vor x Jahren x years ago	*in x Jahren* in x years

vorigen Monat a month ago	*in einem Monat* / *nächsten Monat* } next month
vorige Woche last week	*in einer Woche* / *nächste Woche* } next week
vorgestern the day before yesterday	*übermorgen* the day after tomorrow
gestern yesterday	*morgen* tomorrow
vorhin, eben, gerade just a moment ago	*gleich, bald, nachher* in just a moment

The following adverbs refer to the present moment in time:

gerade just now	*nun* now
jetzt now	*heute* today
schon already	

A secretary or a telephone salesperson who is keeping you waiting on the phone may use:

bald soon
einen Moment bitte just a moment please
sofort / gleich immediately

(ii) In relation to a different point in time

The time adverbs discussed so far are used when the speaker refers to a later or earlier point in time in relation to the present moment of speaking. If a speaker refers to a past or future point in time in relation to yet another point in time, the following set of temporal adverbs may be used:

zuerst → ***dann*** (at) first → then

> *Zuerst wußte ich nicht, was ich tun sollte. Dann wurde mir klar, worum es ging.*
> At first, I did not know what to do. Then it became clear to me what it was about.

zunächst → ***danach*** for the time being → afterwards

> *Zunächst möchte ich mich vorstellen. Danach werde ich über meine Arbeit berichten.*
> First, I will introduce myself. Then I will talk about my work.

vorher / zuvor / davor → ***nachher / hinterher*** before → afterwards

> *Dieses Konzert war besser als je eines vorher / zuvor. Nachher sind wir zum Feiern weggegangen.*
> This concert was better than any one before. Afterwards we went out to celebrate.

zuletzt / schließlich finally / at last
endlich in the end

> *Schließlich hatte er die Schule doch hinter sich.*
> Finally, he had finished school.

N.B. *schließlich* can also be used as a modal particle; it then means 'after all' (cf. section 47).

(b) Duration

bisher so far
immer always
  immer noch still
  immer wieder again and again
lange long
  Wie lange dauert das Konzert? How long is the concert?

nie / niemals never
noch still
seitdem / seither since then
stets always

(c) Repetition

immer wieder again and again
meist(ens) most of the time
oft / häufig often
öfters quite often
manchmal sometimes
selten / kaum rarely
nie never

Adverbs which imply a certain regularity of repetition:

ständig all the time
stets each time / all the time
jedesmal (wenn) each / every time

> *Jedesmal wenn es regnet, bleibt er zu Hause.*
> Every time it rains he stays at home.
>
> *Er kommt jedesmal zu spät.*
> He is late every time.

mehrmals several times
täglich every day
wöchentlich every week

monatlich every month
jährlich every year

★ N.B. *zweimonatlich* can mean either 'twice a month' or 'every two months'. Do not confuse this with *zweimonatig*, which is used as an adjective:

> *Er macht im Sommer ein zweimonatiges Praktikum bei Siemens.*
> In the summer he will do a two-month industrial placement with Siemens.

The same distinction should be made between *jährlich* and *-jährig*:

> *ein dreijähriges Kind*
> a three-year-old child
>
> *Sie zahlen den Versicherungsbeitrag jährlich.*
> You pay the insurance premium annually.

montags, dienstags . . . on Mondays, Tuesdays . . .
morgens in the morning(s)
mittags at lunch time(s)
nachmittags in the afternoon(s)
abends in the evening(s)
nachts at night

> *Nehmen Sie zwei Tabletten morgens.*
> Take two tablets every morning.

This last group of adverbs means 'every morning', 'every afternoon' etc. and should not be used to refer to a particular morning or afternoon.

einmal, zweimal . . . once, twice . . .
wieder again
erneut once again

Erneut is more specific than *wieder* and emphasizes the fact that an action starts all over again from the beginning.

51 Adverbs of manner

(a) Reinforcing a statement

auch / selbst / sogar even

> *Sogar dem Chef war die Sache peinlich.*
> Even the boss was embarrassed about this matter.

besonders particularly

Besonders möchte ich allen Mitarbeitern danken.
I would particularly like to thank all my colleagues.

eben / g(e)rade / genau used to single someone or something out

Genau heute (wo ein Fluglotsenstreik stattfindet) wollte er nach Paris fliegen.
Of all days he wanted to fly to Paris today (although there is an air-traffic controllers' strike).

N.B. *eben* occupies a different position and acquires a different meaning when it is used as a modal particle (see p. 116).

nur only / simply

Er wollte doch nur helfen.
He only wanted to help.

(b) Expressing a degree of certainty

Absolute certainty in a positive sense

zweifellos without doubt / undoubtedly
bestimmt, gewiß certainly

Limited certainty

sicher certainly (though less certain than the above)
wahrscheinlich probably
vielleicht perhaps

Absolute certainty in a negative sense

nicht, nie, niemals never
auf keinen Fall / *keinesfalls* } certainly not (literally: in no case)
unter keinen Umständen not under any circumstances

52 Adverbs of place

(a) Answering the question *Wo?* (Where?)

hier here — *da, dort* there
drinnen inside (indoors) — *draußen* outside (out of doors)

unten down
oben up
links on the left-hand side
rechts on the right-hand side
vorn(e) in front
hinten behind
irgendwo somewhere
nirgendwo / nirgends nowhere

drüben over there
(in)mitten in the middle / centre of
überall everywhere

(b) Answering the questions *Wohin?* and *Woher?* (Where to? Where from?)

hierhin / hierher (to / from) here
dahin / daher (to / from) there
dorthin / dorther (to / from) there
nach / von draußen to / from the outside
hinaus/heraus out(side)
heraus/herein in(side)
hinab / herab, hinauf / herauf, hinüber / herüber, hinunter / herunter, hinein / hervor

The prefix *hin-* is used when the movement originates where the speaker is; *her-* implies that the movement happens at some distance from the speaker and is coming closer (see section 9).

In spoken German, both *hin-* and *her-* are often abbreviated to *r-* (+ preposition), the difference between *hin-* and *her-* being fudged:

hin- / herauf → *rauf* up
hin- / herüber → *rüber* over

Verbs can be prefixed with any of these combinations of *hin- / her-*. For example:

> *Geh doch die Treppe hinauf.*
> Why don't you go upstairs?
> (speaker and hearer are downstairs)
>
> *Komm doch die Treppe herauf.*
> Why don't you come upstairs?
> (speaker is upstairs, hearer downstairs)
>
> *Geh doch die Treppe hinunter.*
> Why don't you go downstairs?
> (speaker and hearer are upstairs)

Komm doch die Treppe herunter.
Why don't you come downstairs? (speaker is downstairs, hearer upstairs)

(c) Combined adverbs of place

irgendwohin to anywhere	*nirgendwohin* to nowhere
irgendwoher from anywhere	*nirgendwoher* from nowhere
überallhin to everywhere	*überallher* from everywhere

53 Prepositional adverbs

In morphological terms a prepositional adverb consists of an **adverb of place** (*da, hier, wo*) + **a preposition**:

QUESTION WORD	ANSWER	
wobei?	*dabei*	*hierbei*
wodurch?	*dadurch*	*hierdurch*
wofür?	*dafür*	*hierfür*
womit?	*damit*	*hiermit*
wonach?	*danach*	*hiernach*
woran?	*daran*	*hieran*
worauf?	*darauf*	*hierauf*
woraus?	*daraus*	*hieraus*
wovor?	*davor*	*hiervor*

Prepositional adverbs are used in the following three ways:

(i) To refer to a whole sentence or phrase:

Wir helfen ihm bei seinem Umzug im Mai. → *Wir helfen ihm dabei.*
We will help him with his removal in May. → We will help him with it.

(ii) To refer to things (rather than persons):

Heute ist das große Fest. Ich habe mich schon lange darauf gefreut.
Today is the great festival. I have been looking forward to it for a long time.

Ich weiß nicht, worauf du dich freust.
I don't know what you are looking forward to.

(iii) If the object to be replaced is not neuter, either the prepositional adverb or a preposition + pronoun may be used:

> *Heute ist die große Party. Ich habe mich schon lange darauf / auf sie gefreut*
> Today is the big party. I have been looking forward to it for a long time.

For people, the prepositional adverb consists of a preposition + the personal pronoun or the question word *wer* in their declined forms. The following list shows examples with *du*:

QUESTION	ANSWER
an wen?	*an dich*
bei wem?	*bei dir*
durch wen?	*durch dich*
für wen?	*für dich*
mit wem?	*mit dir*
nach wessen?	*nach deiner*
nach wem?	*nach dir*
vor wem?	*vor dir*
zu wem?	*zu dir*

> *Vor wem hast du Angst? Vor diesem Mann ? = Vor ihm?*
> Whom are you afraid of? Of this man? = Of him?
>
> *Ich weiß nicht, vor wem du Angst hast*
> I don't know whom you are afraid of.
>
> *Ich weiß nicht, vor was du Angst hast.*
> I don't know what you are afraid of.

54 Conjunctional adverbs

A conjunctional adverb joins two sentences together, and therefore plays a similar role to that of a conjunction (see sections 42 and 56). In contrast to coordinating conjunctions, however, conjunctional adverbs can go in the first position before the conjugated verb (see section 55). They can also be found in the middle of a sentence after the verb.

Common conjunctional adverbs:

allerdings however
außerdem on top of this / beyond this
daher therefore / because of this
demnach according to this
deshalb therefore

deswegen therefore
folglich as a consequence
insofern thus
mithin hence
sonst otherwise/besides
trotzdem nevertheless

> *Er kann nicht Französisch sprechen;*
> *deshalb fährt er nicht nach Frankreich /*
> *er fährt deshalb nicht nach Frankreich.*
> He cannot speak French;
> therefore he does not go to France /
> he therefore does not go to France.

Compare the position of the conjunctional adverb (*deshalb* in the example above) with that of the conjunctions in the following examples. A conjunction is not an independent part of the sentence and therefore cannot be followed by the verb:

> *Er fährt nicht nach Frankreich, weil er nicht Französisch sprechen kann.*
> He does not go to France because he cannot speak French.
>
> *Er fährt nicht nach Frankreich, denn er kann nicht Französisch sprechen.*
> He does not go to France as he cannot speak French.

SENTENCE STRUCTURE

The parts of the sentence

A minimal sentence consists of a noun or pronoun and a verb. In a statement, the noun / pronoun always comes first, and **the verb is in second position:**

I II
Er geht
He goes.

Even in a sentence with the maximum number of elements the verb must still be in the second position. This is often called the 'verb second' rule.

A sentence can start with the object:

II
Den Hund muß ich heute noch ausführen.
I still have to take out the dog today.

The verb remains in the second position and the subject comes immediately afterwards. The emphasis in this sentence would be on *Hund*. It is the dog that has to be taken out, not the baby or anything else.

In the next two examples the adverb or group of adverbs forms the first element of the sentence. Again, the subject must follow the conjugated verb. The emphasis here is on *heute* (as opposed to yesterday and tomorrow) and on *gestern nachmittag* (as opposed to yesterday morning or this afternoon).

II
Heute muß ich den Hund noch ausführen.
Today, I still have to take out the dog.

Gestern nachmittag bei strömendem Regen habe ich den Hund ausgeführt.
Yesterday afternoon I took the dog out in the pouring rain.

But what about the remaining elements of the sentence? The following rules, shown in tabular form on p. 136, should be observed.

The first element is followed by the conjugated verb. The subject comes next (unless it was the first element in the sentence), followed by the position-fixed pronouns.

Pronouns precede nouns, nominative pronouns precede accusative pronouns, which in turn precede dative pronouns (cf. section 6). After this come the objects which are not pronouns, the adverbs (in the order **time** – **manner** – **place**), and modal particles. As a general guideline, these should be ordered according to increasing 'news value' or specificity.

The items that are to be particularly emphasized go as far as possible to the left or to the right – those with special news value tend to go towards the right.

Then follows the remainder of the verb, together with the verbal complement (if there is one). As the parts of the verb encompass or bracket a number of diverse elements, the part of the sentence that comes between them can be called the 'inner field'.

I	IIa	III		IIb
		inner field	*nicht*	
Er	*schreibt*	*seinen Kunden.*		
He writes to his clients.				
Er	*schreibt*	*ihnen.*		
He writes to them.				
Er	*will*	*ihnen*		*schreiben.*
He wants to write to them.				
Er	*will*	*ihnen heute*	*nicht*	*schreiben.*
He doesn't want to write to them today.				
Heute	*will*	*er ihnen*	*nicht*	*schreiben.*
Today he doesn't want to write to them.				
Eigentlich	*will*	*er ihnen heute*	*nicht*	*schreiben.*
He doesn't want to write to them today, really.				
Eigentlich	*will*	*er ihnen heute gerne*		*schreiben.*
He would really like to write to them today.				
Er	*möchte*	*ihnen heute einen Brief*		*schreiben.*
He would like to write a letter to them today.				
Er	*möchte*	*ihnen heute bestimmt*		*schreiben.*
He certainly wants to write to them today.				
Er	*möchte*	*das Geld*	*nicht*	*auf die Bank bringen.*
He does not want to take the money to the bank.				

I	IIa	III		IIb
		inner field	*nicht*	
Er	*wird*	*es heute für ihn*		*auf die Bank bringen.*
He will take it to the bank for him today.				
Er	*will*	*das Geld heute*	*nicht*	*für ihn auf die Bank bringen.*
Today he doesn't want to take the money to the bank for him.				
Er	*hat*	*das Geld heute morgen*		*auf die Bank gebracht*
He has taken the money to the bank this morning.				

Even if a sentence looks much more complex than this, you will be able to reduce it to these elements. This analytical process is essential for understanding complex texts.

6 Main clause and subordinate clause

A subordinate clause can be recognized by the conjunction with which it is introduced. The following subordinating conjunctions automatically send the **conjugated verb to the end of the sentence:**

weil, obwohl, obgleich
während, als, bevor, nachdem, sobald, bis, seit, seitdem, solange, wenn
so daß, ohne daß, um / ohne . . . zu, damit, ob

- **Main clause + main clause**

  Dinkelsbühl ist eine schöne Stadt und es hat einen mittelalterlichen Stadtkern.
  Dinkelsbühl is a beautiful town and it has a medieval centre.

- **Main clause + subordinate clause**

  Dinkelsbühl ist eine schöne Stadt, weil es einen mittelalterlichen Stadtkern hat
  Dinkelsbühl is a beautiful town because it has a medieval centre.

- **Subordinate clause + main clause**

  Weil Dinkelsbühl einen mittelalterlichen Stadtkern hat, ist es eine schöne Stadt.
  As Dinkelsbühl has a medieval centre it is a beautiful town.

You can see that the word order in the main clause, *Dinkelsbühl ist eine schöne Stadt*, remains unchanged in the first two examples. In the subordinate clause, *weil es einen mittelalterlichen Stadkern hat*, the conjugated verb goes to the end.

In the third sentence the subordinate clause counts as the first element of the sentence viewed as a whole, so the verb *(ist)* must immediately follow the subordinate clause. The verb at the end of the subordinate clause and the one immediately following the subordinate clause are separated by a comma: verb – comma – verb.

A subordinate clause may be replaced by either a **preposition + noun** or by a **conjunctional adverb** (see section 54). Which option you choose depends entirely on the style you want to convey and how you want to distribute your information. A subordinating conjunction or a preposition + noun is used to introduce new information and a conjunctional adverb is used to refer to information that is already known. In German a verb phrase is usually preferable to a construction where nouns predominate (see sections 75 and 122–6).

How a subordinate clause can be replaced depends on the conjunction used in the subordinate clause. For example, *weil* is replaced by *wegen*, which takes the genitive:

CONJUNCTION	*weil*	*Dinkelsbühl ist eine schöne Stadt, weil es einen mittelalterlichen Stadtkern hat.*
PREPOSITION	*wegen* (+ genitive)	*Wegen seines mittelalterlichen Stadtkerns ist Dinkelsbühl eine schöne Stadt.* Because of its medieval centre, Dinkelsbühl is a beautiful town.

Furthermore, *wegen* + noun could be replaced by the conjunctional adverbs *deswegen*, *darum* or *deshalb*. Note that the subordinate clause becomes a main clause, with the verb in second position:

ADVERB	*deswegen* *deshalb* *darum*	*Dinkelsbühl hat einen mittelalterlichen Stadtkem, deswegen ist es eine schöne Stadt.* Dinkelsbühl has a medieval centre, therefore it is a beautiful town.

In the same way, nearly every subordinating conjunction (+ subordinate clause) can be replaced by a preposition (+ noun) or by a conjunctional adverb (+ main clause), as shown in the table and examples below.

CONJUNCTION	PREPOSITION	CONJUNCTIONAL ADVERB
weil	*wegen* (+ genitive)	*deswegen* *deshalb* *darum*
obwohl	*trotz* (+ genitive)	*trotzdem*
während (time aspect)	*während* (+ genitive)	*dabei* *währenddessen*
als	*bei* (+ dative) *an* (+ accusative)	
bevor	vor (+ dative)	*davor*
nachdem	*nach* (+ dative)	*danach*
sobald	*bei* (+ dative)	
bis	*bis zu* (+ dative)	*bis dahin* *solange*
seit(dem)	*seit* (+ dative)	*seitdem*

Examples

CONJUNCTION	*obwohl*	*Sie ging zur Arbeit, obwohl sie krank war.* (more elegant) She went to work although she was ill.
PREPOSITION	*trotz* (+ genitive)	*Sie ging trotz ihrer Krankheit zur Arbeit.* She went to work despite her illness.
ADVERB	*trotzdem*	*Sie ging trotzdem zur Arbeit.* She went to work despite it.
CONJUNCTION	*während* (time aspect)	*Er arbeitete, während seine Kinder Ferien hatten.* He worked whilst his children were on holiday.
PREPOSITION	*während* (+ genitive)	*Er arbeitete während der Ferien seiner Kinder.* He worked during his children's holidays.
ADVERB	*dabei* *währenddessen*	*Er arbeitete währenddessen.* He worked in the meantime.

CONJUNCTION	*als*	*Als er kam, waren schon alle Gäste da.* (more elegant) When he arrived, all the guests were already there.
PREPOSITION	*bei* (+ dative) *an* (+ dative)	*Bei seiner Ankunft waren schon alle Gäste da.* On his arrival all the other guests were already there.
CONJUNCTION	*bevor*	*Bitte rufen Sie uns an, bevor Sie kommen.* (more elegant) Please give us a call before you come.
PREPOSITION	*vor* (+ dative)	*Bitte rufen Sie uns vor Ihrem Kommen an.* Please give us a call before your arrival.
ADVERB	*davor*	*Bitte rufen Sie uns davor an.* Please give us a call before(hand).
CONJUNCTION	*nachdem*	*Sie gingen spazieren, nachdem sie gegessen hatten.* They went for a walk after they had eaten.
PREPOSITION	*nach* (+ dative)	*Sie gingen nach dem Essen spazieren.* (more elegant) They went for a walk after the meal.
ADVERB	*danach*	*Sie gingen danach spazieren.* They went for a walk afterwards.
CONJUNCTION	*sobald*	*Ich rufe Sie an, sobald ich Nachricht habe.* (more elegant) I'll call you as soon as I have some news.
PREPOSITION	*bei* (+ dative)	*Ich rufe Sie bei Empfang der Nachricht an.* I'll call you on receipt of the news.

CONJUNCTION	*bis*	*Ich arbeite, bis ich die Lösung gefunden habe.* (more elegant) I work until I find the solution.
PREPOSITION	*bis zu* (+ dative)	*Ich arbeite bis zur Auffindung der Lösung.* I work until the discovery of the solution.
ADVERB	*bis dahin* *solange*	*Ich arbeite solange.* I'll work until then / for the time being.
CONJUNCTION	*seit(dem)*	*Er wohnt hier, seit er Kind war.* He has lived here ever since he was a child.
PREPOSITION	*seit* (+ dative)	*Er wohnt hier seit seiner Kindheit* (more elegant) He has lived here since his childhood.
ADVERB	*seitdem*	*Er wohnt seitdem hier.* He has lived here ever since.

Some subordinate clauses introduced by a conjunction can also be replaced by infinitive constructions (see section 35):

CONJUNCTION	PREPOSITION	INFINITIVE CONSTRUCTION
so daß *damit*	*zu* (+ dative)	infinitive + *zu*
ohne daß	*ohne* (+ accusative)	*ohne* (+ participle) + *zu* + infinitive

CONJUNCTION	*so daß* *damit*	*Er muß im Ausland arbeiten, so daß er Erfahrungen sammeln kann.* He must work abroad so that he can gather experience.
PREPOSITION	*zu* (+ dative)	*Er muß zum Sammeln von Erfahrungen im Ausland arbeiten.* He must work abroad for the gathering of experience.
INFINITIVE + *zu*		*Er muß im Ausland arbeiten, um Erfahrungen zu sammeln.* (more elegant) He must work abroad in order to gather experience.

CONJUNCTION	*ohne daß*	*Wie kann er internationaler Leiter sein, ohne daß er im Ausland Erfahrungen gesammelt hat?* How can he be the international manager without having gathered experience abroad?
PREPOSITION	*ohne* (+ accusative)	*Wie kann er ohne Auslandserfahrungen internationaler Leiter sein?* (more elegant) How can he be the international manager without experience abroad?
ohne (+ PARTICIPLE) + *zu* + INFINITIVE		*Wie kann er internationaler Leiter sein, ohne Auslandserfahrungen (gesammelt) zu haben?* How can he be the international manager without having (gathered) experience abroad?

Obviously, a number of conjunctions function also as a preposition or an adverb, but the position of a conjunction in the clause will always indicate its function.

57 Questions

(a) Yes / No questions

Direct yes / no questions always start with the verb, or, more precisely, with the conjugated verb, i.e. the one that carries the personal ending.

- Simple verb (present tense):

  Kennen Sie den Mann dort? Do you know the man over there?

- Simple verb and auxiliary (perfect):

  Haben Sie den Mann gekannt? Did you know this man?

  Sind Sie in dieser Bar gewesen? Were you in this bar?

N.B. Remember that the German perfect very often has to be translated by using the imperfect tense in English.

- Modal verb (present tense):

  Können Sie den Mann beschreiben?
  Can you describe the man?

- Modal verb (perfect):

  Haben Sie den Mann beschreiben können?
  Have you been able to describe the man?

The verb order for the future tense would, of course, be exactly the same as in the perfect, the appropriate form of *werden* taking the place of *haben* or *sein*.

Indirect questions
An indirect question is introduced by *ob* (whether):

Darf ich fragen, ob Sie den Mann kennen?
May I ask whether you know this man?

Darf ich fragen, ob Sie den Mann beschrieben haben?
May I ask whether you have described the man?

Darf ich fragen, ob Sie den Mann haben beschreiben können?
May I ask whether you have been able to describe the man?

The word order in the subordinate clause, i.e. the indirect question, follows the usual **verb-last** rule (see above, p. 137).

(b) Open questions

Open questions always start with a **question word**. This may be a simple question word, as in 'Who dunnit?'

wer? who?	*was?* what?
wo? where?	*wie?* how?
wann? when?	*warum?* why?

Alternatively, questions can begin with a compound made up of a **question word + preposition**:

wo?+ preposition

womit?	*worunter?*	*wofür?/wozu?*
woher?	*wovon?*	*wovor?*
wogegen?	*wohin?*	*worüber?*
wohinter?		

Womit kann ich dir helfen? How can I help you?
Wovor fürchten Sie sich? What are you afraid of?

wer? + preposition

Wer? + preposition taking the dative → *wem?* (e.g. *mit wem?*)
Wer? + preposition taking the accusative → *wen?* (e.g. *durch wen?*)

Mit wem möchten Sie arbeiten?
Whom do you want to work with?

Durch wen haben Sie ihn kennengelernt?
Through whom did you get to know him?

Welcher?/welche?/welches? and *was für ein?/was für eine?* ask for a particular person or object out of a known group.

If you use *welcher?/welche?/welches?*, the choice is in front of your eyes: for example, there are three apples, a green one, a red one, and a yellow one; you may now be asked which one you want:

Welchen Apfel möchtest du? Which apple would you like?

In your answer you now need to use a demonstrative:

Diesen hier!/Jenen dort! This one here!/That one here!

When you use *was für ein?/was für eine?*, you define what a particular thing or person should be like:

Was für eine Arbeit suchen Sie?
What kind of work are you looking for?

The answer would be:

Eine Arbeit, bei der ich mit Menschen zu tun habe.
A job where I get to meet people.

(c) Introductions to indirect yes/no and open questions

Here are some examples:

Ich weiß nicht, . . . I don't know . . .
Ich habe keine Ahnung, . . . I have no idea . . .
Könnten Sie mir sagen, . . .? Could you tell me . . .?
Ich hätte gerne gewußt, . . . I would like to know . . .
Wer weiß, . . . Who knows . . .
Es spielt keine Rolle, . . . It doesn't matter . . .
Es ist egal, . . . It doesn't matter . . .
Es ist mir gleich/egal, . . . It is all the same to me . . .

58 Question tags

The question tag is characteristic of the spoken language, both in English and in German. The proficiency of a foreign speaker of English is often measured by his or her handling of this device:

Nice day today, isn't it?

Fortunately, the question tag in German is not only used less frequently but it is also invariable.

The formal tag is *nicht wahr?*:

Sie möchten sicher noch etwas trinken, nicht wahr?
You would like another drink, wouldn't you?

It is less formal to add *oder* or *nicht*:

Du bist müde, oder?
You are tired, aren't you?

There are also a number of regional tags which can replace *oder?*: *gell?* or *gellt?* are used more in the southern part of Germany:

Ihr kommt doch pünktlich, gell? You will be on time, won't you?

In the Rhineland and the northern part of Germany, *ne?* (short *e*) is used (for *nicht*):

Ihr kommt doch pünktlich, ne?

You need to be very proficient in German to get away with a dialect question tag when talking to a native speaker. When in doubt, leave it out!

Unlike in English, the question tag can also be used at the beginning of a sentence (with the exception of *oder*):

Nicht wahr, ihr kommt heute pünktlich?
Gell, du bist müde?

A sentence starting with a tag is a statement rather than a (rhetorical) question, and it sounds more familiar and colloquial.

59 Negation

A statement may be negated in two ways, as in English. Quite often, 'not' is translated by *nicht* and 'no' by *kein*. The general rule is therefore as follows.

***Nicht* negates a verb**:

Ich gehe heute nicht ins Büro.
I am not going to the office today.

N.B. For the position of *nicht* in a sentence, see pp. 136–7 and 149–50.

***Kein* negates a noun** and needs to be handled like the indefinite article *ein*. The plural endings are identical to those of adjectives with zero article (cf. section 13).

Heute haben wir kein Geld.
We have no money today.

Während der Rezession macht unsere Firma keine großen Projekte.
During the recession our company is not taking on big projects.

However, not every sentence can be classified according to this general rule.

Nicht is used in a number of idiomatic expressions such as:

Er kann nicht Auto fahren.
He cannot drive.

Er darf nicht Radio hören.
He must not listen to the radio.

Wir sollen nicht Maschine schreiben.
We must not use the typewriter.

If a complement needs to be emphasized, it can be placed at the start of the sentence. The negation would then be *nicht* because it is the verb rather than the noun that is negated. Compare the following examples:

Er ist kein großer Mann.
Ein großer Mann ist er nicht.
He isn't a tall man.

Das ist kein gutes Geschäft.
Ein gutes Geschäft ist das nicht.
This is not a good deal.

60 Modified negation

(a) Adding a nuance to *kein* and *nicht*

This can be done by putting a modifier before *nicht* or *kein.*

(i) Comparison

auch (n)either

Wir sind auch nicht bei der Party gewesen.
We have not been to the party either.

Ich wollte auch keinen Alkohol trinken.
I did not want to drink alcohol either.

(ii) Temporal nuance

(immer) noch still / yet

Immer stresses that you are getting worried or impatient:

Wir haben Ihren Auftrag (immer) noch nicht erhalten.
We have not received your order yet. / We have still not received your order.

Haben Sie denn (immer) noch keinen Gast gesehen?
Have you not seen any guests yet? / Have you still not seen any guests?

nie never

Wir haben Ihren Auftrag nie erhalten.
We have never received your order.

nicht / kein mehr no more / not any more

Wir haben keine Zeit mehr.
We have no more time.

Es ist so neblig, man sieht die Straße nicht mehr.
It is so foggy, you can't see the road any more.

(iii) Stress

überhaupt / gar at all

Ich weiß überhaupt / gar nicht, warum Herr Weidner noch nicht da ist.
I have no idea at all why Mr Weidner is not here yet.

Es gibt gar / überhaupt keinen Grund für Ihr unmögliches Verhalten.
There is no reason at all for your impossible behaviour.

(b) Restricted negation

(i) *nur* only

Ich möchte nur eine Sache besprechen (, nicht mehr).
I only want to discuss one matter (and nothing else).

Note the parallel sentence structure with *brauchen*:

Sie brauchen nicht zu arbeiten.
You do not need to work.

Sie brauchen nur eine Stunde zu arbeiten.
You only need to work for an hour.

Brauchen is being used as an auxiliary and must take *zu* with both *nicht* and *nur* (see section 28).

(ii) *kaum* hardly

Es waren kaum Leute bei der Ausstellungseröffnung.
There were hardly any people when the exhibition opened.

Ich habe kaum geschlafen.
I hardly slept.

(c) Negating an alternative

An alternative can be negated by using *weder ... noch* (neither ... nor):

Weder der Chef noch die Sektretärin wußten von diesem Termin.
Neither the boss nor the secretary knew of this appointment.

Er konnte weder arbeiten noch schlafen.
He could neither work nor sleep.

(d) Negation as a rhetorical figure

A double negation means no negation at all:

Es ist nicht unmöglich, daß die Gäste noch kommen.
It is not impossible that the guests might still come.

Use double negation sparingly as it is part of the 'toolbox' of understatement; and understatement is not a particular feature of German.

61 Position of *nicht*

If a sentence contains a number of complements, *nicht* goes before the adverb of manner and the verb complement (cf. section 55). *Nicht* can itself be classed as an adverb of manner and would precede any other such adverb.

> *Ich konnte heute* [time] *wegen der Verspätung meines Zuges* [cause] *nicht pünktlich* [manner] *zu unserem Gespräch kommen* [verb complement].
> As my train was late I was unable to come to our meeting on time today.

The rule is therefore:

time – cause – negation – manner – place

Modal particles precede the negation:

> *Vor lauter Freude konnte sie sich einfach nicht beruhigen.*
> She was so overjoyed, that she simply could not calm down.

Sentence stress

The position of *nicht* is also determined by the sentence stress. Compare the following sentences, where the stress is indicated by bold type:

Ich habe dir nicht ***geschrieben.***
I did not write to you.

Nicht ***ich*** *habe dir geschrieben.*
It was not I who wrote to you (but someone else).

Ich habe nicht ***Dir / an Dich*** *geschrieben.*
I did not write to you (but to someone else).

In the first sentence we have a clear and unambiguous statement: there was no letter at all. In the second sentence, however, there is a letter, but its author was not the speaker. The stress is on *ich*. In the last sentence, there is a letter, but it was not addressed to the person who is addressed in the statement.

The third sentence poses particular problems for the English speaker because the translation into English is identical with that of the first sentence. However, the gloss given in brackets indicates that the meaning of the first and third sentences is not identical. Be discerning when you decide whether the **dative object** should go before or after *nicht*: more often than not it goes before *nicht*; only if there is a particular stress on the dative object is it preceded by *nicht*.

PUNCTUATION

2 Commas

Commas separate different parts of a sentence. In the spoken language there is a brief pause where a comma would appear in the written language. Generally speaking, however, there are more commas in a German text than you would find in the English version.

(a) Commas in letters

The address lines are never separated by commas.

At one time it was standard practice to use an exclamation mark after addressing someone at the start of a letter; in contemporary usage a comma is preferred:

Sehr geehrter Herr Dr. Schwarzkopf,

There is no comma after the signing-off formula, and none after *Ihr/ Ihre*:

Mit freundlichen Grüßen	Kind regards.
Ihre	Yours sincerely,
Gerlinde Weiß	Gerlinde Weiss

(b) Commas in simple sentences

Compare the following:

London ist die größte englische Stadt.
London is the biggest city in England.

Er hat über dieses Thema einen langen, guten Artikel geschrieben.
He has written a long and good article on this subject.

In the first example, *größte* and *englische* are thought of as a unit. They are interdependent in terms of sense. Therefore, no comma is used.

In the second example, either adjective could apply without reference to the other, so when they occur together they need to be separated by a comma.

Here are some other examples in simple sentences:

Without a comma:

Meine Kollegin Renate ist sehr kompetent.
My colleague Renate is very competent.

Das schöne große Museum ist in der Stadt sehr beliebt.
The beautiful big museum is very popular in town.

No comma is needed here because *Kollegin* and *Renate*, and *schöne* and *große*, are thought of as supplementing each other.

With a comma:

Renate, meine Kollegin, ist sehr kompetent.
Renate, my colleague, is very competent.

Here the phrase *meine Kollegin* functions in apposition. Note that the parenthesis is marked by two commas.

Das Museum, groß und schön, ist in der Stadt sehr beliebt.
The museum, big and beautiful (as it is), is very popular in town.

Language is never so clear-cut that there are no ambiguities:

Zum Essen haben wir einen guten kalten Wein getrunken.
Zum Essen haben wir einen guten, kalten Wein getrunken.
For dinner we had a nice cold wine.

For one speaker, a wine might only be nice if it is served cold and therefore *gut* and *kalt* are considered to be one entity. Another speaker considers the wine to be not only cold, but also good, and thus inserts a comma between the two qualifying adjectives.

(c) Commas in complex sentences

This is an area where the German rules differ most strikingly from English conventions:

(i) Subordination

The subordinate clause is always preceded by a comma:

Alle waren schon im Büro, obwohl es noch nicht 9 Uhr war.
Everybody was already in the office although it was not yet 9 o'clock.

The same applies if several subordinate clauses are linked together:

Wir hoffen, daß sich das Arbeitsklima verbessert, wenn wir neue Computer bekommen.
We hope that the working atmosphere will improve when we get new computers.

(ii) Coordination

Here, rules depend on the meaning.

Without a comma:

Er war reich und arm zugleich.
He was rich and poor at the same time. (sum of characteristics)

Ich fliege und du fährst nach Berlin. (This sentence is condensed from: *Ich fliege nach Berlin, und du fährst nach Berlin.*)
I fly and you drive to Berlin.

With a comma (cf. section 43):

Wir sind nicht reich, aber glücklich.
We are not rich, but happy. (contrast)

Er geht arbeiten, und (= aber) ich bleibe zu Hause.
He goes to work and I stay at home. (contrast, two subjects)

(iii) Commas and *zu* + infinitive

A comma must always be added if *zu* + infinitive is extended by a complement:

Ich höre auf zu rauchen. I stop smoking.

Ich höre auf, Zigarren zu rauchen. I stop smoking cigars.

If *zu* is extended by *anstatt* (instead of), *um* (in order to) or *ohne* (without . . . ing), a comma must be used:

Er rauchte, anstatt zu arbeiten.
He smoked instead of working.

Wir kommen, um zu helfen.
We come to help (you).

Sie verließ das Geschäft, ohne zu zahlen.
She left the shop without paying.

A comma is sometimes needed even in the unextended version of *zu* + infinitive in order to avoid ambiguity:

Es gelang ihnen nicht, zu arbeiten. They did not manage to work.

Es gelang ihnen, nicht zu arbeiten. They managed not to work.

(iv) Participles

The rules are similar to the ones for *zu* + infinitive. If the participle is not extended, a comma is not needed:

Gut ausgeschlafen ging er an die Arbeit.
After a good night's sleep he went to work.

If the participial construction is extended, a comma is needed:

Fest zur Kündigung entschlossen, ging er zum Chef.
Resolved to hand in his notice, he went to see his boss.

However, if the unextended participle introduces a subordinate clause, the participle must go between commas:

Er ging zum Chef, entschlossen, noch heute zu kündigen.
He went to see the boss, resolved to hand in his notice today.

63 Semicolons

The semicolon separates phrases more clearly than a comma does and not as sharply as does a full stop. It is used between two main clauses when the other two options do not seem appropriate.

64 Dashes

Dashes can have the same function as commas when the latter are used to separate insertions that have no direct link with the main line of thought. They should be used sparingly.

Dieser Mitarbeiter hat – mir war das natürlich schon lange klar – überdurchschnittliche Fähigkeiten.
This employee has – and this of course has been clear to me for a long time – capabilities which are above average.

65 Colons

The use of the colon in German is similar to its use in English. A colon is needed before direct speech and before enumerations or explanations. If the sentence after the colon is complete it starts with a capital:

Lassen Sie uns die Ergebnisse zusammenfassen: Erstens muß die Infrastruktur verbessert werden, zweitens . . .
Let us sum up the results: Firstly, the infrastructure needs to be improved, secondly, . . .

But:

Es gibt drei Forderungen: erstens die Verbesserung der Infrastruktur, zweitens . . .
There are three demands: first the improvement of the infrastructure, secondly . . .

Always use a colon before direct speech:

Er sagte zu seinen Mitarbeitern: "Heute müssen Sie alle Überstunden machen."
He told his employees, 'Today you must all work overtime.'

66 Full stops

As in English, the full stop is used to mark the end of a sentence. It is used after reported speech, even if the reported speech is a question:

Er stellte die Frage, ob die Infrastruktur denn so schnell verbessert werden könne.
He asked the question whether the infrastructure could be improved so quickly.

Full stops are used in and after abbreviations, but there are no clear rules. Some party names for example have full stops, some don't: *CDU* = Christian Democrats; but *F.D.P.* = Free Democrats.

Rules for the use of full stops in abbreviations for everyday terms are rather idiosyncratic. The most common ones in written German are listed below.

With full stops

a.a.O	*am anderen / angebenen Ort*	source of the quotation is given elsewhere
bes.	*besonders*	especially
betr.	*betrifft*	referring to (re)
d.h.	*das heißt*	that is (i.e.)
ehem.	*ehemalig*	former
ev.	*evangelisch*	Protestant
kath.	*katholisch*	Catholic
evtl.	*eventuell*	possibly
Fa.	*Firma*	company
gez.	*gezeichnet*	for (pp)

h(rs)g.	*herausgegeben*	edited (ed.)
i.A.	*im Auftrag*	PP
Kto.-Nr	*Kontonummer*	account number (A/C)
Nr.	*Nummer*	number (no.)
og.	*obengenannt (e / en)*	mentioned above
Str.	*Straße*	street (St)
s.o.	*siehe oben*	see above
s.u.	*siehe unten*	see below
u.a.	*unter anderem*	among others
u.ä.	*und ähnliches*	and similar (. . .)
usw.	*und so weiter*	and so on (etc.)
u.U.	*unter Umständen*	possibly
v.Ch(r)	*vor Christi Geburt*	before Christ (BC)
n.Ch(r)	*nach Christi Geburt*	after Christ (AD)
vgl.	*vergleichen Sie*	compare (cf.)
z.B.	*zum Beispiel*	for example (e.g.)
z.H(d)	*zu Händen*	for the attention of (FAO)
z.Zt.	*zur Zeit*	at present

Without full stops

ADAC	*Allgemeiner Deutscher Automobilclub* drivers' club similar to AA / RAC
AG	*Aktiengesellschaft* Public Limited Company (PLC)
AOK	*Allgemeine Ortskrankenkasse* Public health insurance in Germany
CDU	*Christlich-Demokratische Union* German Conservative Party
CSU	*Christlich-Soziale Union* Conservative Party in Bavaria
DB	*Deutsche Bundesbahn* German Railway (cf. BR)
DDR	*Deutsche Demokratische Republik* German Democratic Republic (East Germany until 1990)/GDR
DIN	*Deutsche Industrie Norm* German standard for size and quality of industrial products comparable to British Standard
DM	*Deutsche Mark* German currency
EG	*Europäische Gemeinschaft* European Community (EC)
FH	*Fachhochschule* similar to the former British polytechnics
GmbH	*Gesellschaft mit beschränkter Haftung* Limited Company (Ltd)
KZ	*Konzentrationslager* concentration camp (during *die Nazizeit*)
l	*Liter* litre
LKW	*Lastkraftwagen* HGV
kg	*Kilogramm* kilo
PS	*Pferdestärke* horsepower
qm	*Quadratmeter* square metre (m^2)

S67 Quotation marks

Quotation marks must be used to mark direct speech and quotations. The opening quotation mark used to be a subscript but in the age of international keyboards, both the quotation marks at the beginning and at the end can be superscripts.

If the speaker refers to a specific term within the quotation this is marked by single quotation marks:

> *Der Sprecher meinte: "Der Begriff 'Deutsche Literatur' bedarf der Diskussion."*
> The speaker proposed: 'The term "*Deutsche Literatur*" needs to be discussed.'

Any term which is not in the language of the rest of the text must be printed in italics. However, if it is translated, it should be put in single quotation marks.

GUIDE TO PRONUNCIATION AND SPELLING

68 The relationship between pronunciation and spelling

German is pronounced as it is written, but it is not written as it is pronounced. In other words, whereas the sound of a word corresponds exactly to the letters, a particular sound may be written in more than one way. How does this paradox come about?

The characteristic features of a language are constituted by the range of vowel and consonant quality. The predominant features of German in this respect are long vowels as opposed to short vowels (but virtually no nasals as in French) and soft versus hard consonants (but virtually no gutturals as in Spanish). Whereas it is relatively easy to know from the written text what needs to be pronounced long or short and soft or hard, it is far less clear and predictable how long versus short is conveyed by the spelling of a word.

(a) Vowels

Vowels can be lengthened by adding an *-h* or by using a double vowel (except for *i* and *u*):

a	*Ahnung* suspicion
	Paar pair
o	*Ohr* ear
	Boot boat
u	*Uhr* watch
e	*geht* grey
	Beet (flower)bed
i	*ihm* him
	ziemlich rather

On the other hand, even a simple vowel may be long. Vowels are long before the soft plosives *b, d, g* :

Rabe raven   *radeln* to cycle   *mager* skinny

Vowels are also long before single *m* and *n*:

Mime mime
Mond moon

N.B.:

die Miene facial expression
die Mine mine

On the other hand, vowels are definitely short before a double consonant:

Ratte rat
Wasser water
Motte moth
Rinne gutter

A vowel will be short before *-ss-* and long before *-ß-* if *-ß-* occurs within a word (cf. subsection (c) below).

(b) Umlaut and diphthongs

(i) Umlaut

Vowels which carry a double dot on top are called *Umlaut*. German is the only Indo-European language to make such extensive use of this feature.

ä as in *Bär*

Pronounced exactly like the double vowel in the English 'bear'. The short *ä*, as in *Männer* (men), has the same sound but shorter.

ü as in *Tür* (door), with a long *ü*

There is no direct equivalent in English. If you try to pronounce an *i* as in 'fee' and then form your lips into a funnel you will have the right sound.

München (Munich) has a short *ü*; your mouth opens a little wider.

ö as in *ich möchte* (short and open *ö*) or *mögen* (long and closed *ö*)

Sounds similar to the noise a sheep makes: 'meuh . . .'

(iii) Diphthongs

au as in *Auto* (car) is pronounced like the English 'ow' in 'howl'.

ei

Pronounced as the 'ai' in 'Hawaii'. There are occasions when this sound is spelt completely differently and this is most noticeable in the popular last name of *Meier, Meyer, Maier, Mayr* or *Mayer.*

au / eu as in *Bäume* and *Eule*

Both are pronounced like the English 'boy'. There are no consistent rules for the spelling and unfortunately every word with either of these diphthongs has to be learnt.

(c) Consonants

Consonants can occur in three positions: as an **initial** sound, as a **medial** sound and as a **final** sound. Although there are contrasting pairs in all three categories, the most noticeable difference from English occurs in the category of the final sound:

(i) Voiced plosives (*b, d, g*) versus unvoiced plosives (*p, t, k*)

p versus *b*	INITIAL	MEDIAL	FINAL
Soft	*Bar*	*Rabe*	*Naab*‡
Hard	*Paar*	*Rappe*	*Kapp*

‡ *b* in the final position is by no means as soft as the English 'b' in the same position. It is rather more closely related to 'p' here.

t versus *d*	INITIAL	MEDIAL	FINAL
Soft	*Dach*	*Räder*	*Rad*‡
Hard	*Tasche*	*Retter*	*Rat*

‡ *d* and *t* are homophones (i.e. they sound the same) when they are final sounds. Both are pronounced as hard plosives. Whether the word is spelt with a *t* or a *d* at the end can only be heard by referring to the plural: *das Rad – die Räder, der Rat – die Räte.*

k versus *g*	INITIAL	MEDIAL	FINAL
Soft	*Kuchen*	*Margarine*	*mag*‡
Hard	*Gurke*	*Makel*	*Bank*

‡ Again, the final *g* can hardly be distinguished from the final *k*. The difference between the English words 'rag' and 'rack' is much more obvious.

(ii) *-ig, -ch, sch* and *j*

As a final sound *-ig* is pronounced exactly like *-ich*. Thus, *mutig* and *neulich* have the same final sound. The *-ch* sound is spoken very much in the back of the mouth. Imagine the English word 'shower'. Here, you speak 'sh' (like the German *sch*) in the middle of the mouth. Now try to shift it back. If the vowel preceding the German *-ch* is dark (*o, u, a*), then the *ch* is voiced; if it is preceded by *e* or *i*, and *ä* or *ü*, it is voiceless.

N.B. In Southern Germany, *ch* at the beginning of a word is pronounced like a *k*: *Chemie, Chiemsee* (lake near Munich).

In *Hochdeutsch* try to differentiate clearly between words such as the following, although you will hardly hear the differences in the Rhineland and some southern parts of Germany:

Kirche / Kirsche church / cherry
wachen / waschen to soften / to wash

German *j* is spoken slightly more in the front of the mouth than *ch* and it is voiceless. The sound is quite similar to the *y* in 'paying' or 'yen'.

(iii) *z*

z in German is always spoken as an affricate, i.e. as *t* + a **voiceless** *s*, e.g. in *zum, Zug, Zorn.*

(iv) *w* and *v*

w is spoken with the lips **and** the teeth and it is voiced. Hence, it does not resemble the English 'w' sound but it is very close to the English 'v' in the words 'van' and 'vase'. *v* is voiceless and is pronounced like an *f* (e.g. *brav, von*).

(v) *r*

Two kinds of *r* are distinguished: if *r* is the final sound, as in the name *Peter*, then it is open and sounds rather like a German *a* (as in English 'bath').

If it is the initial or the medial sound, *r* is rolled further back in the mouth, as in the English word 'roots', but there is no hint of an *l*. The *r* is much harder than it is in, say, 'barren': you need to feel your larynx vibrating.

(vi) *ss* versus *ß*

The distinction between *ss* and *ß* is a particular feature of German in Germany. In Switzerland and in Austria *ss* is used throughout.

Both *ss* and *ß* are voiceless consonants. You find *ß*

- after long vowels: *die Füße* (feet)
- if *ß* is the last letter: *der Fuß* (foot), *der Kuß* (kiss)
- if *ß* stands between a short vowel and *t*: *du mußt* (you must)

Remember the following oppositions to help you remember these rules:

Fuß foot – *Füße* feet – *Flüsse* rivers

Maß measure – *Maße* measures – *messen* to measure – *Masse* volume

(d) The final -e

In spoken German the final *-e* of a word is frequently dropped when the last syllable is unstressed. Thus you are likely to hear:

ich hab' instead of *ich habe*
ich laß instead of *ich lasse*
gern instead of *gerne*

However, the final *-e* is pronounced in words such as *Blume, Tante* and *Suppe*. In certain dialects the *-e* in these words too is dropped.

In writing, the dropped verb ending is often (but not always) marked by an apostrophe.

At the same time you will sometimes see a final *-e* added where you would not expect it; this is a faint reminder of the Latin ablative, for which German uses the dative today. You see (and even less frequently hear) it in constructions such as:

Sie stammt aus gutem Hause.
She comes from a reputable family.

Er stand in keinem guten Rufe.
He did not have a good reputation.

Ich weiß nicht, wie ich zu diesem Gotte beten soll.
I don't know how to pray to this god.

69 The alphabet

Even for basic survival in an office or tourist environment you need to be able to spell words out: you may be asked to spell your name at reception, you might want to get through to someone on the phone and have to spell their name, you may have to spell out your own address. In addition, something might be spelt out to you, and it is probably more difficult to get that right, especially over the phone.

In some circumstances (e.g. on the phone) it is difficult to distinguish between certain letters. To get round this problem there is a commonly known and accepted word (mostly a name) for each letter. These are listed below, together with a phonetic guide to pronunciation.

a	a:	*Anton*	o	o:	*Otto*
b	be:	*Berta*	p	pe:	*Paula*
c	tse:	*Cäsar*	q	ku:	*quer*
d	de:	*Dora*	r	er:	*Richard*
e	e:	*Emil*	s	es:	*Siegfried*
f	ef	*Friedrich*	t	te:	*Theodor*
g	ge:	*Gustav*	u	u:	*Ulrich*
h	ha:	*Heinrich*	v	fau	*Viktor*
i	ɪ:	*Ida*	w	ve:	*Wilhelm*
j	jɔt	*Johann*	x	ɪks	*Xaver*
k	ka:	*Kaufmann*	y	*Ypsilon*	*Ypsilon*
l	el	*Ludwig*	z	tset	*Zeppelin*
m	em	*Martha*	ß	*Eszett*	
n	en	*Nordpol*			

PART 2

Contemporary functional language

Christine Eckhard-Black

COURTESY FORMULAS

Speaking good idiomatic German requires not only a sound grasp of grammar and vocabulary, but also a sensitivity to the different registers appropriate to different situations. How speakers adapt the form of expression to the social context has given rise to the branch of research known as sociolinguistics. You will notice in Part II of this book a particular emphasis on differing styles and register. As an introduction, here are some guidelines on courtesy in common situations, i.e. *Höflichkeitsfloskeln* ('polite phrases').

0 Greetings

(a) Saying hello

Guten Tag! is right at any time of day (as long as it is not dark), otherwise say *Guten Abend!* (for times of day see section 141). In southern Germany you will also hear *Grüß Gott!*, and *Grüzi/Grüß Sie!* in Switzerland. Men are expected at least to touch, if not take off, their hats.

★ N.B. When greeting a stranger or an adult you know only slightly, there is no need to include a polite title. *Gnädige Frau, Gnädiger Herr, Gnädiges Fräulein* (Madam, Sir, Young lady) are now considered archaic, but you will still hear them in old-fashioned shops etc. accompanied by very good service! They are also occasionally used in an ironic sense.

For closer or informal acquaintances, it is common to say the name after the greeting: *Guten Morgen, Frau Welsch, Guten Morgen, Dagmar.* An initial greeting is usually accompanied by a (hearty) handshake and looking the other person in the eyes. The same convention applies if people haven't seen each other for a long time.

(b) Saying goodbye

You will be familiar with the ubiquitous *Auf Wiedersehen!* and *Auf Wiederhören* (the latter for telephone conversations). (N.B. The familiar *Tschüß* is now used in shops and offices and even on the phone.) However, there are a number of other ways of taking your leave, depending on what the other person is going on to do:

Bis bald!
Hope to see you again at some time. (i.e. not in the immediate future)

Bis später!
See you later! (maybe even on the same day)

(Gesegnete) Mahlzeit!
Have a good meal! (literally: blessed mealtime) (they are going out to eat, or are eating as you are passing)

Viel Glück!
Good luck!

Viel Spaß!
Have fun! (this could have ironic overtones, if you and they know they've got something difficult ahead of them)

Gute Reise!
Have a good journey! (for any mode of transport)

Gute Fahrt!
Drive safely! (for car journeys)

Schöne Ferien!
Have a good holiday! (from school / university)

Ich wünsche Ihnen einen schönen Urlaub!
I hope you have a good holiday! (from work)

Hals und Beinbruch!
Good luck! (usually when going skiing)

Guten Rutsch!
Have a good (transition into the) New Year!

Alles Gute!
All the best!

Alles Gute für die Zukunft!
All the best for the future! <formal> (e.g. to a student or an employee who is leaving and whom you are unlikely to see again)

Guten Tag!
Good day! (also a way of indicating you are never going to see them again)

Saying goodbye to a friend

Mach's gut!
All the best / Farewell! (literally: do it well)

Tschüß!
≈ Cheers! (but not as a toast) / See you!

Servus!
Cheers! (in Austria)

1 Titles and modes of address

(a) Titles

When addressing someone you have already met, you may have to choose between surname and first name. While the younger generation tends to use first names as freely as the English / Americans, with older people be cautious about dropping courtesy titles unless invited to do so. Because of the complexities of the choice between *Sie* and *du* (see p. 25), some older people may be reluctant to rush onto first-name terms, although the combination of first name and *Sie* is used frequently.

To make a polite reference in the third person to someone, use:

der Herr the gentleman / man
die Dame the lady
die junge Dame the young lady

In formal situations and especially in Austria, people are addressed by their title:

Guten Morgen, Herr Pfarrer. Good morning, Reverend.

Herzlich willkommen, Herr Bürgermeister. Welcome, Lord Mayor.

(b) *Du* or *Sie*

The intricacies of *du* and *Sie* have already been explained in section 6. Suffice it here to say that if in doubt, call someone *Sie (jemanden Siezen)*; it is much safer than calling someone *du (jemanden duzen).*

2 Introductions

As in English-speaking countries, if you have to introduce two people to each other, you should start by telling the woman the man's name, or the more senior person the younger person's name.

(a) Formal

In a formal context, introductions run as follows:

Frau Friedrich, darf ich Ihnen Herrn Dr. Debus, meinen ehemaligen Lateinlehrer vorstellen?
Guten Tag.
Angenehm. / (Es) Freut mich, Sie kennenzulernen.

Mrs Friedrich, may I introduce Dr Debus, my former Latin teacher, to you?
How do you do.
How do you do. / Pleased to meet you.

(b) Informal

In an informal situation you can introduce two people more simply:

Hannelore, das ist Karl-Heinz.
Hallo.
Hallo.

Hannelore, this is Karl-Heinz.
Hello.
Hello.

or:

Ulrike, du kennst doch meinen Freund Michael?
Nein, noch nicht. Guten Tag.
Guten Tag.

Ulrike, you know my friend Michael, don't you?
No, we haven't met. Hello.
Hello.

73 Words to accompany gestures

Ultimately, you cannot speak authentic German unless you adopt some of the gestures – facial expressions, hand movements, shrugs of the shoulders, etc. (see p. 122). The 'paralanguage' of gesture is closely allied to verbal communication; some gestures need a minimum of verbal accompaniment (see section 49):

Offering something with an open hand

Bitte kommen Sie herein! Please come in!

Bitte nehmen Sie Platz! Please have a seat!

Leaving your card

Darf ich Ihnen meine Visitenkarte dalassen?
May I leave my card?

Letting someone go into a room first

Bitte nach Ihnen! After you!

Giving someone flowers

(e.g. your hostess when you are arriving for dinner)

Make sure you have removed the paper (unless it is the elaborate see-through variety) before presenting the flowers (you can leave the paper quite conspicuously by the coat rack).

Darf ich Ihnen ein paar Blumen überreichen?
May I present you with some flowers?

Hier habe ich Ihnen einen Blumenstrauß mitgebracht.
I have brought you a bouquet of flowers.

Giving chocolates, perfume, etc.

Und hier ist eine Kleinigkeit für Sie / für die Gastgeberin.
And here is a little something for you / for the hostess.

Asking formally for a dance

(with a slight bow and right hand behind your back; the old-fashioned school even click their heels)

Darf ich bitten? Would you like to dance?

In a more informal situation you would say *Komm, wir tanzen.*

Accepting a compliment (with a smile)

Usually, a bit more than *Danke* would be appreciated and people often follow it with an understatement:

Ach, das (Kleid) habe ich schon lange.
Oh, I've had this (dress) for a long time.

Entering pubs or public places

The man goes in first (to protect the lady from the unfamiliar), saying:

Darf ich? May I?

If a man were wearing a hat he would take it off as soon as he entered a building, including shops and churches.

Raising your glass to drink someone's health

Never start drinking as soon as your drink is poured. Wait for someone, usually the host or hostess, to raise his or her glass to you saying *Prost* ('Cheers'), then nod slightly, smiling at the oldest lady first and at everybody else in turn, say *Prost*, drink a sip, and, with your glass still raised, look at everybody in turn again. Some people like to clink glasses.

Observe others! These are long-established rituals and *Übung macht den Meister* (practice makes perfect).

Waving in defence

(to stop someone from coming too close or even to wave off an over-the-top compliment):

Nicht doch! Don't!

After sneezing

There is no need to excuse yourself. Instead, the others are expected to say:

Gesundheit! Bless you! (literally: good health)

Looking for a spare seat

(e.g. on public transport or in a cinema) In English you would ask: 'Is this seat taken?' and hope for a 'No' as an answer. However, in German you would say:

Ist der Platz hier noch frei? Is this seat free?

So the answer *Ja* would encourage you to sit down. Young people might even, jokingly, say:

Jetzt nicht mehr! (literally: now (that you are here) no longer (free)).

If you would like to join someone at a table (in many places, especially in the south, a very common practice), say:

Darf ich / Dürfen wir uns zu Ihnen setzen?
May I / May we join you?

ADVICE AND HELP

74 Seeking advice and help

(a) General

When asking for suggestions, advice, help and information, be polite. Don't forget your *bitte* and use the subjunctive:

Könnten Sie mir bitte sagen, . . .
Could you tell me please, . . .

Würden Sie bitte so freundlich sein, . . .
Would you please be so kind, . . .

To get attention, for example if you are trying to stop somebody in the street, introduce your request by saying one of the following:

Entschuldigen Sie bitte, . . .
Entschuldigung, . . .
Verzeihung!
Excuse me!

Hallo! (with the stress on the first syllable) is very informal ('Hey!').

! *He du da!* ('Oi!') is distinctly impolite.

In a real emergency, call:

Hilfe!
Helfen Sie mir bitte!
Hilf mir! (to someone under 16)

Leave space between you and the other person and explain your situation in a short sentence; that will break the ice and is much more likely to produce the desired result.

Ich bin hier fremd. I am a stranger here.

Ich habe mich verirrt. I've lost my way.

Ich habe eine Panne. My car has broken down.

Ich verstehe das nicht. I don't understand this.

Ich habe gehört, hier gibt's ein gutes italienisches Restaurant.
I understand there is a good Italian restaurant around here.

If you want somebody's attention, say in an office, use:

Bitte sagen Sie mir, wie . . . / wo . . .
Please tell me how . . . / where . . .

Ich möchte gern wissen . . .
I would like to know . . .

If you'd like to speak to somebody at length, try:

Darf ich Sie mal stören, bitte?
May I disturb / interrupt you, please?

Hätten Sie vielleicht einen Moment Zeit?
Would you have a minute?

Kann ich Sie eben mal was fragen?
Could I just ask you something?

If you don't understand their answer at first, try:

Wie bitte? Pardon?

Ich spreche nur wenig Deutsch, bitte könnten Sie etwas langsamer sprechen?
I speak very little German, could you speak a little more slowly, please?

Könnten Sie das bitte wiederholen?
Could you repeat that please?

Ich habe das rein akustisch nicht verstanden.
I didn't catch what you said.

In a lecture:

Die ganze letzte Reihe hat das nicht verstanden.
No one on the back row understood / caught that.

Wir können Sie hier hinten nicht hören.
We can't hear you back here.

(b) Phrases for seeking advice and help

Ich brauche Ihren Rat. I need your advice.

Ich wäre sehr dankbar, wenn Sie mir sagen könnten, . . .
I would be very grateful if you could tell me . . .

Ich möchte Sie um Ihren Rat bitten.
I would like to ask your advice.

Was würden Sie mir raten? What would you advise?

Kennen Sie sich hier aus?
Do you know your way around here?

Was soll ich tun? What should I do?

Bitte sagen Sie mir, was ich am besten tun soll.
Please tell me what would be best / to do for the best.

Würden Sie so freundlich sein, mir zu sagen, . . .? <formal>
Would you be so kind as to tell me, . . .?

Würden Sie die Güte haben, . . .? <archaic>
Would you be so kind . . .? (this might have ironical overtones)

Bitte erklären Sie (mir) das. Please explain this to me.

Ich möchte gerne wissen . . . I would like to know . . .

Könnten Sie mir das bitte aufschreiben?
Could you please write that down for me?

In a letter you might use:

Teilen Sie mir bitte mit, . . . (+ indirect question)
Please let me know, . . .

Bitte benachrichtigen Sie uns.
Please inform us.

75 Giving advice

(a) In answer to the initial request

Ja? Yes?

Wie kann ich Ihnen helfen? How can I help you?

Wie / Womit kann ich Ihnen dienen? (in shops)
How can I help / be of service to you?

Ja, worum geht es? What is it about?

Ja, wo fehlt's? <coll.> What's wrong?

Ja, wo hängt's? <coll.> What's up?

Was gibt's? What's the matter?

Tut mir leid, ich bin hier selbst fremd.
I'm sorry, I'm a stranger here myself.

Tut mir leid, ich komme / bin nicht von hier.
I'm sorry, I don't live here.

(b) Giving unsolicited advice

Ich möchte mich ja nicht in Ihre Angelegenheiten (ein)mischen, aber . . .
I don't want to interfere, but . . .

Es geht mich ja nichts an, aber . . .
It is none of my business, but . . .

An Ihrer Stelle würde ich . . . If I were you . . .

In Ihrer Situation . . . In your situation . . .

In Ihrem Fall . . . In your case . . .

Ich würde Ihnen raten . . . I would suggest . . .

Ich würde sagen, Sie müssen . . . I would say you should . . .

(c) Making suggestions

Ich mache Ihnen einen Vorschlag.
If I may make a suggestion?

Ich mache Ihnen folgenden Vorschlag.
If I may make the following suggestion. / Let me suggest the following.

Ich schlage Ihnen vor . . . I suggest . . .

N.B. A noun construction (e.g. *Vorschlag machen*) sounds more formal than the verb phrase (*vorschlagen*). See sections 56 and 122.

Er wäre vielleicht am besten, wenn wir den Absatz auslassen.
Maybe it would be (for the) best to leave out the paragraph.

Vielleicht gibt es doch noch eine andere Möglichkeit.
Maybe there is another possibility.

Machen Sie das so, sonst hat es gar keinen Sinn.
Do it this way, otherwise it is pointless.

Man sollte vielleicht in Erwägung ziehen, . . .
Maybe one should consider . . .

Vielleicht sollte man erwägen, . . .
Maybe one should consider . . .

Es bleibt Ihnen nichts anderes übrig, als nach Hause / zum Direktor zu gehen.
You have no choice but to go home / to the headmaster / director.

Das machen Sie am besten folgendermaßen: . . .
You'd better do this the following way: . . . / You'd better go about it like this: . . .

In a medical prescription:

Dreimal täglich zwei Tabletten mit etwas Flüssigkeit schlucken.
Two tablets to be swallowed with some liquid three times a day.

Vor den Mahlzeiten jeweils 30 Tropfen auf etwas Zucker einnehmen.
Take 30 drops on some sugar before meals.

76 Accepting advice and saying thank you for it

(a) Positive replies

OK! Das ist eine gute Idee!
That's a good idea!

Danke für Ihren Rat, ich komme später darauf zurück.
Thank you for your advice. I'll get back to you (literally: it) later.

Vielen Dank für Ihr großzügiges Angebot
Thank you very much for your generous offer.

Ja, das sehe ich ein, so könnte das gehen.
Yes, I see that, that could work.

Daran hatte ich gar nicht gedacht.
I hadn't thought of that.

Vielen Dank für Ihre Hilfe.
Thank you very much for your help.

Darauf wäre ich allein gat nicht gekommen.
I wouldn't have thought of that myself / on my ovvn.

Das gefällt mir. I like that.
Das war sehr hilfreich. That was very helpful.

Ich bin Ihnen sehr dankbar.
I am very grateful to you. / I appreciate that.

Das ist sehr liebenswürdig. That's very kind.

Doch, das muß ich mal probieren.
Yes, I must try that.

(b) Negative replies

Das finde ich eigentlich nicht so gut.
I don't really like that.

Ich glaube nicht, daß das so geht.
I don't think that'll work like that.

Das ist zwar eine gute Idee von Ihnen, aber . . .
That is a good idea, I grant you, but . . .

Das nützt mir zwar nichts, aber . . .
That's no use to me, though . . .

Eigentlich wollte ich nur ein Glas Wasser.
I really only wanted a glass of water.

Ich wollte wirklich nur ein Glas Wasser.
I **really** only wanted a glass of water.

Trotzdem vielen Dank.
Thanks all the same.

Das muß ich mir noch mal überlegen.
I must think about this.

! *Das geht Sie gar nichts an.*
That's none of your business.

Bitte halten Sie sich da 'raus. <coll.>
Please stay out of this.

77 Responding

Gern geschehen. My pleasure.

Ich wollte ja nur helfen. I only wanted to help.

Ich will nur dein Bestes. I only want the best for you.

Sie brauchen ja nicht gleich böse zu werden.
There is no need to get angry.

OFFERS, REQUESTS AND THANKS

78 Offers

Darf ich Ihnen etwas anbieten?
May I offer you something?

Ich mache Ihnen ein Angebot. <formal>
I'll make / May I make you an offer.

Wir würden Ihnen gern ein Geschenk machen.
We would like to give you a present.

Suchen Sie sich etwas aus.
Do choose something.

Sie dürfen sich etwas aussuchen.
You may choose something for yourself.

Darf ich die Rechnung übernehmen?
May I take care of the bill?

Sie dürfen gerne vor meinem Haus parken.
Feel free to park in front of my house.

Wenn Sie möchten, können Sie gerne mitkommen.
If you like, do come along.

Darf ich Ihnen (bei der Hausarbeit) helfen?
May I help you (with the housework)?

Ich kann Sie gerne mitnehmen.
I'd be pleased to take you / give you a lift.

Darf ich Sie nach Hause bringen?
May I take you home?

Was darf es sein? (in a shop or restaurant)
What may I get you?

Was hätten Sie gerne? What would you like?

Was möchtest du zum Geburtstag?
What would you like for your birthday?

Ich würde dir gern etwas schenken.
I would like to give you a present / gift.

Bitte kommen Sie herein. Please come in.

Bitte bedienen Sie sich.
Please help yourself.

Bitte nehmen Sie Platz.
Please sit down.

Darf ich Ihnen Ihren Hut abnehmen?
May I take your hat (from you)?

Darf ich Ihnen in den / aus dem Mantel helfen?
May I help you on with / out of your coat?

or, more colloquially:

Darf ich? May I?

Hiermit überreiche ich Ihnen den Preis. <formal>
I herewith present the prize to you.

Darf ich Ihnen meine Unterlagen anvertrauen?
May I entrust you with my documents?

Das dürfen Sie gerne behalten, ich brauche es nicht mehr.
Do keep this, I don't need it any more.

79 Requests

Ich hätte gerne . . . I would like . . .

Ich nehme die Tagessuppe. I'll have soup of the day.

★ N.B. Never use *haben* for English 'have' when ordering a meal or shopping. You would be misunderstood because it sounds as if you already have what you are asking for.

Darf ich bitte die Toilette benutzen?
May I use the toilet, please?

Darf ich mir Ihren Rasenmäher aus◊leihen?
May I borrow your lawn mower?

Könnten Sie mir das Buch bis morgen leihen?
Could you lend me the book until tomorrow?

Könnten Sie mir etwas Geld leihen?
Could you lend me some money?

N.B. *leihen* implies you are going to return it. Do not use it the way people say in English 'May I borrow a sheet of paper?' For consumables, use:

Hätten Sie vielleicht ein Blatt Papier für mich?
Would you have a sheet of paper for me?

or: *Könnten Sie mir bitte ein Blatt Papier geben?*
Could you give / spare me a sheet of paper, please?

or: *Darf ich um Feuer / etwas Zucker / Senf / Milch bitten?*
May I have a light / some sugar / mustard / milk please?

Nor is *leihen* used for 'borrow' in the sense of 'I borrowed (took!) your suitcase (while you weren't looking)'. Use instead:

Ich habe mir Ihren Koffer genommen.
I have taken / borrowed your suitcase.

Bitte legen Sie meine Reisetasche ins Gepäcknetz.
Would you put my bag into the luggage rack, please?

Darf ich bitte von hier ins Ausland telephonieren? Ich fasse mich kurz.
May I please ring a number abroad from here? I'll keep it short.

Könnten Sie mir bitte einen Gefallen tun?
Would you do me a favour?

Könnten Sie mir bitte die Briefe einwerfen?
Would you post these letters for me, please?

Würden Sie so gut sein?
Would you be so kind?

Ich flehe Sie an. <formal> I implore you.

Ich möchte Sie dringend bitten, den Brief gleich zu übersetzen.
I (would like to) urge you to translate the letter straight away.

Es wäre mir sehr lieb, wenn Sie die Betten frisch beziehen könnten.
(asking your cleaner or au-pair)
It would be very kind / I would appreciate it if you could put clean sheets on the beds.

Das wäre sehr nett von Ihnen.
I would really appreciate that. / That would be very kind of you.

Wir wären Ihnen sehr dankbar für die Adressen einiger Verlage und Nachrichtenagenturen.
We would be very grateful for the addresses of some publishers and press agencies.

Ich hätte einen großen Wunsch. (to ask a great favour of a friend)
Would you do me a great favour?

Bitte machen Sir mir ein Angebot. <formal>
Please make me an offer.

Ich fordere Sie zur sofortigen Zahlung auf. <formal>
I call upon you for immediate payment.

Ich fordere Sie zum letzten Mal auf.
I am asking you for the last time.

Ich verlange von Ihnen mit größtem Nachdruck, daß Sie . . .
I strongly urge you to . . . / I urgently request you to . . . (literally: I demand of you with the utmost vigour)

Es ist dringend notwendig, daß . . .
It is urgently necessary / of the utmost urgency that . . .

80 Thanks

If you are offered a drink (etc.) and you would like to accept, say:

Ja, bitte. Yes, please.

Do not say *Danke* (thanking someone for the offer). That would be interpreted as *Danke*, short for *Nein, danke*, and you wouldn't get anything!

If you don't want it, say:

Nein, danke. No thank you.

Be prepared for the fact that you will be encouraged to have more.

When declining, it would be polite to elaborate a little, where appropriate. You might say:

Nein danke, ich fahre Auto.
No thank you, I'm driving.

or:

Nein, danke. Es hat köstlich geschmeckt, aber ich kann nicht mehr.
No thank you. It was delicious, but I have had enough.

To say thank you for larger items or services:

Ich bin Ihnen sehr zu Dank verpflichtet. <formal>
I am indebted / much obliged to you.

Sie haben mir damit einen großen Dienst erwiesen. <formal>
You have done me a great favour / service with that.

Sie haben mir gute Dienste getan. <archaic>
You have served me well.

Ich weiß nicht, wie ich Ihnen danken kann.
I don't know how I can thank you.

Das war wirklich sehr nett von Ihnen.
I much appreciate that / that was really very kind of you.

Für das Wiederfinden meiner Handtasche ist eine Belohnung von 100 DM ausgesetzt. (notice)
A 100 DM reward is offered for finding my handbag.

! *Darauf kann ich verzichten.* <impolite>
I can do without that.

In return for small favours it is a nice gesture to give a bottle of wine (at least of *Kabinett* quality) to men and a bouquet of flowers to women.

LIKES, DISLIKES AND PREFERENCES

To express likes, dislikes and preferences, German has a range of verbs and adverbial phrases.

In most cases, the addition of an adverb expresses a more precise shade of feeling.

81 Likes

(a) 'I like something'

German has three ways of expressing this.

- the verb ***mögen**** (+ acc.) (used as a main verb; see pages 67 and 70)

This is used in the same way as 'to like':

> *Ich mag klassische Musik.* I like classical music.

- the construction ***gern haben*** (+ acc.) (*haben* used as main verb)

In relation to things, this is used in the same way as 'to like'. In relation to people, *gern haben* implies affection, even love:

> *Ich habe klassische Musik gern.* I like classical music.
>
> *Ich habe kleine Kinder gern.* I love little children.

- ***gefallen**** (+ dat.)

> *Klassische Musik gefällt mir.*
> I like classical music. (literally: classical music pleases me)

★ N.B. The verb *gefallen* agrees in number with the thing(s) or person(s) that please, i.e. with the subject of the verb. The person that is pleased is in the dative:

> *Klassische Musik gefällt* (= sg.) *uns.*
> We like classical music.
>
> *Diese Bücher gefallen* (= pl.) *mir.*
> I like these books.

(b) 'I like' + verb

For the construction 'I like + verb', use the following:

- verb (+ acc.) + *gern(e)*

  Ich esse gern(e) Fisch. I like eating fish.

  Ich spiele gern(e) Tennis. I like playing tennis.

  Wir kaufen gern(e) Frischgemüse. We like to buy fresh vegetables.

(c) 'I would like . . . to . . .' + verb

For this construction German uses:

- a *daß*-clause

  Ich möchte gerne, daß du die Hausaufgaben machst.
  I would like you to do your homework.

  Ich hätte gern, daß das Spiel verschoben wird.
  I would like the match to be postponed.

N.B. The verb in the dependent *daß*-clause is in the indicative.

(d) Qualifying your likes

To qualify the extent to which one likes something, the following adverbs can be used:

Ich mag / sehe / höre diesen Künstler . . . I like this artist . . .
sehr gern a lot
besonders gern particularly, especially
wirklich sehr gern really a lot
furchtbar gern <coll.> an awful lot
arg gern <coll.> terribly much

Ich finde dieses Gedicht . . . I find this poem . . .
recht gut quite / rather good
ziemlich gut fairly / pretty good
einsame Spitze brilliant
phantastisch fantastic
dufte <now archaic> smashing, great
unheimlich stark incredibly good

Ich finde diesen Typen echt gut. <youth>
I find this chap really great.

For more adjectives see also section 136.

(e) Other phrases to express likes

Der Professor hält den Aufsatz für gelungen.
The professor considers that the essay is well done / inspired.

Hat Ihnen das Essen geschmeckt?
Did you like the meal? (literally: Did the meal taste to you?)

Hast du das Konzert genossen?
Did you enjoy the concert?

Fußball macht ihm Spaß.
He likes football. (literally: Football gives him fun.)

Es freut mich, Sie kennenzulernen.
(I am) Pleased to meet you.

Das macht mir großes Vergnügen.
That gives me great pleasure.

Würden Sie gern mitkommen? – Mit dem größten Vergnügen.
Would you like to come along? – With great pleasure.

Ich bin sehr froh, daß du dich dazu entschieden hast.
I am very glad you decided in favour of that.

Wir sind sehr erfreut über die gute Nachricht.
We are delighted about the good news.

Ich habe dieses Baby zum Fressen gern. <informal>
This baby is so delightful, I could eat him up. (literally: I like this baby enough to eat it.)

Das kommt auf den Geschmack an.
That's a matter of taste.

Er hat einen sehr guten Geschmack.
He has very good taste.

Die Dame mit dem großen Hut ist sehr vornehm.
The lady with the large hat has class.

Den Kindern hat es bei den Großeltern gut gefallen.
The children liked it / had a good time at their grandparents'.

Das kann man Ihnen empfehlen.
This can be recommended (to you).

Das ist gar nicht schlecht.
That's not bad at all.

Das sieht ja ganz gut aus. (see section 47)
That looks quite good.

Es ist ihm recht, wenn wir das liegen lassen.
It's all right with him if we leave this.

Ich bin mit dieser Entwicklung sehr zufrieden.
I am very pleased with this development.

Vater und Tochter mögen sich sehr.
Father and daughter are very fond of each other.

Sie kommen gut miteinander aus.
They get along well (with each other).

Sie empfand eine starke Zuneigung zu ihm. <archaic>
She felt a strong affection for him.

Uns hätte gar nichts Besseres passieren können.
Nothing better could have happened to us.

(f) Idioms

Er ist vor Freude ganz aus dem Häuschen.
He is beside himself with joy.

Sie ist total verliebt, sie ist im siebten Himmel.
She's head over heels in love, she's on cloud nine / over the moon.

82 Dislikes

As well as the idioms below, the phrases in the preceding section on 'likes' can be used in the negative to express dislike.

(a) 'I don't like something'

Ich mag klassische Musik nicht.
I don't like classical music.

Ich mag keinen Kuchen.
I don't like cake.

(For more on *nicht* and *kein* see sections 59 and 60.)

Nelken habe ich nicht so gern.
I don't really like carnations.

Diese Bücher gefallen mir gar nicht.
I don't like these books at all.

Kinder essen Spinat nicht so gern.
Children don't really like spinach.

(b) Using adjectives to express dislikes

The extent to which one dislikes something is shown by the adjective chosen:

Wir finden diesen Prospekt . . . We think this brochure is . . .
schrecklich terrible
geschmacklos in bad taste
nicht so berühmt not so great
nicht so bedeutend <coll.> not so special
unklar unclear
verwirrend confusing
beleidigend insulting
häßlich ugly
scheußlich terrible
ekelhaft disgusting
unverschämt impertinent
unbrauchbar useless
untauglich unsuitable / useless
peinlich embarrassing

Ich finde diesen Typen . . . I find this chap . . .
blöd stupid
! *saublöd* bloody stupid
! *beschissen* bloody awful / shit-awful
! *stinklangweilig* boring as hell

(c) Formal and informal expressions of dislike

As indicated below, expressions of dislike range from the formal to the markedly colloquial.

Der Ton des Briefes gefällt mir nicht.
I don't like the tone of this letter.

Die Ausdrücke des Schreibers mißfallen mir.
The author's expressions displease me. / I don't like the author's style.

Die Ausdrücke des Schreibers gefallen mir nicht.
I dislike the author's expressions.

Es ist mir gar nicht recht, daß ich Ihnen das sagen muß.
I don't like having to tell you that.

Es ist eine unangenehme Sache.
It is an embarrassing matter.

Ich halte diesen Vorschlag nicht für gut.
I don't consider this a good proposal.

Er hat eine Aversion gegen seinen neuen Kollegen.
He has taken against his new colleague.

Er hat etwas gegen ihn. <coll.>
He bears a grudge against him.

Ich halte den Lärm nicht mehr aus.
I can't stand the noise any more.

Ich war von dem Ergebnis sehr enttäuscht.
I was very disappointed by the result.

Das brauchst du dir nicht gefallen zu lassen. <coll.>
You needn't put up with this.

Das würde ich mir auf keinen Fall gefallen lassen. <coll.>
There's no way I'd put up with this.

Das ist wirklich eine Unverschämtheit.
That's really outrageous. (literally: an impertinence)

Das können Sie mit mir nicht machen!
You can't do that to me / treat me like this!

Ich fand diesen Witz äußerst geschmacklos.
I found this joke in very bad taste.

Darüber habe ich mich sehr geärgert.
I was very annoyed about that.

Das ist wirklich sehr ärgerlich.
That really is very annoying.

Die Arbeit ist mir völlig mißraten.
The work went completely wrong / was a total failure for me.

Das kann mich wirklich böse machen.
This can make me really angry.

Zu dumm! <coll.> Oh bother!

Ich finde das sehr beleidigend.
I find this very insulting.

Das ist doch tatsächlich eine unerhörte Beleidigung.
This really is an incredible insult.

Das ist ja unerhört! (see section 47b)
That's quite outrageous.

Das ist aber wirklich schade!
That's really a great pity!

Ich kann den Lehrer nicht ausstehen.
I can't stand the teacher.

Die neue Schreibmaschine taugt absolut nichts.
The new typewriter is no good.
(*taugen* = to be suitable. In the negative = not to be much good / to be useless, worthless.)

Er ist völlig untauglich.
He is completely useless / unsuitable.

Da habe ich nichts davon. <coll.>
That's no use to me.

Eigentlich möchte ich das lieber nicht tun. (see sections 15 and 47)
I'd really rather not do that.

Bitte nehmen Sie es mir nicht übel, aber . . .
Please don't take offence but . . .

Ehrlich gesagt, dazu habe ich gar keine Lust.
Frankly, I don't feel like (doing) that at all.

! *Ich habe die Nase voll von dir.*
I've had enough of you. (literally: full nose)

! *Verdammt nochmal!* Blast! / Damn!

! *Mist!* Shit! / Blast!

! *Scheiße!* Shit!

Since this last expression is so rude, it is often reduced to a mere *Sch . . .* and then another ending is added after a pause, e.g. *Sch . . . eibenkleister!* (literally: putty). This is similar to English 'sh . . . sugar'.

! *Zum Teufel!* Damn!

! *Das stinkt mir aber.* I'm pissed off. (literally: stinks to me)

To express very strong dislikes there is the verb *hassen*, but it should be used with caution:

Er haßt es, wenn die Konferenzen zu lang dauern.
He hates the meetings to go on too long.

Er haßt es, wenn man ihn warten läßt.
He hates to be kept waiting.

Hassen implies much stronger feelings than its English counterpart. 'I hate school' would probably be translated as *Schule ist schrecklich*. Instead of *hassen*, use expressions such as:

Er mag es gar nicht, wenn . . .
He doesn't like it at all when . . .

Es ärgert ihn, wenn . . .
He is annoyed when . . .

(d) Idioms

Wenn er so weitermacht, wird er auf keinen grünen Zweig kommen.
If he carries on like that he won't get anywhere. (literally: he won't get to / onto any green branch)

So ein Pech! Bad luck! / Tough! (literally: Such pitch!)
(Occupiers of medieval castles used to defend themselves by pouring hot pitch through holes in the castle walls onto attackers.)

Die Sache hat nur einen Pferdefuß.
The matter has only one major disadvantage. (literally: horse's hoof)

83 Preferences

German commonly uses the expression ***lieber haben*** (comparative of *gern haben*) for personal preference in relation to people:

Ich habe Karl lieber als Fritz.
I prefer Karl to Fritz. (might even imply: I love him more)

Lieber mögen (comparative of *gern mögen*) and **verb** + ***lieber*** are used more generally, in relation to things, people, activities:

Er mag Rugby lieber als Fußball.
He prefers rugby to football.

Ich lese lieber historische Romane als Krimis.
I prefer reading historical novels to thrillers.

The verb ***bevorzugen*** is now rather archaic and is only used in contexts such as the following:

Der Klassenbeste wurde immer vom Lehrer bevorzugt.
The best / top pupil was always favoured / given preferential treatment by the teacher.

The verb ***vorziehen****** is also slightly archaic, or at least very formal:

Ich ziehe es vor, jetzt zu gehen.
I would prefer to go now.

Other expressions for preference:

Möchtest du lieber jetzt oder später gehen?
Would you prefer to go now or later?

Es wäre ihm lieber, wenn wir nach 22 Uhr leise wären.
He would prefer it if we were quiet after 10 p.m.

Ich buche meinen Flug lieber lange im voraus.
I would prefer to book / booking my flight well in advance.

Ich nehme lieber das andere Kleid.
I would prefer (to take / buy) the other dress.

Ich möchte lieber etwas anderes (essen).
I would prefer (to eat) something different.

Die erste Ausgabe hat mir viel besser gefallen.
I much preferred the first edition.

Es wäre vielleicht besser, erst anzurufen.
It might be preferable / better to ring first.

More formally, the subjunctive could be used (see section 37):

Es wäre vielleicht besser, wenn wir erst anriefen.
It might be better if we rang first.

84 Indifference

It is important to distinguish between polite expressions suggesting you are equally happy to do any of the things under discussion and statements of a total lack of interest.

(a) Polite expressions for indifference

These include:

Ganz wie Sie wollen. Just as you like.

Ich habe keine besondere Vorliebe. <formal>
I have no particular preference.

Das ist mir beides recht. I don't mind.

Das ist mir eigentlich egal.
That makes no difference to me.
(This is difficult to translate into German. *Das macht keinen Unterschied* sounds English.)

Remember, intonation and body language alter the implications considerably.

(b) Expressions for lack of interest, or worse

Das ist mir egal. All the same to me.

Phh. (accompanied by a Germanic shrug of the shoulders)
I couldn't care less.

Das ist mir völlig schnuppe. <coll.> I don't care.

Na und? So what?

(c) Idioms

Du kannst mir den Buckel 'runterrutschen. <coll.>
You can get lost / go and take a running jump as far as I am concerned. (literally: slide down my backside)

Du kannst mir gestohlen bleiben. <coll.>
You can get lost. (literally: remain stolen)

INTENTION AND OBLIGATION

85 Intention and wishes

(a) Useful adverbs and adjectives to express intention

planmäßig (adverb) according to plan

Wenn alles planmäßig verläuft, sind wir bis Januar so weit.
If everything goes according to plan, we'll be ready by January.

planmäßig (adjective) scheduled (timetabled)

planmäßige Abfahrt des Zuges scheduled departure of the train

voraussichtlich (adverb) probably

Der Zug wird voraussichtlich mit zehn Minuten Verspätung ankommen.
The train will probably arrive ten minutes late.

voraussichtlich (adjective) anticipated / expected

Das voraussichtliche Einkommen beträgt ca. 5000 DM monatlich.
The anticipated income will amount to about DM 5000 per month.

(b) Useful verbs to express intention and wishes

Pläne machen to make plans

Sie macht Pläne für die nächste Buchmesse.
She is making plans for the next book fair.

Meine Pläne stehen noch nicht fest.
My plans are not definite yet.

planen to plan

Wir haben schon unseren nächsten Sommerurlaub geplant.
We have already planned our next summer holiday.

Für dieses Frühjahr planen wir fünfzehn Neuausgaben.
We are planning fifteen new editions for this spring.

vor◊haben* to intend to / have planned

Ich habe vor, mir einen großen Wagen zu kaufen.
I am planning to buy (myself) a big car.

Haben Sie für heute Abend schon etwas vor?
Have you made any plans for this evening?

sich etwas vor◊nehmen* to plan

Ich habe mir vorgenommen, in diesem Jahr keine großen Anschaffungen mehr zu machen.
I have decided / planned not to make any more major purchases this year.

The subjunctive of *mögen: ich möchte*

Heute abend möchte ich zu Hause bleiben und einen Roman lesen.
Tonight I would like to stay at home and read a novel.

To express intention the **present tense** is used (see section 21).

Wenn das Wetter am Wochenende schön ist, fahren wir ins Grüne.
If the weather is nice at the weekend, we'll drive out into the country.

Wenn alles gut geht, sind wir vor Einbruch der Dunkelheit am Ziel.
If everthing goes well, we'll be at our destination before it gets dark / by the time it gets dark.

N.B. *ich **will*** (from *wollen*) implies, in the first place, wishes, not necessarily the future tense. Therefore *Ich will tanzen gehen (aber ich muß zu Hause bleiben)* means 'I want to go dancing' and not 'I will go dancing' (see sections 24 and 138).

(c) Phrases used to express intention and wishes

So Gott will und wir leben. <coll.>
God willing (and if we are alive).

Wenn ich groß bin, kaufe ich mir auch einen Jaguar.
When I'm grown up I will buy myself a Jaguar, too.

Ich will Arzt werden.
I want to be (literally: become) a doctor.

Ich hätte große Lust auf einen Eisbecher.
I really feel like / I have a longing for an ice-cream sundae.

Er hat ein starkes Verlangen nach Geborgenheit.
He has a strong desire for security.

Es ist mir wichtig. It is very important to me.

Es drängt sie, mit den Ausgrabungsarbeiten anzufangen.
She is longing to start on the excavations.

Es kommt mir sehr darauf an, daß dieses Projekt sorgfältig zu Ende gebracht wird.
It is very important to me that this project is completed carefully.

Es ist mir ein dringendes Anliegen.
It is a matter of pressing concern to me.

Er macht es zu seinem persönlichen Anliegen.
He takes a personal interest in it.

Das liegt mir sehr am Herzen.
I am very concerned about it. (literally: it lies close to my heart)

Ich wünsche mir sehnlichst, daß etwas geschieht. <archaic>
I am yearning for / I am longing for something to happen.

Es ist mir ein Herzenswunsch.
It is my dearest / fondest wish.

Das größte Glück auf Erden für mich wäre, wenn . . .
For me the greatest happiness on earth would be if . . .

Sie ist sein ganzes Glück.
She means everything to him.

Wenn ich einmal reich wär', . . . (Topol in *Fiddler on the Roof*)
If I were a rich man, . . .

86 Obligation

(a) *sollen* and *müssen*

Obligation is usually associated with the subjunctives of *sollen* and *müssen* (see sections 28 and 29):

Ich sollte vielleicht doch einen Brief schreiben.
Maybe I should write a letter after all.

Eigentlich müßte man sie besuchen.
Really one ought to go and see her.

(b) Other phrases

Ich fühle mich ihr gegenüber verpflichtet.
I feel indebted / obliged to her.

Es ist gesetzlich vorgeschrieben.
One is obliged by law.

Ich bin gezwungen, dich zu bestrafen.
I am obliged to punish you.

Sie sind nicht verpflichtet, diese Fragen zu beantworten.
You are not obliged to answer these questions.

Würden Sie bitte so gut sein und die Post erledigen.
Would you please oblige me by dealing / be so kind as to deal with the post.

Ich bin Ihnen sehr verbunden. <formal>
I am greatly obliged to you.

Besten Dank. Much obliged.

Stets zu Diensten. (as an answer; could be ironical)
Anything to oblige.

Er hat sich bei der Bundeswehr auf acht Jahre verpflichtet.
He signed on with the (Federal) Army for eight years.

Die Schöffen sind zu Verschwiegenheit verpflichtet.
The magistrates are sworn to secrecy.

Das verpflichtet Sie zu nichts.
That doesn't commit you to anything.

Er hat sich vertraglich zu dem Kauf verpflichtet.
He bound himself to the purchase by contract.

Sie sind zu keiner Zahlung verpflichtet.
You are not committed to any payment.

Die Pflege des Gartens ist mir anvertraut worden.
I have been entrusted with the care of the garden.

Sie müssen sich auf einen Kurs festlegen.
You have to commit yourself to a course of action.

Daran ist nun einmal nichts mehr zu ändern.
There is nothing more that can be done about it.

Was sein muß, muß sein.
What must be, must be.

Hier stehe ich, ich kann nicht anders. Gott helfe mir, Amen.
(Luther)
Here I stand, I can do no other. God help me, Amen.

N.B. *sollen* is used for the Ten Commandments:

Du sollst nicht ehebrechen.
Thou shalt not commit adultery.

Du sollst Deinen Nächsten lieben wie dich selbst.
Thou shalt love thy neighbour as thyself.

PERMISSION AND PROHIBITION

87 *dürfen, müssen* and *lassen*

The modal *dürfen* is used to indicate permission:

Du darfst. You have permission. = You may.

It is used in the negative to indicate lack of permission:

Du darfst nicht. You don't have permission. = You must not.
(See section 25)

N.B. A popular range of low-fat dairy and sausage products is called *'Du Darfst'*, implying you may eat this, even if you are watching your cholesterol level or your calorie consumption.

Do not confuse *dürfen* with the modal *müssen*, which implies necessity:

Du mußt. It is necessary for you. = You must.

Du mußt nicht. It is not necessary for you. = You need not.
(See section 28.)

Lassen can also be used for permission (or, rather, absence of prohibition), although it often implies a sense of *laissez-faire* rather than positive permission (see section 32).

Sie läßt die Kinder bis spät abends auf der Straße spielen.
She lets the children play in the street till late at night.

Er läßt seine Tochter abends nicht alleine ausgehen.
He won't let his daughter go out alone at night.

(For more examples of using *lassen* as an auxiliary see section 132.)

88 Seeking permission

(a) Some more formal ways of seeking permission

Würde es Ihnen etwas ausmachen, wenn ich heute nachmittag etwas früher nach Hause ginge?
Would you mind if I went home a little earlier this afternoon?

Darf ich mich zu Ihnen setzen? May I join you (at the table)?

Hätten Sie etwas dagegen, wenn wir vor Ihrem Haus parken?
Would you mind if we parked in front of your house?

Dürfte ich bitte bei Ihnen telefonieren?
May I possibly use your phone?

(b) Official requests for permission

Wir bitten um eine Einfuhrgenehmigung.
We are asking for an import licence.

Wir ersuchen Sie um die Zulassung des Medikaments.
We request you to approve this medicine (for sale).

Ich erbitte die Abdruckgenehmigung für die Kurzgeschichte.
I am asking for permission to copy the short story.

(c) Seeking permission in informal contexts

N.B. *können* is used frequently. See p. 66.

Könnte ich vielleicht dein Rad ausleihen?
Could I possibly borrow your bike?

Macht es dir nichts aus, wenn ich erst morgen komme?
You don't mind if I don't come until tomorrow?

Kann ich dich mal was fragen? Can (may) I ask you something?

Kann ich jetzt aufstehen? (asked by a child)
May I get down now? (i.e. get up from the table)

Kann ich mal kurz deinen Taschenrechner haben?
Can (may) I have / borrow your calculator for a moment?

Laß mich das mal probieren. Let me try / taste that.

89 Granting permission

(a) Official permissions

Hiermit erteilen wir die Abdruckgenehmigung für die Berichte, die Sie uns genannt haben.
We hereby grant permission to copy the reports you have cited to us.

Die nachstehenden Autoren sind mit dem Nachdruck der Beiträge einverstanden.
The following authors agree to the copying of their contributions.

Demonstrationen sind genehmigungspflichtig.
Demonstrations require official permission.

Die zulässige Höchstgeschwindigkeit in einer Spielstraße ist 30 km / h.
The maximum speed-limit in a street officially designated as a play area is 30 km / h. (see p. 111)

Der Wagen ist für den öffentlichen Verkehr zugelassen.
The car is authorized for use on public highways.

Dieses Medikament können Sie ohne Bedenken während der Schwangerschaft nehmen.
You can take this medicine during pregnancy without hesitation.

Ich bin ermächtigt, den Safe aufzuschließen.
I am authorized to open the safe.

(b) Granting permission informally

Aber natürlich. Sure. / Of course.

Das ist mir recht. That's all right with me.

Ja, ja, mach nur. Yes, go ahead.

Wenn es unbedingt sein muß. If you really have to. (grudgingly)

Wenn Sie bei den Weight Watchers sind und auf Ihr Gewicht achten, dürfen Sie pro Tag nur vier 'Portionen' Brot essen.
If you are with Weight Watchers and you are watching your weight, you are only allowed four portions of bread per day.

90 Refusing permission

(a) Formally

Das ist grundsätzlich verboten. That is absolutely forbidden.

Es tut mir leid, aber damit bin ich nicht einverstanden.
I am sorry, but I don't agree with that.

Es wäre mir lieber, wenn Sie das nicht tun würden.
I'd rather you didn't do that.

Ich weigere mich entschieden, das zu erlauben.
I absolutely refuse to give permission.

Ich verbiete Ihnen das ausdrücklich. I expressly forbid it.

Der Arzt hat mir das Rauchen verboten.
The doctor has forbidden me to smoke.

Die Genehmigung zur Eröffnung einer Gaststätte wurde ihm verweigert.
He was refused the licence to open a restaurant.

Solches Unrecht darf man nicht zulassen.
Such an injustice must not be permitted.

Ich lasse keine Ausnahmen zu. I do not allow any exceptions.

Ich lasse Sie nur ungern wieder arbeiten gehen.
I am reluctant to let you go back to work.

Es ist mir gar nicht recht, daß Sie das Risiko eingehen.
I am not at all happy that you are taking this risk.

Das möchte ich mir verbeten haben. I will not have it.

Ich verbitte mir diesen Ton.
I won't be spoken to in that tone of voice.

Das verbietet sich von selbst.
That is out of the question. (literally: that forbids itself)

(b) Informal ways of refusing permission

Nein, das geht nicht. No, that won't do / is not possible.

Nein, lieber nicht. No, better not.

Nein, jetzt habe ich keine Zeit. No, I don't have time now.

Nein, das stört die Nachbarn.
No, that'll disturb the neighbours.

Es ist gegen die Spielregeln. It's against the rules.

Das kommt gar nicht in Frage.
That's completely out of the question. / I won't even discuss it.

Das ist völlig ausgeschlossen.
That's completely out of the question / impossible.

91 Prohibition and warning

(a) Formal prohibitions and notices

Notices use specific verbs that indicate prohibition, together with an infinitive used as a noun:

Das Baden im See ist streng verboten.
Bathing in the lake is strictly forbidden.

Rauchen verboten. No smoking. (literally: smoking forbidden)

Parken verboten. No parking.

Plakatieren verboten. Stick no bills.

Das Betreten des Rasens ist nicht erlaubt.
Keep off the grass. (literally: stepping onto the grass is not allowed)

Baustelle. Betreten und Befahren verboten.
Building site. No entry for pedestrians or vehicles.

Fotografieren ist nicht gestattet.
The taking of photographs is not permitted.

On official notices you often find nouns together with verbs of prohibition:

Gefahrenzone. Eintritt untersagt.
Danger zone. Entry forbidden. / No entry.

Unbefugten ist der Zutritt verboten.
Trespassers will be prosecuted. (literally: entry is permitted only to authorized personnel)

Der *Verkauf von Alkohol an Minderjährige ist nicht genehmigt.*
The sale of alcohol to persons under age (18) is not permitted.

(For adverbs used in official notices, see section 135a.)

(b) More informal ways of indicating prohibition

Kleine Kinder dürfen nicht mit dem Feuer spielen.
Little children must not play with fire.

Das dürfen Sie auf keinen Fall tun.
You mustn't do that under any circumstances.

Ich verbiete dir ein für alle Male, mit dem Motorrad zu fahren.
I forbid you once and for all to ride the motorbike.

Ich würde es gerne tun, finde aber nicht die Zeit dazu.
I would love to do it, but time forbids.

Aber das verbietet der Anstand! But decency forbids!

Gott bewahre! Heaven forbid!

(c) Warning

Sometimes, a prohibition or instruction is followed by a warning or disclaimer:

Betreten der Baustelle verboten. Bei Unfällen wird jede Haftung abgelehnt.
Der Unternehmer.
No entry for unauthorized persons. (literally: Entry to the building site is forbidden.) No liability will be accepted in case of accidents. The Developer.

Parkplatz direkt vor dem Eingang reserviert für Lieferanten.
Wagen ohne Parkbewilligung werden abgeschleppt.
The parking space directly in front of the entrance is reserved for deliveries. Cars without a parking permit will be towed away.

Dauerkarten bitte vorzeigen. Sonst kein Zutritt.
Please show season tickets. Otherwise no entry.

Bitte nicht anfassen. Zerbrochene Ware muß bezahlt werden.
Please do not touch. Breakages must be paid for.

Vorsicht, bissiger Hund!
Beware of the dog.

OPINIONS AND DISCUSSIONS

This topic is divided into seven stages, as they might occur in a discussion: opening, expressing views, clarifying, agreement, concession, disagreement and summing up.

92 Opening

To open a discussion or to ask for an opinion you could use the following expressions:

ab◊stimmen to vote

Auf der heutigen Sitzung soll über den Vorschlag von Herrn Meier abgestimmt werden.
In today's meeting we are to vote on Mr Meier's proposal.

betreffen* to concern

Unser heutiges Thema betrifft die Umweltverschmutzung.
Today's topic concerns pollution of the environment.

sich einigen auf (+ acc.) to agree on

Wir müssen uns auf ein Verfahren einigen.
We have to agree on a procedure.

meinen to think / believe (literally: to be of the opinion)

Herr Schulze, was meinen Sie dazu?
Mr Schulze, what do you think about this?

Was meinen Sie zu dieser Frage?
What do you think about this question?

Stellung nehmen* to voice an opinion (literally: to take a position)

Darf ich Sie bitten, zu folgenden Programmpunkten Stellung zu nehmen?
May I ask you to voice your opinion / make a statement on the following points?

die ***Tagesordnung****(en)* agenda (literally: order of the day)

Heute stehen folgende Punkte auf der Tagesordnung:
Today the following points are on the agenda:

93 Expressing views

angebracht / angemessen appropriate / reasonable

Ich halte das für durchaus angebracht.
I consider this quite appropriate / reasonable.

Ich finde das angemessen. I think this is appropriate.

an◊kommen auf* (+ acc.) to depend on

Es kommt nämlich auf . . . an.
It really depends on . . ., you see. (see section 47)

an◊schneiden* * to raise / touch on

Ich möchte eine andere Frage anschneiden.
I would like to touch on another question.

der ***Antrag*** *(̈e)* application

Soviel ich weiß, liegt noch kein Antrag vor.
As far as I know, no application / request has come in / been handed in yet.

die ***Auffassung****(en)* opinion / view

Ansonsten bin ich der Auffassung, daß . . .
Otherwise I hold the view that . . .

auf◊greifen* * to take up

Ich möchte noch einmal die Idee von Frau Rogalla aufgreifen.
I would like to take up Mrs Rogalla's idea again.

aus◊gehen von* * to assume

Ich gehe davon aus, daß . . .
I assume that . . .

Man geht von der Voraussetzung aus, daß . . .
One assumes that . . . (literally: one starts with the assumption)

bedeuten to mean / signify

Das bedeutet für mich eine große Umstellung.
For me that signifies a big change.

Das bedeutet allerdings . . . However, that means . . .

berücksichtigen to consider / take into consideration

Sie müssen berücksichtigen, daß . . .
You have to take into consideration that . . .

betonen to stress / emphasize

Ich muß allerdings betonen, daß . . .
I must stress, however, that . . .

betreffen * (+ acc.) to concern (see section 92)

Was den Neubau der Schule betrifft, so glaube ich, . . .
As far as the new school building is concerned, I think . . .

bewirken to have an effect

Wenn man etwas bewirken will, dann muß man . . .
If you want to have any effect / get a result, you have to . . .

sich beziehen * auf (+ acc.) to refer to

Ich beziehe mich auf die Tabelle auf Seite drei in Ihrem Bericht.
I am referring to the table on page three of your report.

Ich beziehe mich auf den Punkt fünf der Tagesordnung.
I refer to point five on the agenda.

egal / gleich the same / no difference

Mir wäre das auch egal / gleich.
It wouldn't make any difference to me.

ehrlich honest

Wenn ich ehrlich bin, . . .
To be honest, . . . / Frankly, . . .

eigentlich really (see section 47)

Ich glaube, eigentlich sollte man anders vorgehen.
I think really one should proceed differently.

einerseits on the one hand

Einerseits . . . and(e)rerseits . . .
On the one hand . . . on the other hand . . .

entscheidend crucial / decisive

Das ist der ganz entscheidende Punkt.
This is the crucial point / crux.

entsprechend appropriately

Dem Unfallopfer geht es den Umständen entsprechend gut.
The victim of the accident is as well as can be expected (in the circumstances).

meines Erachtens in my view

Meines Erachtens sollte man das ändern.
In my view one should change that / that should be changed.

erscheinen * (+ dat.) to seem / appear

Folgender Punkt erscheint mir sehr wichtig.
The following point seems very important to me.

fest◊stellen to ascertain / state

Ich möchte einmal folgendes feststellen:
I would like to state / ascertain the following:

(sich) (acc.) ***fragen*** to ask oneself / wonder

Wenn man so etwas hört, kann man sich wirklich fragen . . .
When you hear something like this you really wonder . . .

das ***Gefährliche*** the dangerous (thing) (adjectival noun)

Das Gefährliche sehe ich darin, daß . . .
I see the danger in the fact that . . .

der ***Gegensatz(¨e)*** the contrary

Im Gegensatz zu der Aussage des Vorsitzenden . . .
Contrary to the statement of the chairman . . .

der ***Gesichtspunkt(e)*** point of view

Unter dem Gesichtspunkt der Chancengleichheit . . .
From the point of view / perspective of equal opportunities . . .

glauben to believe / think

Ich glaube, daß . . .
I think / believe that . . .

im Grunde basically

Im Grunde genommen ist es gar nicht so schlimm.
Basically / at the end of the day it is not so bad.

grundsätzlich in principle

Ich würde grundsätzlich sagen . . .
I would say, in principle, . . .

halten * von to think of

Jetzt weiß ich, was ich davon zu halten habe.
Now I know what to think of this. (has negative connotations)

To be more neutral, use:

Ich weiß nicht, was man davon halten kann.
I don't know what to think of this.

die ***Hauptsache*** the main thing

Hauptsache ist, daß wir uns einig sind.
The main thing is that we are agreed.

heikel difficult / delicate / tricky

Das ist ein heikles Thema.
That is a difficult / delicate / tricky subject.

heraus◊kommen * auf (+ acc.) to add up to

Das kommt auf dasselbe heraus.
That adds up to the same thing.

hervor◊heben * to stress / emphasize

Man sollte vielleicht den Absatz sieben besonders hervorheben.
Maybe one should lay stress on paragraph seven particularly.

die ***Hinsicht*** respect

Ich finde, gerade in dieser Hinsicht . . .
I think, especially in this respect . . .

In praktischer Hinsicht ist es . . .
In practical terms it is . . .

hin◊weisen* * *auf (+ acc.) to point out

Ich möchte Sie darauf hinweisen, daß . . .
I would like to point out (to you) that . . .

Ich möchte Sie auf die Nachteile hinweisen.
I would like to point out to you the disadvantages.

auf jeden Fall / jedenfalls in any case

Ich könnte mir auf jeden Fall / jedenfalls vorstellen, daß . . . (usually followed by the subjunctive)
I could imagine in any case, that . . .

auf dem laufenden sein to be *au fait* / up-to-date

Ich bin in dieser Hinsicht nicht auf dem laufenden.
I am not up-to-date in this respect.

lenken auf (+ acc.) to direct / draw to

Ich möchte Ihre Aufmerksamkeit auf folgenden Tatbestand lenken:
I would like to draw your attention to the following matter:

die ***Lösung****(en)* solution

Ich finde, die Lösung des Problems liegt in (+ dat.) . . .
I think the solution to the problem lies in . . .

meinen to think / believe / mean

Ich meine . . .
I am of the opinion that / I think / believe / mean . . . (quite vague, and can be motivated emotionally rather than rationally)

die ***Meinung****(en)* opinion

Meiner Meinung nach sollten wir dafür stimmen.
In my opinion / I think we should vote in favour of this.

die ***vorgefaßte Meinung****(en)* preconceived opinion / prejudice

Das ist eine alte, vorgefaßte Meinung.
That is an old prejudice / preconceived idea.

persönlich personally

Also, ich persönlich meine, wir könnten . . .
Well, personally I think we could . . .

das ***Problem(e)*** problem

Das wahre Problem scheint mir ganz woanders zu liegen.
The real problem seems to lie elsewhere. (literally: somewhere completely different)

richtig◊stellen to put right

Ich muß doch erst ein paar Fakten richtigstellen.
Firstly, I must put a few facts right / straight.

der ***Schritt(e)*** step

Das wäre schon der erste Schritt.
That would be the first step.

selbstverständlich obvious / evident (literally: self-understood)

Das ist fast selbstverständlich.
It almost goes without saying.

(sich) *(dat.)* ***sicher sein*** to be sure / certain

Ich bin mir nicht sicher, ob . . .
I am not sure whether . . .

die ***Sicht*** perspective, sight

Auf längere Sicht sollte man vielleicht ganz davon absehen, (+ *zu* + infinitive).
In the long run perhaps one should do without (-ing) altogether.

der ***Sinn(e)*** sense [FA]

Im weitesten Sinne des Wortes.
In the broadest sense of the word.

sinnvoll making sense / sensible [FA]

Ich persönlich finde das sehr sinnvoll.
I personally think that makes a lot of sense.

stören to annoy / disturb / bother

Das stört mich unheimlich.
This really annoys / bothers me.

die ***Theorie****(en)* theory

Das mag in der Theorie richtig sein, aber in der Praxis sieht es anders aus.
That may be right in theory, but in practice it looks different.

trotzdem despite / still

Trotzdem glaube ich, man sollte . . .
I still think one ought to . . .

zu tun haben * **mit** to have to do with

Das hat nichts mit der Sache zu tun.
That has nothing to do with the matter.

überzeugen ♦ to convince

Ich bin vollkommen überzeugt davon.
I am completely convinced of this / won over by it.

unnötig unnecessary

Ich halte das für völlig unnötig.
I consider this completely unnecessary.

unterschätzen ♦ to underestimate

Man hat das auch nicht unterschätzt.
That has not been underestimated.

der ***Unterschied****(e)* difference

Im Unterschied zu unseren Konkurrenten . . .
Compared with / in contrast to our competitors . . .

unterstreichen ♦* to underline / stress

Ich möchte das noch einmal unterstreichen.
I would like to underline / stress this again.

unverzichtbar indispensable

Ich finde das äußerst wichtig und unverzichtbar.
I think this is most important and indispensable.

der ***Vergleich****(e)* comparison

Im Vergleich zu den Einnahmen im letzten Quartal sind die Gewinnanteile . . .
Compared to the takings of the last quarter the dividends are . . .

verstehen* to understand (cf. *selbstverständlich*)

Das versteht sich ja von selbst.
That goes without saying.

versuchen to try

Ich würde zumindest versuchen, . . . (+ *zu* + infinitive)
I would at least try to . . .

vor allem above all

Vor allem ist es wichtig, . . . (+ *zu* + infinitive)
Above all it is important to . . .

vor allen Dingen more than anything (literally: before all things)

Vor allen Dingen sollte man sofort . . .
More than anything else one should immediately . . .

voraus◊setzen to assume

Darf ich Ihre Zustimmung voraussetzen?
May I count on your agreement? (often rhetorical)

vor◊herrschen to prevail

Es herrscht die allgemeine Meinung vor, daß . . .
The general opinion seems to prevail that . . .

(sich) (dat.) *etwas* ***vor◊stellen*** to imagine

Unter Kapitalismus stelle ich mir immer vor, wie . . .
With capitalism I always imagine how . . . .

etwas (acc.) ***etwas*** (dat.) ***vor◊ziehen**** to prefer something to something (else)

Ich würde immer eine Luxussteuererhöhung einer Lohnsteuererhöhung vorziehen.
I would always prefer an increase in the tax on luxuries to an increase in income tax.

Der erste Vorschlag wäre dem zweiten vorzuziehen.
The first suggestion would be preferable to the second.

wichtig important

Das ist nicht so wichtig wie . . .
That is not as important as . . .

wie gesagt as mentioned / said

Dieses Gebäude sollte, wie gesagt, abgerissen werden.
This building should be torn / pulled down, as I said before.

wirklich really

Ich muß also wirklich sagen . . .
I really have to say . . .

mit anderen Worten in other words

Mit anderen Worten, ich habe festgestellt . . .
In other words, I have noticed . . .

zu◊treffen* auf (+ acc.) to apply to

Das trifft nur auf . . . zu . . .
That only applies to . . .

und zwar namely

Ich würde das anders machen, und zwar ohne Umweltbelästigung.
I would do that differently, namely without harm to the environment.

94 Clarifying

an◊deuten to imply / hint

Wollen Sie damit andeuten, daß . . .?
Do you mean to imply that . . .?

es kommt auf etwas (acc.) ***an*** something matters / is important

Kommt es weniger auf Leistung als auf den guten Willen an?
Is achievement less important than good intentions / goodwill?

bedeuten to mean / signify

Was bedeutet dieses Symbol?
What does this symbol mean?

das ***Beispiel(e)*** example

Könnten Sie uns dafür ein Beispiel geben?
Could you give us an example of that?

die ***Einzelheit*** *(en)* detail

Es sind noch einige Einzelheiten klarzustellen.
Some details have yet to be clarified.

die ***Erfahrung****(en)* experience

Aus meiner eigenen Erfahrung kann ich sagen, . . .
From my own experience I can say . . .

falsch verstehen * to misunderstand

Bitte verstehen Sie mich nicht falsch, aber . . .
Please don't get me wrong, but . . .

gelten * ***für*** to apply to / be valid for

Das gilt natürlich nur für die hiesigen Verhältnisse.
Obviously, this only applies to the local conditions.

der ***Grund****(¨e)* reason / basis

Ein weiterer Grund wäre vielleicht, daß . . .
Another reason might be that . . .

Und was, glauben Sie, ist der Grund dafür?
And what do you think is the reason for this?

heißen * to mean / signify

Was heißt 'in absehbarer Zukunft'?
What is meant / do you mean by 'in the foreseeable future'? (could sound aggressive)

klar werden * to become clear

Man muß sich darüber klar werden, . . . (+indirect question)
You have to be quite clear in your own mind, ...

klar◊stellen to clarify (cf. *richtigstellen* in section 93)

Ich möchte noch einmal klarstellen, daß das nicht beabsichtigt war.
I would like to make it clear once again that this was not intended / deliberate.

sagen to say / mean

Wie soll ich das sagen? How shall I say this?

Was wollen Sie damit sagen? What do you mean by this?

Das sagt gar nichts. That doesn't mean anything.

die ***Seite(n)*** side

Auf der einen Seite . . . auf der anderen Seite . . .
On the one hand . . . on the other hand . . .

verstehen* to understand

Was verstehen Sie unter 'mittelfristig'?
What do you mean by 'in the medium term'?

der ***Vorteil(e)*** advantage

Das hat Vor- und Nachteile.
There are advantages and disadvantages.

weniger . . . vielmehr less . . . rather . . .

Ich meine weniger seine Arbeitsweise sondern vielmehr seine Einstellung.
I don't mean so much his way of working, but rather his attitude.

der ***Zweifelsfall(¨e)*** (case of) doubt

Im Zweifelsfall könnte man . . . If in doubt one could . . .

95 Agreement

auf◊fallen* to stand out

Mir ist die besonders gute Zusammenstellung der Statistiken aufgefallen.
I noticed the particularly good compilation of statistics.

bestimmt definitely

Das ist bestimmt richtig. That is definitely right.

dafür in favour of it / for it

Ich bin sehr dafür. I am very much in favour of it.

dagegen against it

Wenn Sie nichts dagegen haben, . . . Unless you disagree . . .

daran sein to be at it / in it

Da ist 'was dran. There is something in / to that.

doch yes / yet

Doch, doch!
Oh yes! (I do agree, although you think I think otherwise.)

einverstanden sein to be in agreement

Ich bin ganz einverstanden. I am all for it.

Dann wäre ich damit einverstanden.
Then I would agree to that. (If that were the case, then I would agree with it.)

entschieden decidedly / definitely

Das wäre entschieden die beste Lösung.
That would decidedly / definitely be the best solution.

genau precisely / exactly

Genau, das wollte ich auch sagen.
Precisely, that's what I wanted to say as well.

jawohl very well

Jawohl. Fine. / Very well.

klar clear

Das ist ganz klar.
That's quite clear. (i.e. I don't dispute that)

meinetwegen for my sake

Meinetwegen brauchen Sie das nicht zu tun.
You needn't do that for my sake / as far as I'm concerned.

die ***Meinung****(en)* opinion

(Ich bin) ganz Ihrer Meinung. I completely agree with you.
Der Meinung bin ich auch. I think so, too.

natürlich of course/naturally

Natürlich. Of course, naturally. / Naturally.

Okay O.K.

Okay, in Ordnung. All right.

passen to fit / suit

Das paßt mir ausgezeichnet.
That suits me very well.

recht right

ganz recht
quite right

Das ist mir recht.
That's all right with / by me.

*die **Schwierigkeit**(en)* difficulty

Ja, ich glaube, gerade darin liegt die Schwierigkeit.
Yes, I think that's exactly where the problem is / difficulty lies.

selbstverständlich (cf. section 93)

Selbstverständlich!
Certainly! / It goes without saying!

sicherlich certainly

Das ist in Ihrem Fall sicherlich anders.
That is certainly different in your case.

zu etwas (dat.) ***/ zu jemandem stehen**** to stand by something / somebody

Da stehe ich voll und ganz dazu.
I definitely / completely stand by that.

stimmen to be true

Das stimmt schon, aber ich glaube trotzdem, daß . . .
That is true, but I still think that . . .

überein◊stimmen mit to agree with

Da stimme ich mit Ihnen überein.
I agree with you there.

überlegen ⧫ to think / consider / ponder

Ja, ich überlege auch gerade . . .
Yes, I'm also just thinking . . .

zufrieden satisfied / pleased

Jetzt bin ich sehr zufrieden damit.
Now I am very pleased with it.

etwas (dat.) / ***jemandem zu◊stimmen*** to agree with something / someone

Ich möchte dem zustimmen.
I would like to agree with this.

Zustimmung (f.) ***finden*** * to meet with approval

Die neue Regelung hat Zustimmung gefunden.
The new regulation has met with approval.

96 Concession

(a) *ja, schon, zwar*

When these particles are followed by *aber* or *doch* they indicate concession:

Das sehe ich ja ein, aber / doch . . . I do see the point, but / yet . . .

Das meine ich schon, aber . . . I do think that, but . . .

Das ist zwar völlig richtig, aber . . .
(I grant you) That is completely right, but . . .

Das ist ja alles schön und gut, aber . . .
That's all well and good but . . .

(b) Phrases expressing concession

der ***Aspekt(e)*** aspect

Das ist zwar auch ein wichtiger Aspekt, aber . . .
That is, I grant you, also an important aspect, but . . .

eher rather

Nein, ich glaube eher, daß . . . No, I think rather that . . .

entgegen◊setzen (+ dat.) to oppose

Aber wenn . . ., dann habe ich dem auch nichts entgegenzusetzen.
But if . . ., then I have no objection.

grundsätzlich basically / in principle

Grundsätzlich habe ich nichts dagegen einzuwenden, aber / jedoch . . .
Basically / in principle I have nothing against it, but / however . . .

meinetwegen as far as I'm concerned

Meinetwegen. All right then. (agreeing grudgingly)

na schön very well then

Na schön! Very well then! (agreement given reluctantly)

unbedingt necessarily

Nicht unbedingt. Not necessarily.

97 Disagreement

*die **Ablehnung*** disapproval

Dieser Vorschlag wird bei den Wählern auf Ablehnung stoßen.
This suggestion will meet with disapproval / opposition from the voters.

*die **Ansicht(en)*** view / viewpoint

Darüber bin ich ganz anderer Ansicht (gen.).
I couldn't disagree more / I take completely the opposite viewpoint.

*die **Ausnahme(n)*** exception

Es gibt natürlich viele Ausnahmen.
Of course, there are many exceptions.

*der **Begriff(e)*** term / concept

Ich möchte den Begriff 'unreif' gar nicht benutzen.
I really don't like using the term 'immature'.

behaupten to claim / state

Ich würde direkt das Gegenteil behaupten.
I would claim / state the direct opposite.

bezweifeln to doubt / question

Ich wage das zu bezweifeln.
I would question that. (literally: I dare to question that)

(nicht) für etwas sein (not) to be in favour of

Also ich wäre nicht dafür. Well, I am not in favour of it.

gegen etwas sein to be against something

Ich bin sehr dagegen. I am very much against it.

durchaus nicht definitely not

Durchaus nicht, und zwar weil . . .
Definitely not, and that is because . . .

falsch wrong / false

Ich halte beide Extreme für falsch.
I think both extremes are wrong.

gefallen * to please

Es gefällt mir nicht, daß . . .
I don't like it / I am unhappy that . . .

das ***Gegenteil****(e)* opposite

Im Gegenteil! On the contrary!

gehen * to go / work (i.e. be possible)

Das geht nicht. That won't do.

gewiß certainly

Gewiß nicht. Certainly not.

etwas gut finden * to find / consider something (to be) good

Ich finde das nicht so gut.
I don't think this is so good.

nicht in Frage kommen * to be out of the question

Kommt gar nicht in Frage! Out of the question!

im geringsten in the least

Nicht im geringsten! Not in the least!

irren to be wrong / err

Sie irren sich. You are wrong.

der ***Irrtum*** *(¨er)* error / mistake

Sie sind im Irrtum. You are mistaken.

keineswegs

Keineswegs! No way!

langweilig boring

Ich finde es langweilig. I think this is boring.

leider unfortunately

Leider nicht. I am afraid not.

sich lohnen to be worthwhile / worth it (to pay off)

Es lohnt sich nicht. It's not worth it.

nein no

Aber nein! It doesn't! / It won't! / It isn't / It hasn't! / Oh no!

der Quatsch rubbish / nonsense

! *Das finde ich Quatsch.*
I think this is rubbish.

sehen* to see

Das sehe ich überhaupt nicht so.
I don't see it like that at all.

strikt strictly

Da wäre ich ganz strikt dagegen.
I would be completely / totally (literally: strictly) against that.

das ***Thema*** *(Themen)* subject / topic / issue

Zurück zum Thema, bitte. Back to the issue, please.

überzeugen ⧫ to convince

Ich bin nicht überzeugt davon. I am not convinced.

uneingeschränkt without reservation

Uneingeschränkt würde ich das nicht sagen.
I wouldn't say that without reservation / qualification.

unmöglich impossible

Das ist völlig unmöglich. That is completely impossible.

der ***Unsinn*** nonsense

Das ist natürlich völliger Unsinn.
This is of course utter nonsense.

der ***Unterschied****(e)* difference

Man muß aber doch noch Unterschiede machen.
But one does have to differentiate after all.

verallgemeinern to generalize

Das kann man nicht so verallgemeinern.
You can't generalize like that.

verfehlen to miss

Das halte ich für verfehlt.
I think this is missing the point.

wahr true

Das ist gar nicht wahr! That's not true at all!

sich gegen etwas / jemanden wehren to defend oneself against something / somebody

Ich wehre mich dagegen.
I am opposed to this. (literally: defend myself)

jemandem widersprechen* * to contradict someone

Ich möchte dem allerdings widersprechen.
I would however like to contradict that.

Da muß ich Ihnen widersprechen.
There I must contradict you.

der ***Widerspruch****(̈e)* contradiction

Das kann ich nicht ohne Widerspruch hinnehmen. <formal>
I can't accept that without argument.

der Zweck purpose

Das hat keinen Zweck. < coll. > There is no point (to it).

98 Summing up

die Einigung agreement

Da wir noch zu keiner Einigung gekommen sind, müssen wir die Sitzung auf morgen verschieben.
Since we have not reached an agreement, we'll have to postpone the meeting until tomorrow.

einstimmig unanimous

Damit wäre der Vorschlag einstimmig angenommen.
Therefore the proposal is accepted unanimously.

jemanden mißverstehen* to misunderstand someone

Ich glaube, da haben wir uns mißverstanden.
I think we misunderstood each other on / over that.

*das **Protokoll(e)*** minutes (of a meeting) [FA]

Das kann ins Protokoll aufgenommen werden.
That can go into the minutes.

schließen * to conclude

Aus diesem Bericht könnte man schließen, daß . . .
From this report one could conclude that . . .

zurück◊kommen * auf (+ acc.) to return / to come back to

Ich möchte noch einmal auf Ihre Frage zurückkommen.
I would like to return to your question.

zusammenfassend in conclusion

Zusammenfassend möchte ich folgendes sagen:
In conclusion I'd like to say the following:

CERTAINTY, POSSIBILITY AND DOUBT

99 Certainty

(a) Words that express absolute certainty

bestimmt certainly

Das weiß ich ganz bestimmt. I know that for sure.

Das ist bestimmt richtig. That is certainly right.

Es wird bestimmt einige Zeit Unruhe geben.
There is bound to be a period of unrest.

genau exactly

Ich weiß genau, worauf du hinaus willst.
I know exactly what you are aiming at / driving at.

Es läßt sich genau festellen, wer zuletzt am Computer gearbeitet hat.
It is possible to ascertain exactly who was last working on the computer.

Das ist genau die richtige Behandlung für eine Lungenentzündung.
That is exactly the right treatment for pneumonia.

Das ist genau der richtige Werbeträger für unser neues Produkt.
That is exactly the right advertising medium for our new product.

sicher certain / sure

Ich bin mir ganz sicher, daß . . .
I am completely certain that . . .

Bist du dir da auch ganz sicher?
Are you completely certain about that?

(b) Expressions for reasonable certainty

The more common ones are listed first.

überzeugt sein to be convinced

Ich bin davon überzeugt, daß er für die Stelle geeignet ist.
I am convinced that he is suitable for the position / post.

Ich bin davon überzeugt, daß sie es getan hat.
I am convinced that she did it.

selbstverständlich sein to be self-evident (literally: to be self-understood)

Es ist natürlich selbstverständlich, daß Sie bei uns übernachten dürfen.
Of course it goes without saying that you can spend the night with us.

deutlich clearly

Aus den Unterlagen geht deutlich hervor, wie oft Sie im letzten Jahr abwesend waren.
It is clear from the records how often you were absent last year.

100 Prozent / absolut 100 per cent / absolute

Es läßt sich mit 100 prozentiger / absoluter Gewißheit sagen, daß keine Chemikalien benutzt wurden.
It can be said with 100 per cent / absolute certainty that no chemicals were (being) used.

auf keinen Fall no way / definitely not / under no circumstances (literally: in no case)

Das kann er auf keinen Fall ohne Hilfe geschrieben haben.
He can't possibly / No way can he have written this without any help.

Ich möchte auf keinen Fall gestört werden.
I definitely do not want to be disturbed.

keinesfalls by no means / on no account

Die Aufgabe ist schwer, aber keinesfalls unlösbar.
The task / problem is difficult but by no means insoluble.

keineswegs by no means / not in the least / not in any way

Ich fühle mich keineswegs schuldig.
I do not feel in the least / in any way guilty.

★ N.B. *keinesfalls* and *keineswegs* are interchangeable, but *keinesfalls* refers to occasion and *keineswegs* to manner (see section 135b).

unter keinen Umständen under no circumstances

Diese Information darf unter gar keinen Umständen an die Öffentlichkeit weitergegeben werden.
This information must not under any circumstances be passed on to the public.

bedenkenlos / ohne Bedenken unhesitatingly / without hesitation

Ich kann Ihnen diese Ware bedenkenlos empfehlen.
I can recommend this product to you without hesitation.

zweifellos without doubt

Das ist zweifellos mit Abstand der beste Wagen in seiner Klasse.
This is without doubt by far the best car in its class.

nicht in Frage kommen to be out of the question

Es kommt überhaupt nicht in Frage, daß du weggehen darfst, ohne vorher deine Hausaufgaben zu machen.
It's completely out of the question for you to go out before you've done your homework.

leugnen (+ negative) to deny

Niemand kann leugnen, daß er viel Erfahrung auf diesem Gebiet hat.
No one can deny that he has a lot of experience in this area / field.

ab◊streiten* (+ negative) to deny / dispute

Ich möchte nicht abstreiten, daß sie die meisten Verträge bekommen hat.
I do not want to deny that she has got most of the contracts.

zuversichtlich confident

Wir sind zuversichtlich, daß wir gewinnen werden.
We are (quietly) confident that we will win.

(c) More informal expressions of certainty

Das gibt es doch nicht! < informal > But that can't (possibly) be!

Das geht entschieden zu weit! < informal > That definitely goes too far!

100 Possibility

(a) More formal expressions

The more common ones are listed first.

wahrscheinlich probably (literally: true seemingly)

Wir werden wahrscheinlich erst morgen ankommen.
We will probably not arrive until tomorrow.

höchstwahrscheinlich most likely / probably

Dieser Artikel ist jetzt höchstwahrscheinlich ausverkauft.
In all probability they've sold out of this product by now.

möglich possible

Das ist schon möglich. That is quite possible.

möglicherweise (adverb) / possibly

Wir können Ihnen den Rock möglicherweise bis morgen verlängern.
We might be able to lengthen the skirt / let the hem down for you by tomorrow.

vermutlich presumably

Der Täter war vermutlich auf einem gestohlenen Motorrad entkommen.
The criminal had presumably escaped on a stolen motor bike.

vielleicht perhaps / maybe

Vielleicht war er aber auch hinter dem Gebäude verschwunden.
But it is also possible that he had disappeared behind the building.

scheinen* * to seem / to appear

Es scheint alles darauf hinzudeuten, daß der Mörder das Opfer kannte.
Everything seems to point to the fact that the murderer knew the victim.

es mag wohl sein it may well be

Es mag wohl sein, daß er sich das Haus leisten kann, aber vielleicht ist es doch zu groß für ihn.
It may well be that he can afford the house, but perhaps it is too large for him after all.

schwer zu sagen hard to say

Es ist schwer zu sagen, ob wir die Rückstände eintreiben können.
It is difficult to say whether we will be able to collect the outstanding debts.

ab◊hängen* von to depend on

Es hängt alles davon ab, ob sich die Stadtverordneten auf einen Haushaltsplan einigen können.
It all depends on whether the town councillors can agree on a budget.

an◊kommen* auf (+ acc.) to depend on

Es kommt ganz darauf an, wie lange wir für die Reparatur brauchen.
It all depends on how long we need for the repair / the repair will take.

N.B. *es kommt darauf an* can stand on its own but *es hängt davon ab* must be followed by another clause.

vorausgesetzt provided

voraugesetzt, daß die Sitzung noch heute stattfindet
provided the meeting takes place today

unter der Voraussetzung, daß <formal> on condition that

Die Bank gewährte ihm ein Darlehen unter der Voraussetzung, daß er es innerhalb einer bestimmten Zeit zurückzahlen würde.
The bank granted him a loan on condition that he would repay it within a certain period.

voraussichtlich probably

Der Abflug wird sich voraussichtlich verzögern.
The (flight) departure will probably be / is expected to be delayed.

sich (acc.) ***wundern*** to be surprised

Es würde mich nicht wundern, wenn er den Schlüssel aus Versehen mit nach Hause genommen hätte.
I wouldn't be surprised if he had taken the key home by mistake.

soweit as far as

Soweit ich weiß, ist er schon gegangen.
As far as I know he has already left.

(b) Expressions using the subjunctive

es könnte sein it could be / is possible

Es könnte sein, daß der Scheck gefälscht ist.
It is possible that the cheque is forged.

es wäre möglich it might be / it is possible

Es wäre auch möglich, daß sie davon gar nichts gewußt hat.
It might also be that she didn't know anything about it.

(c) More informal expressions of possibility

Glauben Sie wirklich? Do you really think so?

Meinen Sie / Finden Sie? Do you think so?

Ja? Yes? / Really?

101 Doubt

(a) More formal expressions

*der **Zweifel(-)*** doubt
zweifelhaft doubtful
bezweifeln to doubt

Es bestehen noch starke Zweifel über die genaue Anzahl der Verletzten.
Strong doubts still exist / There are still strong doubts about the exact number of casualties. (literally: injured people)

Ob sie das absichtlich getan hat, ist zweifelhaft.
It is doubtful whether she did it intentionally.

Die Richtigkeit seiner Angaben erscheinen mir äußerst zweifelhaft.
I doubt if his information is correct. (literally: The correctness of his statement seems extremely doubtful to me.)

Das möchte ich doch sehr / stark bezweifeln.
I have to say I doubt that very much.

höchst unwahrscheinlich highly / most unlikely

Es ist höchst unwahrscheinlich, daß wir den Auftrag bekommen.
It is highly unlikely that we'll get the job / commission.

nicht sicher not certain / not sure

Sind Sie sich dieser Tatsache ganz sicher?
Are you quite certain of this (fact)?

Ich bin mir nicht ganz sicher.
I am not quite sure.

nicht genau wissen* not to know exactly

Man kann nie genau wissen, wie so etwas ausgeht.
One can never be quite sure how something like that will turn out / what the outcome might be.

notwendigerweise necessarily

Das ist nicht notwendigerweise die beste Lösung.
That is not necessarily the best solution.

keinen Grund haben* to have no reason

Wir haben keinen Grund zu der Annahme, daß die Gefangenen geflüchtet sind.
We have no reason to assume that the prisoners fled.

fraglich sein* to be questionable

Es ist fraglich, ob wir dadurch etwas gewinnen können.
It is debatable whether we will gain anything by this.

die ***Ahnung*** idea / inclination

Ich habe nicht die geringste Ahnung.
I haven't the slightest idea.

(b) Some more informal expressions of doubt

Nicht daß ich wüßte. Not that I would know / know of.

So etwas habe ich ja noch nie gehört.
I have never heard anything like that (before).

Keine Ahnung. No idea. / Not a clue.

Weiß nicht. Don't know.

Huuh! Hum!!

MAKING COMPLAINTS

This section illustrates ways of making complaints. For how to deal with complaints, see sections 105-9 on apologies. For legal matters, see section 148; written complaints are dealt with in sections 111(d) and 112(g).

02 Polite or tentative complaints

Entschuldigen Sie bitte, ich wollte eigentlich Größe 37; dieser Schuh ist Größe 36.
I am sorry but actually I asked for size 37; this shoe is size 36.

Ich glaube, da stimmt etwas nicht.
I think there is something wrong here.

Verzeihung! Ich hatte nur ein Glas Wein bestellt, aber Sie haben mir zwei berechnet.
Excuse me! I only ordered one glass of wine, but you have charged me for two.

Entschuldigung, ich war vor Ihnen dran. <coll.>
Excuse me, it was my turn / I was before you.

Verzeihung! Jetzt bin ich an der Reihe.
Excuse me! It's my turn now.

N.B. The above two sentences are needed more frequently on the Continent, where queuing isn't as customary as it is in England.

Ich fürchte, es handelt sich um ein Mißverständnis. <formal>
I am afraid there is a misunderstanding.

Könnten Sie das bitte noch einmal nachrechnen?
Could you check this amount again, please?

Könnten Sie die Rechnung bitte ändern?
Could you change the bill / invoice, please?

Verzeihung! Mir zieht es. Könnten Sie bitte das Fenster zumachen?
Excuse me! I am sitting in a draught. Could you close the window, please?

103 Forceful or official complaints

Wir möchten bitte sofort mit dem Geschäftsführer / mit dem Besitzer sprechen.
We would like to speak to the manager / the owner straight away.

Die Angelegenheit ist sehr ernst.
The matter is very serious.

Ich muß mich leider über den Zustand des Zimmers beschweren.
I'm afraid I must complain / protest about the state of the (bed)room.

Ich muß Sie darauf hinweisen, daß diese Treppe sehr gefährlich ist.
I must point out to you / I think you should be aware that this staircase is very dangerous.

Mein Mann kann den Lärm nicht mehr ertragen / ausstehen.
My husband can't bear / stand the noise / row any longer.

Ich möchte diese Tischdecke umtauschen. Sie hat einen Webfehler.
I'd like to exchange this tablecloth. It has a flaw (in the weave).

Ich möchte bitte mein Geld zurückhaben. Dieses Gerät funktioniert nicht.
I would like my money back, please. This appliance doesn't work.

Wenn Sie diese Beleidigung / Beschuldigung nicht zurücknehmen, muß ich mich beschweren.
If you don't withdraw your insult / accusation, I shall be forced to make a complaint.

Ich werde eine Klage gegen die Schulverwaltung erheben.
I shall lodge an official complaint against the school administration.

Ich werde mich bei der Verwaltung über Sie beklagen.
I shall complain about you to the management.

104 Adjectives and nouns to strengthen complaints

(a) Adjectives

The following adjectives suggest that something is unacceptable. They can be used to strengthen a complaint. Germans don't usually mince their words. Complaints are stated forcefully, without understatement.

Ihre Frage ist völlig fehl am Platz.
Your question is completely inappropriate.

Die Beleuchtung der Notausgänge ist mangelhaft.
The lighting of the emergency exits is inadequate.

Die Wohnung befindet sich in einem unannehmbaren Zustand.
The flat is in an unacceptable state.

Dieses Benehmen ist ausgesprochen unhöflich.
This behaviour is definitely impolite / uncouth.

Die Kinder sind wirklich unmöglich. <coll.>
The children are absolutely impossible.

Diese Bemerkung ist unverzeihlich.
This remark is unforgivable.

Die Arbeit der Sekretärin ist unzulänglich.
The secretary's work is unsatisfactory / inadequate.

Die medizinische Versorgung ist unzureichend.
The medical provision is insufficient.

Wir finden die Arbeitsbedingungen völlig unzumutbar.
We consider the working conditions completely unacceptable / beyond the pale.

(b) Nouns

So eine Frechheit lasse ich mir nicht gefallen!
I won't put up with such impudence / cheek.

Das ist der Gipfel (der Frechheit)!
That's the height of impudence! / the limit (of impudence)!

Das ist eine Unverschämtheit!
That is an impertinence. / It's outrageous!

Das ist eine Zumutung!
That's a bit much! (an unreasonable demand)

APOLOGIES, EXPLANATIONS AND PROMISES

105 Apologies

(a) General expressions

These are arranged in order from the most sincere to the most cursory:

Es tut mir leid. I'm sorry.

Entschuldigung! / Entschuldigen Sie bitte!
Excuse me!

Verzeihung! Sorry! (literally: forgiveness)

Pardon! (with the accent on the second syllable as in French)
Sorry!

Sorry! Sorry!

(b) Adverbs used to intensify apologies

Es tut mir sehr leid. I am very sorry.
wirklich really
furchtbar awfully
schrecklich terribly
wahnsinnig < coll. > terribly
unheimlich < coll. > terribly / incredibly
außerordentlich extraordinarily / extremely

Entschuldigen Sie bitte vielmals.
I am very sorry. (literally: excuse many times)

(c) Formal apologies

Ich bitte (vielmals) um Verzeihung.
I (do) apologize.

Ich bedaure sehr / außerordentlich.
I very much / sincerely regret it.

Entschuldigen Sie bitte vielmals die Verspätung / das Versehen.
I am very sorry about the delay / oversight.

Ich bin ganz untröstlich darüber, daß . . .
I am completely inconsolable about the fact that . . . (could be ironic)

Bitte haben Sie Verständnis für unsere Lage.
Please understand our situation.

Wir entschuldigen uns für den Lärm / die Unannehmlichkeiten.
We apologize for the noise / inconvenience.

Bedauerlicherweise / Leider ist das passiert.
It is regrettable / unfortunate that this has happened.

Diesen Fehler bitten wir zu entschuldigen.
We would ask you to excuse this error.

Aus unvorhersehbaren Gründen ist es mir nicht möglich, . . .
For reasons I could not have foreseen I am unable to . . .

(d) Informal apologies

Entschuldige! Das war nicht so gemeint.
Sorry! I didn't mean it like that.

Kannst du mir je verzeihen?
Can you ever forgive me? (could also be ironic)

Sei mir nicht böse. Don't be angry with me.

06 Explanations

It is always a good idea to offer some sort of explanation with an apology.

Entschuldigen Sie bitte vielmals, . . .

da muß ich mich vertan haben.
I must have made a mistake / slipped up.

ich habe mich verwählt.
I have got (dialled) the wrong number.

ich habe mich geirrt.
I have made an error / I was wrong.

ich bin schuld.
it's my fault.

aber ich kann nichts dafür. < coll. >
but it's not my fault / it's none of my doing.

Entschuldigen Sie bitte vielmals, . . .

das habe ich völlig / total vergessen.
I completely / totally forgot.

das habe ich nicht extra < coll. > / *absichtlich gemacht.*
I didn't do that on purpose / intentionally.

das war ein Mißverständnis.
that was a misunderstanding.

ich bin so vergeßlich in letzter Zeit.
I have been very forgetful / absent-minded lately.

das war nicht vorhersehbar.
that could not have been foreseen.

daß mein Sohn gestern nicht in die Schule kommen konnte. Er hatte Fieber.
that my son couldn't come to school yesterday. He was running a temperature.

107 Promises

Maybe you'd like to follow up your explanation with a promise:

Ich tue es nie wieder. I'll never do it again.

Das soll nie wieder vorkommen. That will never happen again.

Das wird nicht nochmal passieren. That won't happen again.

Ich werde mich bemühen, daß das nicht mehr vorkommt. < formal >
I will do my best (to make sure) that it won't happen again.

Es wird selbstverständlich korrigiert. < formal >
It will be corrected as a matter of course.

Selbstverständlich bekommen Sie einen Ersatz / eine Gutschrift / Ihr Geld zurück.
It goes without saying that you will get a replacement / a credit note / your money back.

08 Sympathy

Alternatively, you might wish to express or gain some sympathy:

Schade, aber daran kann man nichts ändern.
It is a pity, but you can't do anything about it / nothing can be done about it.

Bitte sei mir nicht böse. Please don't be angry with me.

Das ist wirklich sehr ärgerlich.
That is really most annoying.

Leider kann man nichts dagegen tun.
Unfortunately, nothing can be done about it.

Es ist mir wirklich sehr peinlich.
It is most embarrassing for me. / I am really most embarrassed about it.

Es ist mir wirklich sehr unangenehm.
I am most upset. (literally: it is very embarrassing / awkward for me.)

08 Accepting an apology

(a) Informal expressions

Das kann passieren. It can happen.

Das kann jedem einmal passieren. That can happen to anybody.

Ist schon gut. < coll. > That's all right.

Laß man gut sein. < coll. > Don't worry about it.

Laß doch, du kannst mir das Geld später zurückgeben.
That's all right. You can pay me back later.

Das kann man wieder reparieren. That can be repaired again.

Das ist nicht so schlimm. That isn't (quite) so bad.

Mach dir nichts draus. < coll. >
Don't worry about it. / Don't let it upset you.

Ist O.K. < coll. / youth > It's all right.

Keine Sorge! Don't worry!

Mach dir deswegen keine Sorgen. Don't worry about that.

Macht nichts. It doesn't matter.

Schon vergessen.
It's already forgotten. / It's over and done with.

Laß dir keine grauen Haare darüber wachsen.
Don't lose any sleep over it. (literally: don't grow grey hair about it)

Das hat nichts zu sagen.
That isn't important / doesn't mean anything.

Irren ist menschlich. < proverb > To err is human.

(b) More formal expressions

Nicht der Rede wert. Don't mention it.

Kein Grund zur Aufregung.
No need to worry. (literally: no cause for excitement)

LETTERS AND WRITTEN COMMUNICATIONS

10 Envelopes, lay-out and greetings

(a) The envelope

German conventions for addressing envelopes are different from English and American ones. The first line should be *Herrn* (acc.), *Frau* or *Fräulein* (after a suppressed *an*, which is still used occasionally), followed by the title (except for *Dr.* and *Dipl.Ing.*, which go before the name).

Herrn Professor	*Frau*
G. Funke	*Dr. med. U. Vogt*

N.B. The title *Dr.* is usually made more specific, e.g.:

Dr. med. medical doctor
Dr. med. dent. dentist
Dr. rer. nat. doctor of natural science
Dr. phil. D. phil. / Ph. D. etc.
Dipl. Ing. = *Diplom Ingenieur* engineer with degree

The second line would contain the name, the third line the name of the street, **followed** by the house number. Then there would be a one-line space before the postcode (preceded by *D* for Germany, *CH* for Switzerland and *A* for Austria when writing from abroad), followed by the name of the postal town (with the number of the district). All lines are aligned on the left.

If a particular kind of delivery is required (in German-speaking countries), the following instructions go slightly above the address:

Einschreiben registered
Eilzustellung express
Mit Luftpost airmail
wenn unzustellbar, zurück an Absender if undelivered, return to sender
Drucksache printed matter
Drucksache zu ermäßigter Gebühr printed matter at reduced rate
Päckchen small packet
zu Händen (abbreviated to *z.Hd.*) for the attention of
bei / *c/o* c/o

Example

Einschreiben

Herrn
Dr. med. J. Schwarzhaupt
Frankfurterstraße 17

D 6500 Mainz

On personal letters the sender's address is written on the envelope, preceded by *Abs*: (abbreviation for *Absender* = sender).

(b) Lay-out

Informal letters

No address is needed on the letter itself (since it appears on the back of the envelope. In the top right-hand corner write the name of the town and the date:

Frankfurt, den 1.5.92

or *Wiesbaden, den 8. September, 1993*

All the text is aligned to the left-hand margin. The greeting is followed by a comma and a one-line space, and the first sentence starts with a small letter (unless it is a noun or proper name). Do not start a letter with *ich*. An example of an informal letter between friends is given below on p. 244.

Business letters

Business letters are on either A4 or (horizontal) A5 size paper. The whole letter is aligned to the left-hand margin, without any indentation, except for quoted matter. The addressee's address appears in the top left-hand corner in the same form as on the envelope. The sender's address is usually on the printed letter-head. References and dates of previous correspondence follow; then after a one-line space the *Betreff* or heading giving the subject of the letter; then, after a two-line space, the greeting. The list of enclosures (*Anlagen*) comes directly below the signature. If the letter is signed by someone else (p.p.), *i.V. (in Vertretung)* precedes the name. If the letter runs to more than one page, the pages are numbered and the addressee's name and the date are repeated. Examples of business letters are given on pp. 253–9.

(c) Informal beginnings and endings

To someone you know well

Liebe Ulrike, / Lieber Andreas,
Liebe Ilse und lieber Theo,
Liebe Familie Suffrian
Ihr Lieben, My Dears,

Herzliche Grüße, Dein / Deine
Kind regards, / Best wishes, yours,

Viele liebe Grüße, Dein / Deine
Affectionately, yours, / Best wishes, / Love,

Alles Liebe
Love,

For young people

Bis bald / Tschüß See you soon / Cheers (then just sign your name)

(d) More formal beginnings and endings

Lieber Herr Bauer, / Liebe Frau Simm,

Titles should be included in the greeting and must not be abbreviated:

Lieber Herr Professor Teichner, Dear Professor Teichner,
Liebe Frau Pfarrer Wagner, Dear Reverend Wagner,

However, *Doktor* is commonly abbreviated:

Lieber Herr Dr. Alt,

If you don't know the name of the person you are writing to, use:

Sehr geehrte Damen und Herren,
Dear Sir / Madam, (literally: dear ladies and gentlemen)

You would end the letter:

mit freundlichen Grüßen
Yours sincerely,

Capitalize *mit* if the previous sentence ends with a full stop.

Between professional colleagues, e.g. from one (medical) doctor to another, the title is omitted before the name, and the ending is:

mit kollegialen Grüßen
with greetings from a colleague,

(e) Beginning and ending a formal business letter

Sehr geehrter Herr Debus, / Sehr geehrte Frau Schulze,
Sehr geehrter Herr Direktor Dr. Matthias,

mit freundlichen Grüßen
Yours sincerely, / Yours truly (US),

More formal

mit freundlichen / besten Empfehlungen
With kindest / best regards,

Very formal

Hochachtungsvoll (literally: most respectfully)
Yours sincerely, / Yours faithfully,

N.B. German makes no distinction between people you know / don't know by name.

The name of the signatory is typed out underneath the signature.

(f) Capitalization of *Du* and *Ihr*

In letters, *Du*, *Ihr* and their derivatives, including all possessive adjectives (e.g. *Dein*, *Euer*) are written with a capital letter.

111 Sample letters from private individuals

(a) From a friend

Liebe Verena,

schade, daß wir uns gestern nicht in Heidelberg treffen konnten. Die Zeit war einfach zu kurz. Nächstes mal müssen wir unbedingt etwas ausmachen, damit wir uns wirklich sehen können.

Ich hoffe, es geht Euch allen gut.
Viele liebe Grüße

Sabine

Dear Verena,

It's a great shame we couldn't meet up in Heidelberg yesterday. The time was much too short. Next time we must definitely arrange something so that we can see each other.

I hope you are all well.
Yours,

Sabine

(b) Reservations and bookings

Asking a tourist office for a list of hotels and campsites

Fremdenverkehrsamt
Hochhaus
5400 Koblenz

Sehr geehrte Damen und Herren,

wir haben vor, diesen September am Rhein zu verbringen. Bitte senden Sie uns ein Verzeichnis von Hotels, Pensionen und Campingplätzen in der Gegend von Rüdesheim. Außerdem hätten wir gerne Informationsmaterial über Dampferfahrten auf dem Rhein.

Vielen Dank im Voraus, mit freundlichen Grüßen

Dear Sir / Madam,

We are planning to spend next September in the Rhine valley. Please could you send us a list of hotels, B & B places and campsites near Rüdesheim. In addition we would like some information about steamer excursions along the Rhine.

Many thanks (literally: thank you very much in advance).
Yours faithfully,

Asking a hotel about the availability of rooms

Hotel Waldeck
Straßburger Straße 60
7290 Freudenstadt
Schwarzwald

Sehr geehrte Damen und Herren,

wir würden gerne im nächsten August zwei Wochen in Ihrem Hotel verbringen.

Bitte teilen Sie uns mit, ob Sie noch ein Doppelzimmer mit Bad frei haben, und was die Vollpension bei Ihnen kostet. Es wäre auch sehr nützlich, wenn Sie uns erklären könnten, wie man am besten mit öffentlichen Verkehrsmitteln nach Freudenstadt kommen kann.

Mit freundlichen Grüßen

Dear Sir / Madam,

We should like to spend a couple of weeks in your hotel during August.

Could you please let us know whether you still have a double room with bath available and how much you charge for full board. In addition, it would be very helpful if you could advise us as to how best to get to Freudenstadt by public transport.

Yours faithfully,

Booking a hotel

Bastenhaus am See
Hauptstraße 71
8180 Tegernsee

Sehr geehrte Damen und Herren,

auf unsrer Reise durch Europa würden wir gerne drei Tage am Tegernsee bleiben, und zwar vom 3. bis 6. Juni. Wir benötigen ein Doppelzimmer mit Dusche (möglichst mit Blick auf den See) und ein Einzelzimmer.

Bitte bestätigen sie unsre Buchung und teilen Sie uns den Preis für Zimmer mit Frühstück mit.

Falls Sie uns zur angegebenen Zeit nicht unterbringen können, wären wir für die Empfehlung eines anderen Hotels in der Nähe sehr dankbar.

Mit freundlichen Grüßen

Dear Sir / Madam,

On our trip to Europe we would like to spend three days at the Tegernsee, from the 3rd to 6th of June. We will require a double room with shower (preferably with a view of the lake) and one single room.

Please could you confirm our booking and let us know what you charge for bed and breakfast.

If you cannot accommodate us at this time we would be grateful for a recommendation of another hotel in the vicinity.

Yours faithfully,

(c) Letters requesting information

Asking an institution about language courses and accommodation

Akademisches Auslandsamt
Johannes Gutenberg Universität Mainz
Saarstrasse
D55122 Mainz

Betreff: Feriensprachkurse für Ausländische Studenten

Sehr geehrte Damen und Herren,

als Student der Archäologie an der Universität Oxford würde ich gerne ein Jahr an einer deutschen Universität studieren. Bitte schicken Sie mir Informationsmaterial über Sprachkurse für Ausländische Studenten in Mainz und über die Aufnahmebedingungen für die Universität.

Bitte teilen Sie mir auch mit, wo ich mich für ein Zimmer im Studentenwohnheim bewerben kann.

Vielen Dank im Voraus,
mit freundlichen Grüßen,
Ihr

Dear Sir / Madam,

Re: Vacation (preparatory) language courses for foreign students

As a student of archaeology at Oxford University I would like to study for a year at a German university. Please could you send me information about language courses for foreign students in Mainz and about conditions of admission to the university.

Could you also let me know where to apply to for a room in the hall of residence.

Many thanks,
Yours faithfully,

Asking an institution for a prospectus

> *Europäische Business School*
>
> *Betreff: Informationsmaterial über Kurse*
> *Sehr geehrte Frau Anthes,*
>
> *Ihr Institut wurde mir von einem Kollegen empfohlen. Bitte senden Sie mir Unterlagen über Ihre Kurse, insbesondere in Wirtschaftsdeutsch.*
>
> *Für eine baldige Antwort wäre ich Ihnen sehr dankbar.*

Dear Ms Anthes,

Re: Information about courses

Your institute has been recommended to me by a colleague. Please could you send me brochures about your courses, especially about German for Business.

I would be most grateful for a speedy reply,

(d) Letters of complaint

To a shop in respect of an unsatisfactory purchase

> *Lederhaus Pfeil*
> *Bahnhofstraße*
> *64291 Darmstadt*
>
> *Sehr geehrte Frau Pfeil,*
>
> *am 22. Dezember habe ich bei Ihnen eine 'Enny' Handtasche für 257,50DM gekauft. Vierzehn Tage später riß der Riemen bei normalem Gebrauch plötzlich ab. Dies dürfte bei einer so teuren Handtasche nicht vorkommen. Ich bitte Sie, mir die Tasche umgehend gegen eine neue umzutauschen.*
>
> *Ich lege die defekte Tasche und eine Kopie der Quittung bei und hoffe auf baldige Erledigung der Angelegenheit.*

translation overleaf

Dear Mrs Pfeil,

On the 22nd December I bought an 'Enny' handbag from you for DM 257.50. Two weeks later the strap tore suddenly during normal use. This should not happen with such an expensive bag. I must ask you to exchange the bag for a new one immediately.

I enclose the defective/damaged bag with the receipt.

Please give this matter your prompt attention.

To a travel agent in respect of unsatisfactory (holiday) accommodation

> *Firma Sonnentage*
>
> *Betreff: Unterkunft im Ostertal*
>
> *Sehr geehrte Damen und Herren,*
>
> *bei unserem Ferienaufenthalt im Ostertal (vom 14.-28. August) waren wir mit der Unterkunft leider sehr unzufrieden: die Sauberkeit ließ zu wünschen übrig, die Heizung war für die kühlen Tage unzureichend und die Waschmaschine funktionierte nicht.*
>
> *Wir bitten um Schadensersatz, sonst sehen wir uns gezwungen, die Angelegenheit unserem Rechtsanwalt zu übergeben.*

Dear Sir / Madam,

Re: Accommodation in the Ostertal

We are sorry / regret to inform you that during our holiday in the Ostertal (August 14-28) we were very dissatisfied with the accommodation. The cleanliness left much to be desired, the heating was insufficient for the cool days and the washing machine wasn't working.

We must ask you for compensation. Failing this, we shall have no alternative but to take legal action / refer the matter to our solicitor.

(e) Letters concerning employment

Seeking vacation or short-term employment

Frau L. Pfeffer
Weingut Gebrüder Dr. Becker
6501 Ludwigshöhe / Rhein

Betreff: Bewerbung um Ferienarbeit

Sehr geehrte Frau Pfeffer,

Vor Beginn des Herbsttrimesters würde ich gerne ein paar Wochen in Deutschland arbeiten. Ich stehe den ganzen September und Anfang Oktober über zur Verfügung und könnte Ihnen bei der Weinlese helfen. Ich habe schon einmal auf einem Bauernhof in England gearbeitet.

Ich lege meinen Lebenslauf bei und hoffe, daß Sie sich für meine Bewerbung interessieren.

Dear Ms Pfeffer,

Re: Application for vacation work

I would like to work in Germany for a few weeks before the beginning of the autumn term. I am available for all of September and at the beginning of October and could help you with the grape harvest. I have already worked on a farm in England once.

In the hope that you may be interested in my application, I enclose my CV.

(For CV, see sections 120 and 121.)

Application for a job

Sehr geehrte Damen und Herren,

auf Grund Ihrer heutigen Anzeige in der Morgenpost *bewerbe ich mich um die ausgeschriebene Stelle als . . . Im Laufe meiner Schulzeit besuchte ich Kurse in . . . und erhielt eine praktische Ausbildung in Textverarbeitung / Stenographie.*

Ich verbrachte mehrere Jahre in . . ., um eine gründliche Kenntnis in der Landessprache zu erwerben. Ich beherrsche Deutsch / Französisch in Wort und Schrift, wie die beiliegenden Zeugnisse nachweisen. Ich habe auch etwas Russisch / Italienisch gelernt und kann Übersetzungen aus dieser Sprache übernehmen. Von . . . bis . . . war ich bei . . . als . . . beschäftigt, und ich bin seit . . . Jahren als . . . tätig. Mein jetziger / früherer Arbeitgeber / ehemaliger Schulleiter hat sich freundlicherweise bereit erklärt, mir eine Referenz zu geben / schreiben.

Ich füge Zeugnisabschriften bei. Ich bin jederzeit gern bereit, mich bei Ihnen persönlich vorzustellen.

Dear Sir / Madam,

With reference to today's advertisement in *Die Morgenpost*, I wish to apply for the vacant post of . . . During my time at school, I attended courses in . . . and received practical training in word-processing / shorthand.

I spent several years in . . ., to obtain a thorough knowledge of the language. I speak and write German / French fluently, as confirmed by the enclosed testimonials. I have also learnt some Russian / Italian and can translate from the language. From . . . to . . . I was employed by . . . as a . . ., and for the past . . . years I have been employed as . . . My present / former employer / the principal of my former school has kindly allowed me to give his name as a referee.

I enclose (copies of) testimonials. I should be very pleased to come for an interview at a time convenient for you.

112 Sample business letters

(a) Sending brochures and information to a client

Sehr geehrter Herr Fischer,

bezugnehmend auf unsere Besprechung am 21. 7 übersenden wir Ihnen beiliegend unser Angebot über die Kücheneinrichtung. Weiterhin erhalten Sie einen Küchenprospekt, den Sie uns bitte wieder zurückreichen wollen. Wir hoffen, Ihnen mit diesen Unterlagen gedient zu haben und verbleiben,

mit freundlichen Grüßen

Anlagen

Dear Mr Fischer,

Further to our conversation of 21 July, we are pleased to enclose our quotation / offer for the fitted kitchen. In addition we are sending you a kitchen catalogue, which we would like you to return to us. We hope to have been of service to you and remain,

Yours faithfully,

Enclosures

(b) Asking for a sample

Ja!

☐ **Bitte senden Sie mir kostenlos die Eftapan®-Taschentücher!**

Stempel und Unterschrift

Bitte freimachen, falls Marke zur Hand

Antwort

Merckle GmbH
Im Gehrn 3

89143 Blaubeuren

Yes! Please send me free of charge Eftapan® handkerchiefs
(rubber) stamp and signature

(c) Asking for a quotation

Wir haben Ihren Stand auf der Messe / Ausstellung gesehen.

Wir haben eine Anfrage zwecks Lieferung (größerer Mengen) von . . . Wollen Sie uns bitte einen Kostenanschlag für . . . machen.
Wir wären Ihnen sehr dankbar für Proben / Muster von . . . / nähere Einzelheiten über . . .

Wir bitten um Ihr Angebot von Mengen / Artikeln / Waren, die umgehend lieferbar sind.

In der Anlage befinden sich Listen der uns interessierenden Artikel.

Wir benötigen erhebliche Mengen und können Ihnen größere Aufträge geben, falls uns Qualität und Preis zusagen.

We saw your stand at the Trade Fair / Exhibition.

We would like to enquire about delivery of (large quantities of) . . . Would you please give us a quotation for . . . We should be grateful for samples / patterns / further details of . . .

Please tell us about quantities / articles / goods which can be supplied from stock.

We enclose lists of the goods we require.

We need large quantities and can place substantial orders if both quality and prices suit.

(d) Placing an order

Sehr geehrter Herr,

Wir danken für Ihr Schreiben vom . . . / Ihr Preisangebot / Ihre Preisliste und bestellen zu sofortiger Lieferung: . . .

Wir fügen unseren Auftrag Nr. . . . bei.

Da die Ware dringend benötigt wird, bitten wir um umgehende Lieferung / Lieferung bis zum . . .

Wir müssen darauf bestehen, daß die Lieferung bis zu dem angegebenen Termin erfolgt und behalten uns vor, spätere Abnahme zu verweigern.

Wir bitten, die Ware als Luftfracht / mit Güterzug / als Eilgut / mit nächster Schiffsgelegenheit zu senden.

Bitte sorgen Sie dafür, daß die beiliegenden Verpackungsanweisungen genauestens beachtet werden.

Wir bitten, die obige Auftragsnummer in allen Briefen und Dokumenten anzuführen.

Die Rechnung / Versandanzeige erbitten wir in zweifacher / dreifacher Ausführung sowie eine Ursprungsbescheinigung.

Da dies unser erster Auftrag ist, fügen wir einen Scheck über . . . bei.

Wir bitten, die Ware zum Rechnungswert zuzüglich . . . % zu versichern. / Wir werden die Versicherung von hier aus erledigen.

Mit freundlichen Grüßen

Dear Sir,

Thank you for your letter of . . . / quotation / price lists. We would ask you to send us immediately: . . .

We have pleasure in enclosing our order no. . . .

As the goods are urgently required, we should be grateful for immediate delivery / delivery by . . .

We must insist on delivery within the time stated and reserve the right not to accept the goods should they be delivered later.

Please send the consignment by air / goods train / express / the next boat leaving . . .

Please see to it that the enclosed packing instructions are followed carefully.

We would be glad if you could quote the above order number on all letters and documents.

We require the invoice / a dispatch note in duplicate / triplicate and a Certificate of Origin.

As this is our first order we enclose a cheque for . . .

Please insure at invoice value plus . . .%. / We shall take out insurance ourselves.

Yours faithfully,

(e) Apologizing for a delay

Allbauelemente
D 8500 Nürnberg

ACI (Europa)
Fibres GmbH
z.Hd. Herrn Karwath
7524 Östringen – Faserwerk *2. März*

Betreff: Werkshallen in Östringen

Sehr geehrter Herr Karwath,

wir nehmen Bezug auf das letzte Telefonat mit unserem Herrn Kiener und teilen Ihnen mit, daß am 27.2. die Bauarbeiten am Projekt Östringen, nach Ablauf der Schlechtwetterperiode, wieder aufgenommen wurden.

Hierdurch verzögert sich leider auch die Fertigstellung der Werkshallen bis ca. 20. März.

Wir bitten um Ihr Verständnis und verbleiben,

mit freundlichen Grüßen

Dear Mr Karwath,

Re: workshops in Östringen

We refer to the last telephone conversation with our Mr Kiener and would let you know that the building works were resumed at the Östringen site on the 27 Feb. after a period of inclement weather.

Because of this, the completion of the workshops will unfortunately be delayed until around 20 March.

We ask for your understanding and remain,

Yours sincerely,

(f) Asking for an urgent reply to an earlier letter

Sehr geehrte Damen und Herren,

auf unser Schreiben vom . . . haben wir leider noch keine Antwort erhalten.

Da es sich hier um eine äußerst dringende Angelegenheit handelt, bitten wir die Bestellung postwendend zu bestätigen.

Wir fügen eine Kopie unseres ursprünglichen Schreibens bei.

Vielen Dank im Voraus,

mit freundlichen Grüßen

Dear Sir / Madam,

Unfortunately we have not yet received an answer to our letter of . . .

Since this matter is of the utmost importance, we should be glad if you would confirm acceptance of our order by return.

We enclose a copy of the original letter.

Many thanks,

Yours faithfully,

(g) Complaining about an order

Longlife Rasierklingen
Barthstraße 53
2400 Lübeck

15.9.1991

Sehr geehrte Damen und Herren,
Wir bedauern, Ihnen mitteilen zu müssen, daß die Ware in schlechtem Zustand ankam / nicht den Mustern entspricht / für den hiesigen Markt ungeeignet ist.

Die Ware war so schlecht verpackt / war so schwer beschädigt, daß ein großer Teil unverkäuflich ist / ein Teil des Inhalts fehlte.

Wir bitten, uns die beschädigte Ware zu ersetzen / den Gegenwert der zurückgesandten Ware gutzuschreiben.

Dear Sir / Madam,

We regret to inform you that the goods (we ordered) arrived in poor condition / do not correspond to the sample / are unsuitable for this market.

The goods were so badly packed / were damaged to such an extent, that a large part is unfit for sale / parts of the contents are missing.

We must ask you to replace the damaged goods / to credit us with the value of the returned goods.

(h) Chasing up bills

Teutopress
Internationale Medien-Agentur / Foto-Archiv / Bildbeschaffung / Auftragsreportagen

Frau Angelika Fischer
c/o Dr. Bauer
Georg Treber Str. 18
65428 Rüsselsheim

Bielefeld, den 16. Oktober

Betreff: Unsere Rechnung Nr. A 2870 vom 14. August über

50,– DM

Sehr geehrte Frau Fischer,
nach Mitteilung unserer Buchhaltung ist die o.g. [= oben genannte] Rechnung noch nicht bezahlt worden.

Wir bitten höflich um Überprüfung und baldmögliche Regulierung.

Eine Kopie der genannten Rechnung fügen wir bei.

Mit freundlichen Grüßen

Anne-Marie Pietrek
– Sekretariat–

Anlage

Dear Mrs Fischer,

Re: Invoice no. A 2870 dated 14 August for DM 50.00.

According to information from our accounts department, the above-mentioned bill has not been paid yet.

We would ask you kindly to check on this matter and rectify the oversight as soon as possible. We enclose a copy of the above-mentioned bill.

Yours sincerely,

Anne-Marie Pietrek
– (Secretary's) office –

Enclosure

(i) Notifications from public services

Hessische Elektrizitäts–AG
Jägertorstraße 207
64289 Darmstadt 11
Telefon (06151) 709-1

Sehr geehrte Kundin, sehr geehrter Kunde,

wir haben Sie heute nicht angetroffen und konnten Ihren Stromzähler nicht ablesen. Wir bitten Sie, den Stand Ihres Zählers selbst abzulesen.

Wir danken Ihnen für Ihre Mithilfe.
Mit freundlichen Grüßen

Ihre Hessische Elektrizitäts-AG

Dear Customer,

We didn't find you in today and so could not read your electricity meter. Kindly make a meter reading yourself.

Thank you for your cooperation,
Yours faithfully,

113 Official invitations

Einladung

Am Dienstag, den 14. August, um 19.30 findet im ehemaligen Schulhaus Wallbach eine Sitzung des Ortsbeirates Wallbach statt, zu der hiermit eingeladen wird. Die Sitzung ist öffentlich.

Tagesordnung:

......

......

Bericht des Kassenführers
Verschiedenes.

Für den Ortsbeirat Wallbach:
gez. Bernd Hübner, Vorsitzender

Invitation

On Tuesday, 14 August, at 7.30 p.m. a meeting of the village advisory board will take place in the former school-house in Wallbach. The meeting is public.

Agenda:

.....

.....

treasurer's report
A.O.B. (any other business)

For the village advisory board of Wallbach
signed Bernd Hübner, Chairman

N.B. *gez.* is the abbreviated form of *gezeichnet* (signed).

14 Weddings

(a) Announcement of a wedding

Ihre Vermählung geben bekannt
Klaus und Angelika Gellermann, geb. Knauer.
Die Trauung findet am Samstag, den 30. März in der
Christuskirche in Mainz statt.

Klaus and Angelika Gellermann, née Knauer,
announce their wedding.
The marriage ceremony will take place
on Saturday 30 March at Christ Church in Mainz.

(b) Thanks for letters and wedding presents

Über die zahlreichen Glückwünsche, Blumen und Geschenke anläßlich unserer

Vermählung

haben wir uns sehr gefreut und möchten uns, auch im Namen unserer Eltern, recht herzlich bedanken.

Petra und Walter Schanz

Brensbach-Beuneberg 14,
im Juli

We were delighted to receive numerous good wishes, flowers and gifts on the occasion of our

Wedding

and would like to express our warmest thanks for them, also on behalf of our parents.

Petra and Walter Schanz

Brensbach-Beuneberg 14,
July

115 Bereavement

(a) Annoucement of a funeral

Wir trauern um

Frau Maria Christine Tripp

geb. Benz
die nach einem erfüllten Leben am 7. Januar kurz vor Vollendung ihres
87. Lebensjahres sanft entschlafen ist.

Wir werden sie nicht vergessen.

Im Namen ihrer Angehörigen und Freunde

Horst und Elvira Becker

Auf Wunsch der Verstorbenen findet die Beisetzung in aller Stille statt.

We regret to announce the death of
(literally: we are mourning for)

Mrs Maria Christine Tripp

née Benz
who died peacefully in her sleep on 7 January,
shortly before her 87th birthday.

We will remember her.

On behalf of her relatives and friends

Horst and Elvira Becker

As the deceased wished, the funeral will be private.
(literally: the funeral will take place in quiet)

(b) Thanks for condolences

DANKSAGUNG

Für alle Beileidsbeweise zum Tode unseres lieben Entschlafenen

Dr. Martin Bernges

herzlichsten Dank.

Giesela Bernges, geb. Büchner
Dr. Peter Bernges
und Familie

Frankfurt am Main – Im Juli

Heartfelt thanks for the many expressions of sympathy on the death of our dear late

Dr Martin Bernges

Giesela Bernges, née Büchner
Dr. Peter Bernges
and Familie

Frankfurt on Main – July

THANKS AND BEST WISHES

116 Thanks

(a) General

In a personal letter

Vielen Dank / herzlichen Dank für Deinen Brief / Deine freundlichen Zeilen.
Thank you very much for your letter / your kind note.

In a fairly formal letter

Für Ihren Brief möchte ich mich herzlich bedanken.
I would like to thank you very much for your letter.

In a formal business letter

Wir bestätigen dankend den Eingang / Empfang Ihres Schreibens vom . . .
We acknowledge with thanks your letter of the . . .

(b) Thanking for an invitation

Informally

Herzlichen Dank für die Einladung zum Abendessen / zu Deiner Party. Ich werde bestimmt kommen und freue mich schon sehr darauf. / Leider kann ich nicht kommen, weil . . .

Many thanks for the invitation to dinner / supper / your party. I shall certainly come, and am looking forward to it. / Unfortunately I shall be unable to come because . . .

Formally

Für Ihre freundliche Einladung zum Abendessen / zum Empfang / zur Hochzeit Ihrer Tochter / zum Hauskonzert, die ich gerne annehme / die ich leider nicht annehmen kann (‚da ich schon anderweitig verpflichtet bin <formal> / weil . . .), bedanke ich mich herzlich.

I thank you for your kind invitation to dinner / the reception / the wedding of your daughter / the concert in your home. I am happy to accept. / I regret I am unable to accept (due to a previous engagement / because . . .).

(c) Thanking for a gift

Vielen / Herzlichen / Tausend Dank für das reizende Geschenk / für die schönen Blumen. Das war doch wirklich nicht nötig. / Es war sehr lieb / nett von Dir. Es ist genau das, was ich wollte / gut gebrauchen kann.

Thank you very much / My warmest thanks / Thanks a million for the delightful gift / the pretty flowers. You really shouldn't have. / It was really sweet / kind of you. It is exactly what I wanted / needed.

17 Best wishes

(See also section 70b).

On a postcard

Liebe Grüße / Herzliche Grüße / Grüße vom Bodensee. Deine Inge
Love / warmest greetings / greetings from Lake Constance. Yours, Inge

Einen schönen Gruß aus Berlin.
Dein Peter
Best wishes from Berlin.
Yours, Peter

For a birthday

Alles Gute / Herzlichen Glückwunsch zum Geburtstag und Gottes Segen.
All the best for your birthday / Happy Birthday and God bless.

For Christmas and the New Year

Fröhliche Weihnachten und ein glückliches Neues Jahr. / Frohes Weihnachtsfest und die besten Wünsche zum Neuen Jahr.
Merry Christmas and a Happy New Year / Happy Christmas and all the best for the New Year.

For Easter

Frohe Ostern. / Ein frohes Osterfest. Happy Easter.

For a wedding

Dem glücklichen Paar viel Freude am Hochzeitstag. <formal>
Every good wish to the happy couple on their wedding day.

Zu Eurer Hochzeit wünschen wir Euch Alles Gute und Viel Glück.
All the best and good luck for your wedding.

For an exam

Viel Erfolg bei der bevorstehenden Prüfung. / Alles Gute zum Abitur. < formal >
Wishing you every success in your forthcoming exam. / All the best for / Good luck in your A-levels.

Viel Glück! < informal > Good luck!

For a new home

Viel Glück / Alles Gute im neuen Heim.
Good luck / All the best in your new home.

For a speedy recovery

Gute Besserung. Get well soon.

118 Congratulations

Herzlichen Glückwunsch / Wir gratulieren . . .
Congratulations / We congratulate you . . .
- *zum Baby* on the arrival of the new baby
- *zur bestandenen Prüfung* on passing the exam
- *zum neuen Job* on your new job
- *zur Verlobung* on your engagement
- *zur Beförderung* on your promotion

119 Condolences

Zutiefst erschüttert lasen / hörten wir vom Tode Ihres / Deines Mannes.

We were deeply saddened to read / hear about the death of your husband.

Ich möchte Ihnen unser aufrichtiges Beileid zu Ihrem schweren Verlust ausdrücken. / Bitte nehmen Sie mein tiefempfundenes Mitgefühl zu diesem schweren Verlust entgegen.

I would like to assure you of our deepest sympathy in your tragic loss. / Please accept my heartfelt sympathy for your great loss.

Wir sind alle in Gedanken bei Dir. Laß es uns bitte wissen, wenn wir Dir irgendwie behilflich sein können.

Our thoughts are with you. Please let us know if we can be of any help.

CURRICULUM VITAE

There are two basic types of CV. Many employers still ask for a *handgeschriebener Lebenslauf*, a hand-written CV in narrative style, and there is the so-called *tabellarischer Lebenslauf*, which is much easier to read and gives all the information in note form, arranged in columns.

For both types, use A4-size paper and leave 5-cm margins left and right. Avoid using *ich* at the beginning of a sentence. Sign and date your CV at the bottom.

120 Useful phrases for a narrative CV

(a) Birth and childhood

Am . . . wurde ich als zweite Tochter / erster Sohn des Architekten / Lehrers . . . und seiner Frau / und der Juristin / Sekretärin . . ., geborene . . ., in . . . geboren.
I was born on . . . in . . . as second daughter / first son of the architect / teacher . . . and his wife / and the lawyer / secretary . . ., née . . .

In . . . verbrachte ich meine Kindheit, bis meine Eltern 19 . . nach . . . umzogen.
I spent my childhood in . . . until my parents moved to . . . in 19 . . .

(b) School

Types of school

die Grundschule primary school
die Gesamtschule comprehensive school
das Gymnasium grammar school (not 'gymnasium')
die Privatschule private school
das Internat boarding school
die Realschule ≈ secondary modern school
der Schüleraustausch school exchange

N.B. This list of school types is incomplete. Because of the differences between the German and English school systems, it is not always possible to find exact equivalents.

19 . . wurde ich in die . . . (Schule) in . . . eingeschult.
19 . . I entered the . . . (school) in . . .

Im Juni 19 . . bestand / erlangte / machte ich die mittlere Reife (in den Fächern: . . .) und im Juli 19 . . bestand / erlangte / erwarb ich (mit Erfolg / erfolgreich) das Abitur / die Hochschulreife.
In June 19 . . I passed ≈ O-levels (in: . . .) and in July 19 . . I passed (literally: with success) my ≈ A-levels / university entrance exam.

19 . . wechselte ich in die . . . (Schule).
In 19 . . I moved to . . . (school).

(c) Training and studies

die Ausbildung training
die Lehre apprenticeship
die Universität university
das Studium time at university

19 . . ging ich bei . . . in die Lehre / entschloß ich mich (zunächst) zu einer Lehre als . . .
in 19 . . I started / decided (initially) to do an apprenticeship as a . . . with . . .

19 . . absolvierte ich eine Ausbildung / brach ich meine Ausbildung ab.
In 19 . . I completed training / broke off my training.

19 . . schrieb ich mich an der Universität . . . ein / immatrikulierte ich mich an der . . . Universität . . . für das Fach / die Fächer . . .
In 19. . I matriculated at . . . university for the subject / subjects . . .

Ich studierte mit dem Schwerpunkt auf . . . / mit . . . als Hauptfach.
. . . was my main subject. / I majored in . . .

Das Auslandsjahr verbrachte ich von September 19 . . / bis Juni 19 . . in . . .
My year abroad, from September 19. . to June 19. ., / I spent in . . .

Von . . . bis . . . machte ich mein Auslandsstudium an der . . . Universität.
From . . . to . . . I studied abroad at . . . University.

19 . . absolvierte / machte / bestand / wiederholte ich mein Examen.
In 19 . . I sat / took / passed / re-sat my exam.

In den Semesterferien machte ich ein Praktikum bei der Firma . . . / Mein Anerkennungspraktikum leistete ich bei . . . ab.
In the holidays I did practical training / work experience with the . . . firm. / I served my probationary period with . . .

An der Abendschule holte ich eine Deutschprüfung / Mathematikprüfung nach.
I attended evening classes to sit a German / maths exam. (literally: I caught up on a German / maths exam)

(d) Work experience

das Amt office / authority
die Behörde authority / government office
der Betrieb business / firm
die Fabrik factory
die Firma firm / company
das Unternehmen concern / enterprise

19. . schlug ich die Beamtenlaufbahn ein / ging ich in die Wirtschaft / den Schuldienst.
In 19. . I entered the (higher) civil service / I became a business man / woman / went into teaching.

Ich arbeitete als Sekretärin / Fremdsprachenkorrespondentin / Übersetzerin / Dolmetscherin bei . . .
I worked as a secretary / bilingual / multilingual secretary / translator / interpreter at . . .

. . . wurde ich zu einem Vorstellungsgespräch eingeladen / aufgefordert.
I was invited to / called for an interview.

. . . wurde ich bei . . . als . . . eingestellt.
I was employed as a . . . at . . .

. . . wurde ich angenommen / abgelehnt.
I was accepted / turned down.

. . . kündigte ich / wurde ich entlassen.
. . . I handed in my notice / I was made redundant.

Seit . . . bin ich bei . . . als . . . tätig.
I have been employed as a . . . at . . . since . . .

Seit . . . bin ich stellvertretender Leiter / Leiter der . . . Abteilung.
Since . . . I have been acting (deputy) manager / manager of the . . . department.

(e) Interests and hobbies

Ich interessiere mich für / mein Hauptinteresse gilt (+ dat.) . . .
I am interested in / my main interest is in . . .

motiviert durch . . ., beschloß ich . . .
motivated by . . ., I decided . . .

Ich beschäftige mich mit . . .
I am interested in / I occupy myself with . . .

Ich habe eine Neigung zu / ein Talent für / eine Begabung für . . .
I have an inclination towards / a talent for / a gift for . . .

Ich bin für . . . (besonders) begabt.
I am (especially) gifted in . . .

In meiner Freizeit / In den Ferien beschäftige ich mich mit / mache ich gerne / bin ich verantwortlich für . . .
In my free time / In the holidays I occupy myself with / I like to do / I am responsible for . . .

Meine Hobbies / Lieblingsbeschäftigungen sind . . .
My hobbies / favourite pastimes are . . .

Ich spiele gerne Tennis / Klavier / Schach.
I like playing tennis / the piano / chess.

(See also section 81.)

(f) Useful linking phrases

(See also section 124b.)

To express contrast

aber but	*hingegen* on the other hand, however
jedoch however	*im Gegensatz dazu* in contrast (to that)

To continue ideas

außerdem also, in addition	*zusätzlich* in addition
hinzu kommt, daß added to that	*obendrein* < coll. > on top of that

To give reasons

deshalb therefore	*folglich / infolgedessen* as a consequence
daher for that reason	*aus diesem Grund* for that reason

121 Tabulated CV

Arrange all the information about yourself in the following format. (Translations are given in brackets.) You may wish to leave out the information on your family status.

Name (name):

Geboren (date of birth):

Adresse (address):

Familienstand (family status):

☐ *ledig* (single)
☐ *verheiratet* (married)
☐ *geschieden* (divorced) / *getrennt* (separated)
☐ *verwitwet* (widowed)

	Daten (dates)	*Schule / Arbeitgeber* (school / employer)
Schulbildung: (primary and secondary education)		
Studium: (higher education)		
Berufsausbildung: (professional training)		
Berufserfahrung: (professional experience)		
Kurse und Lehrgänge: (courses)		
Sprachkenntnisse: (foreign languages)		
Besonderes: (other details)		

ESSAY AND PRÉCIS WRITING

22 General: planning and style

School and university students of German are often required to write an essay (*der Aufsatz*) on a topical or literary subject. This section offers some 'skeleton' structures for expressing a cogent and well-expressed argument. For vocabulary appropriate to specific topics, see sections 140-51. Sections 81-4 and 92-8 provide useful further material, as does section 137.

It is worth remembering that your essay will be judged on three criteria: relevant and well-informed content; incisive and well-organized argument; and idiomatic and correct use of German. On the first two points, the most essential key to success is to read the question closely, so that you answer it precisely, and then to prepare a balanced and well-constructed plan. Obviously different types of essays require different approaches, but in all cases your plan (and essay) should comprise the following stages:

1 Brief general introduction to the subject: *die Einleitung*.
2 The main part of the argument, subdivided as appropriate: *der Hauptteil*.
3 Your general conclusions, related back to the question: *der Schluß*.

For the style of an essay keep the following points in mind:

- Be short and precise.
- Use verbs rather than nominal constructions (e.g. use *abliefern*, 'to deliver', rather than *zur Ablieferung bringen*).
- Write short sentences and don't cram too much into them.
- Limit the number of *daß* clauses.
- Start new paragraphs for new thoughts.
- Avoid using pronouns at the beginning of a new paragraph.
- Choose the right register, i.e. use formal language.
- Avoid colloquialisms and fashionable words; instead use the more formal expression. For example, use *keine Lust auf Deutsch (haben)* rather than *Null Bock auf Deutsch (haben)* if you want to say that someone does not like German at all (see section 136 on slang).
- Avoid large numbers of foreign words.

- Use *ich* infrequently, e.g. only when asked to write an *Erlebnisbericht* (personal account), and definitely don't start sentences with *ich*.
- Connect your thoughts by using linking phrases, *Überleitungen* (see section 124b below).

123 Introduction

An interesting introduction captures your reader's attention. You could start with any of the following:

- a definition of the important terms in the question
- an example
- a reference to a TV or radio broadcast
- a reference to a newspaper article
- a recent event
- a short historical survey or a reference to current affairs
- a quotation

The following expressions will be useful if you begin in any of the ways outlined above.

Definitions

Das Lexikon definiert 'Begabung' als 'Anlage zu bestimmten Leistungen'.
The dictionary defines 'talent' as 'an aptitude for certain achievements'.

Der Ausdruck 'Anlage' besagt, daß hier Vererbung im Spiel ist.
The expression / term 'aptitude' implies that heredity is involved here.

Examples

Unter den optischen Täuschungen ist besonders bekannt die sogenannte Müller – Lyersche Täuschung, die als eines der zuerst entdeckten klassischen Beispiele gelten kann.

Among optical illusions / One of the best-known examples of optical illusions is the so-called Müller–Lyer illusion, which can be regarded as one of the first classical examples to be discovered.

In diesem Aufsatz soll erörtert werden, ob es einen angeborenen Unterschied zwischen Männern und Frauen gibt. Dazu möchte ich ein Beispiel aus meinem persönlichen Leben / aus der Zeitung geben.

This essay will debate whether there is an innate difference between men and women. With this in mind I should like to give an example from my personal experience / from the newspaper.

References to broadcasts

Die Sendung QED über Vitamine im Ersten Fernsehprogramm warf die Frage auf, ob Intelligenz durch die Ernahrung beeinflußt wird.
The programme QED on Channel One / BBC 1 about vitamins raised the question whether intelligence is influenced by what we eat / by our diet.

Ein Dokumentarfilm über die 'Befreiung' von Kuweit veranlaßte mich, über folgende Probleme nachzudenken:
A documentary on the 'liberation' of Kuwait made me think about the following problems / issues:

References to newspaper articles

In Der Zeit *war vor kurzem zu lesen, daß . . .*
Recently one could read in *Die Zeit*, that . . .

Neulich war mir in der Frankfurter Allgemeinen (FAZ) *ein Artikel über . . . aufgefallen.*
Recently I noticed an article about . . . in the FAZ.

Letzte Woche berichtete Die Bildzeitung *über einen Mordfall im Schloß.*
Last week the *Bildzeitung* reported the case of a murder in the castle.

Descriptions of events

Bei einem Flugzeugabsturz über Schottland waren damals viele Menschen ums Leben gekommen.
In a plane crash over Scotland many people had died at the time.

Am Jahrestag des Mauerdurchbruchs kam es in den neuen Bundesländern zu mehreren Demonstrationen. Dabei war auf einem Spruchband zu lesen, . . .
On the anniversary of the breakthrough of the Wall several protest marches took place in the new federal states. One banner read . . .

Historical surveys and references to current affairs

Die Industrielle Revolution begann in England.
The Industrial Revolution started in England.

Wer die erste Nachkriegszeit erlebt hat, weiß noch, wie alles gekommen ist.
People who lived through the immediate post-war period remember how everything came about / events fell into place.

Traditionell für die alte vorindustrielle Welt war die ständische Gliederung.
The social structure based on privilege was traditional in the old pre-industrial world.

Alexander von Humboldt legte die Grundlage der modernen Geographie und gilt unter anderem als der Begründer der Klimalehre.
Alexander von Humboldt laid the foundations of modern geography and is regarded among other things as the founder of climatology.

Immer dringlicher wird die Reform der beruflichen Bildung.
The reform of professional training is becoming more and more urgent.

Quotations

Nach Heraklit ist der Krieg der Vater aller Dinge.
According to Heraclitus, war is the father of all things.

Der Verfasser behauptet am Anfang des Artikels, daß die Studenten aus der 'armen Welt' unter erheblichem Erfolgsdruck von daheim stünden.
The author claims at the beginning of the article that students from the 'Third World' are under considerable pressure from home to succeed. (See section 37 for the use of the subjunctive.)

Dieses Zitat aus dem öffentlichen Brief der Freunde der Erde . . .
This quotation from the open / public letter by Friends of the Earth . . .

124 Main part

(a) Structure (*der Aufbau*)

In the main part the important points of the argument are elaborated. The structure has to be logical. Put the most weighty points at the end.

Before you start, make a list of all the points **for** and **against** the argument. For their discussion you have the choice of two basic structures:

(i) Arguments in favour followed by arguments against (*antithetischer Aufsatz*)
List all the positive points first and then all the negative points (or vice versa), i.e.:

positive points
1
2
3
4
5

link
⟶ negative points
1
2
3
4
5

(ii) Alternating arguments for and against (*dialektischer Aufsatz*)
Alternate positive points with negative ones, playing them off against each other.

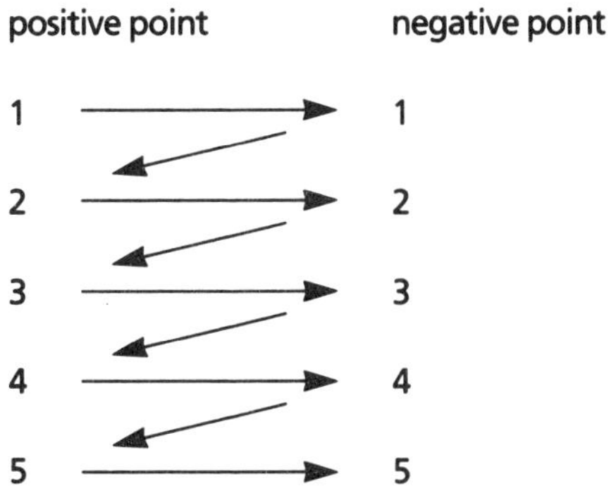

Obviously, the links between the opposing points are crucial and considerably more are required for the second model than for the first.

(b) Linking phrases (*Überleitungen*)

(i) Linking similar thoughts
For the *antithetischer Aufsatz* you can link similar thoughts, i.e. all those that are on one side of the argument, by using the following phrases:

Außerdem ist . . . zu beachten.
In addition one has to keep . . . in mind / remember . . . / consider . . .

Weiterhin gilt . . .
Furthermore / in addition, . . . applies / is generally accepted / it is essential . . .

Darüber hinaus wurde die Erfahrung gemacht, daß . . .
In addition . . . was experienced / found.

Nicht zu vergessen ist . . .
. . . must not be forgotten . . . (literally: not to be forgotten is . . .)

Von besonderer Bedeutung für Y ist Z.
Z is of special importance for Y.

In diesem Zusammenhang sollte man noch erwähnen, daß . . .
In this connection / context one should also mention / point out that . . .

Dafür gibt es Gründe:
There are (good) reasons for this:

Daran knüpfen sich Fragen:
There are questions connected with this / Questions arise from this:

Unabhängig davon:
Independent of this:

Dazu kommt noch folgende Tatsache:
In addition there is the following (fact):

Im Übrigen muß man sich damit abfinden, daß . . .
Besides, one has to come to terms with the fact that . . .

Man muß sich darüber im Klaren sein, . . .
One has to be quite clear about . . .

Darüber hinaus sollte ein Wissenschaftler . . .
In addition to that / Furthermore, a scientist should . . .

(ii) Linking opposites

Use the phrases listed below to link opposing arguments.

For the *antithetischer Aufsatz* you could simply sum up your list of points on one side and then introduce the points on the other side:

Das waren die Vorteile, jetzt kommen wir zu den Nachteilen:
These were the advantages, now the disadvantages:

Diese Argumente sprechen für die These / Aussage und die folgenden dagegen:
These points speak for the thesis / statement and the following against:

For the *dialektischer Aufsatz* you need to link the individual alternate points:

Anders verhält es sich bei . . . It is different with . . .

Im Gegensatz dazu steht (+ nom.) . . .
In contrast to that is . . .

Ganz anders stellt sich . . . dar.
. . . is very different. (literally: presents itself differently)

Dies ist jedoch bei . . . nicht so.
This however is not the case with . . .

Andererseits muß . . . betont werden.
On the other hand . . . has to be stressed.

. . . soll jedoch nicht außer acht gelassen werden.
. . . should not however be overlooked.

Dabei entstehen Gefahren.
With this dangers arise. / There are difficulties involved here.

Dadurch ergeben sich Nachteile.
Through this / Thus disadvantages result. / Problems arise from this.

Allerdings muß man folgendes bedenken:
However, one has to consider the following:

Man darf aber das Ausmaß an Zustimmung nicht unterschätzen.
One mustn't however underestimate the extent of agreement.

Das stimmt natürlich in gewisser Hinsicht, jedoch . . .
That is of course true in certain respects, however . . .

Dagegen läßt sich manches einwenden:
There are a number of things to be said against that:

Damit ist allerdings nicht gemeint . . .
That, however, does not imply / mean . . .

Man darf jedoch nicht vergessen, daß . . .
One must not forget, however, that . . .

Einmal davon abgesehen, daß nach Lage der Dinge . . .
Quite apart from the fact that, as matters stand, . . .

Im Übrigen aber war die Aufgabe ganz anders gestellt.
Besides, the task / question was set quite differently.

(iii) Stressing a point already made

Wie schon gesagt, . . . As was said before / already, . . .

Wie bereits erwähnt, . . . As was mentioned already / before, . . .

Um nochmals auf . . . zurückzukommen, . . .
To come back to . . . (again).

Man kann es nicht oft genug wiederholen, . . .
One cannot repeat often enough, . . .

125 Conclusion

The conclusion of an essay is a summary of the most important points. It could stress the importance of a particular point, point to the future, and / or state the writer's position.

First, decide **how** you would like to conclude. There are several options:

- **Compromise** (*der Kompromiß*): Take up the pros and cons and show possible solutions that could satisfy both.
- **Incompatibility** (*die Unvereinbarkeit*): Point out that both sides have to be taken seriously, but that no *rapprochement* is possible between thesis and antithesis.
- **Personal agreement / disagreement** (*die persönliche Übereinstimmung / Ablehnung*): Having considered both sides, show that you agree / disagree with the thesis given in the question.
- **Synthesis** (*die Synthese*): This is the most difficult option since it is supposed to lift the argument to a higher plane, adding an extra dimension to the discussion.

Here are examples to illustrate the different options for the following question:

Nützt die Technik dem Menschen?
Does technology serve mankind?

Compromise
Die Technik kann dem Menschen einerseits nützen, man denke an Nachrichtentechnik, medizinische Versorgung, Haushaltsgeräte usw., andererseits hat sie durchaus negative Folgen: Verkehrstote, Waffen und Automationsprozesse am Arbeitsplatz, die zu Arbeitslosigkeit führen.

On the one hand, technology can help people: one thinks of telecommunications, medical care, domestic appliances etc. On the other hand, it has negative consequences: deaths in road accidents, weapons, and automation leading to unemployment.

Incompatibility
Wenn die Technik so gefährlich ist, müssen wir zurück in die Steinzeit. Dies ist unmöglich. Wir brauchen die Technik.

If technology is so dangerous then we must return to the Stone Age, which is impossible, for we need technology.

Personal agreement / disagreement

Obwohl ich die Gefahren der Technik sehe, kann ich für meine Person nur sagen, daß ich den technischen Fortschritt bejahe, da er für das Überleben auf einer übervölkerten Erde unumgänglich ist.

Although I do see the dangers of technology, I am in favour of technological progress, because it is absolutely necessary for survival on an overpopulated planet.

Unsere sogenannten technischen Errungenschaften haben sehr viele negative Folgen hervorgebracht. Man sollte sich deshalb fragen, ob man eine Weiterentwicklung der Technik nicht bremsen muß.

Our so-called technical achievements have brought about many negative results. One should ask therefore if one ought not to slow down further technical developments.

Synthesis

Der Mensch kann Die Verantwortung übernehmen und auch lernen, die Technik nutzbringend unter weitgehenderAusschaltung von Gefahren zu verwenden.
Men and women can take on the responsibility and learn to use technology profitably while at the same time largely eliminating dangers.

Remember that your conclusion must follow from the discussion in the main part.

26 Précis writing

General guidelines

- Be precise.
- Concentrate on facts: Who? Where? When? How?
- Do not use *ich*.
  If the original is fiction, refer to the first person narrator as *der Erzähler (der Geschichte)* or by his/her fictitious name (do not use the author's name).
  If the original is a factual text, refer to the author by name or use *der Autor / der Verfasser (des Artikels / des Aufsatzes).*
- Use the present tense throughout for events that took place in the past, but use the pluperfect to refer to any situation or other events prior to those events. (See sections 20–3.)
- Use indirect speech, not direct speech. (See section 137 on alternatives to *sagen* and section 37a for the use of the subjunctive.)

- Do not express your own feelings: be remote and clinical.
- Use your own words as far as possible (when writing a German précis from an English text, do not translate the original first).
- Remember to stay within the required word limit. You might find it helpful to restrict yourself to a certain number of words per line (say 5), and, having beforehand marked on your page multiples of 20 lines, you know automatically when you have written 100 words. This saves frequent recounting.

Structure

A précis consists of an introduction and a main part.

The **introduction** is a vital part of the précis: describe the source of the information and what it refers to. Here are some possible beginnings:

Der Artikel aus Der Zeit *vom 26. März handelt von einer Kindesentführung in Bayern.*
The article from *Die Zeit* of 26 March is about the kidnapping of a child in Bavaria.

Der Zeitungsbericht handelt von einer achtzehnjährigen Schülerin in Bamberg.
The newspaper article is about an eighteen-year-old schoolgirl in Bamberg.

Die Kurzgeschichte beschreibt die Gedanken und Gefühle eines Autofahrers nach einem Autounfall.
The short story describes the thoughts and feelings of a driver after a car accident.

THE TELEPHONE

The Germans divide their lives very strictly between the private and the business sphere. It is therefore considered rude to bother them at home with business matters unless you have been explicitly invited to do so. However, if you do ring anyone at home, ring between about 9 a.m. and 12 noon, and between 3 p.m. and 6 p.m. Many Germans want an afternoon rest (some shops are closed, hotels require absolute quiet, etc.), so respect people's privacy after lunch. Also, business people may be out for lunch at any time between 12 noon and 3 p.m. (Remember, they generally start work at 8 a.m.) Late evening phone calls are reserved for good friends, but even they would be reluctant to ring after 10 p.m.

127 Answering the phone

Whether at home or in the office, you answer the phone by giving your family name. Don't say *Hallo*, and only say *Ja bitte?* if you want to remain anonymous. Children and young people give their full name, all others just use the surname.

If you get the cleaner or the au pair or any guest at a private residence, she / he should say:

> *Hier bei Dr. Schwarzhaupt.* (The *bei* is like *chez* in French.)

At the surgery the phone will be answered with:

> *Praxis Dr. Weicker, guten Morgen / guten Tag.*
> Dr Weicker's surgery, good morning / good afternoon.

(*Guten Morgen* is used until 12 noon, then *Guten Tag*; *Guten Abend* after approximately 6 p.m.)

At an office switchboard the answer is likely to be:

> *Hungsberg und Söhne, guten Tag.*
> Hungsberg and Sons . . .
>
> *Billfinger und Co., guten Morgen.*
> Billfinger and Co. . . .

and if you've dialled an extension you will hear:

Hungsberg und Söhne, hier Weidner.
Hungsberg and Sons, this is (Mr / Ms) Weidner speaking.

If Weidner's secretary answers, she / he will say:

Hungsberg und Söhne, Büro Weidner.
Hungsberg and Sons, (Mr / Ms) Weidner's office.

In return, you are expected to give your own name when you ring:

Hier ist Meyer, könnte ich bitte Herrn Schmidt sprechen?
This is Meyer, could I please speak to Mr Schmidt?

Hier ist Schulze von der IBM in Mainz.
This is Schulze from IBM in Mainz.

If you ring up to speak to the son or daughter of the house and the phone is answered by a parent, you have a much better chance if you introduce yourself:

Hier ist Klaus Hinterwald, dürfte / kann ich bitte mit Ihrer Tochter / mit Sabine sprechen?
This is Klaus Hinterwald, could I speak to your daughter / Sabine, please?

Should you have dialled the wrong number, say:

Entschuldigung, falsch verbunden.
Sorry, wrong number. (literally: wrong connection, blaming the switchboard).

If you haven't given your name, you are likely to be asked:

Wer ist am Apparat, bitte?
Who is speaking, please?

or:

Mit wem bin ich verbunden, bitte?
Who is speaking, please? (literally: who am I connected to?)

or:

Wen darf ich melden, bitte? <formal>
Who is speaking, please? (literally: whom may I announce?)

28 Useful phrases

Bitte verbinden Sie mich mit . . .
Please connect me with / put me through to . . .

Ich möchte bitte Apparat 123.
I would like extension 123 please.
(For numbers, see section 140a.)

Bitte rufen Sie zurück.
Please call back.

Bitte rufen Sie später wieder an.
Please ring back later.

Rufen Sie heute nachmittag / morgen früh / um 11 Uhr wieder an.
Please ring back this afternoon / tomorrow morning / at 11 a.m.
(For the times of day, see section 141.)

Könnte ich bitte mit . . .
Could I please speak to . . .

> *jemandem von der Marketing Abteilung sprechen?*
> someone from the marketing department?
>
> *jemandem von der Rechnungsabteilung sprechen?*
> someone from accounts?
>
> *jemandem von der Verwaltung sprechen?*
> someone from administration?
>
> *der Sekretärin von Herrn Kleinstück sprechen?*
> Mr Kleinstück's secretary?

Könnte ich bitte mit jemandem sprechen, der Versicherungsansprüche bearbeitet?
Could I speak to someone who deals with insurance claims?

Ich rufe an wegen . . . (+ gen.)
I am ringing about . . .

Ich rufe in Verbindung mit meinem Antrag für ein Visum an.
I am ringing in connection with my visa application.

Ich beziehe mich auf . . . (+ acc.)
I am referring to . . .

> *Ihren Anruf vom 1. Juli.* your call of 1 July.
>
> *Ihren Brief vom 5. Juli.* your letter of 5 July.
>
> *Ihr Schreiben vom 8. Juli.* your letter of 8 July.

Ich habe Ihren Namen nicht richtig verstanden.
I didn't quite catch your name.

Haben Sie . . . Do you have . . .

. . . eine direkte Rufnummer? . . . a direct number?

. . . eine Anschlußnummer? . . . an extension number?

Einen Moment / Augenblick, bitte, ich verbinde.
Just a moment, please, I am connecting you.

Bitte bleiben Sie am Apparat. Please hold the line.

Bitte warten. Please wait / hold the line.

Wir wurden unterbrochen. We were cut off.

Würden Sie mich bitte wieder verbinden?
Would you reconnect me, please?

Legen Sie bitte den Hörer auf. Please put down the receiver.

Nehmen Sie bitte den Hörer ab. Please pick up the receiver.

Es tut mir leid, . . .
I am sorry, . . .

Frau Zimmermann ist nicht da.
Mrs Zimmermann is not here.

der Anschluß ist im Moment besetzt.
the number is engaged at the moment.

Wann kommt sie zurück? When will she be back?

Ich rufe später wieder an. I'll ring back later.

Sagen Sie ihr bitte, daß Herr Frisch angerufen hat.
Please tell her that Mr Frisch rang.

Bitten Sie sie, mich anzurufen. Please ask her to ring me.

Würden Sie bitte etwas ausrichten?
Would you please take a message?

Notruf

Polizei

110

Feuerwehr

112

Ich kann Sie schlecht verstehen. I can't hear you very well.

Die Verbindung ist schlecht. The line / connection is bad.

Es meldet sich niemand. There is no reply.

Es meldet sich keiner. / Keiner da. < coll. > No reply.

Kein Anschluß unter dieser Nummer. Number unobtainable.

129 The operator

To ring the operator (*das Fernamt*) from a number in Germany, dial 010 for inland calls (*Inland*) and 0010 for international calls (*Ausland*). You can then ask for an operator-connected call (*ein handvermitteltes Gespräch*). Directory enquiries is *die Auskunft*.

To ask for a collect or transfer charge call within Germany:

Ich möchte ein R-Gespräch bitte.
I would like to reverse the charges, please.

To find out about the cost of a call:

Könnten Sie mir bitte hinterher die Gebühren angeben?
Could you please tell me the charges afterwards?

130 Directory enquiries

The number for inland calls is 01188, for international, 00118.

You will need to state the name of the town and the name of the subscriber (*der Teilnehmer*).

You might want to ask the following questions:

Wie / Was ist die Vorwahl für Frankfurt bitte?
What is the code for Frankfurt, please?

Was / Wie ist die Privatnummer von Herrn Engel bitte?
What is Mr Engel's private number, please?

Was / Wie ist die Geschäftsnummer?
What is the (i.e. his) business number?

You will find sets of phone directories in all public phone-boxes. The individual books refer to certain areas (see map inside front cover), and towns within that area are arranged in alphabetical order. The area codes are given at the top of every page.

131 Answering machines

A message on an answering machine is likely to be similar to one of the following examples:

(a) *Guten Tag, Sie haben den Anschluß von Klaus Anthes gewählt. Rüsselsheim 42337. Ich bin zur Zeit leider nicht zu Hause.*

Bitte hinterlassen Sie Ihre Nachricht nach dem Signal auf dem Band, damit ich Sie so bald wie möglich zurückrufen kann.

Bitte vergessen Sie nicht, Ihren Namen und Ihre Rufnummer anzugeben. Vielen Dank für Ihren Anruf, auf Wiederhören.

Hello, you've dialled Klaus Anthes's number. Rüsselsheim 42337. I am sorry I am not at home at the moment.

Please leave your message on the tape after the signal so that I can ring you back as soon as possible.

Please do not forget to give your name and telephone number. Thank you for calling, goodbye.

(b) *EBS, Europäische Business School. Wir danken für Ihren Anruf, doch leider rufen Sie außerhalb unsrer Bürozeiten an. Legen Sie jedoch bitte nicht gleich auf, Sie haben die Möglichkeit, nach dem Pfeifton eine Nachricht zu hinterlassen.*

Persönlich erreichen Sie uns zwischen neun und siebzehn Uhr. / Unser Büro ist an Werktagen von neun bis siebzehn Uhr besetzt. Auf Wiederhören.

EBS, European Business School. Thank you for your call. However, you are ringing outside our office hours. But don't hang up straight away, you may (literally: have the opportunity to) leave a message after the (whistle) tone.

You can reach us in person between 9 a.m. and 5 p.m. / Our office is staffed Mondays to Fridays from 9 a.m. to 5 p.m. Goodbye.

To leave your own message, say something like:

Hier ist Katrin Long. Oxford 66063. Es handelt sich um die Nachdruckgebühren für Aktuelles, *bitte rufen Sie mich baldmöglichst an. Vielen Dank.*

This is Katrin Long, on Oxford 66063. I am ringing about the copyright fees for *Aktuelles*. Please ring me back as soon as possible. Thank you.

When you ring a surgery, you might get the following message:

> *Hier ist der automatische Anrufbeantworter 06142 68471, Praxis Dr. Vogt. Die Sprechstunden finden montags und freitags von 8 bis 11 und 14 bis 17 Uhr statt. Dienstags und donnerstags nur nach Vereinbarung. In dringenden Fällen rufen Sie bitte die Notdienstzentrale unter Nummer xxx an. Ich wiederhole: ...*
>
> This is the automatic answering service 06142 68471, Dr Vogt's surgery. The surgery is open Mondays and Fridays from 8 a.m. to 11 a.m. and from 2 p.m. to 5 p.m. Tuesdays and Thursdays by appointment only. In cases of emergency, please ring the emergency service on number xxx. I repeat: ...

N.B. Surgeries don't usually let you leave a message: they would be liable if they couldn't act on your call. To find out which doctor / pharmacy is on call / rota, ring 01 1500 or the local hospital.

The number for the police is 110 and for the fire service 112, from all phones within Germany.

PART 3

Word power

Christine Eckhard-Black

SELECTIVE GLOSSARIES OF IDIOMS AND SYNONYMS

132 Building on verbs

Verbs are the backbone of a language – and one of the greatest sources of difficulty for foreign speakers. Part I reviews the uses of different tenses and moods in German (see sections 20-4 and 36-41). This section lists idiomatic structures and expressions based on common verbs, together with key compound forms. Irregular verbs, marked *, are listed in the table of common irregular verbs at the end of the book. Separable verbs are marked with an ◊ between prefix and verb stem, e.g. *sitzen◊bleiben*. All compound verbs are listed with their basic verbs, e.g. *sitzen◊bleiben* would be under *bleiben*. Inseparable verbs (other than the obvious ones) are marked with a ⧫.

bauen to build

erbauen to build up

nicht gerade erbaut sein von etwas / jemandem < coll. >
to be not exactly delighted about something / someone.

bedienen to serve

Ich werde (schon) bedient. I am being served (already).

but: *Ich bin bedient.* < coll. > I've had enough / all I can take.

bekennen* to admit / confess

Farbe bekennen to come clean (in a game, or political tendencies)

bestellen to order

Sie hat sich etwas bestellt. < coll. >
She is (has planned to be) pregnant.

Es ist schlecht um ihn bestellt. He's in a bad way.

Soll ich ihr etwas bestellen? Shall I give her a message?

blasen* to blow

Trübsal blasen < coll. > to mope
jemandem den Marsch blasen to give someone a rocket

> *Ihm werd' ich was blasen.* < coll. >
> I'll give him a piece of my mind.
>
> *Er bläst sich auf.*
> He is showing off / boasting.

bleiben* to remain / stay behind

> *Es bleibt dabei.*
> We'll stick / keep to it.
>
> *Das bleibt unter uns* (dat.).
> That's just between ourselves.

*etwas bleiben lassen** < coll. > to give something a miss
Laß das bleiben! Keep your hands off it! / Leave it!
bei der Stange bleiben < coll. > to stick to it / keep up with something

sitzen◊bleiben (1) to stay down a year / have to repeat a year (at school)

> *Wenn du zwei Sechser im Zeugnis bekommst, mußt du sitzenbleiben.*
> If you get two grade sixes (failure) you will have to stay down a year. (For school grades see p. 395.)

sitzen◊bleiben (2) to be left on the shelf / remain unmarried

brechen* to break

einen Streit vom Zaune brechen to pick a quarrel / start a fight
(literally: to break / pick a quarrel from the fence)

unterbrechen ⧫ to interrupt

> *Bitte unterbrechen Sie mich nicht bei der Arbeit!*
> Please do not interrupt me at work / while I am working!

brennen* to burn

völlig abgebrannt sein <coll.> to be completely broke

> *Es brennt! Es brennt!* Fire! Fire!

(See also *gebranntes Kind* in section 139.)

bringen* to bring / take

Wir bringen jetzt Nachrichten.
We now broadcast the news. / And now for the headlines.

Das Fernsehen bringt eine Sondersendung.
There is a special programme on TV.

Das bringt er nicht. < coll. > He's not up to it.

Das bringt's doch nicht! < coll. > That's no (damn) use!

jemanden zur Strecke bringen to kill / hunt down / bag someone
jemanden aus der Fassung bringen to disconcert / throw someone
jemanden zur Schule / nach Hause bringen to take someone to school / home
Kinder zu Bett bringen to put children to bed
jemanden zum Weinen / Lachen bringen to make someone cry / laugh
jemanden dazu bringen, etwas zu tun to get someone to do something
es zu nichts bringen to achieve nothing / get nowhere
jemanden um etwas bringen to do someone out of something
jemanden um◊bringen < coll.> to kill someone
etwas in Gang bringen to get something going

sich nicht von etwas ab◊bringen lassen* not to be talked out of something / not to be persuaded to change one's mind

denken* to think

Denkste! < coll. > That's what **you** think!

Das hast du dir so gedacht. < coll. >
That's what you thought (but you were wrong).

Ich denke, also bin ich. (Descartes)
I think, therefore I am.

Wo denken Sie hin! What an idea!

Das gibt mir zu denken. That makes me think / worries me.

Daran ist gar nicht zu denken.
That's completely out of the question.

Ich denke nicht daran, das zu tun. < coll. >
There's no way I am going to do that!

Denk' daran! Don't forget!

Das war für mich gedacht.
That was meant / intended for me.

Ich habe mir nichts Böses dabei gedacht.
I meant no harm (by it).

drehen to turn

Der Roman dreht sich um . . . (+ acc.)
The novel is concerned with / about . . .

In meiner Frage dreht es sich darum, ob . . .
My question is about whether . . .

Die Sendung drehte sich um Gleichberechtigung.
The programme was about equal rights.

Alles dreht sich um das Baby.
Everything revolves around the baby.

Sie ist total durchgedreht < coll. >
She has cracked up completely.

ein Ding drehen to pull off a crime (e.g. bank robbery)

fallen* to fall

aus dem Rahmen fallen to go too far (literally: to fall out of the frame)

Er fiel auf der Party völlig aus dem Rahmen, weil er zuviel getrunken hatte.
He showed himself up at the party because he had drunk too much.

ein Buch, das aus dem Rahmen fällt
a book with a difference

jemandem ins Wort fallen to interrupt someone

Das fällt mir schwer. I find that difficult / hard.

auf◊fallen to stand out / attract attention

Erst fiel er auf, dann fiel er hin.
First he attracted attention, then he fell (down).

Es ist mir aufgefallen, wie nervös sie war.
I noticed how nervous she was.

Auffallendes Benehmen im Ausland ist keine gute Eigenschaft.
Conspicuous behaviour abroad is not a good characteristic.

jemandem ein◊fallen to occur to someone

Was fällt dir ein? How dare you?

Das fällt mir nicht im Traum ein! < coll. >
I wouldn't dream of it!

fehlen to miss (intransitive)

Du fehlst mir. I miss you. (literally: you are missing to me)

Wo fehlt's denn? < coll. > What's wrong?

Das fehlt gerade noch! < coll. > That's all that's needed! (ironic)

Er ließ es uns an nichts fehlen. He let us want for nothing.

Fehlt dir etwas? Is there anything the matter / wrong with you?

finden* to find

Das wird sich schon alles finden. Everything will turn out all right.

Ich finde nichts dabei. I think nothing of it.

fliegen* to fly

Der Schwindel fliegt auf.
The fraud is exposed. / The conspiracy's made public.

fressen* to eat (of animals)

Er glaubt, die Weisheit mit Löffeln gefressen zu haben. < coll. > He thinks he knows it all.

Das Baby ist so süß, ich habe es zum Fressen gern.
The baby is so sweet I could eat him.

geben* to give

Gib's ihm (tüchtig)! < coll. > Let him have it (hard)!

es gibt (+ acc.) there is / there are

N.B. The verb is always in the singular, even if the noun is plural.

Gibt es einen Gott?
Is there a God? / Does God exist?

In unserem Sonnensystem gibt es neun Planeten.
In our solar system there are nine planets.

Das darf es doch nicht geben!
That's impossible / cannot be true!

den Ausschlag geben to be the decisive factor
ein Manuskript in Druck geben to have a manuscript printed
jemandem einen Korb geben to turn someone down (usually when a woman is asked for a dance by a man)

an◊geben (1) to show off, boast

Mein Bruder hat als kleiner Junge immer furchtbar angegeben.
My brother always used to show off terribly as a little boy.

an◊geben (2) to state, indicate

wie oben angegeben as stated / mentioned above
a.a.O. = am angegebenen Ort ibid.

Der Zeuge gab an, er habe zwei Schüsse gehört.
The witness stated he had heard two shots.

Er gab an, ihr das Geld schon gegeben zu haben.
He stated he had already given her the money.

einen aus◊geben / eine Runde aus◊geben to stand a round

Ich gebe heute abend einen aus.
It's on me / my treat this evening.

gehen* to go

Morgen geht es nicht. Tomorrow is no good.

Laß es dir gut gehen. Look after yourself.

Wie geht's? < coll. > How are you?

Wie geht es Ihnen? How are you?

Das geht klar. That will be all right.

Es geht mir gegen den Strich.
It goes against the grain (for me).

miteinander gehen < coll., youth > to go out together / go steady
mit jemandem durch dick und dünn gehen to go through thick and thin with someone
jemandem durch die Lappen gehen to slip through someone's fingers

wie warme Semmeln weg◊gehen < coll. > to sell like hot cakes (literally: warm bread rolls)

auf Nummer sicher gehen < coll. > to play safe / hedge one's bets

leer aus◊gehen to go away empty-handed

daneben◊gehen to back-fire

Die Überraschung war völlig danebengegangen.
The surprise had completely backfired.

hoch◊gehen *(explodieren)* < coll. > to explode / go off / go up

Das Chemielabor ist hochgegangen!
The chemistry lab has exploded / gone up!

es geht um . . . . . .is at stake

Holen Sie einen Arzt, es geht um Leben und Tod!
Fetch a doctor, it's a matter of life and death!

Es geht um die Wurst! < coll. >
It's now or never / It's do or die.

Du mußt die Prüfung bestehen, es geht um die Wurst.
You must pass the exam, everything is at stake / hangs on it.

glauben to believe

Ich glaube, ja. I think so.

Das glaubst du doch selbst nicht! < coll. >
You can't be serious!

daran glauben müssen < coll. > to cop it / be lumbered with

Er hat dran glauben müssen. < slang >
He had to buy it.

Heute muß sie dran glauben und Küchendienst machen.
Today it is her turn to be lumbered with working in the kitchen.

haben* to have

Du hast es gut. You've got it made.

Hast du was? < coll. > Are you all right?

Hast du was, dann bist du was. < coll. >
If you've got something (money), then you are somebody.

Das hat es in sich.
That's tough. / That's a tricky one. / That's rich (in alcohol, cream, etc.).

Was hat es damit auf sich ?
What is all this about? / What is all this supposed to mean?

für alles zu haben sein to be game for anything
etwas gegen jemanden haben < coll. > to have something against someone / bear a grudge against someone
nicht mehr alle beisammen haben < coll. > to be not all there / to be a bit soft in the head

etwas satt haben < coll. > to be fed up with something
für jemanden nichts übrig haben to have no time for someone
immer das letzte Wort haben müssen always to want to have the last word

halten * to hold / keep

> *Wir haben das immer so gehalten.*
> We always used to do it like this.
>
> *Der Reissalat hält sich nicht.*
> The rice salad won't keep.

jemanden auf dem laufenden halten to keep someone up-to-date / posted
jemanden zum Narren halten to make a fool of someone
Schritt halten mit to keep pace with
jemanden in Trab halten < coll. > to keep someone on the go / on the trot
dicht halten < coll. > to keep one's mouth shut

sich halten to keep one's post

> *Er hat sich viel zu lange auf dem Posten gehalten.*
> He held out much too long in his post.

hängen * to hang (intransitive)

an jemandem hängen to depend on someone / to be very fond of someone
sich hängen lassen < coll. > to let oneself go

hängen◊bleiben* to get stuck / get left behind / to stay down (i.e. repeat a year at school)

> *Er ist schon zweimal hängengeblieben.*
> He has already twice had to stay down a year.

heißen * to be called

> *Was soll das heißen?* < coll. >
> What is that supposed to mean?

kennen * to know (a person or something by experience)

etwas wie seine Westentasche kennen to know something like the back of one's hand (literally: like one's waistcoat pocket)

kommen* to come

Es kommt darauf an, ob . . . It depends whether . . .

Er ist wegen der Affaire zu Fall gekommen.
The affair caused his downfall.

Das kommt davon, wenn man nicht zuhört.
That's what happens when you don't listen / pay attention.

Wie kommt das? < coll. > How come?

Wie komme ich dazu?
What's that got to do with me? / Why should I do that?

zu nichts kommen to get nowhere / be unsuccessful

zu sich (dat.) ***kommen*** to come round / recover consciousness

Nach dem Schock kam er langsam wieder zu sich.
After the shock he came round slowly.

nicht vom Fleck kommen not to get any further

nicht in Frage kommen to be out of the question

unter die Räder kommen to go to rack and ruin

über die Runden kommen to pull through / manage (especially time / money)

in Schwung kommen to get going / get into full swing

es darauf an◊kommen lassen* to take a chance / chance it

mit knapper Not davon◊kommen *to escape by the skin of one's teeth*

dran◊kommen < coll. > / ***an die Reihe kommen*** to get one's turn

Wer kommt jetzt dran < coll. > */ an die Reihe?*
Whose turn is it now?

heraus◊kommen to come to light

Der Betrug / die Wahrheit wird bald herauskommen.
The deceit (fraud) / truth will soon come to light.

um etwas herum◊kommen to get out of something

Er ist ums Spülen herumgekommen. He got out of the washing up.

lassen* to let / allow / permit (see section 32)

Er läßt sich gern bedienen. He likes being waited on.

Das läßt sich schon machen. That can be done.

Sie läßt sich nichts sagen. She won't be told (anything).

Das kann sich sehen lassen. This is fit to be shown.

sich etwas bringen lassen to have something delivered
sich etwas nicht gefallen lassen not to put up with something
jemanden links liegen lassen to ignore someone / send someone to Coventry
es sich (dat.) *nicht nehmen lassen, etwas zu tun* not to let anything stop one from doing something
sich durch nichts unter◊kriegen lassen < coll. > not let anything get one down
sich vollaufen (voll◊laufen) lassen < slang > to get pissed / get tanked up
jemanden zappeln lassen < coll. > to keep someone in suspense
sich sehen lassen < coll. > to put in an appearance

> *Ich muß mich mal wieder beim Verein sehen lassen.*
> I must put in an appearance at the club.

jemanden im Stich lassen to leave someone in the lurch

leben to live
über seine Verhältnisse leben to live beyond one's means

erleben to experience

> *Warte, sonst erlebst du etwas!*
> Just wait, otherwise you won't know what's hit you!

überleben ♦ to survive

> *Er hatte das Erdbeben überlebt.* He survived the earthquake.
>
> *Das überlebe ich nicht!* < coll. > < figurative >
> That'll be the death of me!

legen to put / lay down (transitive)

> *Man darf nicht jedes Wort auf die Goldwaage legen.*
> One mustn't take everything / every word too literally.

ein gutes Wort für jemanden einlegen to put in a good word for someone

lesen* * to read
jemandem die Leviten lesen to read someone the riot act / tell someone where to get off

liegen* * to lie (intransitive)

> *Das liegt auf der Hand.* < coll.> That's obvious.

machen to make / do

Da ist nichts zu machen.
There is nothing that can be done (about it).

Nun mach' schon! < coll. > Hurry up now!

Macht nichts! < coll. > Never mind, it doesn't matter.

Mach's gut! < coll. > (on saying goodbye)
Look after yourself / Take care!

Mit mir könnt ihr es ja machen. < coll. >
I am game for anything. / You can get away with it with me.

Das macht sich gut. That looks good.

Jetzt mach' mal einen Punkt! < coll. >
Come off it!

einen Besuch machen to pay a visit
sich breit machen to spread oneself / take up a lot of room
sich nichts aus etwas machen not to worry about something / not to like something

Mach' dir nichts draus! < coll. >
Don't let it bother you !

es nicht mehr lange machen < coll. > not to live / last much longer

Er ist schwer krank, er macht es nicht mehr lange.
He is very ill, he won't live / last much longer.

jemanden schlecht machen to denigrate someone / run someone down / blackmail someone
schlapp machen < coll. > to flag / flake out / wilt / collapse

Manche Manager machen mit 45 schlapp.
Some managers are (physically / mentally) finished by the time they are 45.

kurzen Prozeß mit jemandem machen to waste no time with / on someone
Schule machen (used with abstract noun as subject) to set a precedent

Das Beispiel hat Schule gemacht
The example set a precedent.

jemandem einen Strich durch die Rechnung machen < coll. > to upset / mess up someone's plans / put a spanner in the works
ein gutes Geschäft machen to make / get / strike a good deal
Pause machen to take a break

Mach mal Pause. < coll. > (Do) take a break.

nehmen * to take

Man nehme . . . (in recipes) Take . . .

Man nehme 2 Eier, 100g Zucker . . . etc.
Take 2 eggs, 4 oz of sugar . . . etc.

Bitte nehmen Sie Abstand! Please keep your distance!

von einem Plan Abstand nehmen not to get involved with (literally: to take one's distance from) a plan

Sie nahm ihre kranke Mutter zu sich.
She had her sick mother come and live with her.

Diesen Erfolg lasse ich mir nicht nehmen.
I won't be robbed of this success.

etwas an sich (acc.) *nehmen* to pick something up

Ich habe die Papiere [FA] *an mich genommen.*
I've picked up the documents.

etwas zu sich (dat.) *nehmen* to eat something
jemanden zu nehmen wissen to know how to take somebody
jemandem den Glauben nehmen to rob someone of his / her belief
jemandem die Angst nehmen to relieve someone of his / her fears

Die Therapie hatte ihr die Angst vor dem Fliegen genommen.
The therapy had cured her of her fear of flying.

etwas für bare Münze nehmen to take something at face value
jemanden nicht für voll nehmen < coll. > not to take someone seriously

etwas nehmen (in a restaurant, shop etc.) to have (see section 79)

Ich nehme die geräucherte Forelle.
I'll have the smoked trout.

etwas auf◊nehmen to record something

Er hat mir den Film Hilfe, ich habe die Kinder geschrumpft! *auf Video aufgenommen.*
He has videoed the film *Honey I Shrunk the Kids!* for me.

sagen to say / tell

N.B. The person you are telling something (to) is in the dative.

Ich habe ihm gesagt, daß er aufräumen soll.
I've told him to tidy up.

Unter uns gesagt, . . . Between you and me, . . .

Sage und schreibe: 1000DM!
Would you believe it / Believe it or not: 1000DM!

Sagen wir, zum Beispiel . . . Let's say, for example . . .

Laß dir das gesagt sein!
Let me tell you that! / Take it from me!

Du hast mir gar nichts zu sagen! < coll. >
You have no right to order me about!

Er hat im Betrieb etwas zu sagen.
He has a say in the firm.

Das hat nichts zu sagen.
That doesn't mean anything. / That isn't important.

Wem sagen Sie das?
You don't need to tell me, I know that only too well.

Na, wer sagt's denn! < coll. >
There you are (I knew it)!

Sag' nur, du hast es vergessen. < coll. >
Don't say you've forgotten it.

Sie läßt sich nichts sagen. She won't be told anything.

Was soll man dazu noch sagen? < coll. >
What can one say?

Ich hab' dir's gleich gesagt! I told you so.

Ich will dir mal was sagen: . . . < coll. >
Let me tell you something: . . .

Gesagt, getan. No sooner said than done.

etwas auf Deutsch sagen < coll. > to say something clearly, understandably

Sag das doch mal auf Deutsch!
Do express yourself clearly! (not necessarily in German)

jemandem die Wahrheit sagen to tell someone the truth

schaffen (1) (as a regular verb) to manage

Mit ihr will ich nichts zu schaffen haben. < coll. >
I don't want to have anything to do with her.

jemandem viel zu schaffen machen to cause someone a lot of trouble
sich an etwas zu schaffen machen < coll. > to fiddle about with something

es schaffen (etwas zu tun) to manage (to do) something / to make it

Wenn wir uns beeilen, schaffen wir es vielleicht noch.
If we hurry we might still make it.

Er hat es geschafft, das alte Auto wieder in Gang zu bringen.
He managed to get the old car going again.

(er)schaffen (2) (as an irregular verb) to create

Gott schuf die Welt in sieben Tagen.
God created the world in seven days.

schenken to give (as a gift)

Das ist ja fast geschenkt. < coll. >
That's dirt cheap / a give-away.

Uns ist nie etwas geschenkt worden. We never had it easy.

Er hat sich nichts geschenkt. He took great pains.

Das können wir uns schenken. < coll. >
We can skip that / give that a miss.

Sie schenkte ihm sechs Kinder.
She bore (literally: gave) him six children.

jemandem das Leben schenken
(1) to spare someone's life < archaic >
(2) to give birth to a child

schieben * to push / shove

jemandem die Schuld in die Schuhe schieben < coll. >
to put the blame on someone
etwas von einem Tag auf den andern schieben to keep putting something off from one day to the next
mit etwas schieben < coll. > to traffic (deal) in something

Er schob heimlich mit Rauschgift.
He secretly trafficked in drugs.

schreien * to scream / shout

Es ist zum Schreien! < coll. >
It is a scream!

Sie ist so bunt angezogen wie ein Papagei, es ist zum Schreien.
She is dressed in garish colours like a parrot, it's a scream.

Es ist der letzte Schrei. < coll. >
It's the in-thing. (cf. French: *le dernier cri*)

sehen* to see

Das muß man gesehen haben.
It has to be seen to be believed.

Ich sehe was, was du nicht siehst.
I spy with my little eye. (game)

Sehe ich recht?
Am I seeing things?

Das müssen wir erst mal sehen.
That remains to be seen.

Siehste! < coll. > = *Siehst du wohl!*
There, you see!

Siehe oben / unten / Seite 21.
See above / below / page 21.

Von ihm ist nichts zu sehen.
He is nowhere to be seen.

Wir sehen uns morgen.
See you tomorrow.

Abgesehen davon, daß . . .
Apart from (the fact) that . . .

schlecht sehen to have bad eyesight
etwas nicht mehr sehen können not to be able to stand the sight of something any more

Ich kann deinen dreckigen alten Pullover einfach nicht mehr sehen.
I simply can't stand the sight of your filthy old jumper any more.

kein Blut sehen können not to be able to stand the sight of blood
darauf sehen, daß to make sure that / to insist
jemanden vom Sehen kennen to know someone by sight
es auf jemanden abgesehen haben to have it in for someone
es auf etwas abgesehen haben to have one's eye on something

sein* to be

Wie ist es mit dir, kommst du mit?
How about you, are you coming along?

Ist dir etwas?
Are you all right? (literally: is something to you?)

Mir ist kalt / heiß. I am cold / hot.

Mir ist schlecht / nicht gut. I feel sick / unwell.

Es hat nicht sollen sein. < archaic >
It was not meant to be.

Das kann schon sein.
That may well be.

Was darf es sein? (in a shop, restaurant etc.)
What can I get you? (See section 78)

Das kann doch nicht sein!
That's just not possible!

Das darf doch nicht wahr sein!
That can't possibly be true! / I don't believe it!

Was nicht ist, kann noch werden.
Things can always change.

Mit ihm ist zu reden.
He is quite approachable.

Mit ihm ist nicht zu reden.
He is not at all approachable.

Er ist nicht mehr. (euphemism)
He is no longer with us.

Die Sache ist gar nicht so ohne. < coll. >
It's not that easy. / There may be something in this.

bei jemandem unten durch sein < coll. > to be out of favour with someone
auf dem laufenden sein to be well informed
nicht von gestern sein < coll. > not to have been born yesterday
fehl am Platze sein to be out of place

völlig ab◊sein < coll. > to be completely shattered

Nach der Probe war ich völlig ab.
After the rehearsal I was completely shattered.

setzen to put

etwas aufs Spiel setzen to risk something
Wasser auf◊setzen to put water on (to boil)
einen Hut auf◊setzen to put on a hat

sitzen* to sit (intransitive)

Bleiben Sie bitte sitzen! Please don't get up.

(N.B. *sitzen◊bleiben* to remain seated, etc.; cf. *bleiben*, above)

Die Firma sitzt in München.
The firm is based in Munich.

Der Schreck sitzt mir noch in den Gliedern.
I am still recovering from the shock.

Lerne die Vokabeln, bis sie sitzen. < coll. >
Learn your vocabulary until it sticks.

Der Rock sitzt nicht gut.
The skirt doesn't fit too well. (no understatement in German!)

Er sitzt (im Gefängnis). < slang >
He is inside / doing time.

einen sitzen haben < coll. > to have had one too many
in der Klemme / Patsche sitzen to be in a (real) fix

spielen to play

Tennis spielen to play tennis
Geige spielen to play the violin
die erste Geige spielen < figurative > to call the tune
jemandem einen Streich spielen to play a trick on someone
eine Rolle spielen to play a role
seine Beziehungen spielen lassen to bring one's connections to bear

springen * to jump / leap

Das ist gehupft wie gesprungen. < coll. >
That's swings and roundabouts.

etwas springen lassen < coll. > to fork something out

Unser reicher Onkel könnte ruhig mal etwas springen lassen.
Our rich uncle could easily fork out something just once in a while.

stecken to stick / put / be hidden

Der Schlüssel steckt. The key is in the lock.

Steck dein Hemd in die Hose!
Tuck your shirt into your trousers!

Stecken Sie Ihr Ticket ein!
Take your ticket with you!

Er steckt voller Ideen.
He is full of ideas.

Zeige ihm, was in dir steckt!
Show him what you are made of!

Wo steckt er?
Where has he got to? / Where is he hiding?

Da steckt etwas dahinter!
There's someting (hidden) behind it!

sein ganzes Vermögen in etwas (acc.) *stecken* to put / invest all one's money in something
mit jemandem unter einer Decke stecken to be in league / in cahoots with someone
jemanden in den Sack stecken < coll. > to put someone in the shade
Blumenzwiebeln stecken to plant bulbs

etwas ein◊stecken müssen to have to take / swallow a lot (of criticism)

stehen* (1) to stand (intransitive)

Wo steht dein Auto? Where is you car (parked)?

Wie steht es um ihn?
How is he doing? / What is his condition?

Wie stehe ich nun da?
What kind of a fool do I look now?

Es steht dir gut. It suits you (well).

Wie stehen Sie dazu?
What do you think about that?

Das Barometer steht hoch / tief / auf Regen.
The barometer is on high / low / indicating rain.

Die Uhr steht auf 12. The clock shows 12.

but: *Meine Uhr steht.*
My watch has stopped.

Die Chancen stehen 'fifty-fifty'.
The chances are fifty-fifty.

Wie steht das Pfund?
What is the rate of the pound?

Die Aktie steht gut / schlecht.
The share price is good / bad.

etwas steht jemandem zur Verfügung something is at someone's disposal.

Sie steht total auf ihn. < informal, youth >
She is nuts / mad about him.

stehen (2) to be written / printed

Das steht hier schwarz auf weiß.
That's what it says here in black and white.

Das steht in der Bibel.
That's written in the Bible.

Sein Name steht auf der Liste.
His name is on the list.

In der Zeitung steht, daß der Präsident gestorben ist.
It says in the paper that the president has died.

Das Zitat steht bei Goethe / in Goethes Faust.
The quotation is from Goethe / Goethe's *Faust*.

stellen to put / place / stand upright (transitive only)

N.B. *stellen* always implies an upright position:

Eine Flasche in den Kühlschrank stellen.
To put a bottle (upright) in the fridge.

If a horizontal position is implied, use *legen*:

Eine Flasche in den Kühlschrank legen.
To put (lay) a bottle (on its side) in the fridge.

Therefore use *stellen* (to put) only when the object is capable of standing (on legs, casters, etc.)

auf sich selbst gestellt sein to be thrown back onto one's own resources
jemandem eine Frage stellen to put a question to someone
jemanden zur Rede stellen to take someone to task
jemandem etwas zur Verfügung stellen to put something at someone's disposal / to provide someone with something

N.B. *etwas steht jemandem zur Verfügung* something **is** available to someone / something is at the disposal of someone (cf. *stehen* above)
den Wecker auf sieben Uhr stellen to set the alarm for seven o'clock
den Schalter auf Null stellen to turn the switch to zero
jemanden vor Gericht stellen to take someone to court
sich schlafend / taub / tod / dumm stellen to pretend to be asleep / deaf / dead / stupid
sich der Kamera stellen to make oneself available for photographs / filming
sich mit jemandem gut stellen to try to get on good terms with someone

etwas ruhig◊stellen to immobilize

> *Der Arzt hatte mein gebrochenes Bein mit einem Gips ruhiggestellt.*
> The doctor had immobilized my broken leg in plaster.

jemanden ruhig◊stellen (1) (euphemism) to calm, tranquillize someone

> *Der Patient mußte ruhiggestellt werden.*
> The patient had to be tranquillized.

jemanden ruhig◊stellen (2) to manoeuvre someone (too eager or incompetent) into a niche where he or she can do no harm

treten * to step

> *Der Fluß ist über die Ufer getreten.* < formal >
> The river has overflowed its banks.

bei jemandem ins Fettnäpfchen treten (figurative) to put one's foot in it / drop a clanger (literally: to put one's foot into someone's little pot of fat)
in den Ehestand treten < formal > to enter into matrimony
in den Hungerstreik treten to go on hunger strike
auf das Gaspedal / die Bremse treten to step on the accelerator / the brake

verlieren * to lose

> *Das hat hier nichts verloren.*
> It has no business to be here.

> *Diese Bemerkung hat hier nichts verloren.*
> This remark is out of place here.

> *das verlorene Paradies*
> paradise lost

> *Er war in Gedanken verloren.*
> He was lost in thought.

> *Der Hund verliert die Haare.*
> The dog is moulting.

ein Spiel verlieren to lose a match / game
nichts (mehr) zu verlieren haben to have nothing (more) to lose
den Faden verlieren to lose the thread

verstehen * to understand

Das versteht sich von selbst.
That goes without saying. / That speaks for itself.

wünschen to wish

Er wünschte mir gute Besserung.
He said he hoped I would get better soon.

Ganz wie Sie wünschen. < formal > (sometimes ironic)
Just as you like.

Es verlief alles wie gewünscht.
Everything went as they hoped.

Der Herr Direktor wünscht Sie zu sprechen. < formal >
The director would like to speak to you.

viel zu wünschen übrig lassen to leave a lot to be desired
jemandem gute Nacht wünschen to wish / bid someone good night

(N.B. *Nacht* applies to bed-time only; see also section 141e.)

33 Building on nouns

You will probably be familiar with the literal meaning of most of the nouns given below. This section lists some of the common idiomatic expressions in which they are also used, and which are a key to word power in German.

★ N.B. A few of the nouns listed below are considered to be archaic, but they are frequently used in idiomatic expressions. (Plurals are given in brackets.)

(a) Parts of the body

der ***Arm****(e)* arm

jemanden auf den Arm nehmen to pull someone's leg
jemandem unter die Arme greifen to help someone out

das ***Auge****(n)* eye

Augen machen to be wide-eyed
ein Auge zudrücken to turn a blind eye
mit jemandem unter vier Augen sprechen to talk privately with someone / in confidence

etwas mit anderen Augen sehen to see something in a different light
einer Sache ins Auge sehen to face / confront something

Ich habe kein Auge zugetan. I didn't sleep a wink.

Da blieb kein Auge trocken.
There wasn't a dry eye in the place. / There were tears in every eye.

Das kann leicht ins Auge gehen. < coll. >
That can easily go wrong / have dire consequences.

(See also *Auge* in section 139.)

das ***Bein****(e)* leg

etwas auf die Beine bringen / stellen to get something going
die Beine unter die Arme nehmen to look sharp / lively / to hurry
einen Klotz am Bein haben < coll. > to have a millstone round one's neck (lit.: to have a clod / block attached to one's leg)
auf den Beinen sein to be on one's feet
wieder auf die Beine kommen to get back on one's feet / to recover
mit beiden Beinen im Leben stehen to have both feet (firmly) on the ground

Er ist noch gut auf den Beinen.
He is still sprightly.

(See also *Beine* in section 139.)

der ***Daumen****(–)* thumb

jemandem den Daumen halten / drücken to keep one's fingers crossed for someone (literally: to press one's thumb for someone)
über den Daumen peilen to make a rough guess

Über den Daumen gepeilt waren das etwa 7 000 km.
To make a rough guess, that was about 7,000 km.

den Daumen auf etwas halten to keep a tight hand on something

der ***Finger****(–)* finger

jemanden um den kleinen Finger wickeln to twist someone round one's little finger
keinen Finger krumm machen < coll. > not to lift a finger
seine Finger im Spiel haben to have a finger in the pie (literally: in the game)
Fingerspitzengefühl haben to have a sense of tact / a delicate touch

Man zeigt nicht mit nacktem Finger auf angezogene Leute.
< coll. > It is rude to point.

der ***Fuß****(¨e)* foot

auf großem Fuße leben to live the high life
mit dem linken Fuß zuerst aufgestanden sein to have got out of bed on the wrong side (i.e. to be in a bad mood)
festen Fuß fassen to get a firm foothold

Das Publikum lag ihm zu Füßen.
He had the audience at his feet.

das ***Gedächtnis*** memory

ein Gedächtnis wie ein Sieb haben < coll. > to have a memory / head like a sieve, to be a scatterbrain

das ***Haar****(e)* hair

ein Haar in der Suppe finden to find fault with something (literally: to find a hair in the soup)
an den Haaren herbeigezogen far-fetched / stretching things too far
Haarspalterei treiben to split hairs

Mir stehen die Haare zu Berge.
My hair stands on end.

der ***Hals****(¨e)* throat / neck

jemandem den Hals umdrehen < coll. > to drive someone to the wall / to kill someone (in the metaphorical sense)

Ihm steht das Wasser bis zum Hals.
He is up to his neck in it.

Sie fiel ihm um den Hals.
She threw her arms around his neck / embraced him.

! *Das hängt mir zum Halse heraus.* < coll. >
I am sick and tired of it.

die ***Hand****(¨e)* hand

alle Hände voll zu tun haben to have one's hands full
im Handumdrehen < coll. > in the twinkling of an eye (literally: the turn of a hand)

das ***Herz****(en)* heart

ein Herz und eine Seele sein to be bosom pals
etwas auf dem Herzen haben to have something on one's mind
jemandem rutscht das Herz in die Hose one's heart sinks into one's boots

Das liegt mir am Herzen.
This is important to me / close to my heart.

Mir fällt ein Stein vom Herzen. That's a weight off my mind.

der ***Kopf****(̈e)* head

den Nagel auf den Kopf treffen to hit the nail on the head
sich etwas in den Kopf setzen to take something into one's head
Hals über Kopf head over heels / in a mad rush (literally: neck over head)

der ***Leib****(er)* body < archaic >

mit Leib und Seele with body and soul

Er ist mit Leib und Seele Arzt. He is a dedicated doctor.

das ***Mark*** bone marrow < archaic >

Das geht mir durch Mark und Bein. < coll. >
That goes right through me. / That sets my teeth on edge.

N.B. *das Mark* = (bone) marrow; *die Mark* = (Deutsche) Mark. The expression is therefore sometimes changed to *Das geht mir durch Mark und Pfennig.* The meaning remains the same, but with a financial implication.

die ***Miene****(n)* face / expression / air

gute Miene zum bösen Spiel machen to put on a brave face / grin and bear it
ohne eine Miene zu verziehen without turning a hair

der ***Mund****(̈er)* mouth

kein Blatt vor den Mund nehmen not to mince one's words (literally: to put no paper before your mouth)
von der Hand in den Mund leben to live from hand to mouth
nicht auf den Mund gefallen sein < coll. > to have the gift of the gab
Mund und Nase aufsperren to be open-mouthed

*die **Nase**(n)* nose

immer der Nase nach < coll. > just follow your nose
jemanden an der Nase herumführen to lead someone by the nose
von etwas die Nase voll haben < coll. > to be fed up with something
in alles seine Nase hineinstecken < coll. > to stick / poke one's nose into everything

> *Ich sehe es dir an der Nasenspitze an!*
> I can tell by your nose! (literally: tip of your nose) / I can see it written all over your face!

*der **Nerv**(en)* nerve

jemandem auf die Nerven gehen < coll. > to get on someone's nerves

den Nerv haben, etwas zu tun to have the nerve to do something

*das **Ohr**(en)* ear

es faustdick hinter den Ohren haben to be a crafty customer (literally: to have a fistful behind one's ears)
jemandem das Fell über die Ohren ziehen < coll. > to pull the wool over someone's eyes / to take someone for a ride (literally: to pull the skin / hide over someone's ears)
ganz Ohr sein to be all ears
jemandem einen Floh ins Ohr setzen to put ideas into someone's head
die Ohren spitzen to prick up one's ears
die Ohren steif◊halten < coll. > to keep a stiff upper lip / to keep smiling
sich etwas hinter die Ohren schreiben < coll. > to get something into one's thick head (literally: to write something behind one's ears)
bis über beide Ohren verliebt sein < coll. > to be head over heels (literally: right over both ears) in love

*der **Rücken**(–)* back

jemandem den Rücken stärken to back someone up / give encouragement
es läuft einem kalt über den Rücken to send shivers down one's spine

*der **Schädel**(–)* skull

einen dicken Schädel haben to be stubborn / pigheaded / to have a hangover

> *Mir brummt der Schädel.* < coll. >
> My head is throbbing.

der ***Schopf****(¨e)* (shock of) hair < archaic >

die Gelegenheit beim Schopfe packen to jump at the opportunity (literally: to grab the opportunity by the hair)

die ***Schulter****(n)* shoulder

jemandem die kalte Schulter zeigen to give someone the cold shoulder
etwas auf die leichte Schulter nehmen not to take something seriously (enough)

die ***Stirn*** forehead

jemandem die Stirn bieten to face up to someone

> *Das steht dir auf der Stirn geschrieben.*
> It is written all over your face.

die ***Wimper****(n)* eyelash

ohne mit der Wimper zu zucken without batting / lifting an eyelid

der ***Zahn****(¨e)* tooth

jemanden auf den Zahn fühlen to give someone a grilling
die Zähne zusammenbeißen to grit one's teeth

die ***Zunge****(n)* tongue

> *Es liegt mir auf der Zunge.*
> It's on the tip of my tongue.

(b) Animals

der ***Bär****(en)* bear

jemandem einen Bären aufbinden to have someone on / pull someone's leg

die ***Eule****(n)* owl

Eulen nach Athen tragen to carry coals to Newcastle (literally: owls to Athens)

der ***Fisch****(e)* fish

gesund wie ein Fisch im Wasser to be in fine fettle

die ***Fliege****(n)* fly

zwei Fliegen mit einer Klappe schlagen < coll. > to kill two birds with one stone

der ***Hund****(e)* dog

vor die Hunde gehen < slang > to go to the dogs

Da liegt der Hund begraben. < coll. >
That's the cause of it. (literally: there the dog lies buried)

Den letzten beißen die Hunde.
Latecomers must expect to be unlucky. (literally: the last one is bitten by the dogs)

(See also *Hunde* in section 139.)

die ***Katze****(n)* cat

die Katze aus dem Sack lassen to let the cat out of the bag
eine Katze im Sack kaufen to buy a pig in a poke (literally: a cat in the sack)
wie die Katze um den heißen Brei herum◊schleichen to beat about the bush

Es ist alles für die Katz'. < coll. >
It is all in vain / a waste of time.

die ***Kuh****(¨e)* cow

Das geht auf keine Kuhhaut. < coll. >
That is absolutely incredible / staggering / mind-blowing / too much.

die ***Mücke****(n)* midge / gnat

aus einer Mücke einen Elefanten machen to make a mountain out of a molehill

das ***Pferd****(e)* horse

Keine zehn Pferde bringen mich dahin. < coll. >
Wild horses couldn't drag me there.

der ***Pudel****(–)* poodle

wie ein begossener Pudel dastehen < coll. > to look sheepish (literally: to stand there like a wet poodle)

Das also war des Pudels Kern. (Goethe)
So that's what was behind it. (literally: so that's what was the poodle's inmost core)

die ***Sardine****(n)* sardine

wie in einer Sardinenbüchse < coll. > (packed) like sardines

der ***Stier****(e)* bull

den Stier bei den Hörnern packen to take the bull by the horns
brüllen wie ein Stier to roar like a lion (literally: to bellow like a bull)

die ***Taube****(n)* pigeon / dove

Hier geht es zu wie in einem Taubenschlag.
It's like Piccadilly Circus here. (literally: in a dovecot / pigeon loft)

der ***Vogel****(¨)* bird

den Vogel abschießen < coll. > to surpass everyone (ironic)
einen Vogel haben < coll. > to be crazy / weird (see section 49)

(c) Plants

der ***Apfel****(¨)* apple

in den sauren Apfel beißen to grasp the nettle
etwas für einen Apfel und ein Ei kaufen. < coll. > to buy something for a song (literally: for an apple and an egg)

die ***Blume****(n)* flower

jemandem etwas durch die Blume sagen to tell someone something in a roundabout way (usually criticism in a friendly disguise)

die ***Espe****(n)* aspen

zittern wie Espenlaub to tremble like a leaf (literally: like an aspen)

das ***Heu*** hay

Geld wie Heu haben < coll. > to have pots / oodles of money
eine Stecknadel in einem Heuhaufen suchen to look for a needle in a haystack

der ***Hopfen*** hop

Bei ihm ist Hopfen und Malz verloren. < coll. >
He's a dead loss. (literally: hops and malt are wasted on him)

der ***Keim****(e)* seed / bud

etwas im Keim ersticken to nip something in the bud

das ***Korn****(¨er)* grain / corn

die Flinte ins Korn werfen to throw in the towel / to give up (literally: to throw the gun into the grain)

das ***Kraut*** (no pl.) cabbage (South German / Austrian)

wie Kraut und Rüben durcheinanderliegen < coll. > to lie all about / to be scattered all over the place (like cabbage and carrots)
ins Kraut schießen to go to seed / run wild

N.B. *das Kraut(¨er)* herb.

der ***Lorbeer****(en)* laurel

sich auf seinen Lorbeeren ausruhen < coll. > to rest on one's laurels

> *Damit kannst du keine Lorbeeren ernten.*
> That's no great achievement. / That won't get you far.

die ***Palme****(n)* palm

jemanden auf die Palme bringen < coll. > to drive someone up the wall / to make someone's blood boil (literally: to drive someone up the palm tree)

der ***Zweig****(e)* branch

auf keinen grünen Zweig kommen. < coll. > to get nowhere (literally: not to come upon any green branch)

(d) The elements

die ***Erde*** earth

mit beiden Beinen auf der Erde stehen to have both feet firmly on the ground / to be down to earth
in fremder Erde ruhen to rest on foreign soil / to be buried abroad

> *Du wirst mich noch unter die Erde bringen.* < coll. >
> You'll be the death of me yet.

über Stock und Stein up hill and down dale (literally: over stick and stone)

das ***Feuer****(–)* fire

jemandem Feuer geben to give someone a light
wie auf glühenden / heißen Kohlen sitzen to be like a cat on hot bricks / on tenterhooks
mit dem Feuer spielen to play with fire
für jemanden durch's Feuer gehen to go through fire and water / hell and high water for someone

die ***Luft****(¨e)* air

leicht in die Luft gehen < coll. > to be quick to blow one's top
jemanden an die frische Luft setzen to show someone the door
einen Rat in den Wind schlagen to turn a deaf ear to advice / to cast advice to the wind / to throw caution to the wind
auf der gleichen Wellenlänge sein to be on the same wave-length
wie im siebten Himmel sein < coll. > to be on cloud nine

> *Die Luft ist rein.* < coll. >
> The coast is clear.
>
> *Diese Behauptung ist völlig aus der Luft gegriffen.*
> This statement is pure invention.

das ***Wasser*** water

vom Regen in die Traufe kommen (to fall) out of the frying-pan into the fire (literally: to come from the rain into the eaves)
ein Tropfen auf den heißen Stein a drop in the ocean (literally: on a hot stone)
ein Sturm im Wasserglas a storm in a teacup
jemandem das Wasser nicht reichen können not to be able to hold the candle to someone
mit allen Wassern gewaschen sein < coll. > to know all the tricks
aussehen, als ob man kein Wässerchen trüben könnte to look as if butter wouldn't melt in one's mouth (literally: as if one could not muddy any water)
aufs Glatteis geraten * to skate on thin ice
jemanden aufs Glatteis führen to take someone for a ride
die Kuh vom Eis holen < coll. > to save a difficult situation (i.e., to intervene with courage; literally: to fetch the cow from the ice)

134 Colourful adjectives

The most common colour adjectives in German give rise to some idiomatic figurative expressions. Even with the general terms *bunt* and *Farbe*, there are some examples:

bunt many-coloured / colourful

ein bunter Abend a social evening
eine bunte Reihe machen to seat men and women alternately at the table

> *Jetzt wird's mir aber zu bunt.* < coll. >
> This is going too far. / That's too much.

die ***Farbe****(n)* colour

Farbe bekennen to come clean / to make a clean breast of it
die Farben wechseln < figurative > to change sides

blau blue

Associated with faithfulness and frankness: forget-me-nots are pale blue and blue-eyed girls in cheap novels turn out to be honest and good.

blaue Flecken haben to be bruised
blau sein wie ein Veilchen < coll. > to be tight / canned (literally: like a violet)
blau machen to skive / skip work
einen blauen Brief bekommen to receive one's card / warning from school
eine Fahrt ins Blaue a trip / excursion into the unknown / nowhere in particular / a mystery tour
das Blaue vom Himmel herunter versprechen to promise the moon
blaues Blut in den Adern haben (adelige Abstammung) to have blue blood in one's veins (to be of aristocratic descent)
ein großer / kleiner Blauer < coll. > a 100DM / 10DM note (both are actually blue)
mit einem blauen Auge davonkommen < coll. > to get off lightly
jemandem ein blaues Auge schlagen < coll. > to give someone a black(!) eye
der Blaustrumpf < archaic > bluestocking

> *Er wird sein blaues Wunder erleben.*
> He won't know what's hit him.

gelb yellow

Associated with jealousy, envy and anger.

gelb vor Neid green (!) with envy
die gelbe Rübe (Southern German) / *die Karotte* carrot
die Ampel stand auf Gelb the traffic lights were on amber
das Eigelb egg yolk
die Gelbsucht jaundice
das Gelbkreuz / das Senfgas mustard gas

> *Das ist nicht das Gelbe vom Ei.* < coll. >
> That's no great shakes / nothing special.

gold gold

Associated with preciousness and value.

treu wie Gold sein to be faithful and true
Gold in der Kehle haben to have a golden voice (literally: to have gold in your throat)
nicht mit Gold zu bezahlen / aufzuwiegen sein to be (more than) worth one's weight in gold
goldene Worte sprechen to say something important (sometimes words of flattery) / to speak words of wisdom

> *Bei der Hochzeit muß der Brautvater ein paar goldene Worte sprechen.*
> At the wedding the father of the bride has to proffer a few words of wisdom.

der Goldjunge the blue-eyed boy

N.B. A golden handshake is *die Abstandssumme.*

(See also *Gold*, in section 139.)

grau grey

Associated with age and with dreariness.

sich keine grauen Haare über etwas wachsen lassen not to lose sleep over something
der graue Alltag dull routine / the monotony of daily life / nine-to-five existence
alles grau in grau sehen always to look on the gloomy side of things
in grauer Vorzeit / Ferne in the dim and distant past / in the dim future

grün green

Associated with hope, health, vigour, freshness, youth; also has ecological overtones.

grünen <poetic> to spring up anew / to blossom

> *Es grünt so grün, wenn Spaniens Blüten blühen.*
> (from *My Fair Lady*)
>
> When blossoms bloom in Spain, everything springs up anew again. (originally: 'The rain in Spain stays mainly in the plain'.)

grüner Salat lettuce
noch grün hinter den Ohren sein still to be wet behind the ears
der Grünschnabel / grüner Junge greenhorn / know-all
die Grünen (political party) (adjectival noun) the Greens
der Grüne (adjectival noun) < coll., now rare > copper, policeman (colour of the uniform)
die Ampel steht auf Grün the traffic lights are green

> *Grüne Welle bei 50 Km/h.*
> The green lights are phased for 50 km/h. (i.e. you'll ride on a 'green wave' if you travel at a steady 50 km/h)

grünes Licht geben (für) to give the go ahead / give permission / launch something
ins Grüne fahren to take a trip into the country
über die grüne Grenze gehen to cross a border illegally (in the woods etc.)
am grünen Tisch planen to plan from the bureaucratic ivory tower / in theory
die Grüne Woche Berlin's international agricultural fair
der Grüne Plan agricultural aid plan
die grüne Witwe < coll. > lonely suburban housewife (out in the country)
grüne Finger haben to have green fingers (i.e. to be good with plants)

> *Es wird ihm grün und gelb vor den Augen.*
> He is going green around the gills.
>
> *Die beiden sind sich nicht grün.*
> There's no love lost between (the two of) them.
>
> *Das ist dasselbe in Grün.* < colloquial >
> It's one and the same thing.

rot red

The colour of love, so only give red roses if you really mean it! Otherwise it is associated with aggression, as well as left-wing politics.

der rote Oskar (or any other name) socialist Oskar (referring to Oskar Lafontaine, Saarland politician in the 1990s)
in den roten Zahlen stecken to be in the red (financially)
rot vor Wut sein to be red in the face with rage
rot sehen to become very angry / see red
(bis über beide Ohren) rot werden to blush (furiously / violently)
etwas im Kalender rot anstreichen to make something a red-letter day
den Rotstift ansetzen < figurative > to make drastic cut-backs / economies (literally: to apply the red pencil)
jemandem den roten Hahn aufs Dach setzen to set someone's house on fire (literally: to put a red rooster on someone's roof)

> *Bei Rot anhalten!*
> Stop when the lights are red.

> *Gewalt zieht sich wie ein roter Faden durch die Geschichte.*
> Violence runs like a thread throughout history.

> *Das wirkt wie ein rotes Tuch auf ihn.*
> It makes him see red. / It's like a red rag to a bull.

schwarz black

(1) Associated as in English with death and mourning (black-edged stationery, black ties etc.) and misfortune (*das Pech* (pitch) is a symbol of bad luck, cf. p. 191).

das schwarze Brett notice board (not 'blackboard', see below)
der schwarze Mann chimney sweep / bogey man
jemandem den schwarzen Peter zuschieben to pass the buck to someone / give someone the worst deal
warten bis man schwarz wird < coll. > to wait till one is blue (!) in the face / till the cows come home

ins Schwarze treffen to score a bull's eye
das kleine Schwarze the little (short) black dress
das schwarze Schaf in der Familie the black sheep in the family
sich schwarz ärgern < coll. > to get / go hopping mad

Es wurde mir schwarz vor den Augen.
I fainted / blacked out.

Da sehe ich schwarz.
I'm pessimistic about this. / I'm looking on the black side.

Das habe ich schwarz auf weiß.
I've got it in black and white / in writing.

(2) But *schwarz* is also associated with things illegal or with illegality:

im Schwarzhandel on the black market
schwarz arbeiten to moonlight
schwarz fahren < coll. > to dodge paying the fare
schwarz hören / sehen to listen to pirate radio stations / listen to the radio / watch TV without paying or without a licence
schwarz über die Grenze gehen to cross the border illegally
jemanden auf die schwarze Liste setzen to blacklist someone

(3) Black is also associated with Catholicism or conservatism:

Dieser Wahlkreis ist ganz schwarz.
This constituency is out and out conservative.

N.B. Black-out (darkening of windows) is *die Verdunklung*; news black-out is *die Nachrichtensperre*; to have a blackout (medical) is *kurzzeitig das Bewußtsein verlieren*; blackboard (slate) is *die (Schiefer) Tafel(n).*

silber silver

Associated sometimes with money or old age (e.g. *silbernes Haar*).

das Silber silverware
der Silberblick < coll. > (slight) squint
ein Silberstreifen am Horizont light at the end of the tunnel / a ray of hope (literally: a silver stripe on the horizon)

weiß white

Associated with cleanliness and purity.

ein weißes Blatt a blank sheet of paper
ein weißer Fleck auf der Landkarte a piece of uncharted region / territory (literally: a blank area on the map)
Weißer Sonntag Low Sunday (in Christian calendar first Sunday after Easter)
der weiße Tod death in the snow (also death as a result of drugs)
der weiße Sport tennis
der Weißherbst ≈ rosé (wine)

Er gönnt mir das Weiße im Auge nicht.
He begrudges me the very air I breathe.

Er hat eine weiße (reine / saubere) Weste. < coll. >
He is innocent, he has a clean record.

135 Adverbial nuance

Adverbs offer a means to qualify verbs, adjectives or other adverbs. Their standard formation and use are explained in sections 50-4. This section looks at some common German adverbs which have particular nuances. Adverbs marked * can also be used as adjectives in this particular form; others would need to be slightly modified.

(a) Adverbs used primarily in formal notices

andernfalls otherwise

Den Antrag nur ausfüllen, wenn Sie nicht in Ihrem Wahlbezirk wählen. Andernfalls diese Karte zur Wahl mitbringen.
Only fill in the application if you are not voting in your constituency. Otherwise bring this card along to vote.

ausdrücklich* explicitly

Wir weisen Sie ausdrücklich darauf hin, daß . . .
We point out explicitly / specifically draw your attention to the fact that . . .

behördlich* by the authorities / officially

Unbefugten ist der Zutritt bergbehördlich verboten.
Entrance prohibited for unauthorized persons (by the mountain authorities).

dringend* urgently / expressly (associated with polite orders)

Herr Georg Schreiber wird dringend gebeten, sich bei der Information zu melden. (loudspeaker announcement)
Mr Georg Schreiber is urgently requested to report to the information desk.

polizeilich* by the police

Das Betreten der Baustelle ist polizeilich verboten.
Entering the building site is forbidden by the police.

sofort immediately

Bei Rot bitte sofort den Motor abstellen.
When the light shows red, please switch off the engine immediately.

stets always / every time

Denken Sie an die Möglichkeit einer Notbremsung und benützen Sie stets die Haltestangen. (notice on bus / train)
Hold on to the handrails in case there is an emergency stop. (literally: consider a possible emergency stop and always use the handrails)

streng* strictly (associated with prohibition)

Das Betreten der Baustelle ist streng verboten. Eltern haften für ihre Kinder.
Entrance to the building site is strictly forbidden. Parents are liable / responsible for their children.

To express even more severity, ***strengstens*** is used:

Alkoholkonsum ist strengstens verboten.
The consumption of alcohol is strictly / absolutely forbidden.

umgehend* immediately / without further ado (associated with official orders)

Der Fahrer des Wagens mit dem Kennzeichen GG-EC-650 möchte sich umgehend bei der Polizei melden.
The driver of the car registration no. GG-EC-650 is requested / required to report to the police immediately. (radio announcement)

vorübergehend* temporarily

Die Zahnarztpraxis ist vorübergehend geschlossen.
The dental surgery is temporarily closed.

(b) Adverbs used in standard written and spoken German

angeblich * supposedly (associated with doubt)

Er hatte ihr das Geld angeblich schon am Vortag gegeben.
He had supposedly already given her the money the previous day.

N.B. *an◊geben* means 'to state' (but usually there is no doubt implied) (see *geben* in section 32).

anscheinend apparently / seemingly

Die Untersuchung hat anscheinend gar nicht stattgefunden.
Apparently the investigation hasn't taken place at all.

N.B. Do not confuse *anscheinend* with *scheinbar* (see below).

bedingungslos * unconditionally / without condition

Der Absatz wird bedingungslos gestrichen.
The paragraph is (being) deleted unconditionally.

Die Warenprobe wird Ihnen bedingungslos zugeschickt.
The samples (of merchandise) are sent to you without obligation.

Die Soldaten mußten sich bedingungslos ergeben.
The soldiers had to surrender unconditionally.

N.B. Do not confuse *bedingungslos* and *unbedingt* (see below).

besonders especially

Die Prüfungsergebnisse sind in diesem Jahr besonders gut ausgefallen.
The exam results have turned out to be especially good this year.

buchstäblich * literally

Er war buchstäblich nur mit dem, was er auf dem Leibe trug, über die Grenze gekommen.
He had come across the border with literally just the shirt on his back.

(an)dauernd * always / the whole time / permanently

Die Leitung war (an)dauernd besetzt.
The line was continuously engaged. (see also *ständig*)

eilends < archaic, biblical > hurriedly

Die Hirten kamen eilends herbei.
The shepherds hurried hither.

*es **eilig*** * *haben (in Eile sein)* to be in a hurry

Ich habe es eilig. I am in a hurry.

Sie ging eilig die Straße entlang.
She hurried along the street.

eindeutig * clearly / unambiguously

Das konnte eindeutig nachgewiesen werden.
This could be unambiguously proven / demonstrated. / This is demonstrably true.

einzigartig * uniquely

Die Vorstellung war einzigartig schön.
The performance was extraordinarily beautiful.

endgültig * definitely / definitively (literally: valid in the end)

Er sagte ihr, daß es endgültig aus ist zwischen ihnen.
He told her that their affair was over once and for all.

entschieden * decidely / resolutely

Das geht entschieden zu weit!
That is going much / far too far!

enttäuschend * disappointingly

Die Zeugnisse waren enttäuschend schlecht ausgefallen.
The (school) reports had turned out to be disappointingly poor / bad.

mit / ohne Erfolg successfully / unsuccessfully

Der Student hat an dem Seminar mit Erfolg teilgenommen.
The student has successfully participated in the seminar.

eventuell * [FA] maybe

Die Ausgrabungsarbeiten könnten eventuell schon im nächsten Jahr beendet sein.
The excavations might possibly be finished by / as soon as next year.

früh* early

Man soll die Tulpenzwiebeln nicht zu früh stecken.
One should not plant tulip bulbs too early.

gegebenenfalls if necessary / should the occasion arise / if applicable

Diesen Absatz könnte man gegebenenfalls streichen.
This paragraph could be deleted if necessary / need be.

gegenwärtig* at present

Dafür sind gegenwärtig keine Änderungen vorgesehen.
At present no alterations to this are envisaged.

gelegentlich* occasionally / eventually

Note the subtle difference between these two examples:

Er kommt gelegentlich bei mir vorbei.
He drops in every now and again. (i.e. occasionally)

Ich werde mich gelegentlich wieder bei Ihnen melden.
I will get in touch with you sometime. (i.e. when the occasion arises)

An unambiguous alternative for the second example would be:

Ich werde mich <u>bei Gelegenheit</u> wieder bei Ihnen melden.
I will get in touch with you sometime.

gerne with pleasure

Das mache ich sehr gerne. I like doing that.

(For a detailed explanation of the use of *gerne*, see section 81.)

gewissermaßen as it were / to a certain extent / so to speak (adverb expressing uncertainty or used to camouflage something)

Er hat gewissermaßen mit seinem Leben gespielt.
He risked his life. (literally: he played with his life, so to speak)

Er hat den Aufsatz gewissermaßen ohne fremde Hilfe geschrieben.
He wrote the essay almost without help from others.

N.B. *gewiß* means 'certainly':

Er hat gewiß recht. He is certainly right.

gewöhnlich* usually

Er geht gewöhnlich um sieben Uhr aus dem Haus.
He usually leaves the house at 7 a.m.

N.B. *gewöhnlich* as an adjective = 'ordinary', 'common'.

heimlich* secretly

Er hatte ihr heimlich das Puppenhaus gebaut
He had built the doll's house for her in secret.

N.B. *unheimlich* is not the opposite of *heimlich*. Its original meaning is 'uncanny / unfamiliar'. For colloquial use see subsection (c) below.

hoffentlich hopefully / let's hope so

Hoffentlich geht es dir jetzt besser. I do hope you are better now.

in Kürze shortly

Die neue Ausgabe wird in Kürze erscheinen.
The new edition will appear shortly / in the near future.

N.B. *kürzlich* means 'recently' (see section 138a).

innerhalb within / inside

Die Bücher müssen innerhalb von vierzehn Tagen zurückgegeben werden.
The books must be returned within two weeks.

insbesondere (im Besonderen) especially < formal >

Bei der Durchführung des Unterrichts gelten die gleichen Grundsätze, insbesondere das Züchtigungsverbot < officialese >
For classroom management the same principles apply, especially the ban on corporal punishment.

N.B. For less formal purposes use *besonders* (see above).

inzwischen in the meantime / by now

Inzwischen haben die Friedensverhandlungen stattgefunden.
In the meantime the peace negotiations have taken place.

keinesfalls on no account / in no case / no way / under no circumstances (associated with occasion)

Man sollte es keinesfalls unterlassen, dem Gegner zuzuhören.
Under no circumstances should one fail to listen to the opponent.

keineswegs by no means / in no way (associated with manner)

Sein Einfluß darf keineswegs unterschätzt werden.
His influence must in no way be underestimated.

N.B. *keinesfalls* and *keineswegs* are used interchangeably, but there are subtle differences, as the examples show.

kurzerhand without further ado

Sie hatte ihn kurzerhand vor die Tür gesetzt.
She had unceremoniously thrown him out.

meinetwegen for my sake

Meinetwegen brauchst du die Heizung nicht höher zu stellen.
You need not turn up the heating for my sake.

(See section (c) below for the colloquial meaning of *meinetwegen*.)

meistens usually / most of the time

Meine Eltern gehen meistens spät ins Bett.
My parents usually go to bed late.

möglichst as possible

Bitte schicken Sie uns Ihre Antwort möglichst bald zu.
Please send us your answer as soon as possible.

pünktlich* promptly / on time

Das Konzert beginnt pünktlich wie angesagt.
The concert starts promptly as advertised.

scheinbar* seemingly / apparently (but not really)

Der Kunde wollte nur scheinbar bezahlen; an der Kasse bedrohte er die Verkäuferin dann mit einer Pistole.
The customer only made as if to pay; then at the checkout he threatened the assistant with a gun.

N.B. Do not confuse *scheinbar* with *anscheinend* (see above).

sicher* (1) surely / certainly

Sicher hat er sie nach Hause gebracht.
Surely he has taken her home.

sicher * (2) safely

Er hat sie sicher nach Hause gebracht.
He took her home safely.

sicherlich certainly (slightly more formal than *sicher*)

Das war sicherlich nicht meine Absicht.
That was certainly not my intention.

spätestens at the latest < formal >

Das Manuskript ist bis spätestens Ende März abzugeben.
The manuscript has to be delivered by the end of March at the latest.

ständig * permanently / constantly (interchangeable with *dauernd*)

Mußt du denn ständig an mir herumnörgeln? < informal >
Do you really have to nag me all the time?

stetig * steadily / at a constant rate / continuously < formal >

Die Ausgaben nahmen stetig zu.
The expenses increased at a constant rate.

N.B. Compare the meaning of *stets* in subsection (a) above.

täglich * daily

Dusch dich täglich warm und kalt, so wirst du hundert Jahre alt.
Daily showers warm and cold will leave you healthy when you're old.

(See also *werktäglich* below)

umständlich * clumsily / in a roundabout way

Er öffnete den Koffer umständlich.
He clumsily opened the suitcase.

Sie drückt sich oft sehr umständlich aus.
She often expresses herself in a very long-winded way.

N.B. Note the different meaning of *unter Umständen*.

unter Umständen possibly

Das könnte man unter Umständen auch mit der Maschine nähen.
This could also possibly be sewn by machine.

unbedingt* absolutely / whatever happens / definitely

Der Brief muß unbedingt noch heute geschrieben werden.
The letter must definitely be written today (whatever happens).

N.B. Do not confuse *unbedingt* and *bedingungslos* (see above).

urheberrechtlich* by / under copyright

Der Text ist urheberrechtlich geschützt.
The text is protected by copyright.

völlig* completely / wholly

Dieser Kommentar ist völlig irrelevant.
This comment is completely irrelevant.

werktäglich on working days / weekdays

Die FAZ (Frankfurter Allgemeine Zeitung) erscheint werktäglich.
The *FAZ* comes out every working day (including Saturdays).

wirklich* really

Der Abend bei Euch war wirklich schön.
The evening with you was really nice.

ziemlich* rather / quite

Das war eine ziemlich aufregende Geschichte.
That was a rather exciting story.

zugegebenermaßen admittedly < formal >

Ich habe zugegebenermaßen vergessen, ihn zu benachrichtigen.
Admittedly, I forgot to let him know / inform him.

zunehmend* increasingly

Die Lage an der Börse stabilisiert sich zunehmend.
The situation on the stock market is becoming increasingly stable.

Dem Patienten geht es zunehmend besser.
The patient is getting better all the time.

(c) Adverbs used mainly in colloquial German

blöderweise stupidly

Ich habe die Unterlagen blöderweise im Auto liegenlassen.
Stupidly I left the papers / documents in the car.

brennend* literally: with burning (desire)

Ich wüßte ja brennend gern, ob die beiden ein Verhältnis haben.
I am dying to know if those two are having an affair.

Er würde brennend gern nach Indien reisen, aber . . .
He would absolutely / desperately love to travel to India, but . . .

echt* really / truly (often used as a filler, see section 136)

Es tut mir echt leid.
I am really / ever so sorry.

eigentlich* literally: authentically / essentially (now often reduced to a mere filler: really; cf. pp.116–17)

Was willst du denn eigentlich hier?
What do you want here, then?

Eigentlich hast du hier gar nichts verloren.
You have no business to be here, really.

einfach* simply / just

Geh' doch einfach 'rein.
Just go in. / Go right in.

ganz* rather / quite / completly / absolutely / totally (just as with English 'quite', the nuance depends on intonation and context)

Er kann das schon ganz gut. He can (do) that quite well already.

Das finde ich ganz toll! I find that absolutely great!

Das ist mir ganz egal. It's all the same to me.

Das ist mir ganz recht. That's quite all right by me.

Das habe ich ganz vergessen. I completely forgot about that.

N.B. *ganz* can be intensified with *und gar*:

Das ist ganz und gar gelogen.
That is a complete and utter lie.

meinetwegen as far as I am concerned / if you like

Meinetwegen kannst du dir den Schnupfen holen.
You can catch cold for all I care.

N.B. In colloquial usage *meinetwegen* suggests that the speaker doesn't care either way, but compare the meaning given in subsection (b) above.

mords

See section 136.

ruhig * literally: quietly, calmly

Hier kann man ruhig schlafen.
You can sleep quietly / peacefully here.

N.B. *ruhig* also implies peace of mind;

Das kannst du ihr ruhig schenken.
You can give that to her (as a present) by all means / no problem.

Man kann ihm das ruhig ganz offen sagen.
There's no harm in telling him face to face.

unheimlich * incredibly / unbelievably

Ich finde diese CD unheimlich gut.
I find this CD incredibly good.

The original meaning of *unheimlich* is 'strange' or 'eerie' (see subsection (b) above) but used colloquially it intensifies the adjective that follows.

136 Slang and 'youth' language

Popular expressions and slang are a tricky area for foreign speakers for several reasons. They may not be familiar with this register of language from their more formal studies – and in any case slang changes quite quickly. Some of the popular idioms of the late 1960s may not be understood by today's teenagers. Similarily, the youth of today use a vocabulary with their peers that is incomprehensible to their elders. The use of popular expressions, and more particularly slang and youth language, is often indicative of a sense of group identity (peer groups at school, close colleagues at work, friends), and foreign speakers therefore need to be sure they are choosing an appropriate context in which to display their varied vocabulary. Also, there are quite often sexual undertones in these expressions. The foreign speaker may not be aware of them and may not wish to imply them.

In short, it is certainly helpful to recognize all the expressions listed below, but if in doubt stick to the more formal equivalents in spoken language. This is far more *salonfähig* (socially acceptable, literally: 'capable of being used in the drawing room'), as the Germans would say.

Expressions which range from the slightly vulgar to those distinctly liable to shock some people are marked by **!** or **!!**. Youth language is flagged as such and in some instances the areas from which a term originates (psychology, computer science, anglicisms) is given.

The popular terms have been translated, and an attempt has been made to use the same register in the English as in the German.

POPULAR TERM	MORE FORMAL EQUIVALENT
etwas ab◊blocken to block something	*verhindern*
etwas ab◊fackeln to flare / burn off something	*nieder◊brennen**
*auf jemanden ab◊fahren** < youth > to be mad about / attracted by someone	*gut miteinander aus◊kommen**
*auf etwas ab◊fahren ** < youth > to be mad about something	*sich für etwas begeistern*
ab◊hauen to beat it *Hau ab!* Get lost!	*verschwinden* / weg◊laufen**
*ab◊laufen** to go / pass off	*vor sich gehen**
ab◊räumen to clear away (eat) everything (e.g. at a buffet) / eat everything in sight	*tabula rasa machen*
ab◊schlaffen < youth > to wilt / sag (also has sexual connotation) *Er ist total abgeschlafft.* He's lost his vigour. / He's drained.	*schlaff / müde werden**

POPULAR TERM	MORE FORMAL EQUIVALENT
jemanden ab◊schleppen < youth > to drag someone off / get off with someone / pick someone up	*mit jemandem eine (nichtsbedeutende) Affaire beginnen**
sich etwas ab◊schminken to get something out of one's head *Das kannst du dir abschminken.* You can forget that.	*sich etwas aus dem Kopf schlagen**
ab◊schnallen < youth > to be absolutely flabbergasted / gobsmacked *Da schnallste* (for *schnallst du*) *aber ab.* You'll be gobsmacked / so flabbergasted.	*verblüfft / überrascht sein*
*ab◊treten** < youth > to make one's exit / snuff it	*den Ort verlassen* / sterben**
*eine heisse Schau / Show ab◊ziehen** to show off, put on a show	*an◊geben**
sich vom Acker machen to leave the scene	*ab◊hauen*
ackern to slog one's guts out / work like mad / work like hell	*hart arbeiten*
zu viel Action (anglicism) too much fuss / heavy	*zu viel los / zu laut / ungemütlich*
das Allerletzte the absolute limit / the pits	*das Unmögliche*
die / meine Alten my folks	*die / meine Eltern*
das faßt mich an that concerns me / grabs me	*das bedeutet mir etwas / berührt mich*
angesagt on the agenda / to be happening	*auf der Tagesordnung / aktuell / in Mode*
sich mit jemandem an◊legen to pick an argument with someone	*mit jemandem Streit an◊fangen**

POPULAR TERM	MORE FORMAL EQUIVALENT
etwas an◊leiern to get something rolling	*etwas in Gang bringen**
jemanden an◊machen < youth > to chat someone up / give someone a come-on	*Kontakte versuchen / intensiv flirten*
Das macht mich an. That turns me on.	
die Anmache chatting up / cruising / the come-on	*der Kontaktversuch*
an◊tanzen to turn up / show (up)	*an◊kommen**
Und dann tanzt du endlich an und willst warmes Essen. And then you finally show up and expect a warm meal.	
die Asche < youth > dough / dosh	*das Geld*
ätzend < youth > ace / brilliant / wicked grotty / shitty	(literally: *unter die Haut gehend*) *toll* *schrecklich / abstoßend*
etwas auf◊arbeiten (psychology) to look back on and reappraise something	*Vergangenes und Verdrängtes neu untersuchen*♦
*eine Frau auf◊reißen** to pick up a woman	*mit einer Frau Kontakte anknüpfen / intensiv flirten*
(total) aus◊flippen to freak out	*über◊schnappen*
ausgelutscht worn out	*verbraucht* (especially with reference to cars and women)
es rastet bei jemandem aus something snapped in someone / someone's flipped	*jemand regt sich furchtbar auf*
der Balg(¨er) kid / brat (also affectionate)	*der Nachwuchs*
beknackt mad / crazy	*verrückt / blöde*
ein beknackter Typ a berk / jerk / dickhead	
bescheuert barmy / nuts	*dumm / blöde*

POPULAR TERM	MORE FORMAL EQUIVALENT
der / das Betonsilo tower block / high-rise	*das Hochhaus*
die Beziehungskiste(n) (psychology) relationship / emotional entanglement	*die Beziehung*
die Zweierkiste (close / steady) partnership	
die heiße / dufte Biene bird / piece of skirt	*süßes Mädchen*
die Birne nut / head / skull	*der Kopf*
etwas blicken to see the point / to twig	*etwas verstehen**
der Bock < youth > desire	*die Lust*
Null Bock haben auf (+ acc.) not to fancy something at all	*überhaupt keine Lust haben auf*
einen Brass haben < youth > to be hopping mad	*eine Wut / einen Zorn haben*
braun Nazi / fascist	*faschistisch*
brettern to speed along	*schnell (mit dem Auto, Rad) fahren**
das bringt es voll* < youth > that's brilliant / that's lush / it's the best	*es lohnt sich sehr / das ist einfach toll*
das bringt es überhaupt nicht (there is) no point / nothing in it	*es lohnt sich nicht* *das ist langweilig / doof*
die Bullen (pl.) cops	*Polizisten*
!! *mit jemandem bumsen* to have it off with someone / to screw someone	*Geschlechtsverkehr haben*
bunkern < youth > to stash away	*heimlich sparen / an◊sammeln*

POPULAR TERM	MORE FORMAL EQUIVALENT
der Chaot disorganized person / a daisy / slob	*spontaner / unberechenbarer Mensch*
checken (anglicism) to check / twig *Er hat das noch nicht ganz gecheckt.* He hasn't quite got it yet.	*prüfen / kontrollieren*
der Clinch < youth > conflict / scrap *mit jemandem im Clinch liegen* to be locked in dispute with someone	*der Nahkampf*
auf dem falschen Dampfer sein to be barking up the wrong tree *Da bist du aber auf dem falschen Dampfer.* You've got it completely wrong.	*sich völlig irren*
die Demo demo(nstration) *auf der Demo* on the demo	*die Demonstration*
zu dicke too much	*zu übertrieben*
von etwas dicke genug haben to have had a bellyful of something	*etwas gründlich satt haben*
etwas drauf◊haben to be very capable / to show talent / to have what it takes	*im Besitz einer Fähigkeit sein*
*drauf◊sitzen** to sit on something	*belagern / nicht her◊geben wollen**
den Durchblick haben to know what's happening	*etwas verstehen* / Einsicht haben*
durch◊drehen to crack up / go to pieces	*einen Nervenzusammenbruch haben*
'rum◊düsen to dash about	*schnell herum◊fahren**
echt (adverb) < youth > really / absolutely (intensifies the adjective that follows)	*wirklich*

POPULAR TERM	MORE FORMAL EQUIVALENT
Das ist echt gut / blöd. That is really good / stupid.	
eh anyway, in any case *Das weiß man doch eh / eh schon.* That's known anyway.	*sowieso*
die Fehlanzeige < youth > no chance / nil return / anti-climax / wash out / non-event *Ich hatte mich so auf das Fest gefreut, aber es war eine totale Fehlanzeige.* I had been really looking forward to the party, but it was a complete non-event / anti-climax.	*das Mißlingen, das Pech*
*das Flattern bekommen** < youth > to get the jitters / to get your knees knocking	*Angst bekommen*
die Flatter machen to beat it ! *Mach die Flatter!* Beat it / Piss off!	*weg◊laufen**
sich flätzen to loll about / bum around	*herum◊liegen**
der Flop (anglicism) flop	*der Mißerfolg*
die Fluppe(n) fag / ciggy	*die Zigarette*
der Frust (anglicism) frustration / aggro *Seine Arbeit war der absolute Frust.* His work was a real drag.	*der Ärger / die Frustration*
gefrustet < youth > pissed off / frustrated	*frustriert*
der Fummel < youth > gear / drag / rags	*die Kleidung*
! *fummeln* to pet / fondle / grope / feel up	*Petting machen / an jemandem herumtätscheln*

POPULAR TERM	MORE FORMAL EQUIVALENT
garantiert	*bestimmt*
dead certain	
Das gefällt dir garantiert.	
This is bound to please you.	
ist gebongt < youth >	*geht* klar / geht in Ordnung*
fine / okay / right on	
! *geil* < youth >	
was: randy / horny	was: *lüstern / triebhaft*
now: fabulously	now: *faszinierend / toll, super / das Non plus ultra*
! *super echt geilo*	
brilliant / magic	
! *irre geil*	
bloody brilliant / wicked	
das Gelaber	*das Geschwätz*
rabbiting, babbling on	
was gelaufen ist	*was passiert ist*
what has happened	
Die Sache ist gelaufen. It's over and done with.	
gelinkt < youth >	*'reingelegt*
cheated / taken for a ride	
Man hat dich gelinkt. You've been tricked / done.	
gestreßt	*überarbeitet*
harassed / overworked / stressed up	
Ich bin wieder mal total gestreßt.	
I'm completely harassed / exhausted again.	
das große Gewese	*großer Aufruhr*
fuss	
ein großes Gewese um etwas machen	
to kick up a great fuss / make a big scene about something	
die Glotze (1)	*der Fernseher*
(goggle-)box / telly	
vor der Glotze hocken	*vor dem Fernseher sitzen*
to sit in front of the box	

POPULAR TERM	MORE FORMAL EQUIVALENT
die Glotze (2) nut	*der Kopf*
einen an die Glotze kriegen to receive a blow / to get licked / take a beating	*etwas an den Kopf bekommen*
*sich einen greifen** to sort someone out (possibly give him / her a beating)	*sich jemanden schnappen*
einen Hau haben to have a screw loose	*verrückt sein*
ganz schön heavy (anglicism) quite heavy / tough	*schwierig / problematisch*
heiß hot / sexy	*schön / begeisternd*
heiß sein auf etwas to be keen on something	*auf etwas scharf sein*
jemanden heiß◊machen to turn someone on	*jemanden reizen*
*etwas hin◊bringen** to manage something	*etwas fertig◊bringen**
der Hintern behind / bottom	*das Hinterteil*
*jemanden vom Hocker reißen** to knock someone for six / to throw someone off balance	*jemanden schockieren / begeistern / umwerfen**
! *(total) tote Hose* nothing doing / complete non-event	*nichts los / absoluter Mißerfolg*
instandbesetzen to occupy and renovate houses (illegally) / to squat	*heruntergekommene Häuser besetzen und renovieren*
irre terrific / cool	*toll / schön / fantastisch*
! *die Kacke* shit	literally: *der Kot*; as a swear-word: *Mist!* (m.)
Die Kacke ist am Dampfen. There'll be hell to pay.	*Die Geduld ist zu Ende und es gibt Streit / Schläge / große Probleme.*

POPULAR TERM	MORE FORMAL EQUIVALENT
etwas kapieren to get / understand / twig something	*etwas verstehen*
Das geht mir auf den Keks. That gets up my nose.	*Das geht* mir auf die Nerven.*
So ein Keks. What a lot of rubbish.	*So ein Quatsch.*
Kies (m.) *(an den Füßen) haben* to have bread / dough / the dosh	*Geld haben*
die Kippe fag / ciggy / smoke	*die Zigarette*
die Klapse (Klapsmühle) loony bin	*geschlossene Psychiatrie*
in der Klapse landen to end up in the loony bin	*in die geschlossene Psychiatrie kommen*
etwas klar◊kriegen to get something going / cope / pull something off	*etwas fertig◊bringen**
knallhart very tough / as hard as nails	*konsequent / entschieden*
der Knallkopf (stupid) berk / wanker	*blöder / verrückter Mensch*
die Knete dough / dosh	*das Geld*
knutschen neck / snog / smooch	*schmusen*
der Körnerfresser / Körnerfreak muesli freak / rabbit-food eater / veggie (literally: grain-eater)	*Mensch, der sich nur mit Gesundheitskost ernährt*
Kohldampf (m.) *schieben / haben* to be ravenously hungry	*Hunger haben**
die Kohle dosh / dough	*das Geld*

POPULAR TERM	MORE FORMAL EQUIVALENT
der Kopfarbeiter intellectual / white-collar worker	*der Intellektuelle*
der Kumpel pal / buddy / mate	*der Kamerad*
der Kurze the little one / junior	*das Kind / der Kleine / der Jüngste*
labern to rabbit / babble on	*(dumm) daher◊reden*
groß den Larry machen to show off	*sich auf◊regen / sich wichtig machen*
die Latschen (pl.) (worn-out) shoes	*die Schuhe*
aus den Latschen kippen to keel over	*umfallen / sehr überrascht sein*
latschen to trudge / slouch	*laufen**
locker without trouble / problem *Das kannst du doch locker.* You can do that no problem.	*unbesorgt*
logo of course *Ist doch logo!* You bet!	*logisch / klar / selbstverständlich* *Ist doch klar.*
der Macker < youth > guy / bloke / macho	*junger Mann* (pejorative)
mords < youth – now outdated > terrific, tremendous	*ungeheuer*
mosern to gripe / go on about / moan *Du findest aber auch an allem etwas zu mosern.* You always manage to find something to moan about.	*sich beschweren / maulen*
(herum) motzen to grouch / bellyache	*sich über alles beschweren* (stronger than *mosern*)
die Mücke machen to push off	*verschwinden**

POPULAR TERM	MORE FORMAL EQUIVALENT
jemanden naß◊machen < youth > to trounce someone / turn someone on to something	*jemanden auf etwas scharf machen*
jemanden nerven to get on someone's nerves	*jemandem auf die Nerven gehen**
der Ossi East German (still used after unification)	*der Ostdeutsche*
pennen to kip / doss down	*schlafen**
ein◊pennen to fall asleep	*ein◊schlafen**
! *mit jemandem pennen* to sleep with someone	*mit jemandem schlafen*
bei jemandem pennen to spend the night at someone's place	*bei jemandem übernachten* ♦
etwas verpennen to oversleep / forget something	*etwas verschlafen**
die People (anglicism) people	*die Leute*
die Pofe machen < youth > to kip / snooze	*schlafen**
*ein falsches Programm ab◊fahren** (computing; figurative) to run the wrong programme	*auf dem falschen Weg sein*
der Programmabsturz (computing; figurative) programme crash / breakdown	*das Chaos / der Zusammenbruch*
auf den Putz hauen to make something happen	*etwas los◊machen*
quasseln to chatter / waffle	*reden* (pejorative)
etwas raffen to get something / to twig	*etwas verstehen**

POPULAR TERM	MORE FORMAL EQUIVALENT
mit etwas / jemandem zusammen◊rasseln to smash into something / to have an argument with someone	*zusammen◊stoßen**
relaxen (anglicism) to relax	*sich entspannen*
relaxed laid back	*entspannt*
*rum◊hängen** to hang about	nichts tun*, *sich gehen lassen**
sauer sein auf (+ acc.) to be cross with	*beleidigt / verärgert sein**
die Scene the scene / the in-crowd	*die Gruppe der Insider*
die alte Schachtel the old bag / cow	*die (alte) Frau* (pejorative)
! *der Scheiß* shit / crap	literally: *der Kot*; here: *der Quatsch / der Unsinn*
! *wegen jedem Scheiß* for every bloody nuisance *Sie rennt wegen jedem Scheiß zum Arzt.* She runs to her doctor for every bloody little thing.	*wegen jeder Kleinigkeit*
! *Das ist mir scheißegal.* I don't give a shit / damn.	*Das ist mir völlig egal.*
! *die Scheiße* shit / crap	literally: *der Kot*; as a swear-word: *Mist!* (m.)
*etwas 'rüber◊schießen** to pass / chuck something *Schieß mal ne Fluppe 'rüber!* Toss / chuck a fag over! / Give us a ciggy!	*etwas herüber◊reichen* *Gib mir eine Zigarette!*
der Schlamassel mess *Jetzt haben wir den Schlamassel.* A real mess we're in now.	*das Chaos, der Ärger*
! *jemanden voll◊schleimen* to arse-lick someone / lick someone's boots	*jemandem sehr schmeicheln*

POPULAR TERM	MORE FORMAL EQUIVALENT
sich (dat.) *etwas schnappen* to grab / snatch something	*etwas ergreifen**
etwas schnallen to twig	*verstehen**, *begreifen**
der Schwachsinn rubbish / nonsense	*der Blödsinn*
Das ist doch Schwachsinn! But that's complete nonsense / crap.	
Sense (f.) end / finish / that's it (literally: scythe)	*Ende, Schluß*
die große Sense final disaster	*der Atomkrieg*
Jetzt ist Sense. This really is (the end of) it!	
Mach mal Sense. Shut up.	*Mach mal einen Punkt.*
Softie (m.) (anglicism) wimp / softy	*das Gegenteil von Macho*
Spitze brill	*das Beste*
Das ist einsame Spitze. That is absolutely brill.	*Das ist das Beste.*
der Sproß offspring	*der Nachwuchs / der Nachkomme*
stark < youth > great / fantastic	*bewundernswert / klasse / toll*
echt unheimlich stark really incredibly fantastic / bloody brilliant	
jemandem etwas stecken to let someone know something / give someone a piece of one's mind	*jemandem etwas bei◊bringen** / *die Meinung sagen*
der Stift apprentice	*der Lehrling*
! *es stinkt* * *mir* I'm fed up (to the back teeth)	*ich habe es genug / es ärgert mich*
! *stinklangweilig* deadly boring	*unerträglich langweilig*

POPULAR TERM	MORE FORMAL EQUIVALENT
stressig stressful	*anstrengend*
die Stütze the dole	*staatliche Unterstützung*
von der Stütze leben to live on the dole	
nicht mehr richtig ticken to be off one's rocker / trolley	*nicht mehr richtig funktionieren*
tierisch < youth > really	*furchtbar*
tierisch gut incredibly good	*unheimlich gut*
Das hat tierisch wehgetan. That hurt excruciatingly.	*Das hat furchtbar / scheußlich wehgetan.*
los◊tigern to walk off	*los◊ziehen* / los◊gehen**
total (filler word) totally / really	*völlig / gänzlich*
die Tussi (Tussy) female / bird	*die Frau / das Mädchen* (pejorative)
So 'ne Tussi! stupid chick / bitch!	*So ein (blödes) Weib!*
verrammelt barricaded	*verschlossen*
*verschütt◊gehen** to do a vanishing trick / to go for a burton / do a disappearing act	*in Vergessenheit geraten* / verloren gehen**
versiffen to go to pot / become grotty	*versacken / unter◊gehen* / verwahrlosen*
! *vögeln* to screw	*Geschlechtsverkehr haben**
wahnsinnig fantastic / terrific / incredible	*ungeheuer*
Er hat sich wahnsinnig gefreut. He was incredibly pleased.	
die WG (pronounced *WehGeh*) communal living / group sharing a house / flat	*die Wohngemeinschaft*

POPULAR TERM	MORE FORMAL EQUIVALENT
weg vom Fenster sein to be right out of it	*nichts mehr zu sagen haben / keinen Einfluß mehr haben*
der Wessi West German (still used after unification)	*der Westdeutsche*
*jemandem etwas wollen** to want to hurt someone *Der will mir was.* He wants to hurt me.	*jemandem Böses wünschen*
der Zauber fuss / palaver	*der Aufwand*
Was soll der ganze Zauber? What's all this fuss (in aid of)?	*Wozu der ganze Aufwand?*
der ZIVI (*der Zivildienstleistende*) person carrying out community service (as alternative to military service)	*der Ersatzdienstleistende*
der Zoff	*der Ärger*
Zoff machen to pick an argument / row	*Ärger machen*
zu sein (emphasis on *zu*) to be tanked up / plastered / pissed	*betrunken sein*

137 Key synonyms

Both in written and in spoken German, a wide vocabulary is a mark of good style. For that reason, it is useful to find synonyms for over-used words. In addition, English learners of German should note that in formal style, e.g. reports, essays, newspaper articles, *haben*, *sagen* and other common verbs simply do not occur as frequently as do 'to have' and 'to say' (etc.) in English. If you look closely at the *Frankfurter Allgemeine Zeitung*, for example, you will find German has a wealth of verbs which are more precise and elegant, whereas English might use other parts of speech to give comparable variety. Cultivating some of the synonyms below will help you move away from 'translationese' to 'real' German. Included here, in alphabetical order, are the ten words which are most frequently over-used by students. Go through all the synonyms for each word so that you can get a feel for the fine distinctions and areas of overlap. Always try to be as precise as you can.

bekommen [FA] to get / obtain / receive

★ N.B. *bekommen* (or any of the following substitutes) requires the accusative for the thing received, but the recipient is in the nominative:

Er bekam einen Legobausatz zum Geburtstag.
He had / got a Lego set for his birthday.

erhalten* to receive

Er erhielt den Friedensnobelpreis.
He received the Nobel Peace Prize.

sich (dat.) *etwas* ***ergattern*** < coll. > to get hold of something

Die Menschen rannten immer wieder hin, um sich Mauerteile zu ergattern.
The people kept running there trying to grab / get hold of pieces of the (Berlin) Wall.

sich (dat.) *etwas* ***aus◊leihen / borgen*** to borrow

Sie hatte sich von der Stadtbücherei Sprachkassetten ausgeliehen.
She had borrowed language cassettes from the (town) library.

Darf ich mir bitte deinen Rechner borgen?
May I borrow your calculator, please?

kriegen < coll. > to get

Wenn du nicht brav [FA] *bist, kriegst du kein Eis.*
If you don't behave, you won't get an ice cream.

Ich kriege Angst. < coll. >
I'm getting afraid / scared.

empfangen* to receive

Der Schriftsteller hatte endlich seinen Vorschuß empfangen.
The author had finally received his advance.

entgegen◊nehmen* to take / receive

Die Gastgeberin nahm den Blumenstrauß lächelnd entgegen.
The hostess took the bouquet of flowers with a smile.

in Empfang nehmen* < formal > to receive / accept

Die Pakete werden an der Pforte in Empfang genommen.
The parcels will be accepted / received at the porter's lodge.

sich (dat.) (*eine Krankheit*) ***zu◊ziehen**** < formal >

to contract (a disease)

Sie hatte sich bei ihrem Chinaaufenthalt eine Viruskrankheit zugezogen.
She had contracted a virus during her stay in China.

etwas ***an sich*** (acc.) ***nehmen**** to pick up / to take

Er nahm die Aktienpapiere schnell an sich.
He quickly picked up the share certificates.

etwas ***an◊nehmen**** to accept / receive

Sie nahm die Spende dankend an.
She gratefully received the donation.

etwas something

irgendetwas something (but I don't know what)

Ich möchte gerne irgendetwas Hübsches kaufen.
I would like to buy something pretty (but have no idea what).

eine Kleinigkeit a little something

Ich möchte meinem Mann eine Kleinigkeit zum Geburtstag schenken.
I would like to give my husband a little something for his birthday.

Kann man hier eine Kleinigkeit essen?
Can one get a snack / bite to eat here?

ein Anliegen a concern

Ich würde gerne ein Anliegen mit dir besprechen.
I would like to discuss with you something that concerns me.

fahren to go / travel

Fahren is used to indicate all modes of travel except *zu Fuß gehen* (to go on foot) and *mit dem Flugzeug fliegen* (to fly / go by plane). *Mit dem Flugzeug fahren* is very colloquial.

Fahren is followed by *mit*, e.g. *mit dem Bus*, *mit der U-Bahn* etc.

There are, however, a few alternatives to *fahren*:

einen Ausflug machen to take a trip (literally: to make an excursion)

Am Sonntag machen wir einen Ausflug in die Berge.
On Sunday we will take a trip into the mountains.

nehmen * to take

Wir nehmen den Zug nach Heidelberg.
We are taking the train to Heidelberg.

reisen to travel

Der Missionar ist nach Südamerika gereist.
The missionary travelled to South America.

eine (*See-*, *Schiffs-*, *Welt-* etc.) ***Reise machen / unternehmen*** ♦ *
to take a trip

Wenn ich im Toto gewinnen würde, könnte ich eine Weltreise unternehmen.
If I won the pools, I could go on a trip / round the world.

geben to give

Geben (or any of the following substitutes) takes the accusative for the thing given and the dative for the person receiving it (see section 55).

jemandem etwas ab◊schneiden* to cut off something for someone

Sie schnitt ihm ein Stück Brot ab.
She cut off a slice of bread for him.

an◊bieten* to offer

Der Gastgeber bietet zuerst der ältesten Dame ein Getränk an.
The host offers a drink first to the eldest lady.

jemandem etwas ***auf◊zwingen**** to force something onto someone

Lassen Sie sich bloß nichts aufzwingen.
(But) Don't let anything be forced on to you.

aus◊händigen to hand over

Er mußte dem Polizisten seinen Führerschein aushändigen.
He had to hand over his driving licence to the policeman.

jemandem etwas ***ein◊schöpfen*** to ladle something out (literally: in) for someone

Sie schöpfte ihm Suppe ein.
She ladled soup out for him.

jemandem etwas ***ein◊gießen**** to pour something out (literally: in) for someone

Bitte gießen Sie mir nur wenig Wasser ein.
Please give (pour) me only a little water.

jemandem etwas **hinterlassen** ♦ * to bequeath something to someone

Mein Großvater hatte mir viele wertvolle Bücher hinterlassen.
My grandfather had bequeathed me many valuable books.

N.B. *etwas hinterlassen* can also mean 'to leave something behind'.

Der Verstorbene hinterläßt zwei kleine Kinder.
The deceased (man) leaves two small children.

jemandem etwas zum / zur . . . ***schenken*** to give someone something (as a gift) for . . .

Er schenkte ihr einen goldenen Ring zur Verlobung.
He gave her a gold ring for their engagement.

aus◊schenken to pour (out)

Sie schenkte ihm den neuen Wein aus.
She poured him new wine.

spenden to donate

Eigentlich sollte man öfter Blut spenden.
One really ought to give blood more often.

zur Verfügung stellen to make available

Die Direktion [FA] *stellte dem neuen Angestellten einen Computer zur Verfügung.*
The management made a computer available for the new employee.

überbringen ⧫ * to bring / deliver / convey

Der Bote überbrachte dem Feldherrn schlechte Nachrichten.
The messenger took bad news to the commander.

überreichen ⧫ to present

Er überreichte ihm den Europapokal.
He presented him with the European Cup.

verleihen* to confer

1991 wurde der Nobelpreis für Medizin an zwei deutsche Wissenschaftler verliehen.
In 1991 the Nobel Prize for Medicine was conferred on two German scientists.

jemandem etwas ***vererben*** to bequeath / leave something to someone

Die Millionärin hatte ihren Nachfahren ein großes Vermögen vererbt.
The millionairess had left a (huge) fortune to her descendants.

jemandem etwas ***zu◊schieben**** to push something to someone

Er schob seiner Frau das letzte Stück Fleisch zu.
He pushed the last piece of meat towards his wife.

Er wollte ihr die Schuld zuschieben.
He wanted to lay the blame on her.

reichen to pass something to someone

Bitte reichen Sie mir das Salz. < formal >
Please pass me the salt.

jemandem etwas zu◊stecken to slip something to someone

Die Tante Hilda steckte dem Kind einen Schokoladenriegel zu.
Aunt Hilda slipped the child a bar of chocolate.

Wir sollten ihm ein Trinkgeld zustecken.
We should give / slip him a tip.

haben to have

bestehen* aus to consist of

Das Ärztezentrum besteht aus mehreren Einzelpraxen.
The medical / health centre consists of several individual practices.

beherbergen to put up / shelter

Die Unterkunft kann bis zu hundert Wanderer beherbergen.
The accommodation can put up / take up to a hundred ramblers / hikers.

verfügen über (+ acc.) to have (at one's disposal)

Der Wintersportort verfügt über phantastische Pisten und Langlaufloipen.
The winter-sports resort has fantastic pistes and cross-country ski tracks.

umfassen ♦ to comprise

Die Kampfgruppe umfaßt mehr als 50 000 Personen.
The taskforce comprises more than 50,000 people.

rechnen mit to count on / expect

Experten rechnen mit einem Ausbruch der Epidemie in etwa drei Wochen.
Experts are expecting / predicting (literally: counting on) an outbreak of the epidemic in about three weeks' time.

sich erstrecken über (+ acc.) to extend across / over

Der Park erstreckt sich über mehrere hundert Quadratmeter.
The landscaped area / park covers (literally: extends across) several hundred square metres.

genießen* to enjoy

Der Hotelgast genießt eine herrliche Aussicht auf den Bodensee.
The hotel guest enjoys a beautiful view over Lake Constance.

bieten* to offer

Die Freizeitanlage bietet Tennisplätze, ein Freibad und einen Minigolfplatz.
The leisure complex offers tennis courts, an open-air swimming pool and a crazy-golf course.

es gibt* there is / there are

In London gibt es mindestens fünfzig Museen.
In London there are at least fifty museums.

beinhalten (regular) to contain

Das Buch beinhaltet drei Kapitel über die Evolution.
The book contains three chapters on evolution.

sich befinden* to be situated / located

Die Personalabteilung befindet sich im dritten Stock.
The personnel department is (located) on the third floor.

machen (1) to make / produce

backen* to bake

Meine Großmutter hat immer köstliche Apfelkuchen gebacken.
My grandmother used always to bake delicious apple cakes.

basteln to make things (with one's own hands)

Meine Tochter hat mir zu Weihnachten einen Kalender gebastelt
For Christmas my daughter made me a calendar.

her◊stellen to produce

Im Schwarzwald werden traditionelle Kuckucksuhren hergestellt.
Traditional cuckoo-clocks are made in the Black Forest.

produzieren to produce

Opel werden in Rüsselsheim und in Eisenach produziert.
Opel cars are produced in Rüsselsheim and in Eisenach.

zimmern to make (from wood)

Er hat mir einen Schrank aus Eiche gezimmert.
He made me a cupboard from / out of oak.

zu◊bereiten < formal > to prepare

Diese Köstlichkeit bereiten Sie folgendermaßen zu: . . .
Prepare this delicacy in the following manner / way: . . .

machen (2) to do

verbringen* to spend (time)

Womit hast du deine Ferien verbracht?
How did you spend (What did you do in) your holidays?

sich (dat.) ***die Zeit vertreiben**** to pass the time

Womit habt ihr euch gestern die Zeit vertrieben ?
How did you spend your time yesterday?

etwas ***unternehmen*** ⧫ * to do / undertake

Was kann man an einem Regentag unternehmen?
What can you do on a rainy day?

Die Lagerbestände sind veraltet, wir müssen etwas dagegen unternehmen.
The stock is out of date; we must do something about it.

tun* to do

Im Sommer haben wir im Büro viel zu tun.
In the summer there is a lot to do (to be done) in the office.

etwas ***an◊stellen*** to get into mischief (literally: to turn something on)

Man soll kleine Kinder nie alleine zu Hause lassen. Sie könnten etwas anstellen.
One should never leave small children alone in the house. They might get up to mischief.

verbrechen* to commit (a crime) / be up to something (jocular)

Wer hat denn das wieder verbrochen?
Who has been up to this again, then? / Who's responsible for this, then? / Whose doing is this then?

etwas ***fertig◊bringen**** to manage

Wie hast du denn das fertiggebracht?
How did you manage to do that?

das ***Problem****(e)* problem

schwierige Frage (f.) difficult question

Heute müssen wir uns mit der schwierigen Frage der deutschen Wiedervereinigung befassen.
Today we have to deal with the difficult question of German reunification.

verzwickte Angelegenheit *(f.)* complicated / involved matter

Die Unterschlagung von Steuerzahlungen ist eine verzwickte Angelegenheit.
The embezzlement of tax (payments) is a complicated matter.

Schwierigkeiten haben to have difficulties

Sie hatte mit der Erziehung ihres Jüngsten größte Schwierigkeiten.
She had the greatest difficulties in bringing up her youngest son.

hoffnungsloser Zustand (m.) hopeless condition / state

Der Verletzte befand sich in einem hoffnungslosen Zustand.
The injured person / The casualty was in a hopeless condition / state.

trauriger Rekord (m.) sad record

Die Bundesrepublik hat bei den Kinderunfällen einen traurigen Rekord.
The Federal Republic has a sad track record as far as children's accidents are concerned.

wunder / schwacher Punkt (m.) sore / weak point

Ist die Vergangenheitsbewältigung immer noch ein wunder Punkt bei den Deutschen?
Is 'coming to terms with the past' still a sore point for the Germans?

große Erschwernis (f.) great difficulty

Das Reisen im Mittelalter war mit großen Erschwernissen verbunden.
Travelling in the Middle Ages involved great difficulty.

umstrittenes Thema (n.) disputed / controversial topic

Die Anerkennung von Asylbewerbern ist ein äußerst umstrittenes Thema.
The recognition of persons seeking asylum is an extremely controversial topic.

sagen to say

N.B. For reported speech the subjunctive is usually used, see section 37.

äußern to express

Er äußerte größtes Mißfallen über die schlechten Bauarbeiten.
He expressed (his) misgivings about the bad building works.

sich äußern zu to express oneself concerning / to comment on

Sie äußerte sich nicht zu den Beschuldigungen.
She did not comment on / She didn't say anything about the accusations.

an◊geben* to state

Die Befragten gaben mehrere Daten zu ihrem Konsumverhalten an.
Those interviewed stated / gave several facts / data about their consumer habits.

nach Angaben (+ gen.) according to

Nach Angaben der Polizei war keine Schußwaffe aufzufinden.
According to the police report / statement no firearm could / was to be found.

an◊kündigen to announce

Das hessische Innenministerium hat für morgen eine Stellungnahme angekündigt.
The Hesse Ministry of the Interior announced / scheduled a statement for tomorrow.

sich *für etwas* (acc.) ***aus◊sprechen**** to express oneself in favour of something

Der Rektor sprach sich für eine Erweiterung der Grundschule aus.
The headmaster expressed himself in favour / in support of an extension to the primary school.

behaupten to maintain (often associated with claiming something that is not true)

Der Geisterfahrer behauptete, er habe keinen Führerschein bei sich.
The driver on the wrong side of the carriageway (literally: the 'ghost driver') claimed to have no driving licence on him.

bemerken / an◊merken zu to mention / comment

Zu Punkt sieben der Tagesordnung möchte ich gern folgendes bemerken / anmerken.
I would like to make the following remarks on point seven of the agenda.

bemerken to remark / comment

'Eine schlechte Regie', bemerkte der Kritiker.
'Bad (stage) direction' / 'Badly produced', commented the critic. (referring to film / theatre)

berichten to report

Der Kassenführer berichtet über die Finanzlage im letzten Jahr.
The treasurer reports about the state of the finances in the previous / preceding year.

Nach unbestätigten Augenzeugenberichten . . .
According to unconfirmed eye-witness reports . . .

beschreiben* to describe

Der Zeuge beschrieb den Unfallhergang.
The witness described the events leading to the accident.

bestätigen to confirm

Die Sekretärin bestätigte den Eingang des Einschreibens.
The secretary confirmed receipt of the registered letter.

beteuern to affirm / protest / maintain (against doubts)

Er beteuerte, er habe nichts von dem Überfall gewußt.
He affirmed / protested he had known nothing about the attack.

betonen to stress

Er betonte, daß er mit dieser Angelegenheit nichts zu tun habe.
He stressed he had nothing to do with the matter.

bezeichnen to label / describe

Der Redner bezeichnete die Protestaktion als 'geschmacklos'.
The speaker described the protest campaign as 'in bad taste'.

Er bezeichnete die Abrüstung als wichtigste gemeinsame Aufgabe.
He described disarmament as the most important common task / endeavour.

auf etwas (acc.) ***ein◊gehen**** to go into something / be responsive to

Der Arzt ging auf alle Beschwerden der Patientin ein.
The doctor paid attention to every ache and pain of the (female) patient.

jemandem etwas ***entgegen◊halten**** to accuse someone of something

Sie hielt ihm entgegen, daß er seine Frau vernachläßigt habe.
She confronted him with / accused him of the fact that he had neglected his wife.

jemandem ***entgegnen*** to retort / reply to someone

Sie entgegnete ihm, sie habe keine Lust, mit ihm ins Theater zu gehen.
She retorted she did not feel like going to the theatre with him.

sich erfreut zeigen über (+ acc.) to show oneself pleased about

Der Lehrer zeigte sich über die Fortschritte seiner Schülerin sehr erfreut.
The teacher showed (his) pleasure about the progress of his (female) pupil.

erinnern an (+ acc.) to remind of

Er erinnerte die Anwesenden an ihr Versprechen.
He reminded those present of their promise.

N.B. *sich* (acc.) *erinnern an* means 'to remember'.

erklären to explain

Er erklärte, ohne die Lieferung von Ersatzteilen könne das Produkt nicht fertiggestellt werden.
He explained that without the delivery of spare parts the product could not be finished.

erläutern to explain (slightly more formal than *erklären*)

Er erläuterte genauestens, auf welche Weise das Mißverständnis zustande gekommen war.
He explained in great detail how the misunderstanding had come about / arisen.

fordern to demand

Der Oppositionsführer forderte die sofortige Abschaffung der Steuer.
The leader of the opposition demanded the immediate abolition of the tax.

geheim◊halten* to keep secret

Das Versteck der Flüchtlinge hielt er während des ganzen Krieges geheim.
He kept the hiding-place of the refugees secret throughout the entire war.

hin◊weisen* **auf** (+ acc.) to point out / stress

Auf die schädliche Nebenwirkung des Medikaments wird ausdrücklich hingewiesen.
We stress / must point out the harmful side-effect of this medicine.

kritisieren to criticize

Vertreter aller Parteien haben die Waffenverkäufe scharf kritisiert.
Members of all parties heavily criticized the arms sales.

leugnen to deny

Der Angeklagte leugnete, das Opfer umgebracht zu haben.
The accused denied having killed / murdered the victim.

loben to praise

Der Innenminister lobte den schnellen Einsatz der Polizei.
The Home Secretary praised the swift action of the police.

meinen to believe / think (often with emotional connotations)

Meinen is a very vague word and is best avoided in written German, but you will nevertheless find it very frequently in spoken German:

Er meinte, er habe noch nie einen so großen Vogel gesehen.
He thought he had never seen such a big bird.

melden to report

Er meldete dem Geschäftsführer, daß der Computeranschluß mangelhaft sei.
He reported the faulty computer-connection to the manager.

jemandem etwas ***mit◊teilen*** to inform / announce / communicate

Ich teile Ihnen hiermit mit, daß ich meine Versicherung zum 1.7. kündige. < officialese >
I hereby inform you that I cancel / of the cancellation of my insurance from the first of July.

Eine Wissenschaftlerin teilte mit, Hunderte toter Robben würden an der Westküste angeschwemmt.
A (female) scientist said that hundreds of dead seals were washed ashore on the west coast.

nach Mitteilung according to information

Nach Mitteilung des Umweltexperten ist die Wasserqualität jetzt besser.
According to the environment expert the quality of the water is now improved.

Protest ein◊legen gegen to protest against

Er legte Protest gegen die Beschuldigungen ein. < formal >
He made a protest against the accusations.

protestieren gegen to protest against

Ich protestiere heftigst gegen diese Diskriminierung.
I protest most vehemently against this discrimination.

sollen + past participle + ***sein*** supposed to have (+ past participle)

This idiomatic expression implies uncertainty. Something is supposed to have happened (see section 29).

Der Attentäter soll hingerichtet worden sein.
The assassin is supposed / said to have been executed.

vor◊tragen* to present

Der Abgeordnete trug die Beschwerden seiner Wählerschaft vor.
The MP presented the complaints of his constituency.

zu bedenken geben* to ask (someone) to consider

Ich gebe zu bedenken, daß man mit dieser Maßnahme keine Besserung der Umstände erzielen wird.
I would point out that no improvement will be achieved by / through this measure.

zu verstehen geben* to insist / make clear (degree of certainty varies)

Der Herrscher gab zu verstehen, man könne in den nächsten Tagen eine Amnestie erwarten.
The ruler gave to understand / let it be understood that an amnesty could be expected shortly.

jemandem / etwas (dat.) ***zu◊stimmen*** to agree with something or someone

Dieser Meinung kann man nur zustimmen.
One cannot but agree with this opinion.

viel (adjective) much / many

vielfach many (literally: manifold)

auf vielfachen Wunsch unsrer Zuschauer
at the request of many of our viewers

eine Vielfalt von a multitude of

Das Buch enthält eine Vielfalt von Abbildungen.
The book contains copious illustrations.

vielfältig (adjective) a wide range

Der Katalog beinhaltet ein vielfältiges Angebot.
The catalogue contains a wide range of offers.

eine Menge (*von*) a crowd / mass (of)

Vor dem Rathaus demonstrierte eine große Menge von Studenten.
A large crowd of students demonstrated outside the town hall.

Ich habe eine Menge Zeit. < coll. >
I have a lot of time.

massenweise (adverb) masses of / on a massive scale

Das Deutsche Rote Kreuz verteilte massenweise Decken und Kissen.
The German Red Cross distributed many / masses of blankets and pillows.

mehrere (adjective) several

Mehrere Passagiere sind umgeleitet worden.
Several passengers have been diverted.

einige (adjective) some

Einige erlitten schwere Verletzungen.
Some suffered severe injuries.

eine große Anzahl a large number

Eine große Anzahl der Verletzten wurde auf das Lazarettschiff gebracht.
A large number of the injured were taken onto the hospital ship.

umfassend (adjective) comprehensive

Im Museum befindet sich eine umfassende Materialsammlung.
In the museum you will find a comprehensive collection of materials.

unzählig (adjective) innumerable

Unzählige Knochen von Dinosauriern sind in Nordamerika gefunden worden.
Innumerable bones of dinosaurs have been found in North America.

wichtig important

von größter Bedeutung of the utmost importance

Dieser Satz ist von größter Bedeutung.
This sentence is of the utmost importance.

bedeutend significant / important

Er war ein bedeutender Wissenschaftler.
He was a very important scientist.

wertvoll (in)valuable

Vielen Dank für den wertvollen Diskussionsbeitrag.
Many thanks for that invaluable contribution to the discussion.

bemerkenswert remarkable

Das war eine bemerkenswerte Leistung.
That was a remarkable achievement.

einschneidend drastic / decisive

Das war ein einschneidendes Ereignis in meinem Leben.
That was a drastic / decisive event in my life.

nicht zu unterschätzen ⧫ (euphemism) not to be underestimated

Die Kosten der Neuanschaffungen für den Haushalt sind nicht zu unterschätzen.
The cost of new household purchases are not to be underestimated.

entscheidend crucial / decisive

Die Ausbildung ist eine entscheidende Grundlage für die Zukunft Ihres Kindes.
Education is a crucial foundation for the future of your child.

notwendig necessary

Für eine Wohnungseinrichtung ist ein erhebliches Startkapital notwendig.
To furnish a flat a considerable amount of money is necessary at the start. / You need a considerable initial outlay to furnish a flat.

138 *Faux amis*

Faux amis – *Falsche Freunde* or false friends – are words which look almost or completely identical in two languages, but whose meanings are not identical.

For example, to describe a child as *brav* in German indicates good, almost restrained behaviour, whereas the English word 'brave' implies courage and sometimes daring.

This section features the most common German false friends, together with their correct English translation and the German translation of the false English counterpart.

True *faux amis* never share the same meaning in both languages; in other cases, there is some distinction, but also some degree of overlap (partial *faux amis*). These are the two main categories used below:

(a) True *faux amis*

der ***Affekt*** emotional agitation / excitement
(affection *die Zuneigung(en)*)

aktuell topical / relevant
(actual *tatsächlich*)

die ***Allee****(n)* (tree-lined) avenue
(alley *das Gäßchen(–) / die Gasse(n)*)

also therefore
(also *auch*)

die ***Ambulanz****(en)* outpatients' department
(ambulance *der Krankenwagen(–)*)

die ***Angina*** inflammation of the throat / tonsillitis
(angina (pectoris) *die Angina Pectoris / der Herzschmerz(en) / das Herzleiden (–)*)

die ***Art****(en)* kind / species
(art *die Kunst(¨e)*)

arriviert successful; also implies: upstart / parvenu
(arrived *angekommen*)

apart different / out of the ordinary / sophisticated (appearance of woman or girl)
(apart *weg von / getrennt von / außer*)

bekommen to get / receive
(to become *werden**)

das ***Benzin*** petrol
(benzene *das Benzol*; benzine *das Leichtbenzin*)

beraten * to give advice
(to berate *schimpfen / schelten*)

besiegen to defeat
(to besiege *belagern*)

bilden to educate
(to build *bauen*)

die ***Billion*** 10^{12}
(billion (10^9) *die Milliarde*)

der ***Biskuit*** sponge (cake); *die Biskuitrolle* Swiss roll
(biscuit *der Keks(e) / das Plätzchen(–)*)

jemanden ***blamieren*** to embarrass someone
(to blame someone *jemandem die Schuld geben**)

blank bright / clean / shiny
(blank *leer / unbeschrieben (Papier)*)

die ***Box****(en)* loudspeaker
((cardboard) box *die Schachtel(n)*;
(wooden) box *der Kasten(¨)*;
(tool) box *der Werkzeugkasten(¨)*;
(money) box *die Geldbüchse(n)*;
(collection) box *die Sammelbüchse(n)*;
horsebox *der Pferdetransporter(–)*)

brav good / well-behaved
(brave *mutig / tapfer*)

der ***Chef(s)*** boss / chief
(chef *der Koch (¨e) / der Küchenchef(s)*;
(female) chef *die Köchin(nen)*)

die ***Chips*** (pl.) crisps (US chips)
(chips *die Pommes frites* (pl.))

der ***Christ****(en)* Christian
(Christ *Christus*)

das ***Christentum*** Christianity
(Christendom *die Christenheit*)

dann then
(than *als*)

der ***Dealer****(–)* (drug) pusher
(dealer *der Händler(–)*, e.g. car dealer *der Autohändler*)

demolieren to damage / wreck
(to demolish *ab◊reißen* / nieder◊reißen**)

die ***Devise****(n)* (1) slogan / watchword
(2) foreign exchange / currency
(device *das Gerät(e), die Vorrichtung(en)*)

dezent delicate / discreet / muted (colours, music) / restrained / unobtrusive
(decent *anständig / schicklich / sittlich*)

die ***Direktion*** management
(direction *die Richtung(en)*)

der ***Dom****(e)* cathedral
(dome *die Kuppel(n)*)

die ***Dose****(n)* tin / box / container
(dose *die Dosis (Dosen)*)

engagiert committed / active / convinced / involved / dedicated
(engaged (to be married) *verlobt*;
engaged (toilet / telephone) *besetzt*;
engaged / involved (in a fight) *(in einen Streit) verwickelt*)

das ***Etikett****(en)* label
(etiquette *die Etikette / die Verhaltensregel(n)*;
(professional) etiquette *die Berufspraxis*)

eventuell possibly / conceivably / at the most, e.g.:
Bei eventuellen Schäden bekommen Sie Ersatz.
In the event / case of damage you'll get a replacement.
(eventually *mit der Zeit / allmählich*)

die ***Fabrik****(en)* factory
(fabric *der Stoff(e) / das Gewebe(–)*)

famos < archaic > excellent / marvellous
(famous *berühmt*)

fast almost / nearly
(fast (speed) *schnell*; fast (tight) *fest*)

die ***Folklore*** (sg.) traditional dances / folksongs, etc.
(folklore *das Volksgut / die Volksweisheit*)

das ***Formular****(e)* form (e.g. an application form)
(formula *die Formel(n)*)

der ***Fund(e)*** find(ing)
(fund *der Fonds*; (public) funds *öffentliche Mittel*;
to fund *finanzieren*)

das ***Gasthaus(¨er)*** inn / restaurant
(guesthouse (B & B) *die (kleine) Privatpension(en)*)

geistlich religious / ecclesiastical
(ghostly *gespensterhaft / geisterhaft*)

genial brilliant / of genius / gifted / ingenious
((con)genial *freundlich / leutselig / herzlich*)

das ***Gift(e)*** poison
(gift (present) *das Geschenk(e) / Präsent(e)* / (*die Mitgift(en)*
< archaic > dowry);
gift (talent) *das Talent(e) / die Begabung(en)*)

graziös graceful
(gracious *gnädig / huldvoll*)

der / das ***Gully(s)*** drain
(gully / gulley *die Schlucht(en) / die Furche(n)*)

das ***Gymnasium*** *(Gymnasien)* grammar school, often used as loanword 'Gymnasium'
(gymnasium *die Turnhalle(n)*)

handeln to act / trade
(to handle *an◊fassen / sich befassen mit; es handelt sich um* it is a matter of)

der ***Handel*** trade
(handle *der Griff(e) / der Henkel(–)*)

der ***Helm(e)*** helmet
(helm *das Schiffssteuerrad(¨er)*)

hemmen to obstruct / hinder / retard
(to hem *(ein)säumen*; hem *der Saum(¨e)*)

herb bitter / dry / tart
(herb *das Kraut(¨er)*; (medicinal) herb *das Heilkraut(¨er)*)

hissen to hoist (a flag)
(to hiss *zischen / laut flüstern*)

die ***Hose(n)*** (pair of) trousers
(hose *der Schlauch(¨e)*; to hose (down) *bespritzen / (ab◊)spritzen*)

*das **Kanapee(s)*** sofa / settee
(canapé *das Häppchen(–), der Appetithappen(–)*)

*die **Kanne(n)*** pot / jug / churn
(can (tin) *die Dose(n)*; watering-can *die Gießkanne(n)*)

*der **Karton(s)*** (a piece of) cardboard / (cardboard) box (for storing dry goods)
(carton (for fluids) *die Packung(en) (Milch / Saft)*;
carton (of yoghurt) *ein Becher(–) Yoghurt*;
carton (in general) *der Pappkarton(s)*)

*die **Kaution(en)***
(1) deposit (e.g. a month's rent for a flat)
(2) bail (legal)

Er wurde gegen Kaution entlassen.
He was released on bail.

(caution *die Vorsicht* (no pl.) / *die Verwarnung(en)*;
to caution *verwarnen*)

*der **Kipper(–)*** dumper lorry / tipper lorry
(kipper *der (gesalzene) Räucherhering(e)*)

*der **Kitt*** putty / adhesive (for tiles, etc.)
(kit (for soldiers / campers) *die Ausrüstung(en)*;
kit (for making a model) *der (Modell)Bausatz(¨e)*)

*das **Kloster(¨)*** monastery / convent
(cloisters *der Kreuzgang(¨e)*)

*der **Koffer(–)*** suitcase / case / trunk
(coffer *die (Schatz)Truhe(n)*;
coffers (of the government) *der Staatssäckel(–)* (jocular))

*der **Konkurrent(en)*** competitor
(concurrent *gleichzeitig*)

*die **Konkurrenz*** (usually no pl.) competition
(concurrence *die Übereinstimmung(en)*)

konkurrieren to compete / rival
(to concur *überein◊stimmen*)

*der **Konkurs(e)*** bankruptcy / liquidation
(concourse *die Halle(n)*; concourse (station) *die Bahnhofshalle(n)*)

konsequent logical / consistent
(consequently *folglich*)

die ***Krawatte****(n)* tie
(cravat *das (seidene) Halstuch(¨er)*)

der ***Kriminale****(n)* (adjectival noun) < coll. > (abbreviation for *der Kriminalbeamte* (adjectival noun) detective / plainclothes detective)
(criminal *der Verbrecher(–) / der Kriminelle* (adjectival noun))

die ***Kritik****(en)* criticism / critique / review
(critic *der Kritiker(–) / die Kritikerin(nen)*)

das ***Lager****(–)* store / store room / camp
(lager *das Lagerbier(e);*
large / small lager ≈ *ein großes / kleines Helles*)

die ***Lektüre****(n)* reading (material)
(lecture *die Vorlesung(en)*)

die ***Lyrik*** (no pl.) lyrical poetry
(lyrics *der Schlagertext(e) / 'the lyrics'* (anglicism))

man one / you
(man *der Mann(¨er) / der Mensch(en)*)

die ***Mappe****(n)* folder / briefcase / portfolio
((geographical) map *die Landkarte(n) / der Atlas* (pl. *Atlanten*);
(road) map *die Straßenkarte(n);* (town) map *der Stadtplan(¨e)*)

das ***Maß****(e)* measure / dimension
(mass *die Masse(n) / die Menge(n);*
(holy) mass *die (Heilige) Messe(n)*)

mimen to pretend / play
(to mime *mit stummen Gesten zeigen*)

der / das ***Minigolf*** crazy golf
(minigolf *der Miniaturgolf*)

der ***Mist*** (1) dung / manure / muck
(2) < coll., figurative> rubbish
(mist *der (leichte) Nebel / der Dunst* (no pl.))

mondän chic / stylish / showy / flashy / over-dressed
(mundane *alltäglich / gewöhnlich / profan*)

der ***Mörder****(–)* murderer
(to murder *ermorden / um◊bringen** < coll. >)

neulich recently
(newly *neu- / neu;* newly-built *neugebaut*)

nobel superior / select / stylish
(noble *edel*)

notorisch habitual / chronic / constant
(notorious *berühmt / berüchtigt / bekannt*)

die ***Novelle****(n)* novella
(novel *der Roman(e)*)

das ***Objektiv****(e)* lens / lens system
(objective *das Ziel(e)*)

ordinär common / vulgar / rude / coarse
(ordinary *gewöhnlich / normal / üblich*)

die ***Pantomime****(n)* mime (cf. *mimen*, above)
(pantomime *das Märchenspiel(e) im Varietéstil, das um Weihnachten aufgeführt wird)*)

passen to fit / suit
(to pass *vorbei◊gehen** (*verpassen* to miss);
and it came to pass (biblical) *und es geschah**;
to pass (an exam) *(eine Prüfung) bestehen**;
to pass (the salt etc.) to someone *jemandem (das Salz) reichen*)

passieren to happen
(to pass: see above)

peinlich embarrassing

Es ist mir sehr peinlich.
It is most embarrassing for me.

(painful *schmerzhaft*)

die ***Pest*** plague / menace (pestilence)
(pest (bugs etc.) *der Schädling(e) / das Ungeziefer* (no pl.);
pest (annoyance) *die Plage(n)*;
pest (person) < coll. > *die Nervensäge(n)* < coll. >)

pervers perverted / unnatural
(perverse *verstockt / querköpfig*)

das ***Pflaster****(–)* (1) (sticking) plaster
(2) paving
(plaster on walls *der Verputz* (no pl.))

plump ungainly / cumbersome / clumsy
(plump (nicely rounded) *pummelig / mollig*)

prägnant concise / incisive / pithy
(pregnant *schwanger*)

das ***Präservativ****(e)* contraceptive / condom
(preservative *das Konservierungsmittel(–)*)

prinzipiell in principle
(principally *hauptsächlich*)

die ***Probe****(n)* rehearsal / (laboratory) test
(probe *die Sonde(n);* probe (investigation) *die Untersuchung(en)*)

die ***Promotion****(en)* conferment / gaining of doctorate
((job) promotion *die Beförderung(en);*
(sales) promotion *der Werbefeldzug(¨e)*)

der ***Prospekt****(e)* leaflet / prospectus / brochure
(prospect *die Aussicht(en) (auf Erfolg) / die Chance(n)*)

der ***Pudding*** blancmange / custard
(pudding (i.e. dessert) *der Nachtisch(e) / die süße(n) Nachspeise(n) / das Dessert(s)* (French pronunciation))

der Qualm (no pl.) (thick) smoke
(qualms (of conscience) *der Gewissensbiß(sse)*)

rasch quick / prompt / fast
(rash *voreilig;* rash (noun) *der (Haut) Ausschlag(¨e)*)

die ***Rente****(n)* pension (cf. *Pension* in sections 138b and 146b(ii))
(rent *die Miete(n)*)

der ***Ringer****(–)* wrestler
(bell)ringer *der Glockenläuter(–)*)

der ***Schal****(s)* scarf
(shawl *das (Umschlag)Tuch(¨er) / die Stola (Stolen)*)

schauen to look / see
(to show *zeigen*)

der ***Sender****(–)* transmitter / (radio, TV) station
(sender (of a letter) *der Absender(–)*)

sensibel sensitive
(sensible *vernünftig*)

der ***Sinn****(e)* sense / mind
(sin *die Sünde(n)*)

der ***Slip****(s)* a pair of pants (ladies' underwear)
(slip (underwear) *der Unterrock(¨e);*
(pillow) slip *der Kopfkissenbezug(¨e);*
slip (of the tongue) *der Versprecher(–);*
to make a slip *einen Fehler machen;*
to slip (e.g. on ice) *aus◊rutschen)*

solide reputable / sound / trustworthy
(solid *massiv* (cf. *massiv* in section 138b) / *fest)*

sparen to save money
(to spare (protect) *schonen;*
to have something to spare *etwas übrig haben;*
to spare someone something *jemandem etwas* (acc.) *ersparen)*

spenden to donate
(to spend (time) *verbringen**; to spend (money) *(Geld) aus◊geben**

der ***Spleen*** whimsical mood / eccentric or odd idea
(spleen (anatomical) *die Milz;*
spleen (bad mood / anger) *schlechte Laune / die Wut / der Zorn)*

das ***Stadium*** *(Stadien)* stage (of development etc.)
(stadium (football etc.) *das Stadion (Stadien))*

der ***Stall****(¨e)* stable
((market) stall *die Bude(n);*
stalls (theatre) *das Parkett (sg.) / das Parterre* (sg.))

der ***(Gabel) Stapler****(–)* fork-lift truck
(stapler *der Hefter(–))*

stark (1) strong / powerful
(2) (slang / youth) great (cf. sections 81 and 136)
(stark (naked) *unverhüllt / nackt;*
stark (without leaves / decoration etc.) *kahl)*

der ***Stopp*** ban / voluntary cessation / 'freeze'
(stop (transport) *die Haltestelle(n))*

der ***Strand****(¨e)* beach
(strand (fibre) *die Faser(n);* strand(thread) *der Faden(¨);*
strand (hair) *die Haarsträhne(n))*

süffisant complacent / arrogant / conceited / mocking
(sufficient *genügend / ausreichend)*

sympathisch pleasant / nice (positive connotation)
(sympathetic *mitfühlend / bemitleidend / verständnisvoll)*

die ***Taste****(n)* key (instruments / keyboard) / button (machines)
(taste *der Geschmack(̈er)*)

tippen to type
(to tip (give money) *jemandem ein Trinkgeld geben**)

transparent translucent
(transparent *durchsichtig*)

turnen to do gymnastics / acrobatics
(to turn *(sich) drehen / (sich) umdrehen*)

überhören ⧫ to fail to hear / not hear / miss
(to overhear *zufällig (mit◊)hören / unabsichtlich mit◊bekommen**)

übersehen ⧫ to overlook / fail to notice (cf. *Notiz* in section 138(b))
(to oversee *beaufsichtigen, überwachen*)

die ***Übersicht*** overview / control / survey
(oversight *das Versehen*)

vor (1) before / in front of
(2) ago (*vor fünf Jahren* five years ago)
(for *für*)

die ***Vorsicht*** care
(foresight *die Voraussicht*)

die ***Wand****(̈e)* wall / screen
((magic) wand *der (Zauber) Stab (̈e)*)

das ***Warenhaus****(̈er)* department store
(warehouse *das Lagerhaus(̈er) / die Lagerhalle(n)*)

weil because
(while *während*)

wer who
(where *wo*)

die ***Weste****(n)* waistcoat / cardigan / sleeveless pullover
(vest *das Unterhemd(en)*)

wo where
(who *wer*)

Worms name of a city on the Rhine
(worm *der Wurm(̈er)*)

zivil (1) (not military) civilian (*in Zivil* in plain clothes)
(2) < coll. > civilized
(civil *höflich*; civil war *der Bürgerkrieg(e)*;
civil rights *die Bürgerrechte* (pl.))

der ***Zivildienst*** community service (as alternative to military service)
(civil service *der (höhere) öffentliche Dienst / der Staatsdienst*)

der ***Zivildienstleistende*** (adjectival noun) < coll. >
(*der Ersatzdienstleistende*) person carrying out community service
(civil servant *der Beamte* (adjectival noun))

(b) Partial *faux amis*

Partial *faux amis* are those which sometimes have the same meaning in English and in German.

der ***Akademiker(–)*** (1) (university / college) graduate
(2) academic (working in profession or at university)
(3) scientist
(academic *der Wissenschaftler(–) / die Wissenschaftlerin(nen)*;
scholar *der / die Gelehrte* (adjectival noun))

akut (1) burning (question) / of great importance
(2) acute (illness)
(acute *intensiv / fein / scharfsinnig*)

bei (1) with / at / in / in the case of / at the house of (French *chez*)
(2) by / next to (rare)

Er sitzt bei seiner Oma. < coll. >
He is sitting by his grandmother.
(by *von / neben*)

der ***Blinker(–)*** <coll. > (1) indicator light (on vehicle)
(2) blinker (on vehicle) < coll. >
(blinkers (pl.) (for horses) *Scheuklappen* (f.pl.))

der ***Blitz(e)*** (1) lightning
(2) flash (camera)
(blitz *der Bombenangriff(e)*) / *der Luftangriff;* blitz (attack) *die Großaktion(en)*)

die ***Branche(n)*** (1) field / department / trade
(2) branch of industry
(branch (of a tree) *der Ast(¨e)*;
(local) branch (of a shop) *die Filiale(n)*;
(local) branch (of a bank) *die Zweigstelle(n)*)

clever (1) resourceful / quick-thinking / cunning
(2) intellectually clever (rare)
(clever *klug / gewandt / intelligent*)

der ***Fall(¨e)*** (1) case / instance
(2) fall / drop (rare)
(fall) *der Sturz(¨e) / der Absturz(¨e)*

fasten to fast / diet
(to fasten (seat-belt etc.) *an◊schnallen*)

fatal (1) awkward / embarrassing / unfortunate / disastrous / calamitous
(2) fatal (rare)
(fatal *tödlich*)

feudal (1) grand / superior
(2) reactionary
(3) feudal

das ***Format*** (1) reputation / distinguished character (*ein Mann von Format*)
(2) format

frivol (1) indecent / 'naughty' / (a bit) near the bone
(2) frivolous (rare)
(frivolous *albern / kindisch / leichtsinnig / leichtfertig*)

der ***Gag(s)*** (1) gimmick / gimmicky idea
(2) gag
(gag *der Knebel(–) / die Mundsperre(n)*)

der ***Geist*** (1) mind / spirit
(2) ghost (*der Heilige Geist* the Holy Ghost / Spirit)
(ghost *das Gespenst(er)*)

der ***Grad(e)*** (1) degree / extent / stage
(2) grade (intensity of illness)
(grade *die Note(n) / das Niveau(s)*)

groß (1) big / large / great
(2) gross (rare)
(gross *dick / fett / plump*; gross (income, etc.) *Brutto – (verdienst)* (used as a prefix in compounds)

halten (1) to hold / keep / take for
(2) to halt (rare)
(to halt *an◊halten**)

die ***Hosteß****(ssen)* (1) tourist courier
(2) woman at the information desk (e.g. at exhibition)
(3) hostess (looking after special guests at official functions)
(hostess (entertaining guests) *die Gastgeberin(nen)*;
air hostess *die Stewardeß(ssen)*)

die ***Instanz****(en)* (1) responsible authority
(2) (court of) instance (see section 148b)

die Verhandlung in erster Instanz
hearing at the court of first instance
(for instance *zum Beispiel*)

das ***Interview****(s)* interview by the media (rarely: job interview)
(job interview *das Vorstellungsgespräch(e) / das Bewerbungsgespräch(e)*)

irritieren (1) to distract / puzzle / put off
(2) to annoy / irritate (rare)
(to irritate *reizen*)

komisch (1) strange / weird (2) comical

lösen (1) to solve (2) to dissolve (3) to loosen / detach
(to loosen *lockern*)

der ***Magistrat*** (1) municipal authorities / council
(2) (Swiss) magistrate
(magistrate (in magistrates' court) *der Richter(-)*; (police) magistrate *der Polizeirichter*; magistrate (high official) *der Verwaltungsbeamte* (adjectival noun))

die ***Marmelade****(n)* any type of jam (although, according to EC guidelines, only preserves made from citrus fruits should be called *Marmelade*. Other preserves should be called *die Konfitüre(n)*)
(marmalade *die Orangenmarmelade(n)*)

massiv (1) solid (cf. *solide* in section (a) 138a), huge / enormous / immense
(2) massive
(massive *wuchtig / ungeheuer / gewaltig*)

meinen (1) to think / say (to have an opinion)
(2) to mean (wanting to say)
(to mean (having significance of) *bedeuten / heißen**;
mean (adj.) (thrifty) *geizig*; mean (adj.) (nasty) *gemein*)

das ***Menü(s)*** (1) a set meal (on a menu)
(2) menu (on the computer)
(menu (in a restaurant) *die Speisekarte(n)*)

das ***Mittel(–)*** (1) means / medium / average
(2) middle (in compound words), e.g. *das Mittelalter* Middle Ages
(middle *die Mitte(n)*)

der ***Moderator(en)*** (1) (TV or radio) presenter / host (usually serious programme)
(2) moderator (technical)
(Moderator (Head of Presbyterian Church) *kirchliches Oberhaupt(¨er)*; moderator (examiner) *der Prüfer(–)*; moderator (arbitrator) *der Schlichter(–) / der Vermittler(–)*)

das ***Muster(–)*** pattern / sample
(muster (military) *der Appell(e)*; muster-station (e.g. on ship) *der Sammelplatz(¨e)*; to pass muster *den Anforderungen genügen*; to muster *sich versammeln / an◊treten** (*mustern* to inspect / review))

die ***Note(n)*** (1) note (music), *die Noten* (pl.) printed music
(2) note (money)
(3) grade / mark (school)

die ***Notiz(en)*** (1) memo / message
(2) notice (*keine Notiz von etwas nehmen** to take no notice of something)
(3) note (*sich Notizen machen* to take notes)
(notice *der Anschlag(¨e) / der Aushang(¨e)*;
to notice *beachten / feststellen / bemerken*;
noticeboard *das schwarze Brett*;
notice (ending an agreement) *die Kündigung(en)*)

das ***Objekt(e)*** (1) object / thing
(2) subject matter
(object *der Gegenstand(¨e)*)

das ***Organ*** (1) organ (of body)
(2) (administrative) body
(church organ *die Orgel(n)*)

das ***Paket(e)*** (1) large parcel
(2) package (for transportation)
(packet *das Päckchen(–) / kleines Paket(e)*)

pathetisch (1) high-flown / rhetorical (of speech)
(2) pathetic (full of pathos, e.g. music)
(pathetic (pitiful) *mitleiderregend / erbärmlich / jämmerlich*;
pathetic (useless) *lächerlich / armselig*)

die ***Pension****(en)* (1) guest house / boarding house (cf. *Gasthaus* in section 138a)
(2) pension
(pension *die Rente(n)* (cf. *Rente* in section 138a)

die ***Phrase****(n)* (1) bombastic talk (when pl.)
(2) phrase (*leere Phrasen* empty phrases)
(phrase *der Satz(¨e) / der Ausdruck(¨e)*)

die ***Plastik****(en)* (1) sculpture
(2) (medical) plastic surgery operation
(3) < coll. > plastic
(plastic *der Kunststoff(e)*)

das ***Protokoll****(e)* (1) minutes (of a meeting) / record
(2) protocol (only referring to state protocol and computer protocol)

der ***Prozeß****(sse)* (1) trial (in court)
(2) process
(process *der Vorgang(¨e)*)

das ***Puzzle****(s)* jigsaw (puzzle)
(puzzle (game made of metal, plastic etc. to test your patience and skill) *das Geduldsspiel(e)*; puzzle (e.g. mathematical) *das Rätsel(–)*)

die ***Rate****(n)* (1) instalment (see section 144c)
(2) rate (e.g. *die Inflationsrate(n)* rate of inflation)
((interest) rate *der Zinssatz(¨e)*;
rate (telephone, etc.) *die (Telephon)Gebühr(en)*;
failure rate *die Durchfallquote(n)*; to rate *ein◊schätzen*)

der ***Recorder****(–)* cassette recorder
(recorder (musical instrument) *die Blockflöte(n)*)

der ***Rock****(¨e)* (1) skirt
(2) man's jacket < archaic >
(3) rock (music) *Rock(–musik)*
(rock *der Fels(en)*)

scharf (1) hot / spicy (food)
(2) in focus (photographs)
(3) hot (ammunition)
(4) sharp (*ein scharfes Messer* a sharp knife)

*der **Sekretär(e)*** (1) secretary (male)
(2) middle-ranking civil servant
(3) secretaire / bureau (furniture)
(secretary (of state) *der Minister(-)*; cf. section 147a)

*der **Sellerie(s)*** (1) celeriac
(2) celery
(celery *der Stangensellerie*)

stationär (1) in-patient (in hospital)
(2) stationary
(stationary traffic *stillstehender Verkehr*)

*der **Stuhl(¨e)*** (1) chair
(stool *der Hocker(–) / der Schemel(–)*)
(2) stool (excrement) < coll. >
(stool (excrement) *der Stuhlgang* (medical; used in singular))

*der **Tarif(e)*** (1) (pay / wage) agreement, agreed rate of pay
(2) *der (Zoll)Tarif(e)* (customs) tariff (or *die Zollgebühren* (pl.))
(tariff (pubs, hotels, etc.) *das Preisverzeichnis(se)*)

*die **Technik*** (1) technology
(2) *die (Arbeits–) Technik* (work) technique
(technique *die Methode(n)*)

*die **Truppe(n)*** (1) unit (of armed forces)
(2) troupe (of artists)
(3) troops (*die Truppen* (pl.))
(trooper (soldier) *der Soldat(en)*; troop (of cavalry) *die Schwadron(en)*; troop (of artillery and armour) *die Batterie(n)*)

wandern (1) to hike / ramble
(2) to wander
(to wander (aimlessly) *herum◊irren*; to wonder *sich wundern*)

wenn (1) if
(2) when / whenever
(when (referring to past) *als*)

139 Proverbs

Where possible this alphabetical list includes English proverbs which mean the same as the German ones. In some instances the literal translation of the German proverb is given in brackets. The word for 'proverb' is *das Sprichwort(¨er).*

*Wer **A** sagt, muß auch B sagen.*
(If you say A you must also say B.)
In for a penny, in for a pound.

*Der **Apfel** fällt nicht weit vom Baum.*
(The apple falls not far from the tree.)
It's in the blood.

*Aus dem **Auge,** aus dem Sinn.*
Out of sight, out of mind.

*Lügen haben kurze **Beine.***
(Lies have short legs.)
You won't get far by lying.

*Wie man sich **bettet,** so schläft man.*
As you make your bed, so you must lie on it.

***Bleibe** im Lande und nähre dich redlich.*
(Stay in the country and feed yourself honestly.)
Go east, go west, home is best.

*Liebe macht **blind.***
Love is blind.

*Wes **Brot** ich ess', des Lied ich sing.*
(He whose bread I eat, his song I sing.)
He who pays the piper calls the tune.

*Aller guten **Dinge** sind drei.*
All good things come in threes.

***Doppelt** genäht hält besser.*
(Double-stitched lasts / holds (longer).)
It is better to be on the safe side.

***Ehrlich** währt am längsten.*
Honesty is the best policy.

*Kümmere dich nicht um ungelegte **Eier.***
(Don't worry about eggs that haven't been laid yet.)
Don't cross that bridge until you come to it.

***Eile** mit Weile.*
More haste, less speed.

*Was man sich **eingebrockt** hat, das muß man auch auslöffeln.*
(What you have crumbled (into your soup) you must ladle out yourself.)
You've made your bed, now you must lie on it.

*Das **Eisen** schmieden, solange es noch heiß ist.*
Strike while the iron is hot. / Make hay while the sun shines.

***Ende** gut, alles gut.*
All's well that ends well.

*Ohne **Fleiß** kein Preis.*
(Without hard work / diligence there is no prize.)
Success never comes easily.

*Einem geschenkten **Gaul** guckt man nicht ins Maul.*
Don't look a gift-horse in the mouth.

***Gebranntes** Kind scheut das Feuer.*
(The burnt child shuns the fire.)
Once bitten, twice shy.

***Gleich** und gleich gesellt sich gern.*
Birds of a feather flock together.

*Es ist nicht alles **Gold**, was glänzt.*
All that glitters is not gold.

*Morgenstund hat **Gold** im Mund.*
(The morning hour has gold in its mouth.)
The early bird catches the worm.

***Gold** öffnet jede Tür.*
Money rules the world / makes the world go round.

*Was **Hänschen** nicht lernt, lernt Hans nimmermehr.*
(What little Jack won't learn, big Jack will never learn.)
You can't teach an old dog new tricks.

*Das **Hemd** ist einem näher als der Rock.*
(The shirt is closer to you than the coat.)
Charity begins at home.

***Hochmut** kommt vor dem Fall.*
Pride goes before a fall.

Den letzten beißen die ***Hunde.***
(The last one is bitten by the dogs.)
He who hesitates is lost.

Hunde, *die bellen, beißen nicht.*
(Dogs that bark do not bite.)
His bark's worse than his bite.

Viele ***Köche*** *verderben den Brei.*
Too many cooks spoil the broth.

In der ***Kürze*** *liegt die Würze.*
Brevity is the soul of the wit.

Wer zuletzt ***lacht,*** *lacht am besten.*
He who laughs last laughs longest.

Andere ***Länder,*** *andere Sitten.*
(Other countries, other customs.)
When in Rome, do as the Romans do.

Liebe *geht durch den Magen.*
The way to a man's heart is through his stomach.

Alte ***Liebe*** *rostet nicht.*
An old flame never dies.

Ein ***Mann,*** *ein Wort.*
(One man, one word.)
To be a man of one's word.

Es ist noch kein ***Meister*** *vom Himmel gefallen.*
(No master has fallen from heaven yet.)
No-one is born a master.

Übung macht den ***Meister.***
Practice makes perfect.

Der ***Mensch*** *denkt, Gott lenkt.*
Man proposes, God disposes.

Vorsicht ist die ***Mutter*** *der Weisheit / der Porzellankiste.*
(Caution is the mother of wisdom / of the china chest.)
Discretion is the better part of valour.

Müßiggang *ist aller Laster Anfang.*
(Idleness is the beginning of all evil.)
The devil makes work for idle hands.

*Von **nichts** kommt nichts.*
(From nothing comes nothing.)
You cannot build on air.

***Not** macht erfinderisch.*
Necessity is the mother of invention.

*In der **Not** frißt der Teufel Fliegen.*
(In need the Devil feeds on flies.)
Beggars can't be choosers.

***Probieren** geht über studieren.*
(Testing / tasting is better than studying.)
The proof of the pudding is in the eating.

*Der **Prophet** gilt nichts in seinem Vaterland.*
No man is a prophet in his own country.

***Reden** ist Silber, Schweigen ist Gold.*
Speech is silver but silence is golden.

*Keine **Regel** ohne Ausnahme.*
There is an exception to every rule.

*Die Ausnahme bestätigt die **Regel.***
The exception proves the rule.

*Auf **Regen** folgt Sonnenschein.*
(Sunshine follows the rain.)
Every cloud has a silver lining.

*Vom **Regen** in die Traufe kommen.*
(To get from the rain into the eaves.)
To fall out of the frying pan into the fire.

***Ruhe** ist die erste Bürgerpflicht.*
A citizen's first duty is to keep the peace.

*Ein gutes Gewissen ist ein sanftes **Ruhekissen.***
(A clear conscience is a soft pillow.)

***Rom** ist nicht an einem Tag erbaut worden.*
Rome wasn't built in a day.

*Was der Mensch **sät,** das wird er auch ernten.*
As ye sow, so shall ye reap.

*Jeder ist seines Glückes **Schmied.***
Every man is the architect of his own fortune / doing.

*Wer gut **schmiert**, der fährt gut.*
(He who greases well travels well.)
He who pays the piper, calls the tune.

***Schuster** bleib bei deinem Leisten.*
The cobbler must stick to his last.

***Sicher** ist sicher.*
Better safe than sorry / You can't be too sure.

*Wo gehobelt wird, da fallen **Späne.***
(Where there is planing, shavings fall.)
You cannot make an omelette without breaking eggs.

*Besser / Lieber ein **Spatz** in der Hand als eine Taube auf dem Dach.*
(Better a sparrow in the hand than a pigeon on the roof.)
A bird in the hand is worth two in the bush.

*Man soll den **Tag** nicht vor dem Abend loben.*
Don't count your chickens before they are hatched.

*Jeder hat einmal einen guten **Tag.*** Every dog has his day.

*Die **Tat** wirkt mehr als das Wort.* Actions speak louder than words.

*Man soll den **Teufel** nicht an die Wand malen.*
(One should not paint the devil on the wall.)
Talk of the devil (and he will appear).

*Der **Ton** macht die Musik.*
(The tone makes the music.)
It is not what you do, but the way that you do it.

*Auf / Für jeden **Topf** findet sich ein Deckel.*
(A lid can be found for every pot / pan.)
There is a nut for every bolt.

*Alter schützt vor **Torheit** nicht.*
There is no fool like an old fool.

***Träume** sind Schäume.*
All dreams evaporate.

*Steter **Tropfen** hölt den Stein.*
Constant dripping wears away the stone.

*Jeder kehre vor seiner eigenen **Tür.***
(Everyone should sweep outside his own door.)
Put your own house in order first.

__Undank__ ist der Welt Lohn.
The world pays with ingratitude.

Allzuviel ist __ungesund.__
Enough is as good as a feast. / You can have too much of a good thing.

Ein __Unglück__ kommt selten allein.
It never rains, but it pours. / Troubles never come singly.

__Unkraut__ vergeht nicht.
(Weeds won't perish.)
Ill weeds grow apace.

__Unrecht__ Gut gedeihet nicht.
Ill-gotten gains are cursed.

Wer __wagt__, gewinnt. (Who dares, wins.)
Nothing ventured, nothing gained.

__Wasser__ hat keine Balken. (Water has no beams.)
Praise the sea but stay on land. / You must either sink or swim.

Dem Mutigen gehört die __Welt.__
Fortune favours the brave.

Was nicht ist, kann noch __werden.__
Your day may come.

Wo ein __Wille__ ist, da ist auch ein Weg.
Where there's a will, there's a way.

Was du nicht __willst__ das man dir tu', das füg' auch keinem andern zu.
Do unto others as you would be done by.

Wer __Wind__ sät, der wird Sturm ernten.
He who sows a wind will reap a whirlwind.

__Wohltun__ bringt Zinsen.
One good turn deserves another.

__Worte__ sind leerer Schall.
Words are but wind.

Der __Wunsch__ ist der Vater des Gedankens.
(The wish is father to the thought.)

Geld ist die __Wurzel__ allen Übels.
Money is the root of all evil.

Kommt __Zeit__, kommt Rat.
Time will tell.

SPECIAL VOCABULARIES

Sections 140–51 provide selective vocabulary lists for twelve important thematic areas. The first five are of general or everyday interest, and are intended to take your vocabulary beyond the basic expressions common to most phrasebooks. Sections 145–51 are more specialized, and depending whether you want German primarily for business, keeping up with current affairs, scientific research or literary and cultural studies, you will find one or more sections addressed to your needs.

The specialized vocabularies are aimed at the educated layman's choice of words and should help you to understand a quality newspaper article on a particular subject. Of course they are not exhaustive on any topic, but they offer you a practical resource for looking up terms you may meet, and for increasing your own word power. Some of the terms may have other meanings in different contexts.

40 Numbers and statistics

In formal written German, numbers 1–20 are written out in full. After 20, figures are allowed.

(a) Cardinal numbers

0	*null* (see below)		
1	*eins* (*ein / eine*) (see below)	11	*elf*
2	*zwei*	12	*zwölf*
3	*drei*	13	*dreizehn*
4	*vier*	14	*vierzehn*
5	*fünf*	15	*fünfzehn*
6	*sechs*	16	*sechzehn* (no *s* in the middle)
7	*sieben*	17	*siebzehn* (no *en* in the middle)
8	*acht*	18	*achtzehn*
9	*neun*	19	*neunzehn*
10	*zehn*	20	*zwanzig*

21	*einundzwanzig*	30	*dreißig*
22	*zweiundzwanzig*	40	*vierzig*
23	*dreiundzwanzig*	50	*fünfzig*
24	*vierundzwanzig*	60	*sechzig* (no *s* in the middle)
25	*fünfundzwanzig*	70	*siebzig* (no *en* in the middle)
26	*sechsundzwanzig*	80	*achtzig*
27	*siebenundzwanzig*	90	*neunzig*
28	*achtundzwanzig*	100	*(ein) hundert*
29	*neunundzwanzig*		

N.B. The final *–ig* for tens is pronounced *ch* as in *ich* (see section 68).

101 *(ein) hunderteins*
102 *hundertzwei*
etc.

1 000 *(ein) tausend*
1 000 000 *(eine) Million*
1 000 000 000 *(eine) Milliarde*
1 000 000 000 000 *(eine Billion* (see section 138(a))
1 000 000 000 000 000 000 *(eine) Trillion*

Note the capital letters!

(i) *null*

Null is used for the description of the figure 0 and also for the English word 'zero' (e.g. *Null Grad* zero degrees).

(ii) *eins*

Eins is used for the description of the figure 1 (e.g. in telephone numbers: *null sechs eins vier sieben*) and whenever the word 'one' stands on its own:

Es is eins. It is one (o'clock).
Einmal eins ist eins. One times one is one.

But:

Es ist ein Uhr. It is one o'clock.

Er bekam eine Eins in der Prüfung.
He got a (grade) 1 in the exam.

School grades are from 1 to 6:

1 *sehr gut* very good
2 *gut* good
3 *befriedigend* satisfactory
4 *ausreichend* sufficient
5 *mangelhaft* poor (literally: lacking)
6 *ungenügend* unsatisfactory (literally: insufficient)

N.B. If a student gets two 5s or one 6 he or she has to repeat that school year.

(iii) *ein / eine*

Ein / eine is declined when the number refers to a person or a thing. It takes the ending of the noun's grammatical gender, e.g.:

ein Mann	*eine Frau*	*ein Kind*
ein Tisch	*eine Tür*	*ein Sofa*

You cannot usually distinguish between 'one' and 'a / an' (e.g. *ein Mann* one man / a man) unless you stress *ein*, meaning 'one', by intonation, or by double-spacing in written German:

Alle Menschen sprechen eine Sprache, aber nicht alle Menschen sprechen e i n e Sprache. (i.e. *die gleiche Sprache*)
All humans speak a language, but not all humans speak one language. (i.e. the same language)

(iv) *zwo*

Zwo is used for 2 in order to distinguish *zwei* from *drei* when giving numbers orally.

(v) Gender

All numbers (*die Zahl(en) / die Nummer(n)*) are feminine, e.g.

die Eins, die Zwei, die Sechs, die Hundert, die Billion
EXCEPTIONS: *das / die Tausend; das / die Hundert*

(b) Ordinal numbers

Ordinal numbers are used to place people or things into an arithmetical order, such as 'the third' or 'the fifteenth'.

1st *der erste*	6th *der sechste*
2nd *der zweite*	7th *der siebte* (no *en*)
3rd *der dritte*	8th *der achte*
4th *der vierte*	9th *der neunte*
5th *der fünfte*	10th *der zehnte* (etc.)

Usually the ending -*te* is added to the cardinal numbers between 2 and 19. The exceptions are underlined above.

From '20th' onwards -*ste* is added to the cardinal number:

20th *der zwanzigste*
21st *der einundzwanzigste* etc.
100th *der hundertste*

(i) Declension of ordinal numbers

Ordinal numbers are always declined (see section 13):

Sie erhielt den ersten Preis.
She received the first prize.

Er spielte in der zweiten Mannschaft.
He played in the second team.

Sie war seine dritte Frau.
She was his third wife.

Ich komme am vierten Januar. (See section 141(b).)
I am coming on 4 January.

(ii) Sovereigns

Ordinal numbers used in the titles of royalty begin with capital letters and are declined like adjectives treated as nouns (see section 5(e)).

Heinrich der Achte	Henry VIII
die Frauen Heinrichs des Achten	the wives of Henry VIII
Wilhelm der Erste	William I
ein Buch über Wilhelm den Ersten	a book about William I

(c) Round numbers

(i) Approximations

To give approximations, add -*e* to (cardinal) numbers, e.g.

Hunderte (100te), Tausende (1000e).

Round numbers are usually, but not necessarily, followed by *von*:

Tausende von Demonstranten waren nach Bonn gekommen.
Thousands of demonstrators had come to Bonn.

Zehntausende DDR-Flüchtlinge drängten sich in die Aufnahmelager.
Tens of thousands of GDR refugees crowded into the reception camps.

(ii) Other round numbers

ein Dutzend(e) a dozen
in acht Tagen in a week's time
in vierzehn Tagen in two weeks' time / in a fortnight
in ein paar Tagen in a few days' time

(iii) *ein paar / ein Paar*

Ein paar without a capital means 'some', or 'a couple' (in the vague sense, meaning two, three or more)

Ein Paar(e) (with a capital) means 'a pair' or 'a couple' (meaning husband and wife etc.), or 'a pair of' (trousers, shoes).

★ There is never a preposition between the expression of quantity (pairs, bottles, boxes etc.) and the item specified:

ein Paar Schuhe a pair **of** shoes
eine Flasche Wein a bottle **of** wine
eine Schachtel Streichhölzer a box **of** matches

(d) Statistics and percentages

(i) Decimals

Decimals are separated by a comma, e.g. *3,50 DM = drei Mark fünfzig*, but thousands may be divided off by full stops, e.g. *2.000.000*, or spaces.

(ii) Fractions

Fractions are formed by adding *-tel* to the stem of the cardinal numbers 3 to 19, e.g.

ein Viertel, ein Sechstel, ein Sieb(en)tel, ein Zehntel, etc.

N.B.: *die Hälfte* half *ein Drittel* a third

After 19 add *-stel*, e.g.

ein Zwanzigstel, ein Tausendstel

The endings *-tel* and *-stel* are short for *das Teil(e)*, therefore all fractions are neuter.

(iii) Multiples

Multiples are formed by adding *-mal* to the stem of cardinal numbers 1 – infinity, e.g.

dreimal, siebenmal, tausendmal

Man hat Heinrich Heines Gedichte dreitausendmal in Musik gesetzt.
Heinrich Heine's poems have been set to music three thousand times.

You can also use the prefix *ver-* and the suffix *-fachen* to make a (reflexive) verb, e.g. *sich verdreifachen* to triple:

Das Bruttosozialprodukt (BSP) hat sich vervierfacht.
The Gross National Product (GNP) has quadrupled.

N.B. *sich verdoppeln* to double.

Likewise, adjectives can be constructed by adding *-fach*, -fold:

die zehnfache Menge ten times the amount
in vierfacher Ausfertigung in quadruplicate
in dreifacher Vergrößerung enlarged three times

N.B. *einfach* simple (literally: onefold) *doppelt* double

These adjectives can also be used as nouns, e.g. *das Siebenfache* etc.

(iv) Sample sentences

Die durchschnittliche Lebenserwartung der Frauen liegt bei 77 Jahren. Die der Männer bei 72.
The average life-expectancy for women is about 77 years; for men about 72.

Jeder fünfte Schüler wird die Schule ohne Zeugnis verlassen.
One pupil in five will leave school without qualifications.

Ein Drittel der Befragten besitzt einen CD Spieler.
A third of those questioned own a CD player.

N.B. The singular is used after fractions.

Dreißig Prozent der Wählerschaft bevorzugen dieses System.
Thirty per cent of the electorate prefer this system.

Der Anteil der Arbeitslosen ist um 0,3% auf 2,24 Millionen angestiegen.
The percentage (literally: share) of people unemployed has risen by 0.3% to 2.24 million.

Die Gesamtzahl der Erwerbslosen hat sich verdreifacht.
The total number of unemployed (literally: people without earnings) has tripled.

Der Warenexport ist um 2% zurückgegangen.
Export of goods has declined by 2%.

Der Schaden liegt zwischen 5.000 und 6.000 Mark.
The damage amounts to between 5,000 and 6,000 DM.

Die Berechnungen des Statistischen Bundesamtes ergaben eine Inflationsrate von 1,2%.
The Federal Office for Statistics calculated the inflation rate at 1.2%.

Die Lebenshaltungskosten sind im vergangenen Jahr insgesamt um 1,4% gestiegen.
The cost of living rose by 1.4% in the past year.

Der Anteil der Erwerbstätigen im Alter von 20 bis 60 Jahren wird von 58% (1987) auf 48% (2040) sinken.
The proportion of those in paid employment aged between 20 and 60 will fall from 58% (in 1987) to 48% (in 2040).

Ebenso wie im Vorjahr nahm 1988 die Zahl der Geburten in der BRD zu.
As in the previous year, the number of births in the FRG increased in 1988.

Die Volkszählung 1987 ergab, daß sich die Bevölkerung der BRD im Vergleich zur letzten Zählung von 1970 um 432 000 erhöht hat.
The 1987 (national) census revealed that the population had increased by 432,000 compared with the last census in 1970.

Diese Angaben sind 'ohne Gewähr'.
No liability assumed for these data. / No responsibility is accepted for the accuracy of this information.

Ohne Gewähr (on timetables, programmes etc.) means 'subject to change'.

(e) Idiomatic expressions referring to numbers

null

die Stunde Null (the time of) the new beginning (especially in Germany after World War II)

eins

ein für alle mal once and for all
das Einmalhandtuch(¨er) disposable towel
die Einmalbettwäsche disposable bed-linen

> *Ein Unglück kommt selten allein.* (proverb)
> It never rains but it pours.
>
> *Einmal ist keinmal.*
> Once is nothing at all. / Just once won't matter.

auf einmal all at once / suddenly

> *Sie waren alle auf einmal am Ziel angekommen.*
> They all arrived at the finishing line at the same time.
>
> *Wir fuhren langsam durch einen Tunnel, und auf einmal blieb der Zug stehen.*
> We travelled slowly through a tunnel and suddenly the train stopped.

zwei

sich etwas nicht zweimal sagen lassen not to need to be told twice / not to think twice about something
zwischen zwei Stühlen sitzen to sit on the fence / to fall between two stools

drei

> *Alle(r) guten Dinge sind drei.*
> All good things come in threes.

nicht bis drei zählen können not to know how many beans make five (literally: not to be able to count to three)
ehe man bis drei zählen konnte in less than no time / in a trice / before you could say Jack Robinson (literally: before you could count to three)
ein Dreikäsehoch < coll. > a tiny tot (literally: a (person) three cheeses high)

die Dreieinigkeit / die Dreifaltigkeit the (Holy) Trinity
der Dritte im Bunde sein to make a third / to be the third person
in Gegenwart Dritter in the presence of other people
der lachende Dritte the lucky outsider

vier

auf allen vieren kriechen to crawl on all fours
ein Gespräch unter vier Augen a conversation in confidence

fünf

fünf gerade sein lassen < coll. > to turn a blind eye / to let things slide (literally: to let five be an even number)
das fünfte Rad am Wagen sein to be superfluous / in the way
seine fünf Sinne nicht beisammen haben < coll. > not to be quite right in the head

sechs

einen sechsten Sinn für etwas haben to have a sixth sense for something

sieben

seine Siebensachen packen < coll > to pack one's things together / gather up one's stuff
im siebten Himmel sein to be on cloud nine
mit Siebenmeilenstiefeln with giant strides (literally: seven league boots)

acht

die Achterbahn(en) roller coaster

neun

Ach du grüne Neune! < coll.> Oh my goodness! / Good grief!
neunmalklug sein (ironic) to be a smart alec

zehn

das Zehnfingersystem touch-typing (method)
das Zehnersystem decimal system
die Zehn Gebote the Ten Commandments (Old Testament)

elf

einen Elfmeter schießen (football) to take a penalty (kick)

zwölf

in zwölfter Stunde / um fünf vor zwölf at the eleventh hour / in the nick of time / at the last minute

dreizehn

Jetzt schlägt's dreizehn!
That's the limit / too much! (literally: Now the clock strikes 13.)

neunundneunzig

auf neunundneunzig sein < coll. > to be up in arms

hundert

Ich habe dir das schon hundertmal gesagt.
I've told you that a hundred times.

141 Times, dates and temporal expressions

(a) The time

The 24-hour clock is used in all official timetables, e.g.:

Abfahrt 16 Uhr 21	departure 16.21
Ankunft 17 Uhr 15	arrival 17.15

Even in conversation someone might suggest:

Wir treffen uns um 19 Uhr. We'll meet at 7 p.m.

For minutes past the hour, the informal use is:

viertel nach sechs	a quarter past six
halb sieben	half past six

N.B. You are looking towards the next hour; in the South of Germany you might even hear *viertel sieben* (a) quarter past six.

dreiviertel sieben	a quarter to seven
viertel vor sieben	(a) quarter to seven

(i) To ask the time

Wieviel Uhr ist es, bitte? What time is it, please?

Wie spät ist es, bitte? What's the time, please?

Um wieviel Uhr beginnt das Konzert?
What time does the concert start?

Bitte, haben Sie die genaue Uhrzeit?
Would you have the exact / correct time, please?

(ii) To give an approximate time

Wir kommen etwa um vier Uhr an.
We'll arrive at about four o'clock.

Er wird gegen 17 Uhr eintreffen. < slightly more formal >
He will arrive around 5 p.m.

(iii) Clocks and watches

Die Uhr geht vor. The clock is fast.

Die Uhr geht nach. The clock is slow.

Meine Uhr ist stehengeblieben. My watch has stopped.

N.B. *die Uhr(en)* is used for both clock and watch. In order to be more specific a compound noun is needed:

die Armbanduhr	(wrist)watch
die Küchenuhr	(kitchen) clock
die Kuckucksuhr	cuckoo clock
die Standuhr	grandfather clock

(b) Dates

See sections 140(a) and (b) for use of cardinal and ordinal numbers, and section 50 for the word order of time – manner – place.

(i) Giving a day and date

In writing:

Montag, den (acc.) *14. Mai* Monday, 14 May (see section 110).

In conversation:

am Montag, den / dem vierzehnten Mai
on Monday, the fourteenth of May

When giving dates over the phone, use *Juno* instead of *Juni* to distinguish clearly from *Juli.*

To write dates for forms, use day / month / year: *30.04.95* or *30. April 1995*

Remember that ordinal numbers are declined:

Heute ist der dritte Dezember.
Today is the third of December.

Ich habe am 31. (einunddreißigsten) August Geburtstag.
My birthday is on (the) 31(st of) August.

(ii) To ask the date

Welches Datum haben wir heute? < formal >
What is the date today?

Den wievielten haben wir heute? What's the date today?

Der wievielte ist heute? What's the date today?

(iii) To refer to years

The figure relating to a particular year is never preceded by a preposition:

Das war 1992. That was in 1992.

Heinrich Böll starb 1985. Heinrich Böll died in 1985.

Alternatively, you could say:

Das geschah im Jahre 1992.
That happened in (the year) 1992.

Er wurde im Jahre 1917 in Köln geboren.
He was born in Cologne in 1917.

Die Krönung Kaiser Karls des Großen fand im Jahre 800 statt.
The coronation of Charlemagne took place in 800.

A leap year is *das Schaltjahr*:

alle Schaltjahre once in a blue moon (literally: every leap year)

(iv) Historic dates

AD / n. Chr. (nach Christus) AD
v. Chr. (vor Christus) BC

In the former GDR, where the state doctrine was atheist, in books, museums etc. you might well have come across *v.u.Z.*, which stands for *vor unser Zeitrechnung* (before our era).

Centuries, as in English, are referred to as part of the next full century:

das 19. Jahrhundert	the 19th century (1801–1900)
in den zwanziger Jahren (20er Jahren)	in the twenties
in den vierziger Jahren (40er Jahren)	in the forties (etc.)
der Zweite Weltkrieg	the Second World War
vor dem Zweiten Weltkrieg	before the Second World War.

(c) Referring to the past

See also section 50.

die Vergangenheit	the past
gestern	yesterday
vorgestern	the day before yesterday
vorvorgestern < informal >	three days ago
neulich	recently
letzte Woche	last week
vorletzte Woche	the week before last

letztes Jahr	last year
vorletztes Jahr	the year before last
eines Tages (gen.) *geschah etwas*	one day something happened
damals	at the time / then
früher (adverb)	formerly / in earlier times / used to

Früher hatte man die Toilette über dem Hof.
In those days the toilet was across the yard.

Früher fuhr ich mit dem Rad zur Schule.
I used to go to school by bike.

sonst	otherwise / at other times
zu jener Zeit < literary / biblical / archaic >	in those days
es war einmal	once upon a time there was / were

Es war einmal, so fangen alle Märchen an.
Once upon a time, that is how all fairy-tales start.

zu der Zeit als	at the time (when)
als	when (one single occurrence in the past)
wann immer	when / whenever
voriges Jahr	last year
anno dazumal	in olden times
einst	once / some day
kürzlich	recently / later
mein verstorbener Mann	my late husband

★ N.B. *vor* preceding an expression of time means 'that time ago' not 'for' (see *vor* in section 138(a)). Compare the following pairs:

vor acht Tagen a week ago
vor 2 500 Jahren 2,500 years ago

acht Tage lang for eight days
2 500 Jahre lang for 2,500 years

Urgermanisch wurde vor 2 500 Jahren gesprochen.
Primitive Germanic / Proto-Germanic was spoken 2,500 years ago.

Man sprach diese Sprache etwa 1 000 Jahre lang.
People (literally: one) spoke this language for about 1,000 years.

(d) Referring to the present

die Gegenwart	the (abstract) present / (physical) presence
heute	today
jetzt	now
heutzutage	nowadays

gegenwärtig	at the present
zur Zeit (z. Zt.)	at this time / at the moment
schon	already
derzeit (gen.) < formal >	at the moment
vorerst	for the time being
zunächst	first of all / for the time being
soeben	just now
inzwischen	meanwhile
endlich	finally
sofort	at once
bald	soon
alsbald < archaic >	presently
gerade	just (used to express continuous action)

Ich schreibe gerade. I am writing at this moment.

nun	now
eben	just now
aktuell (adjective) [FA]	up-to-date / current (see section 138a)
bis jetzt	up to now
bisher < slightly archaic >	hitherto
manchmal	sometimes
in diesem Jahrhundert	this century
nach wie vor	now as always

(e) Referring to the future

die Zukunft	future
zukünftig	in future
danach	afterwards
daraufhin	thereupon
schließlich	finally / eventually / in the end
auf immer und ewig	for ever and ever
in alle Ewigkeit	for ever and ever (literally: in all eternity)
morgen	tomorrow
übermorgen	the day after tomorrow
überübermorgen < coll. >	in three days' time
morgen früh	tomorrow morning
heute nachmittag	this afternoon
heute abend	this evening / tonight
heute nacht	tonight (after bed-time)

N.B. *heute nacht* could also refer back to the night before (if talked about the next morning).

heute in einer Woche	a week from today
morgen in einer Woche / in acht Tagen	a week from tomorrow
Dienstag in vierzehn Tagen / zwei Wochen	two weeks from Tuesday
am nächsten Tag	the next day
in drei Tagen	in three days' time / three days from now
ab sofort	from now on / as from now
am Sonntag abend	Sunday night
in der Nacht zum Sonntag	Saturday (!) night
in der Nacht von Sonntag auf Montag	in the night from Sunday to Monday

(f) Referring to habitual actions

abends	in the evenings
endlich	finally
gewöhnlich	usually
häufig	frequently
immer	always
immer wieder	again and again
in der Regel	as a rule
jährlich	annually
jederzeit	at any time
jedesmal	each time
meistens	most of the time / mostly
morgens	in the mornings
nachmittags / mittags	in the afternoons
nochmals	once again
normalerweise	normally
oft	often
pro Tag / Stunde / Jahr, etc.	per day / hour / year, etc.
stets	always
täglich	daily

> *Dreimal täglich Zähne putzen . . .*
> Brush teeth three times a day . . .
>
> *. . . und zweimal jährlich zum Zahnarzt.*
> . . . and (go) to the dentist twice a year.

vorzeitig	ahead of time
vorfristig (former GDR)	ahead of time
wiederum	again / afresh
wöchentlich	weekly

All the above adverbs have small initial letters. Note that most can be used as nouns, e.g.:

morgens but *am Morgen*
abends but *am Abend*
samstags but *am Samstag*

142 The weather

For the more common expressions relating to the weather (those based on impersonal verbs), see section 6.

(a) Conversational expressions

Hast du die Wettervorhersage gehört?
Have you heard the weather forecast?

Wie wird das Wetter morgen?
What is the weather going to be like tomorrow?

Das war eine richtige Hitzewelle.
That was a real heatwave.

Es war eiskalt. It was freezing cold.

Vorsicht, es gibt bestimmt Glatteis.
Careful, I'm sure there'll be black ice.

Ein Gewitter zieht auf.
There's a (thunder) storm brewing.

Wir erwarten einen Wettersturz.
We are expecting the weather to turn bad.

(b) Weather reports

(i) Typical weather forecasts on the television or radio

These usually follow the news. Note the telegram-style sentences in the examples below. Forecasts in Germany tend to be much more neutral in tone and more formal than in Britain.

All temperatures are in Celsius.

Nach den Meldungen die Wettervorhersage für Hessen bis morgen abend, ausgegeben vom deutschen Wetterdienst um 18 Uhr 15.	After the news the weather forecast for Hesse until tomorrow evening, issued by the German meteorological office at 6.15 p.m.
Wolkig mit Aufheiterungen, nachmittags und abends zum Teil kräftige Gewitter. Wechselnd, zeitweilig stark bewölkt mit einzelnen Schauern.	Cloudy with bright spells, in the afternoon and evening thunderstorms, which will be heavy in places. Changeable, occasionally very cloudy, with isolated showers.

Tiefsttemperaturen in der kommenden Nacht um zwölf Grad.	Minimum temperatures tonight around 12 degrees.
Morgen wechselnd wolkig und einzelne Schauer. Tageshöchsttemperaturen 18 bis 22 Grad, im Bergland bei 15 Grad.	Tomorrow, frequent cloudy periods and some isolated showers. Maximum temperatures during the day 18 to 22 degrees, in mountain regions around 15 degrees.
Schwacher bis mäßiger, mitunter auch böiger Wind aus westlichen Richtungen.	Light to moderate, occasionally gusty, winds from westerly directions.
Die weiteren Aussichten für Montag und Dienstag: Wechselhaft, bei etwas steigenden Temperaturen.	Outlook for Monday and Tuesday: Changeable, with temperatures rising slightly.

(ii) Other useful expressions

wenig Änderung little change
starke Regenfälle heavy rainfall

Für die zweite Wochenhälfte wird mit Schneeverwehungen gerechnet.
Snowdrifts are expected during the second half of the week.

Von Westen her starke Bewölkung.
Cloud will increase from the West.

Für diese Jahreszeit verhältnismäßig kühl.
Relatively cool for this time of year.

(c) Long-term climatic changes

Klimaexperten fürchten einen globalen Temperaturanstieg.
Climatologists fear a global warming effect.

Man spricht von einer Zunahme des Treibhauseffekts.
There is talk of an increase in the greenhouse effect.

Die Ozonschicht ist bedroht.
The ozone layer is threatened.

Sollen wir uns vor einer neuen Eiszeit fürchten?
Should we fear a new ice age?

Die Wissenschaftler warnen vor den möglichen Folgen einer globalen Erwärmung.
Scientists warn of the possible consequences of global warming.

Die durch die lange Trockenheit hervorgerufenen Probleme verschlimmern sich.
The problems caused by the prolonged dry spell / drought are growing worse.

143 Travel

(a) Motoring

(i) Parts of the car

der Auspuff	exhaust
das Auspuffrohr(e)	exhaust pipe
die Batterie(n)	battery
die Bremse(n)	brake
der Bremsbelag	brake-lining / pad
die Bremsscheibe(n)	brake-disc
die Bremsbacke(n)	brake-shoe
die Birne(n)	(light)bulb
die Ersatzbirne	spare bulb
die Dichtung(en)	gasket / seal
der Druck	pressure

Bitte prüfen Sie den Reifendruck / Ölstand.
Please check the tyre pressure / the oil.

der Fahrtrichtungsanzeiger(–) / der Blinker(–) < coll.>	indicator
die Gangschaltung(en)	gear box
der Schalthebel(–)	gear lever
das Gaspedal(e)	accelerator
die Hupe	horn
der Katalysator(en)	catalytic converter/catalyser
der Keilriemen(–)	fan belt
der Kofferraum(¨e)	boot (US trunk)
der Kühler(–)	radiator
die Kühlerhaube(n)	bonnet (US hood)
die Kupplung	clutch
die Kupplung lösen	to let out the clutch
das Licht(er)	light
das Abblendlicht	dipped headlight
das Fernlicht	full beam
das Standlicht	sidelight
das Bremslicht	brake light
das Nebellicht	fog light
der Motor(en)	engine
die Motorhaube(n)	bonnet (US hood)
das Nummernschild(er) / das Autokennzeichen(–)	number-plate (see note below)
das Rad(¨er)	wheel
der Reifen(–)	tyre
der Ersatzreifen	spare tyre

der Winterreifen	deep-tread tyre (for winter driving)
eine Reifenpanne haben	to have a puncture
der Scheibenwischer(–)	windscreen wiper
der Scheinwerfer(–)	headlight
die Sicherung(en)	fuse
die Ersatzsicherung	spare fuse
der Sitz(e)	seat
der Kindersitz	child seat
der Rücksitz	back seat
der Vordersitz	front seat
der Beifahrersitz	front passenger seat
der Spiegel(–)	mirror
der Außenspiegel	wing mirror
der Rückspiegel	rear-view mirror
der Stoßdämpfer(–)	shock absorber
der Tachometer(–)	speedometer
der Tank	petrol tank
der Ersatztank	reserve tank / can
das Ventil(e)	valve
der Verbandskasten(¨)	first-aid kit
der Vergaser(–)	carburettor
der Wagenheber(–)	jack
die Wagentür(en)	car door
das Warndreieck(e)	warning triangle
das Werkzeug	tool
die Windschutzscheibe(n)	windscreen
die Zentralverriegelung	central locking (system)
die Zündkerze(n)	spark plug
die Zündung	ignition
der Zündschlüssel(–)	ignition key
der Zylinder(–)	cylinder

N.B. You can tell from the number plate where a car is registered. The letters at the beginning signify the town or district, e.g.:

F	stands for *Frankfurt*	*BN*	for *Bonn*
B	for *Berlin*	*HD*	for *Heidelberg*
L	for *Leipzig*	*MTK*	for *Main-Taunus Kreis*

The system is being expanded to take in new registrations from the former GDR. Large cities usually have just one letter, whereas small towns or provincial districts have up to three letters. You can therefore make assumptions about whether or not the driver is used to city traffic. If people move to another district they have to re-register. Old numbers are recycled. There is no way of telling the year of registration from the number plate.

If you take your car to Germany, remember that in addition to the 'green card' (for insurance), it is compulsory to carry a *Warndreieck* (warning triangle) and a *Verbandskasten* (first-aid kit). The ADAC (see below) also recommends that you take *Ersatzbirnen* (spare bulbs) and *Ersatzsicherungen* (spare fuses).

(ii) Travelling by car

ab◊bremsen	to slow down
die Abgase (pl.)	exhaust fumes
ab◊schleppen	to tow away
der ADAC = Allgemeiner Deutscher Automobilclub	Automobile Association
die ADAC Straßenwacht	(ADAC) patrol
der Alcotest(s) (brand name)	Breathalyzer
der Atemalkoholtest	breathalyser (test)
das Pustegerät(e) < coll. >	breathalyser (test)

Er weigerte sich, ins Röhrchen zu blasen.
He refused to be breathalysed.

die Ampel(n)	set of traffic lights
*bei rot über die Ampel fahren**	to go through a red light
*per Anhalter fahren**	to hitch-hike
*an◊lassen**	to start (an engine)

Ich lasse den Motor an. I'm starting the engine.

*an◊springen**	to start (intransitive)

Der Wagen springt nicht an. The car won't start.

die Bahn(en)	track / way
die Autobahn(en) (abbreviated *A*)	motorway (M)
eine vierspurige (Fahr-)Bahn	dual carriageway (tracks are counted in both directions)
bremsen	to brake
eine Vollbremsung machen	to make an emergency stop (by slamming on the brakes)
die Bremsspur(en)	skid mark
der Bremsweg	braking distance
*fahren**	
an◊fahren	to start (up) / move off (e.g. at traffic lights)
auf◊fahren auf	to run / drive into / on to
der Auffahrunfall(¨e)	rear-end collision
die Autobahnauffahrt(en)	slip road on to motorway
los◊fahren	to drive off
überfahren ♦	to run over

der Fahrer(–)	driver
der Beifahrer(–)	front passenger
der Mitfahrer(–)	passenger
*Gas geben**	to increase speed
die Geschwindigkeit(en)	speed
die Geschwindigkeitsgrenze(n)	the speed limit
auf Landstraßen ist 100 km / h	on secondary roads is 100 km / h
in geschlossenen Ortschaften ist 50 km / h	within towns is 50 km / h

Die Richtgeschwindigkeit(en) auf Autobahnen ist 130 km / h.
The recommended speed limit on motorways is 130 km / h.

glatt	slippery
das Glatteis	black ice
hupen	to blow one's horn
die Inspektion(en)	service
die Kreuzung(en)	crossroads
die Einmündung in die Vorfahrtsstraße	T-junction
die Gabelkreuzung	'Y' (forked) junction
der Kundendienst	(customer) service

Könnten Sie bitte den Kundendienst machen?
Could you please service the car?

die Leistung	performance
der LKW (Lastkraftwagen)	HGV (heavy goods vehicle)
der Laster(–) < coll. >	lorry
die Massenkarambolage	multiple crash / pile up
die Panne(n)	breakdown

Er hatte eine Panne mit dem Auto.
His car broke down.

eine Reifenpanne haben	to have a puncture
die Parkkralle(n)	wheel clamp
die Parkscheibe(n)	parking-disc
die Parkuhr(en)	parking-meter
der PKW (Personenkraftwagen)	(private) vehicle / car
einen Platten haben < coll. >	to have a puncture (literally: a flat one)
die Politesse(n)	(female) traffic warden
die Promillegrenze	(alcohol) limit
die (Autobahn)Raststätte(n)	(motorway) service station
*rückwärts fahren**	to reverse
der Service (no pl.)	service
die Sicherheit	safety
der Sicherheitsgurt(e)	seatbelt
die Verkehrssicherheit	road safety

die Spur(en)	lane / carriageway
die Spur wechseln	to change lanes
die Abbiegespur	exit lane (on motorway)
die Überholspur	fast lane
die rechte Fahrspur	inside (!) lane (on the Continent)
auf der falschen Spur überholen ♦	to overtake on the inside
der Stau(s)	traffic jam
ein 15km langer Stau	15km tailback
steuern	to steer
die Steuerung	steering
das Steuerrad(¨er)	steering wheel
die Straße(n)	road, street
die Bundesstraße (abbreviated *B*)	main (A) road
die Landstraße	secondary (B) road
die Schnellstraße	dual carriageway
tanken	to fill up with petrol
*überfahren** ♦	to run over

Er hatte eine Katze überfahren.
He had run over a cat.

überholen ♦	to overtake
die Umgehungsstraße(n)	bypass
die Umleitung(en)	diversion
der Umweg(e)	detour
der Verkehr	traffic
starker Verkehr	heavy traffic
starkes Verkehrsaufkommen	large (increased) volume of traffic
der Verkehrsfunk	radio traffic service
das Verkehrszeichen	traffic sign
die Verkehrsregel(n)	traffic regulation
der Verkehrssünder	traffic offender
das Verkehrssünderverzeichnis in Flensburg	register of traffic offences kept in Flensburg
versagen	to fail

Als sie den steilen Berg hinunterfuhr, versagten plötzlich die Bremsen.
When she drove down the steep hill the brakes suddenly failed.

der Vorsprung	lead / advantage (literally: leap forward / ahead)

Vorsprung durch Technik (VAG slogan)
Ahead through technology

der Wagen(–)	car
der Wegweiser(–)	signpost
*zusammen◊stoßen** mit*	to collide with

For reports on road and traffic conditions listen to the *Verkehrsfunk* (traffic news) on local radio stations. The wavelengths are advertised on motorway boards. Or you could ring the *ADAC Verkehrsservice*, or a local information service (*Straßenzustandsbericht*: Tel. 01169 from most telephone areas).

And please remember: another driver flashing his or her headlights at you is trying to warn you or showing annoyance. It does not mean 'after you'!

(b) Public transport

(i) Tickets and timetables

die Abfahrt(en)	departure (of trains, buses etc.)
der Abflug(¨e)	departure (of planes)
die Ankunft(¨e)	arrival
der Anschluß (-schlüsse)	connection
der Bahnsteig(e) / das Gleis(e)	platform
die Bordkarte(n)	boarding pass
buchen	to book

Flüge zum Spartarif müssen zeitig gebucht werden.
Cheap-rate flights must be booked in good time.

die Ermäßigung(en)	reduction, concession
die Kinderermäßigung	child concession
die Ermäßigung für Rentner / Senioren	concession for senior citizens
die Fahrkarte(n)	(travel) ticket
der Fahrkartenautomat(en)	ticket machine
der Fahrkartenschalter(–)	ticket window / counter
eine Fahrkarte lösen	to buy a ticket
eine Fahrkarte entwerten	to date-stamp a ticket (literally: to de-value a ticket)
die Rückfahrkarte	return ticket
die Einzelfahrkarte	single ticket
die Streifenkarte	ticket valid for several journeys
die Zeitkarte	season ticket
der Fahrplan(¨e)	timetable
der Fahrpreis(e)	fare
der Flugplan(¨e)	timetable (for flights)
der Flugsteig(e)	departure gate
die Kreuzfahrt(en)	cruise
eine Kreuzfahrt machen	to go on a cruise
Nichtraucher	non-smoking (literally: non-smokers)
das Nichtraucherabteil(e)	non-smoking compartment / section

der Paß (Pässe)	passport
der Passagier(e) / der Fahrgast(¨e)	passenger
das Pauschalangebot(e)	package deal
planmäßig	on schedule / scheduled
regelmäßig	regular / frequent

Es gibt eine regelmäßige Zugverbindung zwischen Frankfurt und Mainz.
There is a regular train service between Frankfurt and Mainz.

das Reiseziel(e)	destination
*Schlange stehen / an◊stehen**	to queue
der Schwarzfahrer(-)	fare-dodger
die Seereise(n)	voyage
*um◊steigen**	to transfer / change (trains etc.)
die Verbindung(en)	connection / service

Gibt es eine (direkte) Flugverbindung nach Wien?
Is there a (direct) flight to Vienna?

die Verkehrsverbindung(en)	transport link
der Verkehrsverbund(¨e)	transport authority / network (see note below)
der Verkehrsverein(e)	tourist information office
das Wechselgeld	small change

Bitte Wechselgeld bereithalten. Please have exact fare ready.

der Zeitplan(¨e)	schedule
der Zuschlag(¨e)	additional fare / supplement
die Zwischenlandung(en)	stopover

N.B. The *Verkehrsverbund* is the public transport system in major cities, incorporating trains, buses, underground railway etc. Tickets are valid for certain areas, in which any means of transport can be used. There are different fares for peak and off-peak times. Tickets are purchased from *Fahrkartenautomaten* (ticket machines) and then *entwertet* (date-stamped) in 'orange boxes' (in Frankfurt) or 'blue boxes' (in Munich) (stamping machines). Keep your tickets for inspection. Fines for *Schwarzfahrer* (fare-dodgers) are very heavy.

(ii) Travelling by public transport

*ab◊fahren**	to depart
die Abfahrt(en)	departure (of trains, buses etc.)

Bitte einsteigen. Vorsicht bei der Abfahrt des Zuges. Türen schließen selbsttätig. (announcement on platform)
Please board. Caution as the train is leaving. Doors close automatically.

*ab◊fliegen**	to take off
der Abflug(¨e)	departure (of planes)
das Abteil(e)	(train) compartment
die Ankunft(¨e)	arrival
an◊legen	to dock
die Ansage(n)	announcement
der Anschluß (–schlüsse)	connection
*aus◊steigen**	to get off
der Bahnhof(¨e)	station
der Busbahnhof	bus station
der Bus(se)	bus
die Bushaltestelle(n)	bus stop
der Duty Free Shop	duty free shop
ein◊checken	to check in
ein◊steigen	to get on
die Fähre(n)	ferry, boat
der Flugsteig(e)	departure gate
das Fundbüro(s)	lost property office
das Gepäck	luggage
das Handgepäck	hand luggage
die Gepäckausgabe(n)	baggage claim
das Gleis(e)	platform

Vorsicht auf Gleis eins. Der Zug fährt ein. (announcement)
Caution on platform one, the train is entering the station.

die Grenze(n)	border
der Grenzübergang(¨e)	border crossing
der Hubschrauber(–)	helicopter
der Rettungshubschrauber	rescue helicopter
die Kabine(n)	cabin
die Kreuzfahrt(en)	cruise
eine Kreuzfahrt machen	to go on a cruise
*an Land gehen**	to go ashore
landen	to land
die Mannschaft(en) / die Crew(s)	crew
der Passagier(e) / der Fahrgast(¨e)	passenger
der Schaffner(–)	guard
das Schließfach(¨er)	(left) luggage locker
die Seereise(n)	voyage
die Startbahn(en)	runway
startbereit	ready for take-off
starten	to start
die Störung(en)	disruption
Störung im Betriebsablauf	interruption of services (announcement on a platform, given as apology and reason for delays)

die Straßenbahn(en)	tram
das Taxi(s)	taxi
der Taxistand(¨e)	taxi rank
das Terminal(s)	terminal
*um◊steigen**	to transfer / change (trains etc.)
das Verkehrsmittel	means of transport
öffentliche Verkehrsmittel	public transport
das Verkehrsnetz(e)	traffic network
verpassen	to miss

Wenn wir uns nicht beeilen, verpassen wir den Zug.
If we don't hurry we'll miss the train.

die Verspätung(en)	delay
mit Verspätung	behind schedule

Der Fernschnellzug nach München hat fünf Minuten Verspätung.
The long-distance express (train) to Munich is running five minutes late.

der Wagen(–)	car / carriage / wagon
der Güterwagen	goods / freight wagon
der Schlafwagen	sleeper
der Speisewagen	dining car
der Zeitplan (¨e)	schedule
planmäßig	on schedule / scheduled
der Zoll	customs, duty
die Zollgrenze(n)	border control
die Zollerklärung(en)	customs declaration
zollfreier Einkauf	duty-free purchase / shopping
der Zug(¨e)	train
der Fernschnellzug(¨e)	long distance express (train)
der Nahverkehrszug(¨e)	local train
der Intercity	intercity
der ICE (Intercity Express)	ICE (high-speed train)
der Zusammenstoß(¨e)	collision
die Zwischenlandung(en)	stopover

44 Shopping

(a) Types of shops

die Apotheke(n)	dispensing pharmacy (with small selection of cosmetics and sundries)
die Boutique(n)	boutique
die Drogerie(n)	chemist (no prescriptions)
die Einkaufsstraße(n)	pedestrian shopping area (in town)

das Einkaufszentrum (-zentren)	shopping centre (sometimes out of town)
das Fachgeschäft(e) für . . .	shop specializing in . . .
das Geschäft(e)	shop / business
die Handlung(en) < archaic >	shop / business
das Immobiliengeschäft(e)	estate agents
das Kaufhaus(¨er)	department store e.g.:
der Kaufhof, Aldi, die Quelle, Hertie, Karstadt, Horten	
der Kiosk(s)	kiosk selling cigarettes, drinks and newspapers
das Lebensmittelgeschäft(e)	grocery store
der Markt(¨e)	market
die Markthalle(n)	covered market, usually for wholesale
der Supermarkt	supermarket
der Wochenmarkt	weekly market
der Salon(s) / Friseursalon	salon / hairdresser's
das Selbstbedienungsgeschäft(e)	self-service shop
der Tante Emma Laden(¨)	corner shop
der Verbrauchermarkt(¨e)	discount store
das Versandhaus(¨er)	mail-order firm
der Ottoversand	large Hamburg-based mail-order company
die Bestellung per Katalog	order by catalogue
das Warenhaus(¨er) [FA]	department store

N.B. Many big department stores (see names above) have their own multi-storey car park. Parking there is cheaper, if you get your parking ticket stamped by a store cashier after you have bought something. You then only pay charges for customers, *Gebühren für Kunden*, not for *Benutzer* (users).

(b) Departments within stores

die Abteilung(en)	department / section
die Bäckerei(en)	bakery
die Bastelabteilung	handicraft materials / D.I.Y.
die Bekleidung(en)	clothing
die Damenbekleidung	ladies' fashions
die Campingabteilung	camping department
Damen / Herrenwäsche	lingerie / gents' underwear
Eisenwaren (pl.)	hardware
die Elektro(waren)abteilung	electrical goods department
Gartenartikel (pl.)	gardening items

Haushaltsartikel (pl.)	household items
die Heimwerkerabteilung	D.I.Y.
die Kasse(n)	till / checkout
die Kinderabteilung	children's department
der Kundendienst(e)	customer service
Kurzwaren (pl.)	haberdashery
Lebensmittel(–) (pl.)	food / grocery
die Lederwarenabteilung	leather-goods department
die Metzgerei(en)	butchery
das Möbel(–)	furniture
Obst und Gemüse	fruit and vegetables
die Parfümerie	perfume shop
die Phonoabteilung	hi-fi department
die Photo- / Fotoabteilung	photographic department
die Reinigung(en)	dry cleaner's
das Reisebüro(s)	travel agent
das Restaurant(s)	restaurant
der Schlüsseldienst(e)	key cutters
Schreibwaren (pl.)	stationery
die Schuhabteilung	shoe department
die Spielwarenabteilung	toy department
Sportartikel (pl.)	sports goods

(c) Methods of payment

die Anzahlung(en)	down-payment / deposit
die Barzahlung	cash payment

Hätten Sie vielleicht Kleingeld?
Do you have any small change?

der Geldautomat(en)	cash point
die Geheimnummer eintippen	to key in one's PIN number (Personal Identification Number)
die Kaution	deposit
die Kreditkarte(n)	credit card
mit Kreditkarte zahlen	to pay by credit card (often referred to generically as *das Kärtchen*)
die Quittung(en)	receipt

Könnten Sie mir bitte eine Quittung über Fachbücher ausstellen?
Could you write me a receipt for professional books, please?

die Ratenzahlung(en)	hire purchase, paying by instalments
auf Raten zahlen	to pay in instalments
die Monatsrate(n)	monthly instalment
die Rechnung(en)	bill / account

Das geht auf Rechnung.
That goes on the account.

der Scheck(s)	cheque
mit Euroscheck bezahlen	to pay by Eurocheque

Auf welchen Namen soll ich den Scheck ausstellen?
Who should I make the cheque out to?

Haben Sie einen Stempel?
Do you have a (rubber) stamp?

(d) Sales and reductions

auslaufende Ware	end of line goods
herabgesetzte Ware	lower price goods
der Ladenhüter(–)	non-seller
die Preissenkung	price slashing
der Rabatt	reduction
20% Rabatt	20% reduction
einen Rabatt gewähren / ein◊räumen	to give credit
der Restbestand(¨e)	remaining stock
(der) 'Restposten'	'reduced to clear' (item)
der Verkauf(¨e)	sale
der Räumungsverkauf	clearance sale
der Sommer / Winterschlußverkauf	summer / winter sale

145 Commerce

(a) Production

der Arbeiter(–)	worker
Facharbeiter	skilled worker
der Gastarbeiter	foreign (guest) worker
die Arbeiterschaft(en)	workforce
der Arbeitnehmer(–)	employee
das Atelier(s)	(artist's) studio
die Auflage(n)	edition / print run
eine Zeitung mit einer hohen Auflage	a newspaper with a high circulation

der / die Auszubildende (adjectival noun) (abbreviated *AZUBI*)	person on training scheme
die Baustelle(n)	building site
das Bergwerk(e)	mine
der Betrieb(e)	business / company
die Betriebseinstellung(en)	shut down / closing down of business
die Branche(n)	line of business
die Einfuhr und Ausfuhr	import and export
der Entwurf(¨e)	design
*erfinden**	to invent
das Ersatzeil(e)	spare part
der Ertrag(¨e)	output / yield / return
erzeugen	to produce
der Erzeuger(–)	producer
das Erzeugnis(se)	product
das Etikett(en) [FA]	label (**not** etiquette)
die Fabrik(en)	factory, plant
der Fabrikant(en)	manufacturer
das Fließband(¨er)	assembly line / conveyor belt
die Förderung	(coal) output; also: promotion in the sense of support / encouragement
die Frachtkosten (pl.)	freight cost / carriage
die Landfracht	landfreight
die Seefracht	sea freight
das Gerät(e)	piece of equipment / tool / utensil
das Geschäft(e)	business / shop
das Selbstbedienungsgeschäft(e)	self-service shop
der Geschäftsrückgang(¨e)	(business) recession
der Geselle(n)	journeyman
die Gesellschaft(en)	company
GmbH (*Gesellschaft mit beschränkter Haftung*)	Ltd / Plc (literally: company with limited liability)
die Gewerkschaft(en)	trade union
das Gewicht(e)	weight
herstellen	to produce
der Hersteller(–)	producer
die Herstellung	production
die Herstellungskosten (pl.)	production costs
das Herstellungsverfahren	manufacturing process
die Massenherstellung	mass production
die Industrie(n)	industry

die Bekleidungsindustrie	clothing industry
die Grundstoffindustrie	basic industry
die Schwerindustrie	heavy industry
die Textilindustrie	textile industry
das Industrieerzeugnis(se)	industrial product
der Industriezweig(e)	branch
der Industriestaat(en)	industrial country / state
die Kohlengrube(n)	(coal) pit / coal mine
die Kosten (pl.)	costs
Kosten in den Griff bekommen	to control costs
das Lager(–)	store-room / stock-room / warehouse
Wir haben den Artikel auf Lager.	We have the item in stock.
der Lehrling(e)	apprentice (see also *der Auszubildende*)
das Produkt(e)	product / commodity
das Fertigprodukt	finished / processed product
die Reparatur(en)	repair
der Roboter(–)	robot
der Rohstoff(e)	raw material
die Schicht(en)	shift (also: layer)
die Nachtschicht	night shift
die Tagschicht	day shift
der Standard(e)	standard
die Stillegung(en)	shut- / close-down
der Teilhaber(–)	(business) partner
der Termin(e)	appointed date / time / appointment

Ich habe um elf Uhr noch einen Termin.
I have another appointment at 11 a.m.

das Werk(e)	works / plant
die Werkstatt(¨en)	workshop / garage
das Werkzeug(e)	tool
der Zeitplan(¨e)	schedule

(b) Sales

der Abnehmer(–)	(regular) buyer / customer
der Absatz(¨e)	sales

Die Waren fanden reißenden Absatz.
The goods were sold very quickly.

die Absatzflaute	drop in sales
die Absatzförderung	sales promotion

die Absatzsteigerung	increase in sales
die Anfrage(n)	inquiry
das Angebot(e)	offer
das Sonderangebot	special offer
Angebot und Nachfrage	supply and demand
ein verlockendes Angebot machen	to make an attractive offer
der Auftrag(¨e)	commission / order / instruction
*einen Auftrag erteilen / geben**	to give a commission
einen Auftrag aus◊führen	to carry out an order
der Inkassoauftrag	collection order
die Auskunft(¨e)	information
die Außenstände (pl.)	outstanding debts
die Baisse(n)	slump / fall
bestellen	to order
die Bestellung(en)	order
die Nachbestellung(en)	further / repeat order
das Büro	office
DAX (Deutscher Aktien Index)	German share index
(der) Dienst am Kunden	customer service
der Empfang(¨e)	receipt / reception
den Empfang bestätigen	to confirm receipt
der Empfänger(–)	recipient
zahlbar bei Empfang	payable on receipt
die Erholung	recovery
eine Erholung ein◊leiten	to effect a recovery
die Faktur(en) < archaic >	invoice
die Gewähr (no pl.)	guarantee
gewährleisten	to guarantee / ensure
befriedigende Ergebnisse gewährleisten	to ensure satisfactory results
der Gewinn(e)	profit
der Reingewinn(e)	net profit
der Handel	trade
der Einzelhandel	retail trade
der Großhandel	wholesale
der Außenhandel	foreign trade
die Handelskammer(n)	Chamber of Commerce
die Hochkonjunktur(en)	boom
die Inventur	stocktaking
wegen Inventur geschlossen	closed for stocktaking
der Katalog(e)	catalogue
der Versandkatalog(e)	mail-order catalogue
der Kauf(¨e)	purchase
der Käufer(–)	buyer
der Kunde(n)	customer

der Kundendienst(e)	customer service
der Laden(¨)	(small) shop
liefern	to deliver
der Lieferschein(e)	delivery note
Lieferung per Nachnahme	cash on delivery (C.O.D.)
der Mahnbrief(e)	reminder (letter)
die Menge(n)	quantity
die Messe(n)	(trade) fair
die Frankfurter Buchmesse	the Frankfurt Book Fair
das Muster(–)	sample / pattern / specimen copy
unverkäufliches Muster	sample not for sale
die Nachfrage(n)	demand
steigende Nachfrage	rising demand
das Patent(e)	patent
der Preis(e)	price (also: prize)
die Preisliste(n)	price list
der Preisnachlaß (-lässe)	price reduction
die Probe(n) [FA]	sample (also: test / rehearsal)
die Quittung(en)	(till) receipt
die Rechnung(en)	bill / invoice
*die Rechnung begleichen**	to settle an account
jemandem etwas in Rechnung stellen	to charge someone for something
die Sendung(en)	consignment
die Spesen (pl.)	expenses
der Umsatz(¨e)	turnover / sales
den Umsatz verdoppeln / vergrößern / verbessern	to double / increase / improve sales
verbrauchen	to consume
der Verbraucher(–)	consumer
der Verlust(e)	loss
der Versand	dispatch / shipment
der Vertrag(¨e)	contract
der Vorrat(¨e)	stock / supply
auf Vorrat	in stock
das Vorratslager(-)	store
die Ware(n)	goods
das Warenhaus(¨er) [FA]	department store (**not** warehouse)
die Warenprobe(n)	sample (of merchandise)
die Warenrechnung(en)	invoice
die Fertigware(n)	finished product
die Wirtschaft	economy
der Wirtschaftsaufschwung	(economic boom)
das Wirtschaftswunder	economic miracle

(c) Marketing, advertising and public relations

der Absatz	sales
dieser Roman findet guten / reißenden Absatz	this novel is selling well / like hot cakes
den Absatz steigern	to increase sales
die Absatzchance(n)	sales potential
absatzfähig	saleable
die Absatzflaute(n)	slump / drop in sales
die Absatzforschung(en)	market research
das Absatzgebiet(e)	sales territory
die Altersgruppe(n)	age bracket
*an◊bieten**	to offer
die Anzeige(n)	advertisement (e.g. in newspaper)
*eine Anzeige auf◊geben**	to place an advertisement
der Anzeigenteil(e)	classified advertisement section in paper
der Anzeiger(–)	advertiser / gazette
der Artikel(–)	(sales) item / product (also: (newspaper) article)
der Aufschwung	upswing / boost

Die Wirtschaft erlebt einen Aufschwung.
The economy is experiencing an upturn.

dem Verbraucherkonsum Aufschwung geben	to give a boost to consumer spending
die Auslage(n)	display
der Ausverkauf(¨e)	(clearance) sale
der Räumungsverkauf	clearance sale
der Schlußverkauf	end-of-season sale
billig	cheap (could imply 'of inferior quality')
der Designer(–)	designer
die Einführung(en) auf dem Markt	promotion (literally: introduction to the market)
das Einkaufszentrum (-zentren)	shopping centre
der Entwurf(¨e)	design
ermäßigt	reduced (in price)
fabrikneu	brand new
fortschrittlich	progressive
frei Haus	free delivery
der Geschäftsführer(–)	manager
die Gestaltung(en)	lay-out / arrangement
gewinnbringend	profitable
gratis	free (of charge)
die Güter (pl.)	goods

der Händler(–)	dealer
der Zwischenhändler	middle-man
der Katalog(e)	catalogue
das Kartellamt	≈ Monopolies and Mergers Commission (government body concerned with the control and supervision of cartels)
der Kauf(¨e)	purchase
der Gelegenheitskauf	bargain
der Käufer(–)	customer / buyer
der Konkurrent(en)	competitor
die Konkurrenz	competition
jemandem Konkurrenz machen	to compete with someone
der Konsum	consumption
die Konsumgesellschaft(en)	consumer society
der Konsumzwang(¨e)	pressure / compulsion to buy (created by consumer society)
die Kosten (pl.)	cost
die Einheitskosten	unit costs
die Unkosten	expenses
mit einem Kostenaufwand von einer Milliarde DM	at the cost of one billion marks (see section 140a)
die Kostenerstattung(en)	reimbursement of costs
der Kostenvoranschlag(¨e)	(cost) estimate / quotation
die Herstellungskosten (pl.)	(prime) cost (literally: cost of production)
der Kunde(n)	customer / client
der Kundendienst(e)	customer service
das Lager(–)	store
auf Lager	in store / in stock
die Leistung(en)	performance / achievement
lieferbar	available

Der Artikel ist ab Januar lieferbar.
The item is available from January.

der Markt(¨e)	market
der Marktanteil(e)	share of the market
die Marktforschung(en)	market research
das Monopol(e)	monopoly
die Neuheit(en)	novelty
die Öffentlichkeitsarbeit(en)	public relations (work)
das Plakat(e)	poster
das Poster(–)	poster
die Posterwand(¨e)	billboard
der Preis(e)	price (also: prize)
der Preisnachlaß (-lässe)	reduction (in price)
der Schleuderpreis(e)	crash price

der Selbstkostenpreis(e)	cost price
zum S.k.p.	at c.p.
ein preisgekröntes Produkt	an award-winning product
preiswert	value-for-money

Dieser Anzug ist wirklich preiswert.
This suit really is good value for money.

die Qualität	quality
die Quittung(en)	(till) receipt
die Rate(n)	instalment
die Reklamation(en)	complaint
die Reklame (no pl.)	advertisement
die Reklamezeitung(en)	free paper
die Schlagzeile(n)	caption / headline
das Sonderangebot(e)	special offer
teuer	expensive / dear
die Überschrift(n)	heading / headline
umfangreich	extensive
umfangreiche Auslandsumsätze	extensive overseas sales / sales abroad
um◊tauschen	to exchange

Badebekleidung ist vom Umtausch ausgeschlossen.
Swimwear cannot be exchanged.

die Unterstützung	support
die verkaufsfördernde Unterstützung	promotional support
der Verkauf	sale
der Verkaufsstand(¨e)	stand (e.g. at a fair)
die Verpackung(en)	packaging
das Verpackungsmaterial(ien)	packing material
versteigern	to auction
der Vertreter(–)	sales representative (also: door-to-door salesman)
im Voraus	in advance
der Vorrat(¨e)	supply / provisions
auf Vorrat kaufen	to stock up with something
die Waren (pl.)	goods
das Warenzeichen(–)	trademark
eingetragenes Warenzeichen	registered trademark
die Werbung(en)	advertisement / advertising
Werbung für	promotion / advertisement for
die Radio- / Fernsehwerbung(en)	radio / TV advertising
der Werbefachmann(¨er)	advertising expert / man
die Werbekampagne(n)	advertising campaign
die Werbeagentur(en)	advertising agency
der Werbefunk	(programme of) radio commercials

das Werbefernsehen	TV commercials
der Werbefilm(e)	advertising / promotional film

Wir haben diesen Monat einen 'Vichy' Werbestand im Laden.
We've got a special promotion by Vichy in the store this month.

der Werbefeldzug(¨e)	(sales) promotion
der Werbeslogan(s)	publicity / advertising slogan
der Werbespot(s)	commercial
der Werbetext(e)	advertising copy
das Werbemittel	means of advertising
der Werbeträger(–)	advertising medium
die Werbetrommel für etwas rühren	to beat the big drum for something
die Werbewirksamkeit	publicity value
der Wert(e)	value / worth
die (Kapital)Werterhöhung(en)	capital appreciation
die Wurfsendung(en)	circular
Reklame durch Wurfsendungen	direct advertising
der Zuschlag(¨e)	acceptance of a tender / bid
jemandem für etwas einen Zuschlag geben / erteilen*	to give someone a contract for something
der Zustand(¨e)	condition
in gutem / schlechtem Zustand	in good / bad condition
die Zuwachsrate(n)	growth rate

146 Finance

(a) Government revenue and expenditure

absetzbar	(tax) deductible

Schreibwaren sind steuerlich absetzbar.
Stationery is tax deductible.

das Arbeitslosengeld	unemployment benefit
das Krankengeld	sick pay
die Armut (no pl.)	poverty
die Einfuhrsteuer(n)	import tax
das Einkommen (no pl.)	income (i.e. all earned and 'unearned' income, see below)
die Einkommenssteuer(n)	income tax
die Erbschaftssteuer(n)	death duty / inheritance tax
das Finanzamt	Inland Revenue
das Finanzamt(¨er)	(local) tax office
der Fond(s)	fund
einen Fond ein◊richten	to set up a fund
die Geldentwertung(en)	(monetary) devaluation

Gemeindeabgaben (pl.)	local taxes and rates (including water, sewage, refuse collection etc.)
die Grundsteuer(n)	property tax (based on size and value of property)
der Haushaltsplan(¨e)	budget
die Hundesteuer(n)	dog licence fee
das Kindergeld (no pl.)	child benefit
die Kopfsteuer(n)	poll tax / head tax
die Kraftfahrzeugsteuer(n)	road tax
die Kürzung(en)	cuts

Die Haushaltsmittel mußten stark gekürzt werden.
The budgetary funds had to be cut drastically.

die Lohnsteuer(n)	income tax (paid on salary and wages)
die MWS (Mehrwertsteuer(n))	VAT (Value Added Tax)
öffentliche Mittel (pl.)	public funds
die Pension(en)	(civil service) pension (see below, p. 433)
Regierungsausgaben (pl.)	government spending
der Reichtum	wealth
Sozialabgaben (pl.)	welfare (National Insurance) contributions
die Sozialhilfe	social benefit
die Sozialversicherung(en)	National Insurance
die staatliche Unterstützung	state aid / subsidy
*staatliche Unterstützung erhalten**	to receive state benefits / aid
die Staatsanleihe(n)	government bond
Staatsausgaben (pl.)	public spending
Staatsfinanzen (pl.)	public finances
die Staatskasse (no pl.)	treasury / public purse
Staatskosten (pl.)	public expenses
das geht auf Staatskosten*	that's paid for by the state (literally: that goes on state costs)
die Staatsrente(n)	state pension
der Staatsschatz	national / state reserve
die Staatsschulden (pl.)	national debt
die Steuer(n)	tax
*Steuern erheben**	to levy tax
das Steueraufkommen(–)	tax revenue
der Steuerbeamte (adjectival noun)	tax inspector
der Steuerberater(–)	accountant (literally: tax advisor)
der Steuerbescheid(e)	tax assessment
Steuereinnahmen (pl.)	money acquired from taxation
die Steuererhöhung(en)	tax increase

die Steuererklärung(en)	tax return
die Steuer(rück)erstattung(en)	tax rebate / refund
steuerfrei	tax free
die Steuergruppe / -klasse(n)	tax band
der Steuerhinterzieher(–)	tax evader / dodger
die Steuerhinterziehung(en)	tax embezzlement
die (Lohn-)Steuerkarte(n)	notice of pay received and tax deducted (≈ P60)
das Steuerparadies (no pl.)	tax haven
das steuerpflichtige Einkommen	taxable income
die Steuersenkung(en)	tax reduction
die Steuerumgehung(en)	tax dodging / evasion
die Steuervergünstigung(en)	tax relief
der Steuerzahler(–)	taxpayer
der Stopp(s)	freeze
der Lohnstopp	freeze on wages
die Vermögenssteuer(n)	wealth tax
die Währungsreform(en)	currency reform
der Währungsverfall (no pl.)	(currency) depreciation
der Wohlstand (no pl.)	prosperity
die Wohnungsbeihilfe(n)	rent subsidy / housing benefit
der Zoll(¨e)	(customs) duty / tariff
*Zoll erheben**	to charge toll / duty
die Zölle senken	to reduce tariffs

(b) Salaries and income

If you are enquiring about German salaries and wages, be prepared for the fact that the Germans usually quote their monthly (rather than their annual) salary (*'pro Monat'* = per month): either *Brutto* (gross) or *Netto* (net). Employees are also paid an additional month's (or part of a month's) salary (*das 13. Monatsgehalt*) at the end of the year.

There is a national standard pay structure (*das Tarifgehalt / der Tariflohn* = standard salary / wage) and a minimum wage (*der tarifliche Mindestlohn*) agreed by the *Gewerkschaften* (trade unions).

However, salaries and income are not usually discussed in general conversation – the topic is considered too personal.

(i) Paid income

das Gehalt(¨er)	salary
der Gehaltsempfänger(–)	salaried person
die Gehaltserhöhung(en)	pay (literally salary) rise
der Lohn(¨e)	wages

der Lohnempfänger(–)	wage earner
die Lohnerhöhung(en)	wage rise
die Lohnforderung(en)	wage demand
die Lohnkürzung(en)	wage cut
der Akkordlohn	piece-work pay
der Wehrsold / der Sold (no pl.)	military pay

(ii) Pensions

Traditionally women retired at 63, and men at 65; now there is more flexibility.

die Rente(n)	pension (general)
der Rentner(–)	senior citizen / pensioner (O.A.P.)
die Pension(en)	(retirement) pension (for civil servants – and for their surviving dependants)
der Pensionär(e)	pensioner (on civil service pension)
die Waisenrente(n)	orphan's pension
die Witwenrente(n)	widow's pension

(iii) Other words relating to pay and income

die Bezahlung(en) (für Dienste)	payment (for services)
das Einkommen (no pl.)	income
das verfügbare Einkommen	disposable income
die (Anwalt-)Gebühren (pl.)	(solicitor's) fee
das (Arzt-)Honorar(e)	(doctor's) fee
der Tarif(e)	wage rate / salary scale

Die Gehälter sind tariflich festgelegt.
There are fixed rates for salaries.

das Allgemeine Tarif- und Handelsabkommen	General Agreement on Tariffs and Trade (GATT)
das Trinkgeld(er)	tip (literally: money for a drink)
die Überstunde(n)	overtime
Überstunden machen	to work overtime
der Vorschuß (-schüsse)	advance (payment)

(iv) Sources of unearned income

die Aktie(n)	share
Alimente (pl.)	maintenance (payments) < archaic > (term used especially with reference to illegitimate children)

die Arbeitslosenunterstützung	unemployment benefit
*Arbeitslosenunterstützung beziehen**	to draw unemployment benefit
*stempeln gehen** < coll. >	to be on the dole
das BAFöG Bundesausbildungsförderungsgesetz)	student grant
die Behindertenbeihilfe	disability allowance
die Entschädigung (no pl.)	compensation
das Geschenk(e)	gift / present
der Gewinn(e)	profit / gains
der Gewinnanteil(e)	dividend
der Gutschein(e)	voucher
der Investmentfonds	≈ unit trusts
das Kindergeld(er)	child benefit
die Lebensversicherung(en)	life insurance
die Miete(n)	rent
die Rentenversicherung(en)	annuity
das Stipendium(Stipendien)	scholarship
die Studienbeihilfe	grant / financial aid to students
die Treuhand	trusteeship
die Unterhaltszahlung(en)	alimony / maintenance payment
das Vermächtnis(se)	settlement / bequest / legacy
die Verpachtung(en)	lease
der Wertpapierbesitz(e)	ownership of stocks and shares
der Zuschlag(¨e)	additional pay bonus

(c) Banking and investment

die Aktie(n)	share
in Aktien an◊legen	to invest in (stocks and) shares
der Auftrag(¨e) (über DM 100)	order (for 100 marks)
der Dauerauftrag	standing order
die Bank(en)	bank
die Bundesbank	Federal Bank (of Germany)
der Bankrott	bankruptcy
Bankrott machen / Pleite machen < coll. >	to go bankrupt
der Betrag(¨e)	amount

Der Betrag ist am 25. Mai fällig.
The amount is due on 25 May.

die Börse(n)	stock market / stock exchange
der Börsenkurs(e)	stock-market price
der Börsenmakler(–)	stockbroker

bei Börsenschluß	at the close of the stock market
die Buchung(en)	entry (also: booking)
die Buchführung(en)	book-keeping
für jemanden bürgen	to stand surety for someone
das Darlehen(–)	loan
die Devisen (pl.)	foreign exchange / currency
die Einnahmen (pl.)	receipts
die Einzugsermächtigung(en)	direct debit
*entleihen**	to borrow
die Anleihe	loan / bond
die Entleihung	borrowing
erben	to inherit
die Erbschaft(en)	inheritance
der Erbe(n)	heir
die Erbin(nen)	female heir
die Filiale(n)	branch office
die Gebühr(en)	fee
das Geld(er)	money
die Geldangelegenheit(en)	financial matter
der Geldautomat(en)	cash dispensing machine / cashpoint / ATM
die Geldentwertung(en)	currency devaluation / depreciation
das Kleingeld	(small) change
das Bargeld	(ready) cash
das Geldinstitut(e)	financial institution / bank
*Geld ab◊heben**	to withdraw money
Geld an◊legen	to invest money
Geld auf das Konto ein◊zahlen	to pay money into the account
die Gewähr (no pl.)	guarantee
der Gewinn(e)	profit
der Gewinnanteil(e)	dividend
Gewinnanteile aus◊schütten	to pay / distribute dividends
der Gläubiger(–)	creditor
das Guthaben(–)	credit

Ich habe ein Guthaben von DM 1000.
My account is 1000 marks in credit.

der Haushaltsplan(¨e)	budget
die Hypothek(en)	mortgage
die Immobilien (pl.)	real estate
die Immobilie(n)	(immoveable) property
der Immobilienmarkt	property market
die Kasse(n)	cash desk / till

die Sparkasse(n)	(savings) bank
der Kassierer(–)	clerk / teller
die Kassiererin(nen)	female clerk / teller
das Kassenbuch(¨er)	cash-book
der Konkurs	bankruptcy
den Konkurs an◊melden	to file for bankruptcy / to declare oneself bankrupt
Konkurs machen	to go bankrupt
der (gerichtlich bestellte) Konkursverwalter	(official) receiver
das Konto (Konten)	account
das Konto überziehen ♦ *	to overdraw the account
der Kontostand(¨e)	bank balance
der Kontoauszug(¨e)	bank statement (usually separate sheets for each day's transactions)
das Bankkonto (die Bankkonten)	bank account
das Girokonto	current account / giro account
das Sparkonto	savings / deposit account
der Kredit(e)	credit (second syllable is stressed)
die Kreditkarte(n)	credit card
die Münze(n)	coin
die Nachnahme(n)	delivery (fee)
per Nachnahme	cash on delivery (C.O.D.)
das Portefeuille(s)	portfolio
die Postanweisung(en)	postal order
der Saldo (Salden)	balance
der Scheck(s)	cheque
der Barscheck	open / uncrossed cheque
der Euroscheck	Eurocheque
der Verrechnungsscheck(s)	crossed cheque
einen Scheck ein◊lösen	to cash a cheque

N.B. In order to cross a cheque, you need to write across the top left-hand corner *nur zur Verrechnung* (not negotiable, a/c payee only).

der Schein(e)	note / bill
der Zehnmarkschein	10-mark note
das Schließfach(¨er)	safe deposit box
schulden	to owe
die Schulden (pl.)	debt(s)
die Schulden tilgen	to amortize / pay off debts
der Schuldner(–)	debtor
die Sicherheit(en)	security
das Skonto(s)	cash discount
jemandem Skonto gewähren	to allow someone a cash discount

das Soll und Haben	debit and credit
sparen	to save
das Sparbuch(¨er)	savings book / passbook
das Sparguthaben(–)	savings account
die Ersparnisse (pl.)	savings
sparsam	thrifty / economical
bausparen♦ (intrans.)	to save with a building society (normally used in the infinitive)
die Bausparkasse	building society
stornieren	cancel / reverse
einen Buchungsfehler stornieren	to reverse an entry error
einen Bankauftrag stornieren	to cancel a banking order
überweisen♦*	to transfer (money)
die Überweisung(en)	transfer
*verleihen**	to lend / loan
an jemanden etwas verleihen	to lend something to someone
das Vermögen(–)	property / fortune
die Vorauszahlung(en)	advance payment
der Vorschuß (-schüsse)	advance
*jemandem Geld vor◊schießen**	to advance someone money
die Währung(en)	currency
wechseln	(ex) change
der Wechselkurs(e)	exchange rate
1DM in 10 Pfennigstücke umwechseln	to change 1 mark into 10-pfennig coins

Ich möchte bitte 100 Pfund in DM wechseln.
I would like to change £100 into marks.

das Wertpapier(e)	security / bond
die Wertpapiere (pl.)	stocks and shares
der Wohlstand (no pl.)	prosperity
zahlen	to pay
ab◊zahlen	to pay off
ab◊stottern < coll. >	to pay off by instalments
an◊zahlen	to pay a deposit
ein◊zahlen	to pay in
einen Betrag auf das Girokonto ein◊zahlen	to pay an amount into the current account
zurück◊zahlen	to repay
die Zahlung(en)	the payment
die Zahlungsfrist(en)	period allowed for payment
zahlungsunfähig	unable to pay
die Zahlungsunfähigkeit	inability to pay / insolvency
Zinsen (pl.)	interest
der Zinseszins (no pl.)	compound interest
der Zinssatz(¨e)	interest rate

147 Politics and current affairs

(a) Government

der Beamte (adjectival noun)	civil servant (paid by the state, including teachers)
die Beamtin(nen)	female civil servant
der Bundeskanzler	Federal Chancellor
das Bundeskanzleramt	Federal Chancellery
das Bundesministerium (-ministerien)	federal ministry (see list of ministries below)
der Bundespräsident	Federal President
das Bundespräsidialamt	office of the Federal President
der Bundesrat	Upper House of the German Parliament
der Bundestag	Lower House of the German Parliament
der Bundestagsabgeordnete (adjectival noun)	member of the Bundestag (≈ M.P.)
das Bundesverfassungsgericht	Federal Constitutional Court
der Bürgermeister(–)	town mayor
der Etat(s)	budget
das Grundgesetz(e)	basic law / constitution
der Kreis(e)	district
das Land(¨er)	roughly equivalent to a state or county. (There are now altogether 16 *Länder* in Germany: 11 'old' ones and 5 'new' ones from the former GDR.)
das Land Hessen	the state of Hesse
der Landtag	state parliament
der Magistrat(e) [FA]	municipal authorities
die Menschenrechte (pl.)	human rights
der Minister(–) [FA]	minister (secretary of state)
der Innenminister	Secretary of State / Minister of the Interior
der Finanzminister	Chancellor of the Exchequer
der Ministerpräsident(en)	minister-president (often translated as 'Prime Minister', but has different function, i.e. he / she is head of government in a *Land*)
der Ministerrat	Council of State
das Rathaus(¨er)	town hall

die Regierung(en)	government
die Regierung stürzen	to overthrow the government
der Sekretär(e) [FA]	middle-ranking civil servant
die Sitzungsperiode(n)	(parliamentary) session
der Staatsdienst	civil service
der Staatssekretär(e)	permanent secretary of state (lower ranking than *Minister*, not usually an M.P., tasks similar to that of a junior minister in UK)
der Stadtrat(¨e)	city / town council / councillor
die Verfassung(en)	constitution
die Verwaltung	administration

Ministries in Germany (as at January 1991)

das Auswärtige Amt	the Foreign Office
Bundesministerium	Ministry
des Innern	of the Interior (Home Office)
der Justiz	of Justice
der Finanzen	of Finance (of the Exchequer)
für Wirtschaft	of Economics / Trade and Industry
für Ernährung, Landwirtschaft und Forsten	of Food, Agriculture and Forestry
für Arbeit-und Sozialordnung	for Labour and Social Affairs
für Familie und Senioren	for Family Affairs and Senior Citizens
für Frauen und Jugend	for Women and Young People
für Gesundheit	for Health
für Verkehr	for Transport
für das Post- und Fernmeldewesen	for Post and Telecommunications
für Raumordnung, Bauwesen, und Städtebau	for Regional Planning, Housing and Urban Design
für Bildung und Wissenschaft	for Education and Science
für Forschung und Technologie	for Research and Technology
für wirtschaftliche Zusammenarbeit	for Economic Co-operation
für Umwelt, Naturschutz und Reaktorsicherheit	for the Environment, Nature Conservation and Nuclear Reactor Safety
für innerdeutsche Beziehungen	for Intra-German Relations (abolished in Jan.1991)
der Minister für besondere Aufgaben	the minister for special tasks (also Head of the Federal Chancellery)

(b) Elections

ab◊danken	to resign
der Abgeordnete (adjectival noun)	a member of parliament
die Abstimmung(en)	poll
über etwas ab◊stimmen	to vote on something
die Volksabstimmung	plebiscite
die Volksbefragung(en)	referendum
die Amtszeit(en)	term of office
der Ausschuß (-schüsse)	committee
die Beliebtheit	popularity
der Bundestag (see subsection (a) above)	
die Bürgerrechte	civil rights
der Flügel(–)	wing
der rechte / linke Flügel	the right / left wing
die Fraktion(en)	parliamentary party / coalition
der Kandidat(en)	candidate
für das Amt des Präsidenten kandidieren	to run / stand for president
die (5%) Klausel	5% clause / proviso / stipulation (a party needs at least 5% of the votes to get into the *Bundestag*)
das Mandat(e)	mandate
die 2/3 Mehrheit	2/3 majority
die Meinungsumfrage(n)	opinion poll
der Mißtrauensantrag(¨e)	motion of no confidence
das Mißtrauensvotum	vote of no confidence
die Opposition	opposition
die Partei(en)	political party
das Parteiprogramm(e)	party manifesto
der Parteianhänger(–)	(party) supporter
der Parteigegner(–)	(party) opponent
der Parteivorsitzende (adjectival noun)	party leader
die Stimme(n)	vote
*seine Stimme ab◊geben**	to cast one's vote
das Stimmrecht(e)	right to vote
der Stimmzettel(–)	voting / ballot paper
einstimmig	unanimous

Der Antrag wurde einstimmig abgelehnt.
The motion was rejected unanimously.

die Wahl(en)	election
die Gemeindewahl	local election
die Landtagswahl	election for the *Landtag* (≈ county / state parliament)

die Bundestagswahl	general election
Neuwahlen aus◊schreiben / den Wähler entscheiden* lassen*	≈ to go to the country
wählen	to vote
der Wähler(–)	elector / voter
die Wahlbeteiligung	the turnout (at an election)
der Wahlkampf(¨e)	election campaign
der Wahlkreis(e)	constituency
das Wahlrecht	right to vote / franchise
das aktive Wahlrecht	right to vote for someone
das passive Wahlrecht	right to be elected
die Sendung zur Wahl	≈ party political broadcast (at election time)
die Wahlurne(n)	ballot-box
die (Gesamt)Wählerschaft	electorate
die Mehrheitswahl	majority vote
die Verhältniswahl	proportional representation

(c) Political debate

die APO (die Außerparlamentarische Opposition)	extraparliamentary opposition (in the 60s)
der Beschluß (-schlüsse)	decision
der Mehrheitsbeschluß	majority decision
die Debatte(n)	debate
die Demonstration(en)	protest march
die Tagesordnung(en)	agenda
engagiert [FA]	dedicated
sich für eine Sache engagieren	to be politically active for an issue
die Koalition(en)	coalition
die Ostpolitik	West German policy towards Eastern Europe, in particular East Germany
das Parteimitglied(er)	party member
der Parteitag(e)	party conference
die Protestnote(n)	letter of protest
das Protokoll(e) [FA]	minutes (of a meeting)
das Sommerloch < coll. >	summer recess (literally: summer hole, referring to journalistic void)
das Verfahren(–)	procedure
die Verhandlung(en)	negotiation
*Verhandlungen ab◊brechen**	to break off negotiations

For more vocabulary on (political) discussion, see sections 92–8 and 124–5.

(d) Home affairs

(i) General

das Anerkennungsverfahren(–)	recognition procedure
der antifaschistische Schutzwall (GDR expression for die Mauer)	protection barrier against fascism
der Asylbewerber(–)	person seeking asylum
die Bedingung(en)	condition
Bedingungen auferlegen	to impose terms / conditions
die Besatzung	occupying troops or forces
die Besatzungsmacht(¨e)	occupying power
die Bürgerinitiative(n)	citizens' action group / movement / pressure group
das Gemeinwesen	community / political unit
das Gleichgewicht(e)	balance
das Kräftegleichgewicht	balance of power(s)
das Zünglein an der Waage sein	to hold the balance of power
das politische Gleichgewicht	political balance
die Nachkriegszeit(en)	post-war era
die Nachkriegszeit ist vorbei	the post-war era is over
die Nationalhymne	national anthem
der Persilschein < coll. >	certificate of blamelessness (of Nazi and Stasi past)
die Pressefreiheit	freedom of the press
die Ratifizierung	ratification
Rechte und Pflichten	rights and duties
die Sicherheitspolitik	security policy
der Stasi < coll. >	(abbreviation for GDR *Staatssicherheit*) state security
der Stasi(s) < coll. >	state security man
der Unterzeichner(–)	signatory
der Verfassungsschutz	constitutional protection
der Weltkrieg(e)	world war

> *Heute ziehen wir einen Strich unter den Zweiten Weltkrieg und stellen die Uhr für ein neues Zeitalter.* (Gorbachev, 1990)
> Today we draw a line under the Second World War and set the clocks for a new era.

die Wende	(big political) change
der Wendehals(¨e) < coll. >	turncoat
der (gewaltlose) Widerstand	(non-violent) resistance
die Wiedervereinigung	reunification
der Zivildienst	community service (as alternative to military service)
der Zivildienstleistende(n) (= der Zivi < coll. >)	person doing community service

(ii) Work

das Arbeitsamt(¨er)	employment office
die Arbeitslosigkeit	redundancy / unemployment
der Arbeitsmarkt	employment market
die Entlassung(en)	redundancy
die Kündigung(en)	notice / dismissal
die Kündigung ein◊reichen	to hand in one's notice
*jemandem die Kündigung aus◊sprechen**	to give someone his / her notice
fristlose Kündigung	dismissal without notice
die Kurzarbeit	short time / short-time working
der Ruhestand	retirement
in den Ruhestand treten / gehen**	to retire
der Vorruhestand	early retirement
der Streik(s)	strike
wilder Streik	wildcat strike
die Teilzeitarbeit(en)	part-time work
die Umschulung(en)	retraining

(iii) Social welfare

die Abtreibung(en)	(deliberate) abortion
der Paragraph 218	a paragraph in the penal code which relates to abortion
die Fristenlösung / Fristenregelung	resolution allowing the termination of pregnancy within the first three months / ≈ abortion limit
die Indikationslösung	resolution allowing abortion on ethical, eugenic, medical or social grounds
die AOK (Allgemeine Ortskrankenkasse(n))	the compulsory medical insurance organization, which also pays statutory sick and redundancy pay
das Arbeitslosengeld	earnings-related (unemployment) benefit
die Arbeitslosenunterstützung	unemployment benefit / dole money
der Behinderte (adjectival noun)	handicapped / disabled person
das Krankengeld	(statutory) sick pay
das Mutterschaftsgeld	maternity pay / benefit
die Mutterschaftshilfe	maternity allowance
der Mutterschaftsurlaub	maternity leave
der Sozialarbeiter(-)	social worker
das Sozialamt	(social) welfare office
Sozialabgaben (pl.)	(social) welfare contributions
der Wohlfahrtsstaat(en)	welfare state

(iv) Housing

- General

die Siedlung(en)	(originally: workers') estate
der Soziale Wohnungsbau	public sector housing programme
die Sozialwohnung(en)	council flats (there are very few council houses)
der (eintönige) Vorort(e)	suburbia
Wohnverhältnisse (pl.)	living / housing conditions
das Wohnviertel(–)	residential area

- Types of house

der Bungalow(s)	bungalow
das Einfamilienhaus(¨er)	(small) detached house
das Doppelhaus	semi-detached house
das Herrenhaus	manor house
das Hochhaus(¨er)	high-rise building / flats
das Reihenhaus	terraced house
die Villa (Villen)	villa
das Villenviertel(–)	exclusive residential district
die Wohnung	apartment
die Eigentumswohnung	owner-occupied flat

N.B. *eine Fünf-Zimmerwohnung* would be a flat with five rooms, counting all rooms except the bathroom and kitchen.

das Bad / Badezimmer(–)	bathroom
das Eßzimmer(–)	dining room
die Küche(n)	kitchen
das Schlafzimmer(–)	bedroom
das Wohnzimmer(–)	living / sitting room

(e) Foreign affairs

das Abkommen(–)	agreement
das Handelsabkommen	trade agreement
ab◊schaffen	to abolish
*an◊greifen**	to attack
der Angriff(e)	attack
der Nichtangriffspakt	non-aggression treaty / pact
die Außenpolitik	foreign policy
der Aussiedler(–)	person from the (German-speaking) community in the East resettling in the Federal Republic

der Umsiedler	person from East Germany resettling in the Federal Republic (late 1980s)
der Beitritt	joining
der Beitritt Großbritanniens zur Europäischen Gemeinschaft	accession of UK to the EC
die Blockade	blockade
die Botschaft(en)	embassy
der Botschafter(–)	ambassador
das Bündnis(se)	alliance
der Diplomat(en)	diplomat
*diplomatische Beziehungen ab◊brechen**	to break off diplomatic relations
die Dritte Welt	the Third World
die EG (Europäische Gemeinschaft)	EC (European Community)
das Embargo	embargo
ein Embargo über etwas verhängen	to put an embargo on something
die Entspannungspolitik	(policy of) détente
das Entwicklungsland(¨er)	developing country
die Entwicklungshilfe(n)	(development) aid
die EU (Europäische Union)	EU (European Union)
die EWG (Europäische Wirtschaftsgemeinschaft)	EEC (European Economic Community)
der Frieden	peace
die Geisel(n)	hostage
die Großmacht(¨e)	great power / superpower
die GUS = Gemeinschaft unabhängiger Staaten	CIS = Commonwealth of Independent States
das Konsulat(e)	consulate
die Krise(n)	crisis
der Mitgliedsstaat(en)	member state
der Regierungssprecher(–)	government spokesman
der UNO Sicherheitsrat	U.N. Security Council
der Staatenbund	confederacy
die Vereinten Nationen (pl.)	United Nations
verhandeln	to negotiate

Die Verhandlungen endeten in einer Sackgasse.
The negotiations are at a stalemate / an impasse.

der Vertrag(¨e)	treaty
der Friedenvertrag	peace treaty
der Bündnisvertrag	treaty of alliance
das Völkerrecht	international law
das Zugeständnis(se)	concession
Zugeständnisse machen	to make concessions

(f) Warfare, terrorism and peace

die Abwehr	defence
das landgestützte Abwehrsystem	land-based defence system
der Abzug(¨e)	withdrawal
der Truppenabzug	withdrawal of troops
die Aggression	aggression
blinder Alarm	false alarm / hoax call
die Alliierten (pl.)	allied powers
der Anschlag(¨e)	attack
der Terroristenanschlag	terrorist attack
einen Anschlag auf etwas (acc.) / *jemanden verüben*	to make an attack on something / to make an assassination attempt
(N.B. *einen Anschlag machen*	to put up a notice / poster)
die Aufklärungskamera(s)	reconnaissance camera
der Ausbruch(¨e)	outbreak
ein Ziel aus◊schalten	to 'take out' (destroy) a target
bedrohen	to threaten
der Befehl(e)	order / command
der Befehlshaber(–)	commander
die Befehlsverweigerung(en)	refusal to obey orders
die Befestigung(en)	fortification
die Befreiung	liberation
die finanzielle Belastung(n)	financial burden
der Berufssoldat(en)	professional soldier / regular
beschlagnahmen♦	to impound
die Bewaffnung(en)	arming / weapons
der Bodenkampf(¨e)	ground fight
die Bodentruppe(n)	ground force
das Boden – Boden Raketensystem(e)	ground-to-ground missile system
die Bombadierung(en)	bombardment / bombing
die Briefbombe(n)	letter bomb
die Bundeswehr	Federal Armed Forces (of Germany)
das Bündnis(se)	alliance
der Verbündete (adjectival noun)	ally
der Bunker(–)	bunker
die Demontage	dismantling
in ein Land ein◊marschieren	to invade a country
der Einsatz(¨e)	sortie / deployment

Die Piloten flogen Tausende von Einsätzen.
The pilots flew thousands of sorties.

Man fürchtet sich vor dem Einsatz von chemischen Waffen.
People are (literally: one is) afraid of the deployment of chemical weapons.

die Entspannungspolitik	(policy of) détente
entwaffnen	to disarm
*(sich) ergeben**	to surrender
die Erschütterung(en)	vibration / tremor
die Fahnenflucht	desertion
der Feind(e)	enemy
das Fernaufklärungsflugzeug(e)	long-distance reconnaissance plane
jemanden fesseln	to put someone in chains
flüchten	to flee
der Flüchtling(e)	refugee
die Flugabwehr	air defence
die Fregatte(n)	frigate
die Friedensbemühung(en)	peace effort
die friedliche Lösung(en)	peaceful solution
die Front(en)	front
das Gebiet(e)	area
das Gefecht(e)	skirmish
die Grausamkeit(en)	atrocity
an jemandem Grausamkeiten verüben	to inflict atrocities on someone
das Geschütz(e)	piece of artillery / gun
das Geschwader(–)	squadron / wing
die Grenze(n)	border
die Informationssperre(n)	news blackout / information ban
der Krieg(e)	war
die Kriegsentschädigung(en)	reparations (literally: war compensation)
der Kriegsgefangene (adjectival noun)	prisoner of war
das Kriegsverbrechen(–)	war crime
der Lastenausgleich	≈ burden sharing (compensation paid by the government to members of the public in order to make up for losses and damages they suffered during war)
der Lagebericht(e) / das Briefing	briefing
das Lazarett(e)	field hospital
die Luftaufklärung(en)	air reconnaissance
die Luftbetankung(en)	in-flight refuelling
die Luftbrücke	airlift
die Luftherrschaft	air supremacy
der Luftschutzraum(¨e)	air-raid shelter
die Luftüberlegenheit	air superiority
die Luftwaffe	airforce

der Marschflugkörper(–)	cruise missile
die Meldung(en)	report / announcement
die Mine(n)	mine
der Nachschub(¨e)	supplies
der Niederlage	defeat
der Panzer(–)	tank
die Panzerabwehrrakete(n)	anti-tank rocket
der Panzergrenadier(e)	soldier in the armoured infantry
der Panzerspähwagen(–)	armoured scout car
planmäßig	according to plan
die Raketenabschußrampe(n)	missile launching pad
der Raketenwerfer(–)	rocket launcher
die Räumung	clearing / vacation / evacuation (e.g. of troops and equipment or of civilians)
requirieren	to impound / requisition
die Rettung	rescue
die Rote Armee Fraktion (RAF)	extreme left-wing terrorist organization
der Rückzug(¨e)	retreat
rüsten	to arm
die Rüstung	armament / arms / suit of armour
die Abrüstung	disarmament
der Schaden(¨)	damage
der Schußwechsel(–)	exchange of shots / fire
die Sicherheitszone(n)	security zone
der Sprengkopf(¨e)	warhead
die Sprengladung(en)	explosive charge
die versteckte Sprengladung	booby trap
die Staffel(n)	flight (airforce unit) / escort formation (of ships, police cars etc.)
die Stationierung	deployment (literally: stationing)
die Stationierung von Raketen	deployment of missiles
*in Stellung bringen**	to move into position
die Streitigkeit(en)	quarrel / argument / dispute
Streitkräfte (pl.)	armed forces
der Tote (adjectival noun)	casualty (dead)
die Truppe(n) [FA]	unit of armed forces / battery
die Truppen	troops
der Soldat(en)	trooper / soldier
die Unterstützung	support
'verbrannte Erde'	'scorched earth'
der Vergeltungsschlag(¨e)	retaliatory strike
verhandeln	to negotiate
der Verletzte (adjectival noun)	casualty (injured)

der Verlust(e)	loss
schwere / leichte Verluste	heavy / light losses
vernichten	to annihilate
die Verteidigung	defence
(den Kriegsdienst) verweigern	to refuse (to do military service)
der Kriegsdienstverweigerer(–)	conscientious objector
der Verzicht auf Gebiete	renunciation of territories
*vor◊dringen**	to push forward
ins feindliche Lager vordringen	to push forward into the enemy camp
die Waffe(n)	weapon

Der illegale Waffenhandel nimmt zu.
The illegal arms trade is on the increase.

die Atomwaffen (pl.)	nuclear weapons
der Waffenstillstand(¨e)	cease-fire / armistice
die Warnung(en)	warning
der Wehrpflichtige (adjectival noun)	conscript
das Wettrüsten	arms race
die Wiedereinsetzung der Regierung	reinstatement of the government
das Wüstenschild	desert shield
der Wüstensturm	desert storm
der Zerstörer(–)	destroyer
die Zerstörung(en)	destruction
das Ziel(e)	target / aim
Zuflucht (f.) *suchen*	to seek refuge
*zurück◊treiben**	to drive / force back

148 Legal matters

(a) Crime

an◊stiften	to instigate
jemanden zu einem Verbrechen anstiften	to incite someone to commit a crime
der Anstifter(–)	instigator / ringleader
beeinflussen	to influence
beleidigend	insulting
benachteiligen	to put at a disadvantage
die Benachteiligung	discrimination
beschädigen	to damage
*bestechen**	to bribe
das Bestechungsgeld(er)	bribe

der Betrug	deceit / deception / fraud
betrügen	to deceive / cheat (also: to become unfaithful)
der Betrüger(–)	defrauder
die Beute	loot / haul / swag
der Dieb(e)	thief
der Diebstahl(¨e)	theft
die Drohung(en)	threat
entführen	to kidnap
*entkommen**	to get away / escape
entwenden	to steal / purloin
erdrosseln / erwürgen	to strangle
erpressen	to blackmail
die Erpressung	blackmail
*erschießen**	to shoot dead
*erschlagen**	to strike dead / kill
*erstechen**	to stab (to death)
fälschen	to forge / fake / falsify
*fliehen**	to flee
das Gesetz(e)	law
gesetzwidrig	illegal / unlawful
die Gewalt	violence
die Gewalttat(en)	act of violence
gewissenhaft	conscientious
gewissenlos	unscrupulous / without conscience
die Grausamkeit(en)	cruelty
die Hinterziehung(en)	evasion / appropriation
klauen < coll. >	to nick
lügen	to lie
morden	to murder
der Mörder(–) [FA]	murderer
die Nötigung	coercion
Nötigung zum Diebstahl	coercion to theft
der Raub	robbery
die Rechtsverletzung(en)	infringement / violation (of the law)
der Schauplatz(¨e)	scene of crime
der Schuft(e) < coll. >	cad
straffällig werden	to commit a criminal offence
die strafbare Handlung	punishable offence
die Tat(en)	crime (but: die *gute Tat* = good deed)
der Täter(–)	criminal / culprit
der Tatort(–)	scene of crime
die Tatsache(n)	fact

unterdrücken ♦	to suppress
unterschlagen ♦ *	to embezzle / misappropriate
Beweise unterschlagen	to withhold proof
die Unterschlagung(en)	embezzlement / misappropriation
untreu	unfaithful / disloyal
jemandem untreu werden	to become unfaithful to someone
die Veruntreuung(en)	embezzlement
*verbieten**	to forbid
das Verbrechen(–)	crime
ein Verbrechen begehen / etwas verbrechen**	to commit a crime
Er hat etwas verbrochen.	He has committed a crime.
der Verbrecher(–)	criminal
der Schwerverbrecher(–)	serious offender
der Verdacht	suspicion
jemanden wegen etwas (gen.) *verdächtigen*	to suspect someone of something
das Vergehen(–)	crime
die Vergewaltigung(en)	rape
jemanden zu etwas (dat.) *verleiten*	to lead someone astray / entice someone into something
gegen etwas (acc.) *verstoßen**	to offend against something
gegen das Gesetz verstoßen	to contravene the law
jemanden in Versuchung führen	to lead someone into temptation
jemandem etwas (acc.) *weg◊nehmen**	to take something away from someone
der Zwang(¨e)	force / compulsion
jemanden zwingen etwas zu tun*	to force someone to do something

(b) Legal proceedings

die Abfindung(en)	settlement / compensation
an◊klagen	to accuse
der Angeklagte (adjectival noun)	the accused
die Anklage(n)	accusation
der Anwalt(¨e)	advocate (short for *der Rechtsanwalt*) / defence lawyer / solicitor / barrister
an◊zeigen	to report
eine Anzeige erstatten	to start legal proceedings
eine Anzeige gegen jemanden liegt vor	someone has been reported to the police / authorities

auf◊klären	to solve / explain
die Aufklärung	resolution / solution / elucidation

Hinweise, die zur Aufklärung des Falles beitragen, werden mit einer Geldsumme von DM 100 belohnt.
A reward of 100 marks will be given for information leading to prosecution. (literally: Hints leading to the solution of this case will be rewarded with a sum of 100 marks.)

die Aussage(n)	statement
die Zeugenaussage	witness's statement / testimony
begnadigen	to reprieve
begutachten	to give expert advice / survey
belangen	to prosecute

Dafür kann man belangt werden. You can be prosecuted for this.

jemanden wegen Verleumdung belangen	to sue someone for libel / slander
belasten	to incriminate
das Belastungsmaterial(ien)	incriminating evidence
jemanden (völlig) entlasten	to exonerate someone
beordern	to summon
beschädigen	to damage
der Schaden(¨)	damage
jemanden zur Leistung von Schadenersatz verurteilen	to award damages against someone
Schadenersatz zugesprochen bekommen	to be awarded damages
der Schädiger(–)	perpetrator
der Geschädigte (adjectival noun)	victim
beschlagnahmen♦	to confiscate / seize / impound
die Beschlagnahmung(en) / die Beschlagnahme(n)	confiscation / seizure / impounding
jemanden wegen etwas (gen.) *beschuldigen*	to accuse someone of something
die Beschuldigung(en)	accusation
bestrafen	to punish
die Bestrafung	punishment
betrügen	to deceive / cheat
der Betrug	deceit / deception / fraud
*beweisen**	to prove
der Beweis(e)	evidence / proof
bezeugen	to testify / attest

Können Sie das bezeugen? Will you testify to this (effect)?

der Zeuge(n)	witness
das Bundesfassungsgericht	Federal Constitutional Court
die Drohung(en)	threat

der Eid(e)	oath
*einen Eid schwören**	to swear an oath
die Eidesstattliche Erklärung	statutory declaration
die Eingabe(n)	petition
sich einigen	to agree
die Einigung	agreement
der Einspruch(¨e)	objection

Ich erhebe Einspruch!* Objection!

enthüllen	to reveal
der Ersatz	replacement
für etwas Ersatz leisten	to pay / provide compensation for something
der Fall(¨e)	case
die Folge(n)	consequence
der Freiheitsentzug	imprisonment

Er wurde zu 15 Jahren Freiheitsentzug verurteilt.
He was sentenced to 15 years imprisonment.

*jemanden von etwas frei◊sprechen**	to acquit someone of something
der Freispruch(¨e)	acquittal
*jemanden gefangen◊halten**	to hold someone prisoner
das Gefängnis(se)	prison
die Gefängnisstrafe(n)	prison sentence
das Untersuchungsgefängnis(se)	remand prison
gerecht	just
das Gericht(e)	court
gerichtlich	judicial
das Gerichtsverfahren(–)	legal proceedings
die Gerichtsverhandlung(en)	trial / hearing
der Gerichtsvollzieher(–)	bailiff
*gestehen**	to confess
ein Geständnis ab◊legen	to make a confession
das Gutachten(–)	expert advice
die Haft	custody / detention
jemanden in Haft nehmen	to take someone into custody / remand someone
die Untersuchungshaft	custody / period of imprisonment awaiting trial
der Häftling(e)	prisoner / detainee
verhaften	to detain
der Hausdurchsuchungsbefehl(e)	search warrant
die erste Instanz [FA]	the court of first instance
die zweite Instanz	appeal court
die dritte Instanz	court of final appeal
die Berufung in zweiter Instanz	second appeal
das Urteil letzter Instanz	final judgement

*die Interessen einer Partei vertreten**	to represent the interests of a party
der Jurist(en)	lawyer
die Justiz	justice / judiciary
der Justizirrtum(¨er)	miscarriage of justice
die Justizbehörde(n)	judicial authority
die Kaution(en)	bail

Er wurde gegen eine Kaution von 30 000 DM entlassen.
He was released on bail of 30 000 marks.

klagen	to sue
auf Scheidung klagen	to petition for divorce
der Kläger(–)	plaintiff / petitioner / prosecuting party
das Laiengericht(e)	magistrates' court (literally: lay court)
der Milderungsgrund(¨e)	mitigating circumstance
mildernde Umstände geltend machen	to invoke mitigating circumstances
der Nachweis(e)	proof
der Notar(e)	notary
der Prozess(e)	trial / court case
prozessieren	to go to court
das Recht(e)	law / justice
das Arbeitsrecht	labour law
das Erbrecht	law of inheritance
das Familienrecht	family law
das Naturrecht	natural law
das Strafrecht	criminal law
das Verwaltungsrecht	administrative law
das Zivilrecht	civil law
rechtlich	by law / legal
rechtmäßig	lawful / legitimate
der Rechtsanwalt(¨e)	defence lawyer (solicitor or barrister)
das Rechtsanwaltsbüro(s)	legal practice / solicitor's office
der Rechtsbeistand(¨e)	legal advice / advisor
der Rechtsberater(–)	legal advisor
der Rechtsstreit	law suit
der Rechtsweg	legal action

Der Rechtsweg ist ausgeschlossen.
The judge's decision is final. (literally: Recourse to legal action is excluded – e.g. in a raffle)

unter Ausschluß des Rechtswegs	without recourse to legal action / the courts / the law
der Richter(–)	judge

der Sachverständige (adjectival noun)	expert witness
die Schilderung(en)	description / account
die Schuld	guilt / fault

Es ist meine Schuld. It is my fault.

schuldig	guilty
jemandem die Schuld geben / zu◊schieben**	to blame someone

Wer auffährt, hat immer Schuld.
The person who drives into another car is always at fault.

die voreilige Schuldanerkenntnis	premature admission of guilt
das Schuldgefühl(e)	sense / feelings of guilt
die Selbstanzeige(n)	self-denunciation
der Staatsanwalt(¨e)	public prosecutor
strafbar	punishable
sich strafbar machen	to make oneself liable to prosecution

Das ist strafbar. That's a punishable offence.

die Strafe(n)	punishment
gegen jemanden Strafanzeige erstatten	to bring charges against someone
straffällig werden	to commit a criminal offence
das Strafgesetzbuch(¨er) (StGB)	criminal / penal code
die Strafkammer(n)	division for criminal matters (of a court)
strafmündig	of the age of criminal responsibility
unschuldig	not guilty
die Sühne	expiation / atonement
das Urteil(e)	judgement / decision
das Fehlurteil	error of judgement
ein Fehlurteil fällen	to return a wrong verdict / pass a wrong judgement
die Verhandlung(en)	hearing / trial
die Verleumdung(en)	slander / libel
der Vermerk(e)	note / remark / observation
versichern	to assure / assert / affirm
etwas hoch und heilig / eidesstattlich versichern	to swear blind to something / attest something in a statutory declaration
die Versicherung(en)	assurance
die eidesstattliche Versicherung	statutory declaration
die Versöhnung	reconciliation
der Verteidiger(–)	defence lawyer
der Verteidiger des Angeklagten	the counsel for the defence

die Vorladung(en) vor Gericht	summons (to court)
*Zeugen vor Gericht vor◊laden**	to subpoena witnesses
das Zuchthaus(¨er)	prison for capital offenders (US penitentiary)
der Zufall(¨e)	coincidence

(c) Insurance

die Versicherung(en)	insurance
*eine Versicherung ab◊schließen**	to take out insurance
der Versicherungsbetrug(¨e)	insurance fraud
die Versicherungspolice	insurance policy
die Versicherungsprämie(n)	insurance premium
der Versicherungsschutz	insurance cover
die Versicherungssumme(n)	sum insured
das Versicherungsunternehmen(–)	insurance company
die Berufsunfähigkeitsversicherung	disability insurance (insurance against incapacity to follow one's profession / trade)
die gesetzliche Brandversicherung	legally required fire insurance
die Feuerversicherung	fire insurance
die Gebäudeversicherung	building insurance
die Haftpflichtversicherung	personal liability insurance / third-party insurance
die Hausratversicherung	contents insurance
die Krankenversicherung	health insurance
die Rechtsschutzversicherung(en)	insurance for legal protection
die Unfallversicherung	accident insurance

149 Computers, technology and research

Vocabulary specifically related to word-processing is listed separately in subsection (b) below.

(a) Computers: hardware

die Anlage(n)	system
angeschlossen	on-line
nicht angeschlossen	off-line
die Anzeige	indicator
der Ausdruck(e)	print-out
die Bedienerkonsole(n)	user console

benutzerfreundlich	user-friendly
die Betriebsart(en)	mode
betriebsbereit	ready
der Bildschirm(e)	screen
der Chip(s)	chip
der Computer(–)	computer
Daten (pl.)	data
die Datenbank(en)	data bank
der Datenbestand(¨e)	data base
der Datenempfang	data reception
die Datentechnik	data technology
die Datenverarbeitung	data processing
der Drucker(–)	printer
die EDV Anlage = elektronische Datenverarbeitungsanlage	data-processing system
(das) Ein- / Ausschalten	switching on / off
die Einsteckkarte(n)	(plug in) card
das Einzelpapier	single sheet paper
die Einzelpapierzuführung(en)	(cut) sheet feeder
das Endlospapier	continuous stationery / paper
die Festplatte(n)	hard disk
der Freigabehebel(–)	release lever
der Hacker(–)	hacker
das Handbuch(¨er)	manual
die Hardware	hardware
(die) Informatik	computer science
das Interfacekabel(–)	interface cable
per Knopfdruck	by pressing the button
die Kompatibilität	compatibility
der Laptop = tragbarer Computer	laptop
die Leistungsfähigkeit	power / performance
die Maus(¨e)	mouse
das Memory (no pl.) / *der Speicher(–)*	memory / storage
das Megabyte(s)	megabyte
der Modus (Modi)	mode
der Netzanschluß (schlüsse)	mains connection
die Netzspannung(en)	mains voltage
netzunabhängig	network-independent
der Papierwahlschalter(–)	paper selection button
der Personalcomputer(–)	personal computer
der Rechner(–)	computer / calculator
der Selbsttest(s)	selftest
die Software (no pl.)	software
der Speicher(–)	memory / storage
die Speicherkapazität(en)	memory / storage capacity
das Stachelrad(¨er) / die Stachelwalze(n)	tractor

der Superrechner(–)	supercomputer
das System(e)	system
der Systemberater(–)	systems analyst
die Tastatur(en)	keyboard
das Terminal(s)	terminal
die Verkabelung	installation of cables / connection (computer to printer)
die Vernetzung	networking / interlinkage (several systems)
die Walze(n)	platen
die Druckerwalze	printer platen

(b) Computers: software, especially word-processing

The following word list is intended to help with the terminology of word-processing and its various commands. Some of the terms may have other meanings in different contexts (i.e. unrelated to computing).

When keying-in German on an English / American keyboard use ASCII codes for umlauts and *ß*.

der Absatz(¨e)	paragraph
die Änderung(en)	alteration
die Anzeige(n)	indicator
das Arbeitsblatt(¨er) / das Spreadsheet(s)	spreadsheet
der Ausschnitt(e)	window
(das) Bearbeiten	edit
der Befehl(e)	command
das Befehlsmenü(s)	command menu
der Bereich(e)	division
die Betriebsart(en)	mode
das Betriebssystem(e)	operating system
(die) Bibliothek(en)	library
der Bildlauf	scroll
die Bildlaufarretierung	scroll lock
der Bildschirm(e)	screen
(das) Bildschirm löschen	clear (screen)
die Bildschirmseite(n)	(screen) page
rechtsbündig / linksbündig	right / left justified
CUU (der computerunterstützte Unterricht) / CAL	CAL (Computer-assisted Learning)
die Datei(en)	document / file
(das) Dateilöschen	delete document
der Dateimanager	manager / document retrieval

drucken	to print
der Druck	print
das Druckformat(e)	style (sheet)
drücken	to press
Drücken Sie die Alt-Taste.	Press the alt-key.
(das) Einfügen	insert
die (DOS) Eingabeforderung	(DOS) prompt
(das) Ende	end
das Expertensystem(e)	expert system
(das) Festhalten	record
die Festplatte(n)	hard disk
die Flüssigkeits-Kristall Anzeige(n)	liquid crystal display
(das) Formattieren	formating
die Funktionstaste(n)	function key
Gehe zu	jump (go-to)
Gesamt	all
(das) Gesamtlöschen (Tabs)	reset all (tabs)
Grundbegriffe (pl.)	basics
(die) Hilfe	help
die Kopf- // Fußzeile(n)	running head / header // footer
(die) künstliche Intelligenz	artificial intelligence
(das) Laden	load
das Laufwerk(e)	(disk) drive
(das) Layout	layout
die Lektion(en)	lesson
das Lernprogramm(e)	tutorial
(das) Löschen	delete
das Mausverfahren	working with the mouse
(das) Muster(–)	format
der Nadeldrucker	dot matrix printer
(der) Neustart	restart
(die) Option(en)	options
(die) Paginierung	page numbers / pagination
der Papiereinzug	paper feed
der Papierkorb	scrap / waste basket / bin
der Papierstau(s)	(paper / printer) jam
der Papiervorschub(¨e)	paper feed to the next top of form / page advance
(die) Position 1	home
(der) Rahmen(–)	border
die Rechtschreibung	spelling
das Rechtschreibprogramm	spell check
(das) Register(–)	index
(das) Return	return / enter
die Returntaste	return key

die Richtungstaste(n)	cursor / direction key
rückgängig machen	to undo
die Schriftart(en)	(type) face / font / character font
der Seitenrand(¨er)	margin
der Seitenumbruch(¨e)	gutter
senkrecht	vertical
setzen	to set
sofort (Druck)	direct (print)
(das) Speichern	save
(der) Stopp(s)	stop
(das) Suchen	search
die Tabulaturtaste	tab key
die Taste(n)	key
die Tastenkombination(en)	key combination
der Textbaustein(e)	block (of text)
die Textverarbeitung	word-processing
die Trennhilfe(n)	hyphenate
das Typenrad(¨er)	daisywheel
(das) Überarbeiten und Fertigmachen zum Druck	edit (and get ready for print)
(die) Überarbeitung	revision (marks)
überschreiben ♦ *	to overtype
(das) Übertragen	transfer
(das) Umbenennen	rename
(das) Umschalten	shift
(das) Unterbrechen	escape
verarbeiten	to process
(das) Verbinden	attach
verborgen	hidden
(das) Verknüpfen	link
(das) Verlassen	quit
(das) Verschieben	move
das Verzeichnis(se)	index / register / dictionary
waagrecht	horizontal
wählen	to choose
die Warteschlange(n) (Druck)	(print) queue
(das) Wechseln	replace
weiter	continue
die Wiederaufnahme	resume
das Zeichen(–)	character / sign
der Zeichenabstand(¨e)	print pitch / horizontal spacing
die Zeile(n)	line
der Zeilenabstand(¨e)	line spacing
die Zeilennummer(n)	line number
(das) Zusammenführen	merge

(c) Domestic technology

die Alarmanlage(n)	alarm system
der Anrufbeantworter(–)	answering machine
der CD Spieler(–)	CD player
die Fernbedienung	remote control
der Gefrier(kühl)schrank(¨e)	(upright) freezer
die Gefrier(kühl)truhe(n)	(chest) freezer
die Geschirrspülmaschine(n) / die Emma (jocular)	dishwasher
das Haushaltsgerät(e)	domestic appliance
das Kabelfernsehen	cable television
das kabellose Telefon(e)	cordless phone
die Mikrowelle(n)	microwave
der Mixer(–)	mixer / blender
die Sprechanlage(n)	intercom
die Stereoanlage(n)	hifi system
der Telefonanschluß (-schlüsse)	telephone line / connection
der Videorekorder(–)	video recorder
der Zauberstab(¨e)	(hand-held) mixer (literally: magic wand)

(d) Recent technology

die Anlage(n)	system / installation
der Bildschirmtext(e) (BTX)	Viewdata (Prestel / Ceefax)
der Bildschirmtextanschluß (-schlüsse)	Viewdata connection
das Bildtelefon(e)	video telephone
die Digitaltechnik	digital technology
die Elektromagnetbahn(en)	electromagnetic track
das Elementarteilchen(–)	elementary particle
das Endgerät(e)	terminal
der Energieverlust(e)	energy loss
das FAXgerät(e)	fax machine
(tele)faxen	to fax
GS = Geprüfte Sicherheit (f.)	safety mark / ≈ kite mark (literally: tested safety)
herkömmlicher Rechner	conventional computer
die Kernforschung	nuclear research
die Kernfusion(en)	nuclear fusion
das Kernkraftwerk(e)	nuclear power station
die Kernspaltung(en)	splitting of the atom
die Kühlung	cooling
der Laserstrahl(en)	laser beam
die Lasertechnik	laser technology
die Lichtgeschwindigkeit	speed of light

die Lichtwelle(n)	light wave
das Modem(s)	modem
die Raumsonde(n)	space probe
die Rechengeschwindigkeit(en)	processing speed
der Satellitenempfänger(–)	satellite dish
das Satellitenfernsehen	satellite TV
der Speicherring(e)	storage ring / ring buffer
die Sprungtemperatur(en)	critical temperature (for superconductor)
der Supraleiter(–)	superconductor
supraleitendes Material	superconducting material
der Tageslichtprojektor / der Overheadprojector	OHP (overhead projector)
die Technikbewertung(en)	technology assessment
der Teilchenbeschleuniger(–)	particle accelerator
das Tele Shopping	tele-sales
der Widerstand(¨e)	resistance
der Zusammenprall(e)	collision

(e) Some 'green' issues and technology

das Abfackeln (des Öls)	flaring / burning off (of oil)
der Altglascontainer(–)	bottle bank
die Altkleidersammlung(en)	collection of old clothes
die (Ölteppich-)Barriere(n)	(oil slick) booms
bleifreies Benzin	lead-free petrol (in fact *bleifrei* is now considered and called *Normal* whereas leaded petrol is called *Verbleit*)
chlorfreigebleichter Zellstoff(e)	non-chlorine-bleached cellulose
die Entsorgung	(waste) disposal
die Entsalzungsanlage(n)	desalination plant
der Katalysator(en)	catalytic converter / catalysor / exhaust emission control
die Kläranlage(n)	sewage / waste-water treatment plant
krebserregend	carcinogenic / cancer-producing

Rauchen ist krebserregend.
Smoking is carcinogenic / can lead to cancer.

die Müllverbrennungsanlage(n)	refuse incinerator
die Müllvertwertung	waste recycling
der Ölskimmer(–)	oil skimmer
phosphatfreies Waschmittel(–)	phosphate-free washing powder
der radioaktive Abfall(¨e)	radioactive waste
der saure Regen	acid rain

schadstoffarm	low in harmful / toxic substances
der Schadstoffausstoß(¨e)	emission of harmful substances
die Umweltampel(n)	signal at traffic light indicating a long wait (drivers should switch off their engines)
die Umweltbelastung(en)	environmental pollution
der Umweltsünder(–)	someone who deliberately pollutes the environment
umweltfreundlich	environmentally friendly
die Umweltverträglichkeitsprüfung (U.V.P.) / der Umwelt TÜV < coll. >	test for pollution control
TÜV = der Technische Überwachungsverein	≈ M.O.T. (for all kinds of technical equipment)
die Wiederaufbereitungsanlage(n)	recycling plant
die Wiederverwertung / das Recycling	recycling

(f) Research

die Aufgabe(n)	task
die Befragung(en)	questioning
beobachten	to observe
die Beobachtung(en)	observation
*beschreiben**	to describe
die Beschreibung(en)	description
bestätigen	to confirm
die Bestätigung(en)	confirmation
*beweisen**	to prove
der Beweis(e)	proof / evidence
endgültig	definitive / final
die Erfahrung(en)	experience
erforschen	to research in great depth
*ergeben**	to result

Die Untersuchungen haben ergeben, daß . . .
The investigations have yielded / given / shown that . . .

das Ergebnis(se)	result
*erkennen**	to perceive
die Erkenntnis(se)	perception
der Fall(¨e)	case
forschen	to research
die Forschung(en)	research
der Forscher(–)	researcher
*gelten**	to be valid

Es gilt für diesen Fall. It applies in this case.

die Grenze(n)	limit (also: boundary / border)
die Grundlagenforschung(en)	basic / pure research (literally: research into the foundations of science)
die Lehre(n)	teaching / theory
das Lehrbuch(¨er)	teaching book / textbook (usually **the** authoritative version)
prüfen	to check / examine
überprüfen ♦	to (double) check / examine / scrutinize
die Überprüfung(en)	(double) checking
die Technik [FA]	technology
die Arbeitstechnik(en)	technique / method
unterscheiden ♦ *	to differentiate / distinguish
der Unterschied(e)	difference
untersuchen ♦	to investigate
die Untersuchung(en)	investigation
die Verantwortung(en)	responsibility
verdeutlichen	to clarify / explain
der Versuch(e) / das Experiment(e)	experiment
die Voraussage(n)	prediction
der Vorgang(¨e)	process
die Wahrnehmung(en)	perception
widerlegen	to refute
*widersprechen**	to contradict
der Widerspruch(¨e)	contradiction
das Wissen	knowledge
die Wissenschaft(en)	science
die Naturwissenschaften	natural sciences
die Geisteswissenschaften	arts / humanities
der Wissenschaftler(–)	scientist / academic
der Zeitpunkt(e)	date

150 Cinema, theatre and the fine arts

(a) Cinema and theatre

der Akt(e)	act
ein Drama mit fünf Akten	a play in five acts
der Applaus	applause
auf◊führen	to perform
der Auftritt(e)	entrance / appearance (on stage)

die Bühne(n)	stage
der Darsteller(–)	actor / performer
das Drama (Dramen)	drama
das Drehbuch(¨er)	film script

Die Dreharbeiten fangen morgen an. Filming starts tomorrow.

das Fernsehen / der Fernseher(–)	television
der Film(e)	film
der Dokumentarfilm(e)	documentary
der Spielfilm(e)	feature film
der Kurzfilm(e)	short film
die Filmindustrie(n)	cinema industry
der Filmausschnitt(e)	film clip
der Filmstreifen(–)	filmstrip
einen Film drehen	to make / shoot a film
vor Ort filmen	to film on location
fotogen	photogenic

Sie ist sehr fotogen. She films well / is photogenic.

die Halbtotale(n)	medium shot
die Handlung(en)	action
das Kino(s)	cinema
komisch	funny / comic
die Komödie(n)	comedy
die Kritik(en) [FA]	critique
der Kritiker(–)	critic
der Lautsprecher(–)	(loud) speaker
die Leinwand(¨e)	screen
Mitwirkende (adjectival noun)	cast

Mitwirkende in der Reihenfolge ihres Auftritts:
Cast in order of appearance:

die Montage(n)	montage
die Nachrichten (pl.)	TV / radio news
der Nachspann / Vorspann	credits (at the end / beginning of the film)
die Nahaufnahme(n)	close-up
das Parterre / das Parkett	stalls
die Person(en)	person
der Platzanweiser(–) / die Platzanweiserin(nen)	usher / usherette / steward
Probeaufnahmen (f.pl.) *machen*	to give someone a film test
der Produzent(en)	producer
das Programm(e)	programme
im vierten Programm	on Channel Four
das Publikum	audience

der Rang(¨e)	circle
erster / zweiter Rang	first (dress) / second (upper) circle
die Regie(n)	direction
die Regie führen / haben	to direct
unter der Regie von	directed by
die Regieanweisung(en)	stage direction
der Regiestuhl(¨e)	director's chair
der Regisseur(e)	film director
die Rolle(n)	role
der Schauspieler(–)	actor
die Schauspielerin(nen)	actress
der Schnitt	film editing
der Sender(–)	(broadcasting) station
die Sendung(en)	broadcast
spielen	to play
der Sprecher(–)	speaker / announcer / narrator
der Star(s)	star
die Synchronisation / das Dubbing	dubbing
das Theater(–)	theatre
das Theaterstück(e)	play
das Tonarchiv(e)	sound archives
die Tragödie(n)	tragedy
der Trailer(–)	trailer
die Veröffentlichung(en)	release
der Vorhang(¨e)	curtain

Der Vorhang geht auf. The curtain rises.

der Vorspann(¨e)	opening credits
die Vorstellung(en)	performance
die Wochenschau(en)	weekly news (mainly 1930s)
in Zeitlupe (f.)	in slow motion
der Zuschauer(–)	spectator
im Zuschauerraum	in the auditorium

(b) Fine arts

The suffix *-mus* always makes the noun masculine, e.g. *der Realismus* (realism), *Impressionismus, Expressionismus, Naturalismus, Symbolismus* etc.

abstrakt	abstract
das Acryl	acrylics
der Akt(e)	nude
die Allegorie(n)	allegory

*an◊streichen**	to decorate / paint
das Aquarell(e)	water-colour
das Atelier(s)	artist's studio
die Ausstellung(en)	exhibition
der Barock	baroque
die Batik(en)	batik
die Biedermeierzeit	Biedermeier period
das Bild(er)	picture
der Bildhauer(–)	sculptor
die Bildhauerei / die Bildhauerkunst	sculpture
die Blütezeit(en)	Golden Age (literally: blossoming time)
die Collage(n)	collage
die Darstellung(en)	representation
das Detail(s)	detail
der Druck(e)	print
die Epoche(n)	epoch
epochemachend	epoch-making
die Fälschung(en)	forgery / fake
die Farbe(n)	colour
die Federzeichnung(en)	pen-and-ink drawing
kolorierte Federzeichnung	a drawing in ink and wash
der Flügel(–)	panel (of screen / altar)
das Fresko (Fresken)	fresco
die Galerie(n)	gallery
gegenständlich	representational
das Gemälde(–)	painting
das Genie(s)	genius
genial [FA]	of genius / gifted
der Geschmack(¨er)	taste
der Gewebefilmdruck(e)	screenprinting
der Hintergrund / Vordergrund	background / foreground
der Jugendstil	art nouveau
der Katalog(e)	catalogue
die Keramik(en)	ceramics
die Klassik	classical period
die Kunst(¨e)	art
die bildenden Künste	the fine arts
der Künstler(–)	artist
der Kupferstich(e)	copperplate print / engraving
die Leinwand(¨e)	canvas
die Lithografie(n) / Lithographie(n)	lithograph
malen	to paint
bemalen	to decorate
handbemalt	hand-painted
der Maler(–)	painter

die Malerei(en)	painting
der Mäzen(e)	patron
das Mäzenatentum	patronage
der Meister(–)	master
das Modell(e)	model (fashion / nude)
das Museum (Museen)	museum
die Ölmalerei(en)	oil (painting)
das Ornament(e)	ornament
das Paneel(e)	panel (of door / wall)
der Pinsel(–)	brush
plastisch	sculptural
das Porträt(s)	portrait
die Radierung(en)	etching
der Rahmen(–)	frame
das Raster(–)	grid / halftone / raster screen
der (Bild)Raster(–)	screen (printing)
das Relief(s) (pronounced as three syllables)	relief
die Reproduktion(en)	reproduction
das Rokoko	rococo period / style
die Romantik	(age of) Romanticism
der Schmuck (no pl.)	jewellery
das Schmuckstück(e)	(piece of) jewellery
schnitzen	to carve
die Holzschnitzerei(en)	wood carving
die Skizze(n)	sketch
die Skulptur(en) / die Plastik(en)	sculpture
die Statue(n) (pronounced as three syllables)	statue
die Stickerei(en)	embroidery
das Stilleben(–)	still life
die Stukkatur(en)	stucco (work) / ornamental plasterwork
die Tönung	shade / tone
eine leichte / schwache Tönung mit brauner Tünche	a wash of brown ink
die Tünche(n)	whitewash / distemper / wash
zeichnen	to draw
die Zeichnung(en)	drawing
die Ziselierung(en)	engraving / chasing

51 Literature and music

(a) Literature

(i) Books, plays and poetry

der Abriß (-risse)	synopsis / overview / (shorter than *Inhaltsangabe*)
der Abschnitt(e)	paragraph
absurd	absurd
der Akt(e)	act
der erste / zweite Akt	first / second act
die Anekdote(n)	anecdote
der Anfang(¨e)	beginning
auf◊führen	to perform
die Aufführung(en)	performance
die Aufklärung(en)	the Enlightenment / explanation
die Auflösung(en) / der Ausgang(¨e)	denouement
der Ausdruck(¨e)	expression
die Ausgabe(n)	edition
die kommentierte Ausgabe	annotated edition
*heraus◊geben**	to edit
der Ausgangspunkt(e)	point of departure
die Aussage(n)	statement / meaning
der Autor(en)	author (of a particular work)
die Bedeutung(en)	meaning / significance
die Betrachtung(en)	contemplation / examination / reflection
das Buch(¨er)	book
die Bildgeschichte(n)	picture story
der Chor(¨e)	chorus / choir
der Comic(s)	comic / comic strip / cartoon
dar◊stellen	to present
die Darstellung(en)	presentation / performance
der Darsteller(–)	actor
der Dichter(–)	poet
die Dichtung	poetry
das Gedicht(e)	poem
dichten	to write poetry
erdichtet	fictitious
das Drama (Dramen)	drama
die Eigenschaft(en)	characteristic
der Eindruck(¨e)	impression
die Einheit(en)	unit / unity
(die) Einheit der Handlung	unity of action

(die) Einheit des Ortes	unity of place
(die) Einheit der Zeit	unity of time
die Einleitung(en)	introduction
das Ende	end
glückliches Ende	happy ending
tragisches Ende	tragic ending
das Epos (Epen)	epic (poem)
die Entwicklung(en)	development (of plot)
die Erklärung(en)	explanation / source of interpretation
erzählen	to tell / narrate
der Erzähler(–)	narrator / story-teller
die Erzählerin(nen)	female narrator
der Ich-Erzähler	first-person narrator
die Erzählung(en)	story / narrative
die Erzählerperspektive(n)	narrator's perspective
die Fabel(n)	fable
der Fachausdruck(¨e)	specialist term
der rote Faden	central theme / leitmotif
die Fee(n)	fairy
die Folge(n)	sequence / consequence / episode
der Gag(s)	gag
der Gedanke(n)	thought
der Hauptgedanke	main thought
das Gefühl(e)	feeling / sentiment
das Gesamtwerk (no pl.)	complete works
die Geschichte(n)	story / plot
die Geschichte (no pl.)	history
der Gesichtspunkt(e)	point of view / perspective
das Gespräch(e)	conversation
das Gleichnis(se) / die Allegorie(n)	allegory
das Gleichnis(se) / Parabel(n)	parable
das Gleichnis vom verlorenen Sohn	parable of the prodigal son
gleichnishaft / allegorisch	allegorical
gleichnishaft / parabolisch	parabolical
die Gleichzeitigkeit	simultaneity
die Gliederung(en)	structure / division
die Handlung(en)	plot / action / deed
es handelt von	it is about
der Handlungsablauf(¨e)	plot / action
die Nebenhandlung	sub-plot
der Hauptteil(e)	main part
die Hauptrolle(n)	main role
der Held(en)	hero

die Heldin(nen)	heroine
der Antiheld(en)	anti-hero
die Antiheldin(nen)	anti-heroine
der Herausgeber(–)	editor
die Herausgeberin(nen)	female editor
die Hexe(n)	(wicked) witch
der Hintergrund(¨e)	background
der Höhepunkt(e)	climax
das Hörspiel(e)	radio play
sich (acc.) *identifizieren mit*	to identify with
die Identifizierung(en)	identification
die Identität(en)	identity
die Illustrierte(n)	magazine
der Inhalt	contents
die Inhaltsangabe(n)	(table of) contents / synopsis
das Inhaltsverzeichnis(se)	table of contents
die Interpretation(en)	interpretation
das Kapitel(–)	chapter
die Karikatur(en)	caricature
die Katharsis	catharsis
die Klassik	classical period
klassisch	classical
der Krimi(s) < informal >	whodunnit / thriller
die Kurzgeschichte(n)	short story
das Leitmotiv	dominant theme / leitmotif
das Lied(er)	song
das Lustspiel(e)	comedy
die Lyrik (no pl.)	lyric poetry, verse
das Märchen(–)	fairy tale
das Märchenspiel(e) (‚das um Weihnachten aufgeführt wird)	pantomime
der Märchenprinz(en)	Prince Charming
die Märchentante(n)	story-hour presenter (female)
das Merkmal(e)	characteristic / feature
die Metapher(–)	metaphor
die Pantomime(n) [FA]	mime
die Parodie(n) / die Persiflage(n)	parody
der Poet(en)	poet
die Quelle(n)	source / spring
der Raubdruck(e)	pirated edition
die Reihenfolge(n)	sequence
der Reim(e)	rhyme
das Reimpaar(e)	(rhyming) couplet
die Reportage(n)	report
der Rhythmus (Rhythmen)	rhythm
die Rolle(n)	role

der Roman(e)	novel
der Fortsetzungsroman	serialized novel
der Kriminalroman / der Krimi(s)	thriller
die Rückblende(n)	flashback
der Sachtext(e)	non-fiction (text)
die Satire(n)	satire
der Schluß (Schlüsse)	ending
die Schlußfolgerung(en)	conclusion / inference
der Schriftsteller(–)	author (of a particular work) / writer
die Schriftstellerin(nen)	female author / writer
die Science-fiction	science fiction
die Silbe(n)	syllable
die Spannung(en)	tension
Die Spannung steigt.	Tension is building up.
die Sprechblase(n)	speech-bubble / balloon
die Steigerung(en)	intensification / heightening / aggravation
der Stil(e)	style
die Strophe(n)	stanza / verse
das Symbol(e) für	symbol of
der Symbolismus	symbolism
die Szene(n)	scene
die Tatsache(n)	fact
die These(n)	thesis / proposition
die Antithese	antithesis
die Tragödie(n)	tragedy
die Tugend(en)	virtue
der Überblick	survey / overview
die Überleitung(en)	transition
die Verfremdung	alienation
der Verfremdungseffekt(e)	alienation effect (Brecht)
der Verlauf(¨e)	course (of events)
der Handlungsverlauf	course of events
der Vers(e)	verse / line / stanza
das Versmaß(e)	metre
das Verspaar(e)	couplet
der (Vers)Fuß(¨e)	(metrical) foot
der Vordergrund(¨e)	foreground
der Wendepunkt(e)	turning point
das Werk(e)	work / opus
zitieren	to quote
das Zitat(e)	quotation

(ii) Journalism

die Anzeige(n)	advertisement
der Anzeigenteil(e)	advertising section
die Ausgabe(n)	edition
die Wochenendausgabe	weekend edition
die Beilage(n)	supplement
die Wochenendbeilage	weekend supplement
die Literaturbeilage	literary supplement
der Bericht(e)	report
der Berichterstatter(–)	reporter
die Berichterstatterin(nen)	female reporter
die Besprechung(en)	review
die Buchbesprechung(en)	book review
die Filmbesprechung(en)	film review
das Blatt(¨er)	(news)paper
das Abendblatt	evening paper
das Monatsblatt	monthly paper
das Blättchen(–) / das Käseblatt / Käseblättchen < informal >	rag
die Boulevardpresse (no pl.)	the tabloids
die Boulevardzeitung(en)	tabloid paper
der Entwurf(¨e)	draft (also: design)
die (Druck)Fahne(n)	galley proof
das Feuilleton(s)	arts section
der freie Mitarbeiter(–)	freelance (worker / writer)
der Herausgeber(–)	editor
die Herausgeberin(nen)	female editor
der Kommentar(e)	commentary
der Kommentator(en)	(political) commentator
der Korrespondent(en)	correspondent
der Auslandskorrespondent	foreign affairs correspondent
die Korrespondentin(nen)	female correspondent
die Kritik(en) [FA]	review / critique
der Leitartikel(–)	editorial / leader
der Leserbrief(e) / Brief an den Herausgeber	letter to the editor
die Meldung(en)	report / information / news
der Mord(e)	murder
der Mörder(–) [FA]	murderer
die Nachricht(en)	news
die öffentliche Meinung(en)	public opinion
das Opfer(–)	victim
die Regenbogenpresse (no pl.) < informal >	gossip papers / magazines
der Reporter(–)	reporter / sports commentator

die Reporterin(nen)	female reporter / sports commentator
der Schauplatz(¨e)	scene of crime
das Schlagwort(¨er)	slogan
die Schlagzeile(n)	headline
der Sensationsjournalismus	tabloid journalism
die Spalte(n)	column
die Stellungnahme(n)	commentary
der Teil(e)	section
der Sportteil(e)	sports section
der Wirtschaftsteil(e)	business section
der Umbruch(¨e)	page proof
das Urteil(e)	judgement
das Verbrechen(–)	crime
der Verbrecher(–)	criminal
die Verbrecherin(nen)	female criminal
verfassen	to write / draw up
einen Bericht verfassen	to write a report
der Verfasser(–)	writer
die Verfasserin(nen)	female writer
der Verlag(e)	publishing house
die Verlagsanstalt(en)	publishing house / firm
der Verlauf(¨e)	course
der Handlungsverlauf	course of events
verlegen	to publish
der Verleger(–)	publisher
die Verlegerin(nen)	female publisher
veröffentlichen	to publish / publicize
die Veröffentlichung(en)	publication
das Voruteil(e)	prejudice
der Werbetext(e)	advertising text
die Zeitschrift(en)	illustrated paper / periodical / journal
die Monatszeitschrift	monthly (journal)
die Jahreszeitschrift	annual (journal)
die (heutigen) Zeitläufte	≈ current events / the present (day)
die Zeitung(en)	newspaper
die Tageszeitung	daily (paper)
die Wochenzeitung	(weekly) paper
eine Zeitung von Rang (und Namen)	a quality paper
der Zeitungsschreiber(–) / der Lohnschreiber / der Auftragsschreiber	(newspaper) hack

(b) Music

(i) Vocal

a capella	voices only
der Alt	altos (section of choir)
die Altistin(nen)	alto (individual singer)
der Baß	basses (section of choir)
der Baß (Bässe)	bass (individual singer)
Contra- / Kontra-	counter-
der Sopran	sopranos (section of choir)
die Sopranistin(nen)	soprano (individual singer)
Ich singe Sopran. I am a soprano.	
die Stimme(n)	voice
der Tenor	tenors (section of choir)
der Tenor(¨e)	tenor (individual singer)

(ii) Instruments

das Blasinstrument(e)	wind (usually brass) instrument
die Blaskapelle(n)	brass band
das Bläserensemble(s)	wind ensemble
das Blechblasinstrument	brass instrument
die Blechbläser (pl.)	brass section (in an orchestra)
die Blockflöte(n)	recorder
die Bratsche(n) / die Viola (Violen)	viola
das Cello / Celli	cello
das Cembalo(s)	harpischord
das Fagott(e)	bassoon
der Fagottbläser(–) / der Fagottist(en)	bassoonist
der Flügel(–)	grand piano
die Geige(n) / die Violine	violin
die Gitarre(n)	guitar
die Baßgitarre	bass (guitar)
die Elektrogitarre	electric guitar
die Konzertgitarre	acoustic guitar
die akustische Gitarre	acoustic guitar (folk / pop)
das Glockenspiel(e)	glockenspiel / carillon / chimes (literally: bell play)
die Harfe(n)	harp
das Holzblasinstrument(e)	woodwind instrument
das Horn(¨er)	horn
das Waldhorn	French horn
das Instrument(e)	instrument
das Kammerorchester(–)	chamber orchestra
die Klarinette(n)	clarinet

das Klavier(e)	piano
das wohltemperierte Klavier	the Well-Tempered Clavier
Kontra-	counter-
der Kontrapunkt	counterpoint
die Oboe(n)	oboe
die Orgel(n)	organ
die Pikkoloflöte(n) / das Pikkolo(s)	piccolo (flute)
die Posaune(n)	trombone
das Quartett(e) / Quintett(e) / Sextett(e) etc.	quartet / quintet / sextet
die Querflöte(n)	flute
das Saxophon(e)	saxophone
das Schlaginstrument(e)	percussion instrument
das Schlagzeug	set of drums
die Stimmgabel(n)	tuning fork
das Streichinstrument	string instrument
der Synthesizer(–)	synthesizer
das Tasteninstrument(e)	keyboard instrument
die Trommel(n)	drum
trommeln	to beat the drum
die Trompete(n)	trumpet

(iii) Notes and keys

N.B. Major keys are capitalized and minor keys are written as a small letter.

A Dur	A major
c moll	C minor
B	(key of) B flat
H	(key of) B
die Hohe Messe (h moll)	B minor Mass (Bach)
-is	-sharp
Fis	F sharp
-es	-flat
Des	D flat
Es	E flat
der Baßschlüssel(–)	bass clef
der Halbton	semitone
die Kadenz(en)	cadence
die Note(n)	note
die Viertelnote	crotchet (US quarter note)
die Achtelnote	quaver (US eighth note)
die Sechzehntelnote	semiquaver (US sixteenth note)
die Noten (pl.)	sheet music
der Quintenzirkel	cycle of fifths

der Takt(e)	time / bar
die Tonart(en)	key
die Tonfolge(n)	succession of notes / melodic line / scale
die Tonleiter(n)	scale
der Violinschlüssel(–)	treble clef
das Vorzeichen(–)	sharp / flat (sign) / key signature

(iv) Performance

der Applaus (no pl.) / *der Beifall* (no pl.)	applause
Applaus / Beifall spenden	to applaud / give applause
Applaus / Beifall ernten	to receive applause
das Ballett	ballet
der Chor(¨e)	choir
die Collage(n)	medley
der Dirigent(en)	conductor
das Duo(s) / Trio(s)	duo / trio
(das) Heavy Metal	heavy metal
der Jazz	jazz
die Kammermusik	chamber music
die Kapelle(n)	band (also: chapel)
der Klang(¨e)	sound
der Komponist(en)	composer
komponieren	to compose
das Konzert(e)	concert
der Konzertmeister(–)	leader / (US concert master)
das Lied(er)	song
der Liedtext(e)	lyrics
der Marsch(¨e)	marsh
die Melodie(n)	melody / tune
das Musical(s)	musical
die Musik	music
der Musiker(–)	musician
die Musikerin(nen)	female musician
musikalisch sein	to be musical
die Oper(n)	opera
die Operette(n)	operetta
das Orchester(–)	orchestra
die Ovation(en)	ovation
stehende Ovationen (pl.)	standing ovation
die Probe(n)	rehearsal
die Generalprobe	dress rehearsal
(der) Rap / Rythmischer Sprechgesang	rap
der Refrain(s)	chorus (at the end of each verse)

(der) Reggae	reggae
(der) Rock [FA]	rock
die Rockmusik	rock music
der Rock and Roll	rock and roll
das Solo(s)	solo
der Solist(en)	soloist
die Solistin(nen)	female soloist
die Sonate(n)	sonata
die Soulmusik	soul
der Stab(¨e) / der Taktstock(¨e)	baton
stimmen	to tune
richtig gestimmt sein	to be in tune
verstimmt sein	to be out of tune
die Symphonie(n) / die Sinfonie(n)	symphony
die Tonlage(n)	pitch
das absolute Gehör haben	to have perfect pitch
die Tonleiter(n)	scale
die Tournee(n) / die Tour(en)	tour
die Tournee durch die Provinz	provincial tour
üben	to practise
das Volkslied(er)	folksong
der Vorhang(¨e)	curtain
der Walzer(–)	waltz
die Zugabe(n)	encore

PART 4

Exercises

Geran Jones

152

Gender of nouns

(See S1)

A *Translate into German:*

1. In the photograph you can see a small girl riding the white horse.
2. The victim was the forty-two-year-old editor of a famous newspaper.
3. The crocodile was swimming in the lake.
4. The Far East attracts me.
5. The Urals form the border between Europe and Asia in Russia.
6. The sorcerer's apprentice had a problem with the broom.
7. The people of this country speak an incomprehensible language.
8. Health is the most important thing in life.
9. There is a famous brewery in this part of town.
10. Do you like the Hilton? I prefer the Penta.
11. I don't recognize the instrument that the beggar is playing.
12. The first person to throw a six starts.
13. What I like most about Scotland is the picturesque landscape.
14. This university was founded in 1350.
15. The explorer never returned from his expedition.
16. We are travelling to Turkey next summer.
17. We bought the encyclopaedia at an antique dealer's yesterday.
18. Christmas falls on a Thursday this year.
19. The hostage was released unharmed.
20. Yesterday we saw a red squirrel in the oak tree.

B *Setzen Sie die fehlenden Artikel ein:*

Für d___ frühe westdeutsche Bundesrepublik bedeutete 'Europa' außerdem zweierlei: d___ Entréebillet für d___ Rückkehr in d___ zivilisierte westliche Welt und ein___ Ersatzidentität für d___ verlorengegangene und tabuisierte nationale Einheit. Was folgt nun aus d___ Umstand, daß inzwischen sowohl d___ Anschluß an d___ westliche Zivilisation als auch d___ Wiedervereinigung zustande gekommen ist? Sind d___ kompensatorischen Komponenten ein___ postnationalen, ja anationalen Redens damit erledigt, oder weisen sie noch ein___ Weg in d___ Zukunft?

(excerpted from *Die Zeit*)

153 The article

(See S2)

A *Translate into German:*

1. My daughter plays the flute.
2. He is a plumber.
3. There are no snakes in Ireland.
4. The government is responsible for the money supply.
5. Do you sell garlic?
6. The conference takes place at Lake Constance.
7. Some applicants were not interviewed.
8. Both my sisters live in Switzerland.
9. Which watercolour did you buy?
10. This plug doesn't fit the socket.
11. Those voters who supported your party will not regret it.
12. His suitcase went missing, so he had to wear the same shirt for a week.
13. That's not a solution.
14. Do you have some cloth or other I could use in the garage?
15. He has blisters on both hands.
16. In your position I would have done the same.
17. Of all the countries in the Middle East, Lebanon is the one I'd like to visit.
18. I've got some good news for you.
19. These trousers suit you.
20. My neighbour's fence is behind the trees.

B *Setzen Sie die fehlenden bestimmten Artikel ein und ergänzen Sie die Endungen der übrigen Artikel und Pronomen:*

'____ Bild von einem selbst als Baby auf ____ Bärenfell für ____ Bewerbungsphoto, das kann ____ Personalverantwortlichen ein____ Unternehmens schon mal ____ entscheidenden Kick geben,' sagt Herbert Fossler, Personalberater aus Wiesbaden. Mit zwanzig seiner Berufskollegen beriet er während ____ Hannover Messe all jen____, die auf ____ Suche nach ein____ Stelle sind: Wie man Unterlagen präsentiert, ein Vorstellungsgespräch führt oder ____ weitere Karriere planen soll.

In ___ Tat sehen sich ___ Unternehmen und ihre Mitarbeiter in ___ Personalabteilungen einem stetig wachsendem Berg von Bewerbungunterlagen gegenüber: vierhundert Bewerbungen auf ein___ Stellenausschreibung sind kein___ Seltenheit. 'Was denken Sie, nach welch___ Methode der Personalmensch ein___ solchen Stapel durcharbeitet? Ein___ Chance hat nur der- oder diejenig___, deren Unterlagen absolut einwandfrei sind und ohne übertriebenen Gag ___ Interesse ___ Lesenden wecken – ___ vielzitierte Hürde also. Darum bitten die Personalberater auch immer, zu ___ Beratunsgespräch ___ vorbereitete Kandidatur mitzubringen.

(excerpted from *Süddeutsche Zeitung*)

154 Formation of the plural

(See S3)

A *Translate into German:*

1. There are no easy solutions.
2. The cabinet must share responsibility for decisions.
3. Parents are responsible for their children.
4. Which diseases have you suffered from?
5. These new channels do not have a greater range of programmes.
6. More and more families are living beyond their means.
7. Men and women have the same rights.
8. Maths, English and a foreign language are compulsory subjects in all schools.
9. The birds were twittering in the trees.
10. The twins went to the same two universities.
11. Travellers to Israel and Syria need two passports.
12. Blood transfusions have become safer.
13. This compartment is for non-smokers.
14. Subsidies in this area must be abolished.
15. There are some interesting antique shops under the arches.
16. Open the curtains.
17. They got into difficulties at the border.
18. Too many lorries use our roads.
19. In his suitcase he had two suits, four shirts, three ties and an assortment of socks.
20. He pricked up his ears and listened carefully to the speaker.

B *Setzen Sie die Ausdrücke in Klammern in den Plural:*

Die großen britischen (Zeitung) haben in den vergangenen (Monat) so ziemlich alles versucht, um den wundersamen Schwund der Leserschaft aufzuhalten: (Gewinnspiel), (Buchpreis), verbilligte (Reiseangebot) und (Umfangerweiterung) . . . (Schätzung) zufolge kostet das Preis-Dumping bei der *Times* Rupert Murdoch jährlich 45 (Million) Pfund; Conrad Black wird für die Verbilligung des *Daily Telegraph* jedes Jahr 40 (Million) Pfund veranschlagen müssen. Wenn es langfristig nicht gelingt, diese finanziellen (Loch) mit Hilfe von höheren (Verkauf) und vor allem mit Hilfe von gesteigerten Werbe- und Anzeigen(einnahme) zu stopfen, dürften (Kürzung) der (Produktionskosten) angesagt sein.

(excerpted from *Die Presse*)

C *Übersetzen Sie die Ausdrücke in Klammern:*

Bulgarien: Herrliche, flach ins Meer abfallende (beaches) ziehen sich an der bulgarischen Schwarzmeerküste entlang. Das Hinterland säumen (vineyards) und (orchards). Gute (hotels), zahlreiche (sports) und interessante (excursions) zu günstigen (prices) machen Bulgarien zu einem Urlaubsziel für groß und klein.

(excerpted from ITS Broschüre)

155 Declension of weak nouns

(See S5b)

A *Translate into German:*

1. We saw an elephant at the circus.
2. Mr Schmidt had a conversation with his neighbour.
3. Germany has elected a new president.
4. I listened to an argument between a Communist and a Christian on the radio.
5. The lawyer put several questions to the witness.
6. The barber is cutting the customer's hair.
7. Does man resemble an ape at all?
8. We were stopped by a policeman in town.
9. In the film the nurse took her leave of the hero.
10. The force of his belief grows stronger every day.
11. Yesterday we bumped into a French farmer.
12. The story is about a giant and a dwarf.

13. The plans for this building were drawn up by a well-known architect.
14. Many Jews have left Russia in the last twenty years.
15. Mr Klein went to Detmold to visit his nephew.
16. Good heavens! What are you doing there?
17. On the Berlin coat of arms one sees a large bear.
18. This castle belongs to a count.
19. He had forgotten the name of that famous conductor.
20. We never gave it a thought.

B *Gleichen Sie die schwachen Nomen in Klammern an:*

Der mittelalterliche (Glaube), daß böse Macht ihre Gewalt über den (Mensch) verliert, wenn man sie bei (Name) nennt, bildet den Kern des alten deutschen Märchens Rumpelstilzchen. Rumpelstilzchen ist ein Zwerg, der einem armen Mädchen zu Reichtum, Glück und Ehe verhilft. Als Lohn dafür verlangt er ihr erstes Kind. Als das Kind geboren ist, erscheint er am Bett der Mutter, um es zu holen. Der gute Helfer wird jetzt zum bösen Geist. (Wir erinnern uns, daß die Zwerge, auch wenn sie den (Mensch) manchmal helfen, im Grunde böse sind.) Auf die Bitten der Mutter, das Kind behalten zu dürfen, antwortet der Zwerg: 'Wenn du meinen (Name) herausfindest, kann das Kind bei dir bleiben.' Nach drei Tagen erfährt die Frau durch einen (Bote) den seltsamen (Name) des Zwerges. Als dieser nun wiederkommt, um das Kind wegzunehmen, sagt sie zu ihm: 'Heißt du etwa Rumpelstilzchen?' Darauf verschwindet der Zwerg sofort. Sein (Name) ist ausgesprochen worden, und in diesem Augenblick verliert er seine Macht.

(excerpted from O. Koischwitz, *Reise in die Literatur*)

156 Declension of adjectival nouns

(See S5e)

A *Translate into German, using adjectival nouns:*

1. Many young people meet up in the town centre.
2. Is your boyfriend French? No, he's German.
3. One of his acquaintances was spending the night in the same hotel.
4. The fire brigade is made up of volunteers.
5. At what time did you see the accused?
6. The official spoke with the unemployed man.

7. Do you know that many wealthy people live in this suburb?
8. Yesterday I bumped into a Hungarian in front of the town hall.
9. Do you have anything interesting to report?
10. We always do something special at the weekend.
11. After the break there was nothing edible left in his briefcase.
12. The Foreign Office could say nothing further on this matter.
13. We did not know anything definite about the contents of the files.
14. Dieter is working with an apprentice in his workshop.
15. Sabine introduced me to her fiancé.
16. They took the injured person to hospital.
17. A prisoner has escaped.
18. Our colleague turned to his immediate superior.
19. Molière wrote a comedy about a miser.
20. Brussels should promote the employment of the disabled.

B *Machen Sie aus den Adjektiven in Klammern Substantive:*

Was ich getan habe, ist nichts, nicht viel, so gut wie nichts. Ich werde (besser) machen, Lisaweta: dies ist ein Versprechen. Während ich schreibe, rauscht das Meer zu mir herauf, und ich schließe die Augen. Ich schaue in eine ungeborene und schemenhafte Welt hinein, die geordnet und gebildet sein will, ich sehe in ein Gewimmel von Schatten menschlicher Gestalten, die mir winken, daß ich sie banne und erlöse: tragische und lächerliche und solche, die beides zugleich sind – und diesen bin ich sehr zugetan. Aber meine tiefste und verstohlenste Liebe gehört den (blond) und (blauäugig), den hellen (lebendig), den (glücklich), (liebenswürdig) und (gewöhnlich).

(excerpted from Thomas Mann, *Tonio Kröger*)

157 Personal pronouns

(See S6)

A *Translate into German:*

1. We observed you during the conference.
2. Did she write him a letter in the end?
3. How is she? She's fine.
4. Did the police come? Yes, they came straight away.
5. The new teacher is lacking in confidence.
6. Do you remember the Braun family? I ran into them in the supermarket.

7. Franz, can you help me with this account?
8. Why do you keep calling us? We already have double-glazing!
9. Sit down and tell me all about it.
10. Where's the frying-pan? I'm sure it was in the cupboard.
11. The detective lit a cigarette, then put it in an ashtray.
12. Pass me the spoon, please. It's resting on the jug.
13. Put the cold meat in the fridge, otherwise it will go off.
14. He succeeded in convincing the archbishop of his sincerity.

B *Setzen Sie die Personalpronomen in Klammern in den richtigen Fall:*

Manchmal wird's (ich) ganz dunkel vor den Augen, vielleicht kann ich diesen Brief nicht einmal zu Ende schreiben – aber ich will alle Kraft zusammentun, um einmal, nur dieses eine Mal zu (Du) zu sprechen, Du mein Geliebter, der (Du) (ich) nie erkannt.

Zu (Du) allein will ich sprechen, (Du) zum erstenmal alles sagen; mein ganzes Leben sollst (Du) wissen, das immer das Deine gewesen und um das (Du) nie gewußt. Aber (Du) sollst mein Geheimnis nur kennen, wenn ich tot bin, wenn (Du) (ich) nicht mehr Antwort geben mußt, wenn das, was (ich) die Glieder jetzt so kalt und heiß schüttelt, wirklich das Ende ist. Muß ich weiterleben, so zerreiße ich diesen Brief und werde weiter schweigen, wie ich immer schwieg. Hältst Du (er) aber in Händen, so weißt Du, daß hier eine Tote (Du) ihr Leben erzählt, ihr Leben, das das Deine war von ihrer ersten bis zu ihrer letzten wachen Stunde.

Fürchte (Du) nicht vor meinen Worten; eine Tote will nichts mehr, (sie) will nicht Liebe und nicht Mitleid und nicht Tröstung. Nur dies eine will ich von (Du), daß Du (ich) alles glaubst, was mein zu (Du) hinflüchtender Schmerz (Du) verrät. Glaube (ich) alles, nur dies bitte ich (Du): man lügt nicht in der Sterbestunde eines einzigen Kindes.

(excerpted from S. Zweig, *Brief einer Unbekannten*)

C *Setzen Sie die fehlenden Pronomen ein:*

Vielerorts griff der Mensch seit dem vergangenen Jahrhundert freilich auch direkt in das Wasserregime ein. Kaum einem der größeren Flüsse, von denen ____ einst respektvoll Abstand hielt, ließ ____ seinen natürlichen Lauf. ____ wurden begradigt, kanalisiert und aufgebaut, in enge Betten gezwängt und von ihren Auen abgeschnitten. Einzige Ausnahme ist die Elbe, die auch als der letzte 'richtige Fluß' Europas gilt. Der Rhein dagegen zählt wohl zu den bekanntesten Beispielen für intensiven Wasserbau. Es begann vor 175

Jahren mit den 'Rheinkorrektionen' des badischen Ingenieurs Johann Gottfried Tulla, welche die Gemeinden am Oberrhein gegen Hochwasser schützen sollten. ____ folgte zu Beginn dieses Jahrhunderts eine zweite Korrektur zugunsten der Schiffahrt und schließlich seit den dreißiger Jahren der 'Moderne Oberrheinausbau' zum Zwecke der Energiegewinnung. Nach dem Ende des Krieges wurde ____ im Jahr 1955 aufgenommen, 1977 war ____ abgeschlossen.

(excerpted from *Frankfurter Allgemeine Zeitung*)

158 Possessives

(See S7)

A *Translate into German:*

1. Where have I put my glasses?
2. Could you lend me your calculator?
3. Our negotiations haven't led to anything so far.
4. I fell asleep during his long talk .
5. Thanks to your speedy help the problem has been solved.
6. The PM has resigned. His decision is irreversible.
7. In their opinion the asylum seeker should be deported.
8. The traveller put the rolled-up newspaper into his case.
9. Do you still live with your parents?
10. The broker wrote to his accountant.
11. I would do the same in his position.
12. How do you make ends meet with your salary?
13. Our house is to let.
14. To her great delight she learned that she had won first prize.
15. I saw the UFO with my own eyes.

B *Füllen Sie die Lücken:*

Zuckmayer über seinen Bruder

____ Bruder hatte das nicht unproblematische Schicksal, ein Musterschüler zu sein, allzeit der beste in ____ Klasse – der Lernstoff flog ihm zu, und er war von Natur aus strebsam und fleißig, so daß er mir oft als mahnendes Beispiel vorgehalten wurde. Das hat uns aber nie entzweit, ich ärgerte mich nicht einmal darüber, sondern quittierte solche Hinweise mit einer lächelnden Indifferenz, die ____ Erzieher zur Weißglut brachte. Was den Bruder für mich weit über die Gestalt des

Musterknaben hinaushob, war ____ ungewöhnliches Musiktalent. Schon im Volksschulalter hatte er die Klavierkenntnisse des Dorforganisten, der ihn unterrichtete, überflügelt, und bald konnte ihm auch die brave Musiklehrerin in Mainz nicht mehr vorspielen: denn statt der Bravourstücke von Chopin oder Schumanns 'Aufschwung', womit das alte Fräulein gern brillierte, hatte er für sich das 'Wohltemperierte Klavier' entdeckt und Bach als Gipfel und Leitgestirn – was um die Jahrhundertwende keineswegs selbstverständlich war. 'Er bachelt wieder,' sagten ____ Eltern, wenn man stundenlang aus dem Musikzimmer nichts anderes hörte oder wenn er sich bereits mit der Komposition von Fugen und Kantaten beschäftigte. Ich aber habe ____ ersten Schreibversuche unterm Klang dieses strengen und systematischen Klavierübens vollbracht (und ____ Bruder war der erste Mensch, der sie ernstnahm).

(excerpted from C. Zuckmayer, *Als wär's ein Stück von mir*)

59 Reflexive pronouns

(See S8)

A *Translate into German:*

1. I washed my hands.
2. May I introduce myself?
3. You two boys, get changed straight away!
4. They wanted to complain about the Spanish hotel.
5. Our new colleague dyes his hair.
6. I must quickly put some make-up on before the guests arrive.
7. The Teutons imagined the afterlife to be dark, misty and cold.
8. How can you afford it?
9. He enquired about the departure times of the trains.
10. I have applied for a well-paid job in Brussels.
11. Have you broken your leg?
12. Before she goes to bed my daughter combs her hair.
13. Do you ask yourself whether we could have done it differently?
14. We are looking forward to the trip to Italy.
15. He imagines he is going to be promoted next year.
16. Do you remember the decision we made?
17. The child was afraid of ghosts.
18. The customer will be annoyed about the poor quality of the goods.
19. I have fallen in love with an actor.
20. Did you apologize to the boss for the interruption?

B *Fügen Sie die richtigen Reflexivpronomen ein:*

Schließlich entschied ich ____, Pförtner zu werden. Und ich wurde Pförtner in einer Spielzeugfabrik. Ich kann ____ vorstellen, daß viele meiner Kollegen durch diesen Beruf hochmütig werden, daß sie auch nach Feierabend noch mit kaltem Gesicht herumlaufen und abweisende Handbewegungen um sich her streuen.

Ich bin nicht so geworden, obwohl ich ____ nach Kräften bemühe, meinen Dienst tagsüber gewissermaßen unbarmherzig zu tun. Ich fühlte ____ von Anfang an zu Hause in meiner gläsernen Loge.

(excerpted from Martin Walser, *Die Klagen über meine Methoden häufen sich*)

C *Entscheiden Sie, ob die unterstrichenen Reflexivpronomen im Akkusativ oder im Dativ stehen:*

Der Liberale hält <u>sich</u> mit John Locke von all diesen übersteigernden Verzerrungen frei. Er verfällt, was die Menschen angeht, weder dem absoluten Pessimismus noch dem blinden Optimismus. Er wird auch die Macht weder diktatorisch noch anarchisch verteufeln. Er macht <u>sich</u>, wie Ralf Dahrendorf bemerkt hat, weder Illusionen über die Macht noch über die Möglichkeit, sie abzuschaffen. Er kann <u>sich</u> keinen absoluten Staat ohne pluralistische Gesellschaft vorstellen – aber eben auch keine zufällige Gesellschaft ohne den ordnenden Staat. Der Liberale plädiert für aufgeklärte, dann aber auch verbindliche Gesetze.

Um es anekdotisch auszudrücken: Als es in den Justizreformen der sechziger und siebziger Jahre darum ging,vernünftige Gesetze auf der Höhe der Zeit zu formulieren, an die man <u>sich</u> dann halten konnte und deshalb halten mußte, waren die Liberalen ganz bei der Sache. Als es wenig später für 'liberal' galt, <u>sich</u> je nach Gusto an Gesetze nicht mehr zu halten, war der wahre Liberale als erster entsetzt.

(excerpted from *Die Zeit*)

160 Demonstratives

(See S9)

A *Translate into German:*

1. This steam iron is far too expensive for me.
2. Those social problems discussed by the politicians remain unresolved.
3. What is the quickest way there?

4. He must have come from there.
5. Those people who travel without paying will be fined.
6. Does anyone object?
7. This computer works much more quickly than that one.
8. Up to now everything has gone well.
9. Whoever finds my key will get a reward.
10. We hereby inform you that your camera has been handed in to the lost property office.
11. You can drive up to there; then you have to walk.
12. It was one of those phone numbers which was always engaged.
13. I hereby acknowledge receipt of your letter.
14. I shall come back to that point.
15. What do you understand by that?
16. He had big losses from that.
17. I didn't think anything of it.
18. You are not able to borrow those books from the library.
19. We shall talk about this again.
20. That's debatable.

B *Setzen Sie die entsprechenden Endungen ein:*

Dies____ war kaum geschehen, da rief eine Glocke zum Abendessen, und ich überließ mich der größen Strömung, die zum Speisesaal trieb. Dies____ gewaltige Raum enthielt neun lange Tische für die neun Klassen des Gymnasiums. Nahe dem Eingang, zwischen den Reihen der Kleinsten, die noch am meisten der Aufsicht bedurften, stand ein Tischchen für den Herrn Direktor und die zwei Präfekten. Fern gegenüber, bei den höheren Klassen, schimmerte und plätscherte etwas nie Gesehenes, ein ungeheurer Pokal, aus dem sich königskerzenhoch ein blütentragender Kolben erhob; dies____ entsprangen zwei Röhrchen, die unaufhörlich Wasser spendeten. Dies____ metallene Wunder war mit mit blauer Farbe frisch angestrichen, der Flor der Kolbenblumen sogar mit etwas Gold bemalt.

(excerpted from H. Carossa, *Verwandlung einer Jugend*)

C *Setzen Sie die richtigen Formen für derjenige, usw. ein:*

Es liegt auf der Hand, daß intelligente Menschen, seit 1960 zumindest, fragten, wofür sie denn weiter arbeiten sollten und immer effizienter, wenn der Tisch gedeckt ist. Sei es, weil die Eltern fleißig weiter wirkten und der Brut die eigene schwere Jugend ersparen wollten, sei es, weil der Staat bei wachsender Wirtschaft _____ viel abnahm, die arbeiteten

– um es ______ zu geben, die nicht, noch nicht, nicht mehr arbeiteten. Nicht weil sie nicht könnten, sondern weil sie anderen Lustgewinn der Erwerbsarbeit vorziehen. Von ______, denen geholfen werden muß in einer zivilisierten Gesellschaft, ist hier nicht die Rede. Selbstverständlich soll auch ______ essen, der nicht arbeitet; aber eben karger, damit sich Fleiß lohnt.

(excerpted from *Die Zeit*)

D *Geben Sie die richtige Form für da + Präposition an:*

Was kostet ein Prozeß?

Jeder Prozeß kostet Geld. Wird er – wie häufig – durch Urteil beendet, entscheidet der Richter auch (______), wer von den Parteien die Prozeßkosten zu tragen hat. Grundsatz ist (______), daß die unterliegende Partei die gesamten Kosten des Rechtsstreits zu tragen hat. (______) gibt es im Strafprozeß keine 'Partei' wie im Zivilprozeß. Ob hier der Angeklagte zahlen muß, hängt (______) ab, ob er verurteilt oder freigesprochen wird. Um welche Kosten handelt es sich (______)? Die Kosten eines Rechtsstreits setzen sich zusammen aus den Gerichtskosten und den außergerichtlichen Kosten.

(excerpted from *Bayerischer Rechtswegweiser*, 11. Auflage, 1991)

161 Relative pronouns

(See S10)

A *Translate into German:*

1. I am looking for a calculator which is mains-operated.
2. A vacuum cleaner is a machine with which one cleans carpets.
3. The house we want to buy is a long way from the station.
4. The girl you are thinking about has just got on the bus.
5. The novel I'm reading has been translated from Russian.
6. The baby slept right through the night, which we did not expect.
7. The students, whose exams were over, were drinking champagne in the garden.
8. Everything he told me I recorded on tape.
9. The furniture you like has been imported from Sweden.
10. There is a ticket for buses and trains which the whole family can use.
11. Germany fortunately counts as one of those countries in which there is no shortage of water.

12. In the summer we used to bathe in a lake whose water was cold and clear.
13. The engineer we bumped into yesterday has just been promoted.
14. That which is most fun is forbidden here.

B *Setzen Sie die fehlenden Relativpronomen ein:*

Schwierige Frage das: Wie bewegt man sich auf der Oberfläche eines Planeten, ______ kein Mensch je betreten hat? Von ______ also nicht bekannt ist, wie hoch der Staub herumliegt? Auf ______ eine schwächliche Schwerkraft herrscht, nämlich genau ein Sechstel der Gravitation, ______ unsereins gewohnt ist? Und auf ______ man einen dicken Raumanzug samt schwerem Pack mit sich herumschleppen muß, ______ einen in eine leichte, dafür aber um so beständigere Rückenlage bringt? Richtig: Man hopst herum wie ein Känguruh.

(excerpted from *Zeit Magazin*)

C *Setzen Sie die fehlenden Relativpronomen ein:*

Weizsäcker war sicher der politischste Präsident auf eine Weise, ______ zu Dank verpflichtet. Aber er war auch ein Präsident, ______ uns von Politik freistellte. Vielleicht verdankt sich seine Beliebtheit dem Umstand, daß wir das ahnten, aber nicht eingestehen mußten. Weizsäcker hat nämlich Distanzen hergestellt, er war Repräsentant. Der Staat und seine Institutionen, ______ die Politik doch anvertraut ist, erhielten in ihm noch einmal bildhaft Gestalt. So war es, so könnte es eigentlich wieder sein. . . In politisch aufgeladenen Zeiten, in ______ die Bürger selber aktiv sind, richten sich die Blicke gar nicht so sehr auf das Präsidentielle. Das sind die Zeiten für Bundespräsidenten.

(excerpted from *Die Zeit*)

62 Indefinites

(See S11)

A *Translate into German:*

1. No hurry! Everybody will get a turn.
2. Absolutely all the events at the festival were sold out last week.
3. The building of the Brandenburg Gate was begun in 1789.
4. Anybody can say that!
5. Every third adult in this country is overweight.

6. If one looks around one realizes how beautiful the countryside is.
7. One doesn't have to come to terms with that.
8. Everyone's got only one thing on their mind.
9. This sheet doesn't give one enough information.
10. He has already applied for several jobs.
11. 'All the best', he said, and got into the car.
12. Nobody could have predicted that Germany would be unified in 1990.
13. When everybody was dancing, someone or other called the police.
14. He who arrives too late is punished by life.
15. The first person to have no counters left is the winner.
16. Water is the source of all life.
17. Did you manage to reach someone in the embassy?
18. All products are being made CFC-free this year.
19. Some people had bought their tickets in advance.

B *Setzen Sie die entsprechenden Endungen ein:*

All____, was die Bundesrepublik in einem halben Jahrhundert an Wohlstand, Friedlichkeit und Duldsamkeit – also an besonderer Kultur – hervorgebracht hat, begründet eine gemeinsame Herkunft für all____, die dabeigewesen sind. Diese gemeinsame Herkunft teilen auch die 'deutschen' Italiener, Spanier, Portugiesen, Griechen, Türken. Aber auch der offensten Gesellschaft fiele es schwer, diese Offenheit gegenüber all____ späteren Zuwanderern zu beweisen.

(excerpted from *Die Zeit*)

C *Füllen Sie die Lücken und übersetzen Sie die Ausdrücke in Klammern:*

Hugo ging es nicht anders als mir; auch er lebte ein Doppelleben und war zu jed____ kindlichen Torheit bereit, während er sich sehnsüchtig den Wellen großer Dichter öffnete . . . Auch war noch nirgendwoher die Meinung zu uns gedrungen, daß ein Dichter den andern beschatten oder daß (*one*) den einen durch den andern überwinden könne; sie waren uns alle nur Äste und Zweige eines unsichtbaren Geisterbaums, der (*somewhere*) im deutschen Norden stand und über all____ Seelen rauschte. So hatte auch kein____ den andern zu beneiden; jed____ lief seiner in Bahn, jed____ kam einmal an den Punkt höchster Beglänzung, wo kein____ anderer ihn ersetzen konnte, jed____ schlug einmal die Stunde, wo sich die Finsternis eines Herzens in ihm aufhellte, in ihm allein. Wenig galt uns das Persönliche, und wenn uns (*someone*) gesagt hätte, Goethe habe nichts für Kleist und Hölderlin getan, so würden wir das nicht verstanden haben – hatte er nicht auch für sie geschaut und gesungen?

(excerpted from H. Carossa, *Verwandlung einer Jugend*)

163 Interrogatives

(See S12)

A *Translate into German:*

1. Which novel did you like best?
2. Whom did you ask?
3. What are you thinking about, in fact?
4. He asked whether there was a direct bus to Schwandorf.
5. Whose office is on the top floor?
6. Which film would you prefer to see?
7. Who handed the passport in to the police?
8. In which laboratory was this experiment carried out?
9. Why doesn't the engine start?
10. What time did the bank close?
11. What sort of company car do you drive now?
12. Where and when shall we meet?
13. What did you talk about in the hotel and with whom?
14. What do you attach great importance to?
15. Whom can I rely on?
16. What are you waiting for?
17. Whom did you advise to buy these shares?
18. What's it all about?

B *Lesen Sie den Text und fragen Sie:*

Zu Mersburg bei Konstanz lebte gegen Ende des 15. Jahrhunderts ein ehrlicher Bursch, Heinz Klöpfgeißel geheißen und Faßbinder seines Zeichens, von guter Gestalt und Gesundheit. Er stand in inniger Wechselneigung mit einem Mädchen, Bärbel, der einzigen Tochter eines verwitweten Glöckners, und wollte sie ehelichen, doch stieß des Pärchens Wunsch auf väterlichen Widerstand, denn Klöpfgeißel war ein armer Kerl, und der Glöckner fordete erst eine stattliche Lebensstellung von ihm, daß er Meister würde in seinem Gewerbe, bevor er ihm seine Tochter gäbe. Die Neigung der jungen Leute aber war stärker gewesen als ihre Geduld, und aus dem Pärchen war vor der Zeit schon ein Paar geworden. Denn nächtlich, wenn der Glöckner glöckeln gegangen war, stieg Klöpfgeißel ein bei Bärbel, und ihre Umarmungen ließen das eine dem andern als das herrlichste Wesen auf Erden erscheinen.

(excerpted from Thomas Mann, *Doktor Faustus*)

Hier sind Antworten auf Fragen zum Text. Wie lauten die Fragen?

1. Er war ehrlich und gesund.
2. In Mersburg.
3. Er war Faßbinder.
4. Des Glöckners.
5. Weil Klöpfgeißel arm war.
6. Er ging abends aus.
7. Er traf Bärbel.
8. Jede Nacht.

164 Declension of adjectives after definite article

(See S13a)

A *Translate into German:*

1. At last I've found the right place.
2. They have sold the old farmhouse.
3. Did you rent the French villa you saw?
4. The wide streets of the capital were full of cars.
5. The exhausted refugees at last arrived safely.
6. Two men had the same ingenious idea.
7. She got off the bus at the next stop.
8. The fire threatened houses and one of the best-known hotels.
9. The measures which were implemented have succeeded more quickly than expected.
10. Trains are now using the newly opened tunnel.
11. Put the peeled potatoes into the boiling water.
12. The new Mercedes is now available.
13. Put this book on the top shelf, would you?
14. You are staying in one of the most expensive hotels in town.
15. The driver did not see the red light.

B *Setzen Sie die Adjektivendungen ein:*

Nur aus Liebe (ARD)

Ein Mann zwischen zwei Frauen, immer noch und immer wieder eine Geschichte wert. In der Variante des italienisch____ Dreiteilers steht der jung____ begabt____ Modedesigner Nicola zwischen dem schön____, aber launisch____ Modell Camille und der lieb____ und treu____, dabei auch hochintelligent____ und tüchtig____, vielleicht aber nicht so mondän attraktiv____ Literaturstudentin Francesca. Wie das ausgeht, kann man sich denken. Bis sich die Richtig____ finden, passiert allerhand, jedenfalls viel, viel mehr als in einem normalen Leben, aber gerade deshalb schaut man sich's ja an .

(excerpted from *Stuttgarter Zeitung*)

C *Setzen Sie die Adjektivendungen ein:*

Insel Mallorca: Die Insel der lang____ Badestrände und romantisch____ Buchten, des bunt____ Küstenlebens und der ungezählt____ Unterhaltungmöglichkeiten. Und das ander____ Mallorca, die fast unbekannt____ Insel der verschlafen ____ Bergdörfer, der weit____, fruchtbar____ Ebenen im Südwesten und der bizarr____ Gebirgslandschaften im Norden und Nordwesten. Schon nach etwa zwei Stunden Direktflug finden Sie die ideal____ Kulisse für einen erholsamen Urlaub.

(excerpted from ITS Broschüre)

165 Declension of adjectives after indefinite article

(See S13a)

A *Translate into German:*

1. My wife gave me an expensive watch for my birthday.
2. Your brown leather case has gone missing.
3. She was leafing through a German magazine.
4. I drive an environmentally friendly car.
5. A Japanese factory now stands on the site of his old school.
6. When are you going to visit our Berlin office?
7. They were photographed by a hidden camera.
8. We saw a man with a funny hat in Spain.
9. Go past an old church and turn right.
10. The broker was wearing a blue shirt and a grey suit.
11. The company will have to negotiate a new contract.
12. A further rise in interest rates is expected.
13. This is a small step for man and a giant leap for mankind.
14. This development is part of a new investment plan.
15. After dinner the guests sat round an open fire.

16. I've had a very hectic day today.
17. Do you need a woollen blanket tonight?
18. He's looking for a comfortable hotel.
19. Did you bring a sharp knife with you?

B *Setzen Sie die Adjektivendungen ein:*

Ein Geruch von Zwiebeln und Kohl erfüllt die Luft mit einem süßlich-herb____ Aroma. Die Fahrradreifen kerben ihre tief____ Spuren in den sandigen Feldweg, der gradlinig auf den Sebalder Reichswald zuführt. Auch hier trifft man einen Bauern bei der Feldarbeit. Mit einem klein____ Messer erntet eine alt____ Frau in grauen Filzpantoffeln Petersilie. Sie gruppiert die Suppenpflanzen zu Sträußchen und legt sie in eine Holzkiste. Ein schwarz____ Kopftuch hält ihr schlohweiß____ Haar zurück. Mit den Petersilienzweigen beliefert sie in Nürnberg und Fürth die Kaufhäuser.

Aus der Ferne rückt am Waldrand ein massiv____ Steinportal in Sicht. Beim Näherkommen kann man die Inschrift 'Irrhain' erkennen. Dahinter öffnet sich eine lang____ dunkel____ Baumallee aus knorrigen Eichen, Kastanien und Buchen, die ihre Äste zu einem dicht____ Blätterdach verwoben haben. Am Ende dieses ein wenig unheimlichen Ganges steht man in einem lichtdurchflutet____ Waldstück.

(excerpted from *Süddeutsche Zeitung*)

166 Declension of adjectives after no article

(See S13a)

A *Translate into German:*

1. He still had three Italian stamps in his wallet.
2. This film is suitable for small children.
3. We bought fresh fruit at the local market.
4. Old medicines should be thrown away.
5. The meat should be served on warm plates.
6. Despite thick fog they decided to drive to Scotland.
7. This firm builds houses with good-quality materials.
8. According to German doctors ozone does not cause lasting damage to health.
9. One sees more and more foreign lorries on the roads.
10. The manager spoke with striking workers.
11. The government has created favourable conditions for an economic recovery.

12. He has a passion for fast cars.
13. The meeting is taking place behind closed doors.
14. Unripe bananas are not good for you.
15. Sprinkle chopped parsley over it.
16. The financial advisers were criticized for certain shortcomings.
17. This company has a beautiful selection of good games.
18. All products are manufactured according to strict quality guidelines.

B *Setzen Sie die entsprechenden Endungen ein*

(i) Inzwischen leben im Freistaat 18,3% aller über Zwanzigjährig____ alleine (1972: 12,7%), wobei die Zahl alleinlebend____ Männer insgesamt vergleichsweise stärker zugenommen hat als die alleinlebend____ Frauen. Grund ist der überproportionale Anstieg (Verdreifachung) der Zahl männlich____ Singles in der Altersgruppe der 30- bis 59-jährigen Männer.

(excerpted from *Bayerische Staatszeitung*)

(ii) Skoda 'Comfort-Line'
In limitiert____ Stückzahl sind ab sofort die Skoda Favorit und Forman in metallisiert____ Sonderfarbe 'Seegrün' mit folgend____ Zusatzausstattung zu haben: Veloursitzbezüge, abgedunkelt____ Heckleuchten, getönt____ Scheiben, Mittelkonsole, Schalthebelknopf mit Lederbezug und Ledermanschette, Fernentriegelung der Heckklappe, gepolstert____ Türfüllungen, Zentralverriegelung und speziell____ Sportraddeckel.

(excerpted from *Basler Zeitung*)

(iii) Industriell____ Herz, führende Wirtschaftsregion und spannend____ Erlebnisland-Nordrhein-Westfalen ist überraschend vielseitig: erholsam____ Naturlandschaften vor der Haustür, lebendig____ Miteinander mit regional____ Traditionen, Sport und Freizeitgestaltung nach Talent und Laune.

(excerpted from *NRW Werbung*)

67 Comparative and superlative adjectives

(See S15 and S16)

A *Translate into German:*

1. I would like to see the latest film.
2. The highest mountain in Germany is situated in Bavaria.

3. You will find a better racket over there.
4. The nearest underground station is 500 m away.
5. Illiteracy is widespread in the poorest countries.
6. The coffee could be stronger.
7. Here the river is deepest.
8. The longest days in the year are normally the warmest.
9. Could you please drive more slowly?
10. The most expensive cars are the most comfortable.
11. The telephone is one of the most useful inventions of the twentieth century.
12. Do you have something cheaper?
13. Mirror, mirror on the wall, who is the fairest of them all?
14. In which town does it rain most frequently?
15. I need a faster computer.
16. Russian is much easier to learn than Japanese.
17. Is our new colleague more ambitious than the head of department?
18. At the moment Edinburgh is colder than Moscow.
19. The greater the quantities you order, the lower the prices you pay.
20. Herr Schwarz is the most reliable worker.

B *Übersetzen Sie die Ausdrücke in Klammern:*

Obgleich zwischen den Fjorden Norwegens und den sonnigen Stränden Siziliens die Lebensformen, Normen und Werte zum Teil deutlich voneinander abweichen, stellt Eurostat dennoch einige Trends fest: in Europa wird (less and less) geheiratet, und die einmal eingegangenen Ehen werden (more and more often) wieder geschieden. Die Ehe scheint auch für (more and more) Menschen nicht mehr die gesellschaftliche und juristische Voraussetzung für die Familiengründung zu sein. . . . Die traditionellen Regeln der gesellschaftlichen Moral werden (soonest) noch in den südlichen Ländern respektiert ... Der Umbruch von Moral und Gesellschaft wird in den skandinavischen Ländern (most noticeably) sichtbar: in Dänemark zum Beispiel wurden im vergangenen Jahr 224 Ehen zwischen homosexuellen Paaren geschlossen. Überall in Europa wird (less) geheiratet.

(excerpted from *Der Tagesspiegel*)

C *Setzen Sie die unterstrichenen Adjektive in den Superlativ:*

Da gräbt man jahrelang die lang Stollen, bohrt die tief Löcher und vergißt darüber völlig, sich in der nah Nähe umzuschauen.

Nach einem der interessant Rohstofflieferanten. Kaum zu sehen, aber allgegenwärtig: alte Kunststoff-Fenster. In Behringen/ Thüringen haben wir, VEKA Umwelttechnik, das weltweit modern Recycling-Werk für Kunststoff-Fenster gebaut und seit November '93 im Betrieb.

(excerpted from Werbung, *VEKA Umwelttechnik GmbH*).

168 Present tense

(See S21a, b)

A *Translate into German:*

1. I collect stamps from all over the world.
2. Are you going to buy that second-hand car?
3. He knows what he's doing.
4. These sources show that his aim was clear.
5. The lecture ends at about 10 p.m.
6. She always forgets her passport.
7. The world champion is stepping into the ring.
8. Do you speak fluent Greek?
9. I like fishing in the Ammersee.
10. Where are you running to?
11. The doctor regularly takes the patient's blood pressure.
12. Watch that you don't bump yourself on it.
13. The Schmidt family invites us every year.
14. I am changing £500 this week.
15. Breathe through your nose.
16. It's getting dark.
17. Werner is helping him with his work.
18. What's your name?
19. Hans doesn't eat any meat – he's a vegetarian.
20. Mummy, Franz is tying Lotte to a tree!

B *Setzen Sie die Verben in Klammern ins Präsens:*

Die Demokratie (sein) nicht ein Denkmal, das man einmal (errichten) und das (ausstrahlen) auf die Gesellschaft, ihr Orientierung (geben). Gerade weil sie dem einzelnen große Freiheit (gewähren), Raum (lassen) zur eigenen Lebensgestaltung, (sein) sie ständig in Bewegung, (entwickeln) sich zum Guten oder zum Schlechten. Nur wenn viele

Bürger sich dafür (engagieren), (haben) die Demokratie eine Zukunft und dieses Engagement (beginnen) in der Selbstverwaltung der Städte und Gemeinden, der Landkreise und Bezirke. . . .

Die Parteien (tragen) unsere Demokratie. Das (können) sie nur, wenn sie in deren Mutterboden, der kommunalen Selbstverwaltung, verwurzelt (sein). Das bewährte Miteinander von Parteien und unabhängigen Gruppierungen (dürfen) weder von diesen noch von jenen gefährdet werden. Vielmehr (gelten) es, gemeinsam den radikalen Kräften zu wehren, die sich immer ungenierter (gebärden). (Können) es denn einen größeren Gegensatz geben als den zwischen parteifreien Bürgern, die sich für ein friedliches Miteinander in Städten und Gemeinden (engagieren), und Radikalen? Deren Radikalität (zulassen) keinen Kompromiß.

(excerpted from *Bayerische Staatszeitung*)

C *Setzen Sie die Verben in Klammern ins Präsens:*

Nach Kaliningrad und an die Küste

Es (sein) Freitag, 19 Uhr, schon seit einer Stunde (stehen) auf dem Berliner Hauptbahnhof ein 'Königsberg-Expreß' genannter Zug unter Diesel. Auf kürzester Strecke, über Bydgoszsc (Bromberg) und Elblag (Elbing) ohne Zwischenhalt nach Kaliningrad fahrend, (benötigen) er für die knapp 700 Kilometer lange Strecke kaum 14 Stunden, was einer Durchschnittsgeschwindigkeit von etwa 50 Stundenkilometern (entsprechen). Demgemäß (sein) der Zug mit Schlaf- und Liegewagen ausgestattet. . . . Ich (fahren) gern mit Schlafwagenzügen, weil sie mich in sanftem Schlummer ins Zielgebiet (befördern). Grenzbeamte, die Nachtdienst (haben), (müssen) dagegen wach bleiben. Sie (sich rächen) per Dienstvorschrift: um 5 Uhr (rumpeln) die polnische Paßkontrolle durch den Zug, um 6 Uhr die russische, um 7 Uhr (sich anschließen) der Zoll. . . .

Für 2300 Rubel, umgerechnet zwei Deutsche Mark, (bringen) uns der Überlandbus in drei Stunden die 110 Kilometer von Kaliningrad nach Sowjetsk, dem ehemaligen Tilsit. Aus unerfindlichen Gründen (sich weigern) sich der Fahrer, die Taschen und Koffer der Reisenden im Gepäckfach zu verstauen, weshalb das Innere des Busses rasch ein leicht chaotisches Aussehen (annehmen). . . . Im Vergleich zu der Bahn (gelten) der Bus als teuer. Wer aufs Geld schauen (müssen), (benutzen) den langsameren Zug. Die Landschaft recht zu würdigen (fallen) in beiden Verkehrsmitteln schwer, da in der Verbindung mit öffentlichem Eigentum saubere Scheiben sowenig bekannt (sein) wie der Begriff der Erhaltungsinvestition, wovon das krachende Getriebe des Ikarus-Busses bei jedem Schalten gequält (ablegen). . . .

Am nächsten Tag (fahren) wir über den Grenzfluß Memel nach Litauen. Drei Stunden (nehmen) auf der russischen Seite die Abfertigung von sechs Personen in Anspruch. Woran es (liegen), (wissen) keiner, denn kontrolliert (werden) nicht. Bei den Litauern (dauern) der entsprechende Vorgang ganze fünf Minuten.

(excerpted from *Die Zeit*)

169 Imperfect tense (weak verbs)

(See S19b and S21a)

A *Translate into German:*

1. He bought a Japanese car last autumn.
2. She waited for the bus in the pouring rain.
3. He nodded and opened his diary.
4. He offered the princess a packet of cigarettes.
5. The plane took off from Hanover on time.
6. The plumber repaired the pipe in under an hour.
7. The fire caused damage estimated at 500,000 DM.
8. The colonel opened an account at the Dresdner Bank.
9. She was afraid that her mobile phone was not working.
10. A spy observed their meeting on Tuesday.
11. It hailed all over town yesterday.
12. The girls smiled and waved until the ferry left.
13. From the A road a small path branched off towards the wood.
14. The chef sat down at the writing-desk and held his head in his hands.
15. She considered whether he ought to ask her friend for a loan.
16. Suddenly you directed your gaze at me.
17. The building contractor scribbled a few figures on a piece of paper.
18. We negotiated for months with the Arabs over this contract.
19. The politicians congratulated the footballers on their success.
20. We saved up money for a Mercedes.

B *Setzen Sie die Verben in Klammern ins Präteritum:*

Der Alte lag da, blau, sein Atem ging wie eine rostige Säge durchs Zimmer. Von Zeit zu Zeit (bäumen) sich sein Oberkörper, seine verkrümmten Hände (zerren) an der dunkelroten gesteppten Decke. Der Doktor (anfeuchten) ein Handtuch, (spritzen) Essig darauf und (legen) es dem Sterbenden auf den Kopf. Zweimal stieg ich die Treppe zu Elisabeth empor. Das erste Mal blieb alles still. Das zweite Mal (hören) ich sie laut schluchzen. Ich (klopfen) stärker. . . . Es (mögen) gegen drei Uhr morgens gewesen sein, ich (hocken) am Bettrand Jacques, der Doktor schlief, ohne Rock, den Kopf in die Hemdärmel gebettet, über dem Schreibtisch. Da erhob sich Jacques mit ausgestreckten Händen, (öffnen) die Augen und (lallen) etwas. Der Doktor erwachte sofort und trat ans Bett.

(excerpted from J. Roth, *Die Kapuzinergruft* [1938])

170 Imperfect tense (strong verbs)

(See S21b)

A *Translate into German:*

1. Did you like his new film?
2. He always lost his notes before meetings.
3. The trade fair took place in Leipzig last year.
4. The waiter recommended this Australian wine.
5. The businessman flew to Munich and arrived in his office at three o'clock.
6. He jumped from his horse, ran to the bar and drank two whiskies.
7. The puppy fell off the chair.
8. The Meyers remained in the waiting lounge.
9. The Finns scored seven goals in eighteen minutes in the ice-hockey match.
10. We forgot to buy onions and garlic.
11. She promised to accompany him to the exhibition.
12. Soldiers tore down the Berlin Wall in 1989.
13. They travelled to his uncle's by underground.
14. At the station he ate a sausage and drank a glass of water.
15. We got into difficulties at the border.
16. The sun shone all day on Saturday.
17. The surgeon found himself in a difficult situation.
18. Before the operation the patient weighed 85 kilos.
19. The representative left the hotel at 6.30.
20. My nephew owned several valuable oil paintings.

B *Setzen Sie die Verben in Klammern ins Präteritum:*

Angefangen (haben) das Drama um die Banane mit dem europäischen Binnenmarkt. Bis dahin (haben) jedes EU-Mitgliedsland sein eigenes Bananenregime. Die Südländer (bevorzugen) ihre heimische Produktion und die aus den befreundeten AKP-Ländern, die Nordländer (greifen) zur billigen Dollarbanane aus Südamerika und (erheben) einen Zoll von 20%, und die Deutschen (erstreiten) für sich das Privileg, Bananen für den eigenen Markt zollfrei einzuführen – in einem gemeinsamen Markt ein untragbarer Zustand.

Der Vorschlag der Kommission zur Vereinheitlichung der Regeln (stoßen) freilich stets auf Widerstand. Nur mit einem in Brüssel als Paketlösung titulierten Kuhhandel (gelingen) es den Bürokraten, die Sperrminorität der Verordnungsgegner zu sprengen. Einmal (lassen) sich die deutschen Unterhändler dazu hinreißen, gegen die Interessen niederländischer Milchbauern zu votieren. . . Ein anderes Mal (scheren) die Dänen aus der Front der Neinsager aus, weil sie turnusgemäß gerade den Ratsvorsitz (führen) und nicht mit dem Makel leben (wollen), ein wichtiges Vorhaben blockiert zu haben. So (werden) Realität, was die Beobachter bis dahin nur amüsiert (haben).

(excerpted from *Die Zeit*)

C *Setzen Sie die Verben in Klammern ins Präteritum:*

Autodieb gab zu viel Gas

Nach Auskunft der Polizei war die unsichere Fahrweise des 18-jährigen Steglitzers bereits an der Finckensteinallee Beamten einer Zivilstreife aufgefallen. Sie (verlieren) das Auto zunächst aus den Augen, (spüren) es aber an der Leonorenstraße wieder auf. Kaum hatte der jugendliche Fahrer die Haltekelle der Zivilstreife erkannt, (geben) er Gas. Er (rasen) bei rotem Ampellicht über zwei Kreuzungen. Jenseits der Kreuzung Malteserstraße/Paul-Schneider-Straße (prallen) das Fahrzeug mit dem linken Hinterreifen gegen den Bordstein der Mittelinsel, (mitteilen) die Polizei.

Durch die Wucht des Aufpralls (überschlagen) sich das Auto zweimal, (schleudern) gegen einen Baum und (landen) im Zaun des Preußenstadions.

(excerpted from *Der Tagesspiegel*)

171 Perfect and pluperfect tenses (weak verbs)

(See S22a, b)

A *Translate into German:*

1. Before we drove onto the ferry we had filled up with petrol.
2. Let's go, I've already paid.
3. Before the widow left the house she packed her suitcase.
4. Do you know if he has been able to ring from Siberia?
5. They had wanted to build a petrol station on this site originally.
6. Have you ever had the urge to give up everything and retire to a monastery?
7. When you were children were you interested in stamps?
8. The washing-machine was broken, so I repaired it myself.
9. I've made you a huge meal – I hope you're hungry.
10. The businessmen had been followed everywhere.
11. All day long I've only heard sirens.
12. The chairman has just given a report on the negotiations.
13. My friend has put his car at my disposal.
14. Oedipus had been pursued by fate all his life.
15. The police had arrested the culprit several times before.
16. The team fought tenaciously right to the end of the game.
17. Dr Schneider has worn himself out working for that company.
18. The new professor has aroused the students' curiosity.
19. The manager has taken the decision to make fifteen staff redundant.
20. The passenger pressed the red button.

B *Setzen Sie die Verben in Klammern in die angegebene Form:*

Volle Medienfreiheit für Sinn Fein

In einem überaus geschickten Schachzug (verkünden; perfect) Premierminister Major während eines überraschenden Besuches in Nordirland am Freitagnachmittag die Aufhebung der geltenden Medienbeschränkungen gegen Sinn Fein sowie die verschiedenen paramilitärischen Gruppierungen in der Provinz. Gleichzeitig betonte er aber, daß sich die Republikaner nunmehr direkt den Fragen nach der Permanenz des von der IRA vor zwei Wochen verkündeten Waffenstillstandes stellen müßten. Zugleich (ankündigen; perfect) der britische Regierungschef ein Referendum, welches in der Provinz nach Abschluß der Friedensgespräche über die Zukunft Nordirlands abgehalten werden soll. In einer weiteren versöhnlichen Geste (anordnen; perfect) der Nordirlandminister Mayhew die Wiedereröffnung von zehn Grenzübergängen zwischen der Republik und Ulster .

Die britische Regierungen (einführen; pluperfect) die Medienbeschränkungen gegen Sinn Fein im Oktober 1988. Unmittelbarer Anlaß war ein blutiger IRA-Anschlag, bei welchem acht britische Soldaten in der nordirischen Grafschaft Tyrone ums Leben gekommen waren. Doch die damalige Premierministerin Thatcher (vorbereiten; pluperfect) das Terrain bereits mit ihrer klassisch gewordenen Beschwörung , Terroristen und Hijackern müsse nunmehr der 'Sauerstoff der Publizität' verweigert werden.

(excerpted from *Neue Zürcher Zeitung*)

72 Perfect and pluperfect tenses (strong verbs)

(See S22a, b)

A *Translate into German:*

1. In the last few years the number of cars on the road has increased considerably.
2. He had taken a vow never to talk about it.
3. I have seen much worse.
4. A nineteen-year-old has mugged a pensioner.
5. The mother screamed with anger after her child had spilt orange juice on the carpet.
6. Fritz has gone for a walk with the Alsatian.
7. Of course, the judge took the circumstances into consideration.
8. Whilst climbing the Zugspitze he got into difficulties.
9 This well-known forward scored nine goals in the World Cup.
10. After the last guest had gone, the host did the washing up in the kitchen.
11. The cost of living has gone up 7 per cent in the last year.
12. The law has already come into effect.
13. The owner has had his kitchen extended.
14. The electrician had cut his finger.
15. I had never managed to resist temptation.
16. Did you like the opera?
17. The decision turned out to be just as we had hoped.
18. After he had carried the fridge into the kitchen, he sat down on a chair.

19. I was sure I had understood his instructions correctly.
20. Did you compare this result with the survey carried out yesterday?

B *Setzen Sie die Verben in Klammern in die angegebene Form:*

Zwanzig Jahre später, im Juli 1958 bezogen wir hier unser Haus, das schönste und – wenn es uns vergönnt ist – letzte Haus unseres Lebens.

Auch dieses habe ich nicht gesucht, sondern es (zufallen; perfect) mir, wie die Farm in Vermont. Oft (vorbeigehen; pluperfect) ich daran und hatte seine prachtvolle Bauart bewundert, die in der ursprünglichen Form und Proportion der alten Saaser Höfe (halten; perfect), und das umliegende, von immergrünen Arven, Bergkiefern und Fichten abgeschirmte Grundstück. Aber wir wußten nicht, daß die Erbauer (versterben; pluperfect), daß es keine Erben gab, die es halten wollten, daß der jetzige Besitzer im Begriff war, es zum Verkauf anzubieten. Eine beiläufige Begegnung machte uns mit alledem vertraut.

Wir (sein; pluperfect) inzwischen, nach dem zweiten Weltkrieg, vierzehnmal in Saas-Fee, es zog uns immer wieder hierher. Ich (besteigen; pluperfect) am Seil und in der guten, schweigsamen Gesellschaft eines älteren Bergführers, bei dem wir auch wohnten, die Berge, ich kannte die alten Geißenpfade und Schafalmen der Umgebung so gut wie die Holzfällersteige und Wildwechsel in Vermont oder die Bauernwege und Hochwälder bei Henndorf.

(excerpted from C. Zuckmayer, *Als wär's ein Stück von mir*)

C *Setzen Sie die Verben in Klammern ins Plusquamperfekt:*

Die Sonne brannte noch immer stark, ihr Licht brannte nie schneidender, als wenn es schräg (richten). Mir war es wie immer fremd, daß es hier keine Dämmerung gibt, sondern immer nur jähen Übergang von Tag zu Nacht. Ich nahm mich zusammen und schritt jetzt kräftiger aus, obwohl der Anstieg in einem unbezwinglichen Abgrund verloren war. Das Treppengeländer drehte und wölbte sich auf einem mächtigen, pfähleartigen Zaun aus Orgelkakteen. Ich konnte nicht mehr unterscheiden, was Bergkämme und was Wolkenzüge waren. Ich fand den Weg zu der Kneipe, wo ich nach dem Abstieg aus dem höher gelegenen Dorf (sitzen). Der Hund (weglaufen). Zwei Truthähne, die vorhin noch nicht da (sein), weideten jetzt auf dem Weg . . . Mein Wirt machte keine Bewegung, als ich zurückkam. Ich war es nicht wert, ich (einreihen) schon in die gewöhnlichen Sinneseindrücke. Ich war jetzt zu müde, nur noch einen Schritt zu machen, ich setzte mich vor meinen alten Tisch. Ich wollte in die Berge zurück, sobald ich ein wenig (ausschnaufen).

(excerpted from A. Seghers, *Der Ausflug der toten Mädchen*)

173 Future tense and future in the past

(See S24)

A *Translate into German:*

1. Mercedes will obtain the new six-cylinder engine from Volkswagen.
2. The company will invest more than 2 billion DM in the project.
3. Up to 3,000 people will work in the factory.
4. The product will cost less than the previous model.
5. My friend will be able to repair the washing-machine.
6. The guests will have gone home.
7. The Prime Minister will have to negotiate with other parties.
8. We will have found a solution by the end of the month.
9. The last bus will have gone by now.
10. By the end of the year my daughter will have learned to read.
11. The election campaign will probably take place in October.
12. I shall probably inherit my uncle's house.

B *Setzen Sie die Verben in Klammern ins Futur und setzen Sie sie an die richtige Stelle im Satz:*

(i) Der Berliner Senat hält an der Zielzahl von 100.000 Studienplätzen in Berlin fest. Weil diese Zielzahl verbindlich ist, (geben) es auch im Doppelhaushalt 1995/96 zunächst keine Senkung der Staatszuschüsse. Aber es (kommen) zu einem Abbau von Doppel- und Dreifachangeboten an den Berliner Hochschulen.

(Excerpted from *Der Tagesspiegel*)

(ii) Manches (sein) auch billiger zu machen, ohne daß die Umwelt darunter leidet . . . Doch das alles (hinweghelfen) nicht über die Erkenntnis : Staatsziele und Parteiprogramme mögen recht und billig sein, ihre Ausführung ist oftmals teuer. Selbst bei bestem Willen (gehen) es oft nicht ohne weitere Belastungen für die Unternehmen, Bürger und Kommunen.

(excerpted from *Frankfurter Allgemeine Zeitung*)

174 Modal verbs

(See S25 to S31)

A *Translate into German:*

1. May I open the window?
2. We shall not be allowed to go to the reception.
3. She is said to be very rich.
4. He will never be able to speak Dutch.
5. She has never had to commute.
6. He always wanted to travel to the Czech Republic.
7. He wasn't allowed to enter the laboratory.
8. That may be true.
9. He had to repeat it.
10. They were to come in the afternoon.
11. He can summarize reports very fast, can't he?
12. He was able to read the Russian newspaper.
13. Do you like carrots?
14. He must have done it at six o'clock.
15. You had wanted to work at a fast-food outlet.
16. Will you be able to finish it by next week?
17. May I come in?
18. I should like two bottles of olive oil and a kilo of oranges.
19. We wanted to buy a crystal vase.
20. Thou shalt not steal.

B *Setzen Sie die entsprechenden Modalverben ein:*

Einsatz der Bundeswehr außerhalb des NATO-Gebietes

Kinkel: Wir ______ weder Zwerg noch Riese sein, Deutschland hat nach 1945 bis zur Wiedervereinigung bewußt auch sicherheits- und militärpolitisch eine zurückhaltende Politik gespielt. Auch nach dem Karlsruher Urteil ______ wir nicht in präpotentes Gehabe verfallen; es bleibt bei der Kultur der Zurückhaltung. Ich sage immer wieder – wir werden in Zukunft auch mehr nein als ja sagen ______. Nie habe ich der Bundesrepublik eine militärische Rolle zuschreiben ______. Aber wir haben durch das Urteil des Bundesverfassungsgerichts nun eine Lage, daß wir – andere Länder auch – über Bundeswehreinsätze außerhalb des NATO-Gebietes in jedem Einzelfall jeweils frei entscheiden ______.

(excerpted from *Süddeutsche Zeitung*)

C *Füllen Sie die Lücken mit Modalverben in der entsprechenden Form:*

In der Schweiz ist dies aber nicht Usus, so daß einige Restaurateure zum 'Overbooking' übergegangen sind: die Tische werden überbucht – wenn trotzdem alle Gäste kommen, _____ sich einige bei einem Apéritif gedulden. Im Normaltarif-Flugverkehr ist solches 'Overbooking' schon lange Tradition. 'Auf stark frequentierten Strecken buchen wir beispielsweise zehn Personen mehr als ein 100-Sitz Flugzeug an Platz bietet, um so weniger leere Plätze hinnehmen zu _____,' sagt Swissair-Sprecher Peter Gutknecht. Wenn alle Flugkunden kommen, _____ die zuletzt gebuchten Passagiere auf einen späteren Flug ausweichen. Von den 'No-shows' seien auch die Borddienste betroffen, betont Gutknecht, da man nie abschätzen _____, wieviele Essen man mitnehmen _____, was zu einem Abfallproblem geführt habe.

(exerpted from *Basler Zeitung*)

175 *Lassen*

(See S32)

A *Translate into German:*

1. Unfortunately her parents got divorced recently.
2. These mistakes can easily be corrected with a macro.
3. I have had my hair cut.
4. 'Richard sends his regards,' he added.
5. After the accident she had to be thoroughly examined.
6. Water consumption can be considerably reduced with this device.
7. Certainly even more can be done.
8. That can easily be changed.
9. His friends left him in the lurch.
10. I wanted to have my permit extended.
11. I am not going to stint myself.
12. The minister sent for his adviser.
13. She had dropped a saucer whilst doing the washing up.
14. We weren't impressed.
15. The general has had additional troops transferred to the town.
16. You can cut down a lot of rubbish if you use returnable bottles.
17. I know that he has had to have his car repaired.

18. The butcher has grown a beard.
19. I shall leave my tennis racket at home.
20. Don't be put off by anyone or anything.

B *Übersetzen Sie die unterstrichenen Satzteile ins Englische:*

Der Erzähler Leo Perutz

Ohnehin habe das Leben mit dem Traum eine längst anerkannte und oft ausgesprochene Ähnlichkeit. Perutz hat sich lange darüber belehren lassen müssen. Ganze Romane von ihm lassen sich als Traumprotokolle lesen, seine Welt ist überhaupt aus traumartigem Stoff. Darum auch sind seine Bücher ausnahmslos Märchen: nicht weil es in ihnen schiefe Würfel, Teufelspakte, Verwünschungen und Wunder hagelt, sondern weil das Märchen die Form ist, in der sich die Welt als Traum fassen läßt.

(excerpted from *Frankfurter Allgemeine Zeitung*)

176 Verbs with separable and inseparable prefixes

(See S34)

A *Translate into German:*

1. What did the waiter recommend?
2. We signed the contract immediately.
3. The customs official asked what we had to declare.
4. He left his nephew a fortune.
5. He had not stressed the correct word.
6. He went into town to draw out money from the bank.
7. He has failed the exam for the second time.
8. That ugly tower block is going to be pulled down.
9. The professor interrupted his lecture to have a drink of water.
10. The dog ran into the street and caused an accident.
11. The size of the cathedral impressed them.
12. Bayern München, his favourite team, suffered a defeat.
13. The diplomat was wary of the peace in the Balkans.
14. A monkey attacked a tourist in the nature reserve.
15. I'll repeat the sentence one more time.
16. The bell-tower was destroyed by an earthquake.
17. The army crushed all opposition in that country.
18. Stamp your ticket before you get on the train.
19. The student overdrew his account.
20. I can resist everything except temptation.

B *Setzen Sie die Verben in Klammern ins Präsens:*

Das Feld (sich vorbeidrehen) mit ihnen langsam; der Zug (umgehen) sie, die Zwischenräume (sich verringern), sie werden ein Block, und einen Augenblick sehe ich nur eine einzige; dann (sich herausschieben) die anderen wieder hinter der vordersten, und sie sind noch lange allein am Himmel, bis sie von den ersten Häusern verdeckt werden.

Ein Bahnübergang. Ich stehe am Fenster, ich kann mich nicht trennen. Die andern (vorbereiten) ihre Sachen zum Aussteigen. Ich spreche den Namen der Straße, die wir (überqueren), vor mich hin – Bremer Straße – Bremer Straße – Radfahrer, Wagen, Menschen sind da unten, es ist eine graue Straße und eine graue Unterführung – sie (ergreifen) mich, als sei sie meine Mutter.

Dann hält der Zug, und der Bahnhof ist da mit Lärm, Rufen und Schildern. Ich (aufpacken) meine Tornister und (festmachen) die Haken, ich nehme mein Gewehr in die Hand und (hinunterstolpern) die Tritte.

Auf dem Perron (sich umsehen) ich; ich kenne niemand von den Leuten, die da hasten. Eine Rote-Kreuz-Schwester (anbieten) mir etwas zu trinken. Ich (abwenden mich), sie (anlächeln) mich zu albern, so durchdrungen von ihrer Wichtigkeit: Seht nur, ich gebe einem Soldaten Kaffee. Sie sagt zu mir 'Kamerad', das hat mir gerade gefehlt.

(excerpted from E. M. Remarque, *Im Westen nichts Neues*)

177 The infinitive and *zu*

(See S35)

A *Translate into German:*

1. I intend to arrive on Friday afternoon.
2. He hoped to avoid the traffic jams on the ring road.
3. I suggested playing a round of golf.
4. It is forbidden to smoke on the Underground.
5. The waiter had forgotten to bring some mustard.
6. She wants nothing to do with it.
7. Eurotunnel succeeded in building a tunnel under the Channel.
8. It is important to bring the right documents to the meeting.
9. He convinced several banks to invest heavily.
10. The Russians have promised to help Chinese industry.
11. Tomorrow we will try to contact the embassy.
12. Do you have time to read through this report?

13. The policemen came in without knocking.
14. Every type of political extremism is to be resisted.
15. I don't feel like doing the weeding.
16. To make a pizza you need pastry, tomatoes and cheese, amongst other things.
17. It will never be possible to prove the motives of the criminals.
18. The Rhine holds the sad record of being the most heavily polluted river in Central Europe.
19. It is necessary to take precautions.

B *Setzen Sie zu ein, wo es notwendig ist: (14 mal!)*

Lutz hatte gerade noch Zeit, die Liste des Nationalrats durchsehen und sie, stöhnend über die Berühmtheit der Namen, sinken lassen – in was für eine unselige Angelegenheit bin ich da verwickelt, dachte er – als Bärlach eintrat, natürlich ohne anklopfen. Der Alte hatte vor, die rechtlichen Mittel verlangen, bei Gastmann in Lamboing vorsprechen, doch Lutz verwies ihn auf den Nachmittag. Jetzt sei es Zeit, zur Beerdigung gehen, sagte er und stand auf. Bärlach widersprach nicht und verließ das Zimmer mit Lutz, dem das Versprechen, Gastmann in Ruhe lassen, immer unvorsichtiger vorkam, und der Bärlachs schärfsten Widerstand befürchtete. Sie standen auf der Straße ohne reden, beide in schwarzen Mänteln, die sie hochschlugen.

Er verzichtete jedoch nicht darauf, den gewohnten Weg durch die Stadt und über die Bundesterrasse gehen, halb schlafend zwar, aber jeder Schritt in der reingefegten Luft tat ihm wohl. Lutz, dem er bald darauf im Bureau gegenübersaß, bemerkte nichts, war vielleicht auch zu sehr mit seinem schlechten Gewissen beschäftigt, um etwas bemerken können. Er hatte sich entschlossen, Bärlach über die Unterredung mit von Schwendi noch diesen Nachmittag orientieren, nicht erst gegen Abend, hatte sich dazu auch in eine kalte, sachliche Positur mit vorgereckter Brust geworfen, wie der General auf Traffelets Bild über ihm, den Alten in forschem Telegrammstil unterrichtend. Zu seiner maßlosen Überraschung hatte jedoch der Kommissär nichts dagegen einwenden, er meinte, es sei weitaus das beste, den Entscheid des Bundeshauses abwarten und die Nachforschungen hauptsächlich auf das Leben Schmieds konzentrieren.

(excerpted from F. Dürrenmatt, *Der Richter und sein Henker*)

178 The subjunctive

(See S37)

A *Translate into German:*

1. He says he has too much work.
2. The secretary maintains the boss is running in the park.
3. The patient said he had been ill for a long time.
4. Would you do me a favour please?
5. Could you pass me the pepper?
6. The businesswoman explained that her children were visiting her uncle.
7. Hans said he would be home late.
8. The couple stated that they had gone to the cinema on Sunday.
9. Her boss says she must work harder.
10. The doctor advised the patient that he should not smoke.
11. Might I ask you to post this letter please?
12. The journalist reports that the law will be passed by the end of the month.
13. I almost missed the train.
14. Could you come by at about six o'clock?
15. We've done it!
16. He said he had good news to report.
17. The minister agreed that this represented an excellent prospect for ending the war.

B *Übersetzen Sie die Verben in Klammern:*

Humphrey wieder unter Verdacht

Nur zwei Wochen, nachdem Humphrey, die Katze aus Downing Street 10, von Premierminister John Major vom Verdacht freigesprochen wurde, vier Rotkehlchen erlegt zu haben, gibt es neue Vorwürfe gegen das Tier. Die *Times* berichtete am Donnerstag, mehrere Augenzeugen (had seen), wie Humphrey im nahegelegenen St James Park auf Beutezug (had gone) und Enten (had caught). Ein Polizist, der am Sitz des Regierungschefs in der Downing Street im Einsatz war, soll gesagt haben, er (had seen), wie die schwarz-weiße Katze mit eindeutiger Absicht in Richtung Park geschlichen und 'noch mit Federn rund um die Schnauze' (had returned).

(excerpted from *Frankfurter Allgemeine Zeitung*)

C *Setzen Sie die Verben in Klammern in den Konjunktiv:*

De Klerk sagte, es (sein) zwar zu verstehen, daß manche Investoren angesichts der politischen Unwägbarkeiten vorerst eine wartende Haltung (einnehmen), doch (haben) Südafrika eindrucksvoll bewiesen, daß es seine Differenzen durch Verhandlungen lösen (können); man (haben) jetzt eine ausgewogene Verfassung, einen 'Rechtsstaat' (de Klerk benutzte das deutsche Wort), eine Koalitionsregierung, die mehr als 90 Prozent der Bevölkerung (repräsentieren), und – was die wirtschaftliche Seite (angehen) – geordnete Verhältnisse: die Inflation (sein) unter Kontrolle, man (üben) monetäre und fiskale Disziplin und (verfügen) unter anderem über eine exzellente Infrastruktur, reiche Bodenschätze, genügend Energie und eine funktionierende Verwaltung.

(excerpted from *Frankfurter Allgemeine Zeitung*)

D *Schreiben Sie den folgenden Absatz in der indirekten Rede. Beginnen Sie mit 'Er sagte. . . .'*

Keine Generation vor uns hatte so viel Freizeit wie wir. Vor 40 Jahren bemaß sich die 'freie Zeit' pro Werktag gerade auf 1,5 Stunden; heute sind es mehr als vier Stunden. Die Wochenendfreizeit hat sich von 1,5 auf zwei Tage ausgedehnt; für viele beginnt das Wochenende schon am Freitagmittag. Und die Urlaubsdauer hat sich mehr als verdreifacht. Die Freizeit ist auch zu einem wichtigen Wirtschaftsfaktor in Milliardenhöhe geworden. Ein durchschnittlicher Arbeitnehmerhaushalt gibt zur Zeit knapp 8800 DM im Jahr für seine Freizeitbedürfnisse aus. Und unter diesen Bedürfnissen der Freizeit, Erholung – und Gesundheitspflege – rangiert der Sport ganz oben an. Rund 1100 DM der Freizeitausgaben entfallen allein auf Sport und Camping. Im Freizeitbereich gehört der Sport nach Urlaub und Auto zum drittgrößten Ausgabenposten.

(excerpted from *Bayerische Staatszeitung*)

179 The conditional

(See S38)

A *Translate into German:*

1. If I have time I'll visit you in Venice.
2. If he knew that he wouldn't ask.

3. Had the tram arrived at the station on time we would not have missed the train.
4. If he had gone to Berlin he could have finished the job.
5. If the project works it could be extended later.
6. What would have happened if there had been a power cut?
7. If you worked more quickly you could earn more.
8. It would be wiser if you phoned me in advance.
9. With a bit more effort you could have kept the appointment.
10. Would the European Union be in a better position if Britain had joined earlier?
11. If pollution is not limited further, the greenhouse effect will worsen.
12. If we bought that tumbledown house we would have to spend a lot on renovation.
13. Had he gone to the lecture he would have learned a good deal about Rilke's poetry.
14. If I had had time I would have had my hair cut.
15. If he had not said anything at the meeting his conscience would have troubled him.
16. Even if all the check-outs were open they wouldn't be able to cope with these crowds.
17. If the alarm bell sounds, leave the building immediately.
18. You would not be indifferent to the subject if you had seen that programme on TV.
19. Even if I had won the lottery I would not have stopped working.
20. If you don't know the German word, look it up in a dictionary.

B *Schreiben Sie die Verben in Klammern in den Konjunktiv II (in der Vergangenheitsstufe). Das Partizip II soll in die Lücken eingesetzt werden:*

Stefan Heym (geb. Helmut Flieg), deutscher Schriftsteller aus jüdischer Familie, denkt an seine Schulzeit:

(sich entscheiden), um ein Beispiel zu nehmen, der junge Flieg an diesem Morgen _____, beim Frühstück nicht die Zeitung zu studieren, sondern sein Schulbuch, er (stoßen) nie auf die Nachricht _____, daß die Generalität der Reichswehr eine Anzahl ihrer Offiziere als Instrukteure der Kuomintang-Armee nach China zu entsenden beabsichtige; und (einfallen) ihm_____, nachdem er während der ersten Schulstunde des weiteren über die Sache nachgedacht hatte, in der zweiten nicht der ziemlich banale Reim 'exportieren-Offizieren', so (sich entschließen) er wohl kaum _____ ein ganzes Gedicht zu diesem Thema unter der Schulbank zu schreiben und (tragen) dieses Gedicht auch nicht während des protestantischen Religionsunterrichts in der dritten Stunde, von dem er dispensiert war, zur Redaktion der Chemnitzer Volksstimme ______ und (werden) somit auch nicht der Mittelpunkt eines politischen Provinzskandals ______, in dessen Folge er gezwungen war, Deutschland bereits im März 1933 zu verlassen; vielmehr (bleiben) er im Lande wie andere seinesgleichen ______ und (enden) mit großer Wahrscheinlichkeit als Wölkchen über Auschwitz ______.

(excerpted from S. Heym, *Nachruf*)

180 The imperative

(See S39)

A *Translate into German, giving both du and Sie forms:*

1. Ask him the way to the village.
2. Help that old woman.
3. Walk round the corner.
4. Buy a day ticket – it's very cheap.
5. Stay here.
6. Give him your pen.
7. Get dressed immediately.
8. Get on the train.
9. Be good.
10. Listen carefully.
11. Wake me up at six o'clock, please.
12. Write it down in your diary.
13. Put the light out.
14. Sign the form at the bottom.
15. Pick up the visitor from the airport.
16. Lift that crate up.
17. Check those figures.
18. Change in Stuttgart.
19. Guess what I've bought.
20. Hang in there!

B *Schreiben Sie die folgenden Imperativformen in die* Du *form um:*

Sparsamer Umgang mit Wasser
Ziehen Sie das Duschen einem Wannenbad vor. Für ein Vollbad benötigen Sie 150–180 Liter, für ein Duschbad dagegen nur 30–50.
Stellen Sie während des Einseifens die Dusche ab.
Benutzen Sie beim Zähneputzen einen Zahnputzbecher.
Achten Sie auf wassersparende Einrichtungen.

Sparsamer Umgang mit Wasser beim Geschirrspülen und beim Wäschewaschen.

Nutzen Sie immer die volle Geräteauslastung aus.
Achten Sie beim Kauf eines neuen Haushaltsgerätes auf die Angaben in Bezug auf Energie- und Wasserverbrauch.
Benutzen Sie für gering verschmutzte Wäsche oder für kleinere Füllmengen die Sparprogramme.
Verzichten Sie bei 95° Programmen auf eine Vorwäsche.

Sparsamer Umgang mit Wasser bei der Hausgartenbewässerung

Bewässern Sie nur, wenn es wirklich nötig ist, und achten Sie auf die Bedarfsmengen der Pflanzen.
Gießen Sie nur die Pflanzen und nicht die Betonplatten.
Geben Sie den Pflanzen nur Wasser, wenn es kühl ist, d.h. nicht tagsüber, sondern abends.
Zeigen Sie, daß Sie umweltbewußt denken, und verzichten Sie auf das Rasensprengen.
Verwenden Sie zur Gartenbewässerung Regenwasser, das in Regentonnen gesammelt wurde.

(excerpted from Länderarbeitsgemeinschaft Wasser: Wer den Tropfen nicht ehrt. . . . Empfehlungen zum sparsamen Umgang mit Trinkwasser im Haushalt.)

81 The passive voice

(See S40 and S41)

A *Translate into German:*

1. The Rhine is endangered by pollutants.
2. The consequences of acid rain were first noticed in Scandinavia.
3. There was singing and dancing.
4. The railway will be subsidized by increases in taxes on fuel oil.
5. The Beetle has not been produced in Germany for a long time.
6. We hope that a vaccine will be developed.
7. Illegally parked cars will be towed away.
8. They were arrested in the middle of the night.
9. The film has been seen by more than 5 million people in Germany.
10. The accused were charged with stealing cars.
11. Towards the end of the year operations are postponed because of costs.

12. Electric vacuum cleaners were shown at an exhibition in Vienna in 1883.
13. In Germany a flat is broken into every two minutes.
14. Your suit can be picked up from the cleaner's next Tuesday.
15. Answers must not be written in pencil.
16. Measures must be taken to prevent further air pollution.
17. The car was stopped by customs officials at the border.
18. The task will have been done before your return.
19. Co-operation between both companies is to be continued in the future.
20. The European Parliament is elected for five years.
21. The price of a pound of coffee has gone up by two DM.

B *Setzen Sie die Verben in Klammern in den Passiv. Sie stehen alle im Präsens:*

In einem zweiten Schritt (zulassen) Charterflüge zwischen Miami und Havanna künftig nur noch für den Transport legaler Immigranten. Drittens werden die Vereinigten Staaten die Sendungen von Radio Marti und TV Marti nach Kuba intensivieren, um die kubanische Bevölkerung unter anderem auf die neuen Asylbedingungen für Kubaflüchtlinge hinzuweisen; um die Störaktionen der kubanischen Regierung zu umgehen, sollen diese Radio- und Fernsehprogramme von amerikanischen Flugzeugen aus (senden). Als vierten Schritt kündigte President Clinton schließlich an, die USA werde sich bei der UNO bemühen, daß Kuba wegen Verletzung der Menschenrechte (verurteilen).

(excerpted from *Neue Zürcher Zeitung*)

C *Setzen Sie die Verben in Klammern in den Passiv. Sie stehen alle im Präsens:*

Arbeitsmarktpolitik

Auch zeigen gerade die Erfahrungen in den neuen Ländern, daß eine Dezentralisierung der Arbeitsmarktpolitik und Entscheidungsprozesse der Bundesanstalt notwendig sind. Nur so können regionale Besonderheiten (berücksichtigen) und die arbeitsmarktpolitischen Instrumente entsprechend (wichten). Dieser Prozeß muß (verbinden) mit einer Stärkung der Selbstverwaltung, damit der Dialog der Ämter mit den Akteuren des ersten Arbeitsmarktes (intensivieren). Langfristig sollten (wahrnehmen) von der Bundesanstalt für Arbeit nur noch die originären Versicherungsaufgaben. Der Bereich der arbeitsmarktpolitischen Instrumente würde (umsetzen) dann von entsprechenden Landesbehörden.

(excerpted from *Vereinigung der Unternehmensverbände in Berlin und Brandenburg e. V. Jahresbericht*, 1992)

D *Translate into German, without using the passive:*

1. The quantity of rubbish removed from households is increasing each week.
2. The medicine which has been prescribed by the doctor must be taken twice a day.
3. Has a black wallet been handed in to you?
4. Behind the road blocks guarded by police the streets were full of cars.
5. Night driving must be avoided as it disturbs children's sleep pattern.
6. The success of learning from the Japanese is not to be underestimated.
7. In the library not a sound could be heard.
8. The question should be asked why the firm has not invested in South Africa.
9. The amount of beer which is drunk in Germany has decreased.
10. An increase of 25 per cent in single people has been registered.
11. This product is being sold in all our branches.
12. Of course, we are afraid that industrial secrets could be divulged.
13. Too much paper is being used.
14. Account should be taken of the fact that he has no experience.
15. The number of accidents had been reduced.
16. This contentious issue can be settled in our next meeting.
17. Hair should be washed every three days.
18. Bus tickets can be purchased in this shop.

82 Coordinating conjunctions

(See S43)

A *Translate into German:*

1. In small bars men talk about football and make bets about the coming Italian game.
2. The water in the open-air pool is cold, but we are still going swimming.

3. He wanted to be a writer. However, he had too little imagination.
4. The town council was no longer in the old tower but had moved into a new office block.
5. He put on his sun-hat and began to mow the lawn.
6. These cables offer you not only British television but also programmes from all over Europe.
7. For the ramble bring an anorak, boots and a map.
8. This car has a diesel engine, i.e. you can't put normal petrol in it.
9. He went into the kitchen since he wanted to switch on the dishwasher.
10. He wanted to go shopping on Saturday afternoon but all the shops were shut.
11. At this university you can study European, African and Asian languages.
12. I rang up my accountant, for I had to make a new tax return.
13. She looked for her purse for hours but couldn't find it.
14. In those days salt was worth as much as gold, but today salt is strewn on the streets by the ton.
15. It's going to be a long journey. Bring a novel, some playing cards and something to eat with you.

B *Setzen Sie die fehlenden Konjunktionen ein:*

Rover 114 Cabrio

Weniger gut gefallen hat uns, daß der 114er sicherheitstechnisch nicht auf der Höhe der Zeit ist. Airbag und ABS sind ___ für Geld ___ für gute Worte lieferbar. Da sind Konkurrenten wie das neue Fiat *Punto Cabriolet* ___ der offene *Peugeot 205* einfach weiter. ___ der Kofferraum des Rover ist wirklich nur als kleine, dunkle Höhle zu bezeichnen, in die sich gerade mal eine Reisetasche verkriechen kann. ___ da sich die Rücksitzlehnen umklappen lassen, können auch zwei Koffer und mehr mit auf die Reise genommen werden, wenn nur zwei Personen mitfahren.

___ genug der Mäkelei, schließlich dient ein Cabrio vor allem einem Zweck: es soll dem Fahrer oder der Fahrerin Spaß bereiten. ___ das tut der 114er schon dann, wenn man das Verdeck lüften möchte.

(excerpted from *Süddeutsche Zeitung*)

C *Setzen Sie die fehlenden Konjunktionen ein:*

Der Fall Günter Deckert

Wenn gesagt wird, die Urteilsbegründung im Fall Deckert schade dem Ansehen Deutschlands, ____ ist dieser Schaden jetzt verdoppelt, ____ es kann nun noch behauptet werden, es sei auch in Deutschland die richterliche Unabhängigkeit nicht mehr gesichert. Hier waren die Richter nicht nur auf dem rechten oder linken Auge blind, ____ auf beiden Augen. Das entspricht zwar den verbundenen Augen der Justitia, ____ Blindheit gegenüber der Verfassung hält diese nicht aus. Die Bundesjustizministerin hatte keine verbundenen Augen, ____ihre Bemerkung, die richterliche Unabhängigkeit sei kein 'Freibrief', ist zwar richtig, ____ wird übersehen, daß nur das Delikt der Rechtsbeugung eine entsprechende 'Briefzensur' zulässig macht. Der Zwiespalt zwischen richterlicher Unabhängigkeit und 'political Correctness' ist unüberbrückbar.

(excerpted from Prof. Doehring, 'Briefe an die Herausgeber,' *Frankfurter Allgemeine Zeitung*)

83 Subordinating conjunctions

(See S44)

A *Translate into German:*

1. I am looking forward to my holiday in Greece, especially as I have lots of friends there.
2. I hope that the baby soon learns to walk.
3. Most people, when they come home from work, just want to slump in a chair.
4. She did not ring me, even though she was visiting Britain.
5. The longer he waited, the worse his toothache became.
6. The article may not be published before he has given his authorization.
7. The acid contained in citrus fruit is so strong that it can damage tooth enamel.
8. When they moved to Berlin they had two small children.
9. He read the director's report so that he would be better prepared for the interview.

10. As soon as he arrived at his holiday destination he twisted his ankle.
11. As the exchange rate is so unfavourable we can afford only a few souvenirs.
12. Before she went to the theatre she put on her make-up.
13. Instead of doing something useful with them they were put on the scrap-heap.
14. His wife asked whether he had any small change on him.
15. The child lay in bed and pretended to sleep.
16. He opened the letter without hesitating.
17. Since he has taught here, many students have chosen Latin.
18. Instead of doing his homework Franz spent all evening watching television.
19. As far as I know no houses are going to be built in this field.
20. We have had a new window put in so that there is more light in the room.

B *Setzen Sie die fehlenden Konjunktionen ein:*

In einer zwanzigminütigen Pause setzen wir uns auf die Eisentreppe, wo etwas weniger Staub ist. Die türkischen Kollegen bestehen darauf, ____ ich von ihren Broten mitesse, ____ sie sehen, ____ ich nichts dabei habe. Nedim, der älteste von ihnen, gießt mir aus seiner Thermoskanne warmen Tee ein. Sie geben untereinander von ihrem Wenigen ab und gehen insgesamt miteinander sanft und freundlich um, wie ich es bei deutschen Arbeitern selten erlebt habe. Es fällt auf, ____ sie während der Pause meist getrennt von den deutschen Kollegen sitzen und nur selten Türkisch miteinander reden. Meist verständigen sie sich in sehr schlechtem Deutsch oder sie schweigen, ____ die deutschen Kollegen das große Wort führen. Nedim klärt mich später einmal den Grund auf. 'Die Deutschen meinen, wir reden schlecht über sie. Und ein paar meinen, wir werden zu stark, ____wir Türkisch zusammen reden. Sie wollen alles mitkriegen, ____ sie uns besser kommandieren können.' Ich erlebte es später selbst, ____ Alfred, ein Wortführer der Deutschen, einmal wutentbrannt dazwischenfährt, ____ die türkischen Kollegen in der Pause miteinander Türkisch reden: 'Sprecht gefälligst deutsch, ____ ihr was zu sagen habt.'

(excerpted from G. Wallraff, *Ganz unten*)

184 Prepositions which take the accusative

(See S45a)

A *Translate into German:*

1. Galileo asserted that the earth revolves around the sun.
2. The shop is shut until next Monday.
3. The lovers strolled along the riverbank.
4. Against all expectations that lazybones passed the exam.
5. I would never have been able to do it without your help.
6. The family sit around the table.
7. When I was in Belgium they took me for a German.
8. After the walk he leaned against an oak tree.
9. Turnover went up by a quarter last year.
10. He peeped through the window, but couldn't see anyone.
11. How much did you pay for your satellite dish?
12. She held the slide up to the light.
13. We have rented the office for half a million DM.
14. Go round the corner and through the subway.
15. The mouse ran along the wall.

B *Setzen Sie die entsprechenden Endungen ein:*

Der Ausbau von Kindergartenbetreuungsplätzen und der Rechtsanspruch auf einen Kindergartenplatz seien ungewiß, und die Verwirklichung von Verkehrsberuhigungsmaßnahmen oder Kinderspielplätzen sei verschoben worden. Als unverständlich bezeichnete es Schmidt, daß an deutschen Gerichten gegen d___ Bau von Kindertageseinrichtungen oder gegen 'd___ Lärm spielender Kinder auf Spielplätzen' geklagt werde.

Die Arbeiterwohlfahrt fordert mehr Büros für Kinderbeauftragt___, die sich alltäglicher Probleme annehmen und für d___ Kinder eintreten. Wirtschaft, Gewerkschaften, Verbände und kommunale Persönlichkeiten sollten sich verstärkt für Kinder engagieren.

(excerpted from *Süddeutsche Zeitung*)

185 Prepositions which take the dative

(See S45b)

A *Translate into German:*

1. Many greetings from Turkey!
2. Since my holiday I have only dreamed of Egypt.
3. At the moment I am living with my parents-in-law.
4. From the outset the married couple have done nothing but quarrel.
5. Apart from the mayor, there was nobody to be seen.
6. He looked out of the window.
7. According to the rumour, we're all getting a salary increase.
8. At the last party he was sitting opposite me.
9. The new timetable is valid from next week.
10. One cannot cope with drug problems on one's own.
11. The party suffered a heavy defeat in the local elections.
12. Her parents come from a wealthy background.
13. To my great disappointment she turned down my invitation.
14. In karate you must fight with your hands as well as your feet.
15. Opposite the petrol station is a splendid half-timbered house.
16. The accountant has been working for this firm for three years.
17. My cousin makes no secret of his concern.
18. He went to the concert by tram.
19. The young mother pushed the trolley out of the supermarket.
20. The manager asked about the competitiveness of the German steel industry.

B *Setzen Sie die fehlenden Präpositionen ein:*

(i) _____ einer Umfrage benützt jede vierte österreichische Frau täglich einen Lippenstift. Grund genug, einmal der Geschichte des 'Zauberstab des Eros', wie er anfangs genannt wurde, nachzugehen. . . . Rote Lippen sind schon _____ Menschengedenken ein Symbol für Erotik und Schönheit. Die ersten Hilfsmittel, um den Lippen eine andere Färbung zu geben, gehen bis _____ den Sumerern, vor 3500 Jahren zurück. Die Ägypterinnen, die, wie man _____ Geschichtsbüchern weiß, sehr viel Wert auf ihr Äußeres legten, betonten ihre Lippen _____ einer Mischung _____ natürlichem Eisenoxyd und Ocker. _____ den Griechen hingegen war der Lippenschmuck nur für Männer (!) und Huren bestimmt. Im Mittelalter benützte man das Innenleben der weiblichen Schildlaus, um den Lippen das gewünschte Rot zu geben.

Erst das ___ dem Orient kommende Hennapulver bot eine einfachere (und auch appetitlichere) Möglichkeit, die Lippen zu betonen.

(excerpted from *Werbung aus Die Presse*)

(ii) Kurz gemeldet

Ein nackter Autodieb ist der Polizei ___ längerer Verfolgungsjagd in Hannover ins Netz gegangen. Der etwa 25-jährige Mann hatte den Wagen in Garmisch-Partenkirchen gestohlen. ___ seiner Amokfahrt rammte er mehrere Autos, mißachtete rote Ampeln und überfuhr beinahe einen Polizisten.

Vier antike Vasen im Wert ___ mehreren Millionen Mark sind ___ den Vatikanischen Museen in Rom gestohlen worden. Sie wurden ___ einer stark gesicherten Vitrine entwendet.

Kinderlähmung ist weltweit auf dem Rückzug. Die Zahl der gemeldeten Poliofälle ist ___ Angaben der Zentren für Seuchenkontrolle und -vorbeugung ___ 1988 um 70% auf 9700 zurückgegangen.

Den Sohn seiner früheren Freundin hat in Berlin ein Mann ___ dem ehemaligen Jugoslawien entführt. ___ zwei Komplizen drang er ___ Polizeiangaben in deren Wohnung ein.

___ einem Brand in der über 100 Jahre alten Markthalle ___ Hanoi sind ___ Angaben von Augenzeugen vier Menschen ums Leben gekommen.

20 Kilo Heroin hat die Polizei in Bremervörde beschlagnahmt. Das Rauschgift wurde im Auto eines 33-jährigen Mannes entdeckt, der ___ einem Rumänienurlaub zurückkam.

(excerpted from *Süddeutsche Zeitung*)

C *Füllen Sie die Lücken:*

Der flüchtige Chef der Geiselnehmer von Englschalking dürfte nur mehr im Besitz von höchstens 20 000 Mark aus d__ 1,5 Millionen-Beute sein. Nachdem 1,05 Millionen Mark beschlagnahmt wurden, als vier Gangster nach d__ Geiselnahme und d__ erpreßt__ Tresoröffnung in der Bank für Gemeinwirtchaft am Promenadeplatz vor drei Wochen in einer Wohnung am Hasenbergl bei__ Geldzählen von d__ Polizei überrascht wurden, führte ein V-Mann aus d__ Münchner Roma-Szene Beamte der Mordkommission nun zu d__ Verstecken von weiter__ 430 000 Mark aus der Beute. Sie waren bei Mutter und Schwester von Bandenboß Zvonko Todorovic, 24, gebunkert.

Nach d__ Coup war der aus d__ Woiwodina nördlich von Belgrad stammende Roma im Auto mit sein__ Beuteanteil von 450 000 Mark in Begleitung seiner Ehefrau Biljana, 25, geflüchtet. Sie befand sich in d__ Wohnung von Todorovics Mutter in Taufkirchen, als die Polizei noch am Tattag zu ein__ Razzia erschien, behauptete, von d__ Tat nichts gewußt zu haben: ihr Mann habe sie nur nach Hause gefahren. Damals wurde in ihren gemeinsam mit der Schwiegermutter bewohnten Taufkirchner Räumen und im Keller kein Geld gefunden.

(excerpted from *Süddeutsche Zeitung*)

186 Prepositions which take either the dative or the accusative

(See S45c)

A *Translate into German:*

1. He escaped via Switzerland to the United States.
2. The thief disappeared over the garden fence.
3. The farmer sat down at a table in the corner.
4. He sat down next to the chairman's wife.
5. We waited for half an hour at the bus stop.
6. In your position I would take the risk.
7. Over the bed hangs an old bearskin.
8. My niece lives in the country.
9. The actress kissed Helmut on the cheek.
10. In no circumstances are you allowed to leave this room.
11. The butcher can drink you under the table.
12. To understand what he means you have to read between the lines.
13. I shall wait for you outside the cinema.
14. There you see the new bridge over the Thames.
15. I am still working on my thesis.
16. You don't need to bang on the table.
17. The dog fell into the river, then swam to the bank.
18. The tiger paced up and down in its cage.
19. The neighbour's child has locked himself into our wardrobe.
20. He knocked on the door and went into the office.

B *Setzen Sie die fehlenden bestimmten Artikel ein und ergänzen Sie die Endungen der übrigen Artikel und Pronomen:*

Unter d__ vielen Mängeln fallen die Schwächen in d__ Agrarpolitik auf, ein__ überlebenswichtigen Wirtschaftsbereich für Afrika, in d__ fast drei Viertel der Schwarzafrikaner arbeiten. Auf kein__ anderen Kontinent werden die Bauern so stark mit Steuern, Exporttarifen, überbewerteten Wechselkursen und künstlich verteuerten Einfuhren belastet. . . . Die Reformen auf d__ Agrarbereich zu konzentrieren, zumal auf d__ Lande der Großteil der Armen lebt – dazu rät auch die Weltbank und verweist auf d__ Erfolgsgeschichten in Ostasien. Die Stärkung der Landwirtschaft war für die Tigerstaaten und ihre Nachahmer der Ausgangspunkt ihres Aufstiegs. Gestützt auf d__ Wachstumsimpuls aus der Landwirtschaft, investieren die Staaten in sozial__ Programme, in d__ Gesundheitsversorgung und in d__ Erziehung. Der Anteil der Bevölkerung, der in dies__ Region unter d__ Armutsgrenze lebt, ist seither spürbar gesunken.

(excerpted from *Frankfurter Allgemeine Zeitung*)

187 Prepositions which take the genitive

(See S45d)

A *Translate into German:*

1. During his stay he spoke a lot of German.
2. Because of the traffic jam they arrived in Mannheim three hours late.
3. He owns a piece of land outside town.
4. The old town of Prague lies below the castle.
5. Instead of a radio we bought a hi-fi.
6. Despite the heavy rain the children played football in the garden.
7. The sheep do not graze above a certain height in the mountains.
8. I must find a buyer within the next two weeks.
9. Instead of a birthday card he received a gas bill.
10. Outside surgery hours Dr Schmidt can be contacted at home.
11. The flight has been delayed because of technical difficulties.
12. The court sentenced him to life imprisonment for attempted murder.
13. Despite his education he still can't mend a fuse.
14. He had to ring his wife during the meeting.
15. The hostess did all that because of me.

B *Lesen Sie den Text und beantworten Sie die Fragen:*

Deutlich mehr Alkoholismus in der Dritten Welt

Washington Vor den sozialen Folgen des zunehmenden Alkoholismus in der Dritten Welt hat das amerikanische 'Worldwatch Institute' gewarnt. Der ursprünglich sehr niedrige Alkoholkonsum in den

Entwicklungsländern sei inzwischen fast so hoch wie in den Industrienationen, heißt es in einer Studie. In vielen Entwicklungsländern habe sich der Bier- und Schnapsverkauf in den vergangenen 25 Jahren vervielfacht. Schon jetzt vertränken dort vor allem die Männer einen Großteil ihres Einkommens. In Burkina Faso gäben viele Männer fast die Hälfte ihres Verdienstes für Bier aus. Die erhöhten Kosten machten sich schon jetzt im Gesundheitsbereich bemerkbar. So habe in Trinidad jeder zweite Krankenhauspatient Probleme mit dem Trinken. In Chile sei Alkohol indirekt für 53 Prozent aller Todesfälle verantwortlich. Als Ursache für den steigenden Alkoholkonsum wird in der Studie unter anderem die Werbung genannt, mit der Hersteller aus den Industrieländern Drinks zu Statussymbolen machten. Viele afrikanische Regierungen förderten zudem wegen der beträchtlichen Steuereinnahmen die Herstellung von Bier in eigenem Land.

(excerpted from *Süddeutsche Zeitung*)

Die folgenden Satzteile beziehen sich auf den obigen Text. Vervollständigen Sie die Sätze mit Präpositionen, Artikeln usw.:

1. Europa __ ist Alkoholkonsum auch gestiegen
2. Die Männer in vielen Entwicklungsländern __ Bier __ Lebensmittel kaufen
3. Gefahr __ Alkohol __ die Bevölkerung __ die Regierung läßt Alkoholkonsum nicht bremsen
4. Trinken __ muß Trinidad viel Geld im Gesundheitsbereich ausgeben
5. hohe Preise __ viel Geld für Alkohol ausgegeben.
6. __ die letzten 25 Jahre hat sich Bierverkauf in der Dritten Welt vervielfacht
7. Alkoholkonsum gestiegen __ Werbung

188 Verbs and adjectives with prepositions

(See S46)

A *Translate into German:*

1. Nobody doubts your abilities.
2. The engineer is very proud of his invention.
3. In the holidays he suffered from a tropical disease.
4. The chairman is married to a Frenchwoman.

5. She had to wait a long time for the next hovercraft.
6. In the recession he was worried about his job.
7. These policemen are in charge of guest security.
8. He reacted straightaway to the price reduction of his rival's products.
9. He insisted on his right to speak to a lawyer.
10. The mayor reported on his visit to the twin town.
11. During her stay in Italy Ruth took part in a demonstration.
12. He laughed about our experiences in the hotel.
13. We are most grateful for your help.
14. In his speech he made several allusions to the Bible.
15. Are you working on your novel still?
16. Let's drink to the future!
17. The local council is responsible for rubbish collection.
18. I am not satisfied with this explanation.
19. Have you apologized for your impoliteness?
20. Herr Ahrens doubts the veracity of that story.

B *Setzen Sie die fehlenden Präpositionen ein:*

Falls ich Weihnachten noch hier im Loch sitzen sollte, laß Dich dadurch nicht bekümmern. Ich habe eigentlich keine Angst da____. Weihnachten kann man als Christ auch im Gefängnis feiern – jedenfalls leichter als Familienfeste. Daß du Sprecherlaubnis beantragt hast, da____ danke ich Dir ganz besonders. Ich glaube auch, daß es jetzt ohne Komplikationen möglich war. Allerdings hätte ich nicht gewagt, Dich da____ zu bitten. Aber da Du es nun von Dir aus getan hast, ist es ja noch viel schöner. Es ist meine ganze Hoffnung, daß es nun wirklich dazu kommt! Aber weißt Du, auch wenn es abgelehnt wird, so bleibt doch die Freude, daß Du es versucht hast, und nur der Zorn über gewisse Leute wird für den Termin etwas größer, was nichts schadet. (Ich denke nämlich manchmal, ich bin ____ die ganze Sache noch nicht wütend genug!) Also wollen wir dann auch diese bittere Pille herunterschlucken – da____ gewöhnen wir beide uns in letzter Zeit ja allmählich. Ich bin froh, daß ich Dich im Augenblick der Verhaftung noch sah und vergesse das nicht.

(excerpted from D. Bonhoeffer, *Widerstand und Ergebung*)

C *Setzen Sie die fehlenden Präpositionen ein:*

Von oben betrachtet ist Bayern 70.554 Quadratmeter groß. Fast jeder Quadratzentimeter ist ideal ____ einen Erholungsurlaub. ____ den Gast warten großartige Landschaften, kristallklare Seen, romantische Städte

– wie gesagt, oberflächlich betrachtet. Denn die Attaktivität des Landes setzt sich ____ vielen facettenreichen Details zusammen, wie traumhafte Schlößer, stolze Burgen, traditionsreiche Heilbäder und berühmte Museen . . . In einer Umwelt, die vom Gast noch als sauber und intakt empfunden wird. Da____ tragen nicht unwesentlich die National- und Naturparks bei . . . ____ den Berühmtheiten des Landes gehören auch die Bereiche Kultur und Brauchtum. Alles zusammen ergibt ein einzigartiges Ganzes: Das Ferienland Bayern . . . Das persönliche Wohlbefinden hängt heutzutage immer mehr ____ Können denn ____ Wollen ab. Auch wenn man etwas ganz für sich selbst tun will – Streß, Hektik, falsche Ernährungsgewohnheiten oder Bewegungsmangel sorgen da____, daß man es noch lange nicht so kann, wie man sich das vorstellt.
(excerpted from *Münchner Tageszeitung*)

189 Adverbs of time

(See S50)

A *Translate into German:*

1. Ten years ago there were only fields here. Now a road runs through this district.
2. In those days one had to work at the weekend.
3. She took her driving test the day before yesterday.
4. First we are going to discuss the details of this plan, then we'll call it a day.
5. The financial director is getting a new company car next month.
6. When we were in Denmark it rained the whole time.
7. As the telephone number was constantly engaged he kept on having to redial it.
8. When I am particularly busy I sometimes eat at a snack bar.
9. Most shareholders never come to the AGM.
10. In the end the company went bust.
11. Do you go swimming in the morning or the evening?
12. Where once the old castle stood, a multi-storey department store now towers.
13. The balance of trade has been in the red for some years; since then we have had to pay higher taxes.
14. Do you think that foreigners should be entitled to vote in future?
15. *Die Zeit* appears weekly.
16. I am just coming / I am on my way.
17. The new law comes into effect the day after tomorrow.

B *Füllen Sie die Lücken mit den folgenden Adverbien: noch niemals, dann, sofort, gleich, gleichzeitig, eines Morgens, diesmal, jeden Tag*

Jemand mußte Josef K verleumdet haben, denn ohne daß er etwas Böses getan hätte, wurde er ____ verhaftet. Frau Grubach, seine Zimmervermieterin, die ihm ____ gegen acht Uhr das Frühstück brachte, kam ____ nicht. Das war ____ geschehen. K. wartete noch ein Weilchen, sah von seinem Kopfkissen aus die alte Frau, die ihm gegenüber wohnte und die ihn mit einer an ihr ganz ungewöhnlichen Neugierde beobachtete, ____ aber, ____ befremdet und hungrig, läutete er. ____ klopfte es und ein Mann, den er in dieser Wohnung ____ gesehen hatte trat ein. Er war schlank und doch fest gebaut, er trug ein anliegendes schwarzes Kleid, das ähnlich den Reiseanzügen, mit verschiedenen Falten, Taschen, Schnallen, Knöpfen und einem Gürtel versehen war und infolgedessen, ohne daß man sich darüber klar wurde, wozu es dienen sollte, besonders praktisch erschien. 'Wer sind Sie?' fragte K. und saß ____ halb aufrecht im Bett. Der Mann aber ging über die Frage hinweg, als müsse man seine Erscheinung hinnehmen, und sagte bloß seinerseits: 'Sie haben geläutet?'

(excerpted from Franz Kafka, *Der Prozeß*)

90 Adverbs of manner and place

(See S51 and S52)

A *Translate into German:*

1. He is undoubtedly at the peak of his career.
2. Next year we shall probably go to Spain.
3. The rep is waiting outside.
4. It has to rain today of all days!
5. He will certainly have checked it over carefully.
6. Put the parcel over there.
7. A visa is certainly not necessary for entry.
8. The children went out into the fresh air.
9. Come in immediately!
10. Flags were hanging out of the windows.
11. Mrs Fisch took a black skirt out of her suitcase.
12. When the bell went the schoolgirls rushed down the steps.
13. Come over here!
14. I particularly like playing badminton.

15. The file is down there on the shelf.
16. In German buses does one get on at the front or at the back?
17. What's the best way for me to get there?
18. You should sign correspondence at the bottom on the left.

B *Füllen Sie die Lücken mit den folgenden Adverbien: daher, besondes, drastisch, besonders, selbst:*

Wissen Sie, daß gerade Gewässer mit ihren Schilf- und Röhrichtbeständen als Lebensraum für Pflanzen und Tiere ____ wertvoll sind und z.B. 80% der gefährdeten Vogelarten auf solche Feuchtgebiete angewiesen sind? Diese wichtigen Flächen werden durch Badeanstalten, öffentliche Badeplätze, Ferienhäuser, Bootstege usw. ____ eingeengt. ____ die wenigen noch verbliebenen Teilflächen müssen Pflanzen und Tiere mit einer ständig steigenden Zahl von Wassersportlern teilen. Der Lebensraum Wasser mit seinen ____ gefährdeten Randzonen kann ____ nur durch Ihr verständnisvolles Verhalten in seiner Bedeutung für die Pflanzen- und Tierwelt, den Naturhaushalt und die Schönheit des Landschaftsbildes erhalten werden.

(excerpted from: *Schwimmer und Badende – Naturschutz-Informationsblatt des Bayerischen Staatsministeriums für Landesentwicklung und Umweltfragen*)

C *Füllen Sie die Lücken mit den folgenden Adverbien: verzweifelt, her, rund, darüber, nie, auch, überall, nicht, wiederum, auch:*

Ein Trend ist ein Trend

Bis zum Jahr 2000 dauert es noch ____ 56000 Stundeneinheiten. Wir machen uns Gedanken ____ oder auch ____ – im Unterbewußtsein aber schwärt das Fin-de-Siècle. Es macht uns zu schaffen. Wir wollen auf der richtigen Arche einschiffen, um ins neue Jahrtausend zu schaukeln. Die Verunsicherung ist ____ und nicht klein. Sie macht ____ den Marketingleuten zu schaffen, die ____ nach griffigen Begriffen in der immer formloser werdenden Gesellschaft suchen. Trends müssen ____, Trends, die Minireligionen der Jetztzeit. Wir glauben nicht mehr an den Messias, der kommen wird. Aber der nächste Trend wird uns erretten. . . .

Wer keinen Trend weiß, ist von gestern – was aber bei manchem Trend ja ____ bedeuten würde, daß er oder sie von morgen ist. Das Magazin *Wiener* war ____ um einen Trend verlegen, und war noch so dumm. *Wiener* ist tot. Trendinfarkt. Kurzschluß. ____ das Tempo legte sich ein neues Layout zu und tendiert zu einem bunten *Nachrichten*-Magazin. Trends funktionieren nicht mehr, zu schnell sind die Konsumzyklen geworden. Zuviele Medien haben zu schnell sich Trends erredet.

(excerpted from *Basler Zeitung*)

191 Word order

(See S55)

A *Translate into German:*

1. I gave them our new telephone number.
2. Every day I travel to work by bus.
3. He has left the country for financial reasons.
4. The teachers are working in the school only until noon because of the heat.
5. Bring it to me straight away!
6. I'll come to your dinner party next week with pleasure.
7. Jutta went to the university yesterday filled with fear because of the exam.
8. Stupidly she left her purse in the open-air pool yesterday.
9. You told me that story yesterday.
10. The president gave his inaugural speech in Berlin yesterday.
11. From tomorrow the buses will go past our flat because of the roadworks.
12. The teacher only told me the exam result the day before yesterday.
13. The firm did not deliver the goods to the customer yesterday.
14. During his stay in the capital Hans often went to the theatre.
15. He gave the secretary a bunch of flowers on her birthday.
16. Did he prove it to you?
17. The policeman took them away from him.

B *Ordnen Sie die folgenden Elemente, so daß korrekte Sätze entstehen:*

1. Bringen/ Sie/ das Brathähnchen / mir / bitte.
2. Darf / ihr / es / ich / abnehmen?
3. Blut / öfters / eigentlich / man / sollte / spenden.
4. Zur Arbeit / ich / fahre / mit der U-Bahn / jeden Tag.
5. Das Salz / mir / bitte / reichen Sie.
6. Dir / hat / der Professor / noch / wegen seiner Krankheit / geschrieben / keinen Brief.
7. In der Straßenbahn / vergessen / ich / dummerweise / meinen Regenschirm / vorgestern / habe.
8. Gesprochen / mit ihr / auf der Party / du / hast / gestern?
9. Die Tante / eine Tafel Schokolade / steckte zu / dem Kind.
10. Ins Zimmer / nervös / gegen 20 Uhr / sie / kam.

192 Negation and position of *nicht*

(See S59, S60 and S61)

A *Translate into German:*

1. We didn't buy any peaches.
2. If I don't tackle this problem, nobody will.
3. They no longer have to queue up but usually get individual appointments.
4. The results show that no appliance is free from environmentally damaging substances.
5. It is not publicly announced who is flying with whom.
6. Children should not be treated as machines.
7. The lawyer says that his client cannot be sentenced by the courts.
8. There are enough orders, it's just that purchasers are often not able to pay.
9. We are not afraid of spiders.
10. This document is not of great importance.
11. The patient is not allowed to drink alcohol.
12. Although our son is studying engineering he's not going to be an engineer.
13. The priest doesn't drive.
14. The director's travelling expenses alone come to 6000 DM.
15. This edition is so outdated that it is no longer read.
16. Because of the loud music in the disco I hardly slept last night.

B *Verneinen Sie die folgenden Sätze mit nicht:*

1. Wie sich mittlerweile abzeichnet, scheint dieses Vorhaben befriedigend lösbar zu sein.
2. Obwohl sich Wissenschaftler in den letzten Monaten intensiv mit diesen Fragen befaßt haben, ist Klarheit in Sicht.
3. Die SPD kann, was beeindruckendes Personal angeht, aus dem Vollen schöpfen.
4. Das ist sein Eingeständnis, daß er die Wahl nach dem Muster des Duells gewinnen kann.
5. Ein Zweikampf findet statt, auch weil der Herausforderte sich darauf einläßt. (both clauses!)
6. In dieser Frage macht sich beliebt, wer abseits steht.
7. Es blieb ihm anders übrig.
8. Ich werde diese Diskussion neu vom Zaun brechen.

9. Zu mehr Klarheit haben diese Arbeiten beitragen können.
10. Auch für den Verbraucher ist der Umgang mit Abfall einfacher geworden.

(taken from *Frankfurter Allgemeine Zeitung*)

193 Key to exercises

152A

1. In dem Foto kann man ein kleines Mädchen sehen, das auf das weiße Pferd steigt.
2. Das Opfer war der 42-jähriger Herausgeber einer berühmten Zeitung.
3. Das Krokodil schwamm im See.
4. Der Ferne Osten zieht mich an.
5. Der Ural bildet die Grenze zwischen Europa und Asien in Rußland.
6. Der Zauberlehrling hatte ein Problem mit dem Besen.
7. Die Bevölkerung dieses Landes / die Leute in diesem Land spricht eine unverständliche Sprache.
8. Die Gesundheit ist das Wichtigste im Leben.
9. Es gibt eine bekannte Brauerei in diesem Stadtviertel.
10. Gefällt Ihnen das Hilton? Ich bevorzuge das Penta.
11. Das Instrument, das der Bettler spielt, erkenne ich nicht.
12. Der erste Spieler, der eine Sechs würfelt, fängt an.
13. Was mir in Schottland am besten gefällt, ist die malerische Landschaft.
14. Diese Universität wurde 1350 gegründet / ist 1350 gegründet worden.
15. Der Forscher ist nie von seiner Expedition zurückgekehrt.
16. Wir fahren nächsten Sommer in die Türkei.
17. Wir haben die Enzyklopädie gestern bei einem Antiquitätenhandler gekauft.
18. Der erste Weihnachtstag fällt in diesem Jahr auf einen Donnerstag.
19. Die Geisel wurde unverletzt entlassen.
20. Gestern sahen wir ein rotes Eichhörnchen auf der Eiche.

152B

die, das, die, die, eine, die, dem, der, die, die, die, eines, einen, die

153A

1. Meine Tochter spielt Flöte.
2. Er ist Klempner (von Beruf).
3. In Irland gibt es keine Schlangen.
4. Die Regierung ist für die Geldmenge verantwortlich.
5. Verkaufen Sie Knoblauch?
6. Die Tagung / Konferenz findet am Bodensee statt.
7. Manche Bewerber wurden nicht interviewt.
8. Meine beiden Schwestern wohnen in der Schweiz.
9. Welche Aquarelle haben Sie gekauft / erworben?
10. Dieser Stecker paßt nicht in die Steckdose.
11. Die jene Wähler, die Ihre Partei unterstützt haben, werden es nicht bereuen.
12. Sein Koffer ist verlorengegangen, deshalb mußte er eine Woche lang das gleiche Hemd tragen.
13. Das ist keine Lösung.
14. Haben Sie (irgend)einen Lappen, den ich in der Garage benutzen könnte?
15. Er hat Blasen an beiden Händen.
16. An deiner Stelle hätte ich dasselbe gemacht.
17. Von allen Ländern im Nahen Osten möchte ich den Libanon besichtigen.
18. Ich habe eine gute Nachricht für dich.
19. Diese Hose steht dir (gut).
20. Der Zaun meines Nachbarn ist hinter den Bäumen.

153B

das, dem, das, dem, eines, den, der, jene, der, einer, die, der, die, den, eine, keine, welcher, einen, eine, diejenige, das, des, die, dem, die

154A

1. Einfache Lösungen gibt es nicht.
2. Das Kabinett muß die Verantwortung für Entscheidungen teilen.
3. Eltern haften für ihre Kinder.
4. An welchen Krankheiten haben Sie gelitten ?
5. Diese neuen Kanäle haben kein erweitertes / größeres Angebot an Sendungen.
6. Immer mehr Familien leben über ihre Verhältnisse.
7. Männer und Frauen sind gleichberechtigt.
8. Mathe, Englisch und eine Fremdsprache sind Pflichtfächer in allen Schulen.

9. Die Vögel zwitscherten auf den Bäumen.
10. Die Zwillinge gingen auf dieselben zwei Universitäten.
11. Reisende nach Israel und nach Syrien brauchen zwei Pässe.
12. Blutübertragungen sind sicherer geworden.
13. Dieses Abteil ist für Nichtraucher.
14. Subventionen in diesem Bereich müssen abgebaut werden.
15. Einige interessante Antiquitätenläden befinden sich unter den Bögen.
16. Mach / Machen Sie die Vorhänge auf!
17. An der Grenze gerieten sie in Schwierigkeiten.
18. Zuviele Lastkraftwagen fahren auf unseren Straßen.
19. In seinem Koffer hatte er zwei Anzüge, vier Hemden, drei Krawatten / Schlipse und eine Auswahl an Socken.
20. Er spitzte die Ohren und hörte dem Vortragenden gut zu.

154B

Zeitungen, Monaten, Gewinnspiele, Buchpreise, Reiseangebote, Umfangerweiterungen, Schätzungen, Pfund, Millionen, Löcher, Verkäufen, Anzeigeneinnahmen, Kürzungen, Produktionskosten

154C

Strände, Weinberge, Obstgärten, Hotels, Sportmöglichkeiten / Sportarten, Ausflüge, Preisen

155A

1. Wir haben einen Elefanten im Zirkus gesehen.
2. Herr Schmidt hat sich mit seinem Nachbarn unterhalten.
3. Deutschland hat einen neuen Präsidenten gewählt.
4. Im Radio habe ich einen Streit zwischen einem Kommunisten und einem Christen gehört.
5. Der Anwalt hat dem Zeugen mehrere Fragen gestellt.
6. Der Frisör / Der Barbier schneidet dem Kunden die Haare.
7. Ähnelt der Mensch einem Affen überhaupt?
8. Wir wurden in der Stadt von einem Polizisten angehalten.
9. Im Film hat sich die Krankenschwester vom Helden verabschiedet.
10. Die Stärke seines Glaubens nimmt jeden Tag zu / Seine Glaubensstärke wächst jeden Tag.
11. Gestern sind wir einem französischen Bauern begegnet.
12. Das Märchen handelt von einem Riesen und einem Zwerg.
13. Die Pläne dieses Gebäudes wurden von einem bekannten Architekten entworfen.
14. In den letzten zwanzig Jahren haben viele Juden Rußland verlassen.

15. Herr Klein fuhr nach Detmold, um seinen Neffen zu besuchen.
16. Um Gottes Willen! Was machst du denn da?
17. Auf dem Berliner Wappen sieht man einen großen Bären.
18. Dieses Schloß gehört einem Grafen.
19. Er hatte den Namen jenes bekannten Dirigenten vergessen.
20. Wir haben uns nie darüber Gedanken gemacht.

155B

Glaube, Menschen, Namen, Menschen, Namen, Boten, Namen, Name

156A

1. Im Stadtzentrum treffen sich viele Jugendliche.
2. Ist dein Freund Franzose? Nein, er ist Deutscher.
3. Einer seiner Bekannten übernachtete im selben Hotel.
4. Die Feuerwehr besteht aus Freiwilligen.
5. Um wieviel Uhr / Wann haben Sie den Angeklagten gesehen?
6. Der Beamte sprach mit dem Arbeitslosen.
7. Wissen sie, daß viele Reiche in diesem Vorort wohnen?
8. Gestern bin ich vor dem Rathaus einem Ungarn begegnet.
9. Haben Sie etwas Interessantes zu berichten?
10. Am Wochenende machen wir immer etwas Besonderes.
11. Nach der Pause war nichts Eßbares mehr in seiner Aktentasche / Mappe.
12. Das Auswärtige Amt konnte über diese Sache nichts Näheres / Weiteres sagen.
13. Wir wußten über den Inhalt der Akten nichts Genaues.
14. Dieter arbeitet in seiner Werkstatt mit einem Auszubildenden.
15. Sabine hat mich ihrem Verlobten vorgestellt.
16. Sie brachten / Man brachte den Verletzten ins Krankenhaus.
17. Ein Gefangener ist entflohen.
18. Unser Mitarbeiter hat sich an seinen unmittelbaren Vorgesetzten gewandt.
19. Molière hat eine Komödie über einen Geizigen geschrieben.
20. Brüssel sollte Arbeitsplätze für Behinderte fördern.

156B

Besseres, Blonden, Blauäugigen, Lebendigen, Glücklichen, Liebenswürdigen, Gewöhnlichen

157A

1. Wir haben dich / Sie während der Tagung beobachtet.
2. Hat sie ihm schließlich einen Brief geschrieben?

3. Wie geht's ihr? Ihr geht's gut./ Es geht ihr gut.
4. Ist die Polizei gekommen? Ja, sie ist sofort gekommen.
5. Es fehlt dem neuen Lehrer an Selbstvertrauen.
6. Erinnerst du dich an die Brauns? Ich bin ihnen im Supermarkt begegnet.
7. Franz, kannst du mir bei dieser Rechnung helfen?
8. Warum rufen Sie uns immer wieder an? Wir haben schon Doppelfenster (im Haus).
9. Setz dich mal hin und erzähl mir alles!
10. Wo ist denn die Bratpfanne? Ich war sicher, daß sie im Schrank war.
11. Der Detektiv zündete (sich) eine Zigarette an, dann legte er sie auf den Aschenbecher.
12. Geben Sie mir bitte den Löffel. Er liegt auf dem Krug.
13. Leg den Aufschnitt in den Kühlschrank, sonst wird er schlecht.
14. Es gelang ihm, den Erzbischof von seiner Ernsthaftigkeit zu überzeugen.

157B

mir, dir, du, mich, dir, dir, du, du, du, du, mir, mir, ihn, dir, dich, sie, dir, mir, dir, dir, mir, dich

157C

er, er, Sie, Ihnen, er, er

158A

1. Wo habe ich meine Brille hingelegt?
2. Kannst du mir deinen Rechner leihen?
3. Unsere Verhandlungen haben bis jetzt / noch zu nichts geführt.
4. Während seines langen Vortrags bin ich eingeschlafen.
5. Dank deiner / Ihrer schnellen Hilfe hat sich das Problem gelöst.
6. Der Premierminister / Kanzler ist zurückgetreten. Seine Entscheidung ist unwiderruflich.
7. Ihrer Meinung nach soll der Asylbewerber abgeschoben werden.
8. Der Reisende tat die zusammengerollte Zeitung in seine Mappe.
9. Wohnst du immer noch bei deinen Eltern?
10. Der Makler schrieb an seinen Steuerberater.
11. An seiner Stelle würde ich dasselbe tun.
12. Wie kommen Sie mit Ihrem Gehalt aus?
13. Unser Haus ist zu vermieten.
14. Zu ihrer (großen) Freude erfuhr sie, daß sie den ersten Preis gewonnen hatte.
15. Ich sah das UFO mit eigenen Augen.

158B

mein, seiner, meine, sein, meine, meine, mein

159A

1. Ich habe mir die Hände gewaschen.
2. Darf ich mich bei Ihnen vorstellen?
3. Ihr zwei Jungen, zieht euch sofort um!
4. Sie wollten sich über das spanische Hotel beschweren.
5. Unser neuer Kollege färbt sich die Haare.
6. Ich muß mich schnell schminken, bevor die Gäste (an)kommen.
7. Die Germanen hatten sich das Totenreich/die Hölle dunkel, neblig und kalt vorgestellt.
8. Wie kannst du dir das (denn) leisten?
9. Er erkundigte sich nach den Abfahrtszeiten der Züge.
10. Ich habe mich um / für eine gut bezahlte Stelle in Brüssel beworben.
11. Hast du dir das Bein gebrochen?
12. Bevor sie ins Bett geht, kämmt sich meine Tochter die Haare.
13. Fragst du dich, ob wir das anders hätten machen können?
14. Wir freuen uns auf die Reise nach Italien.
15. Er bildet sich ein, daß er nächstes Jahr befördert wird.
16. Erinnern Sie sich an den Entschluß, den wir getroffen haben?
17. Das Kind fürchtete sich vor Gespenstern.
18. Der Kunde wird sich über die schlechte Qualität der Waren ärgern.
19. Ich habe mich in einen Schauspieler verliebt.
20. Hast du dich bei dem Chef wegen der Unterbrechung entschuldigt?

159B

mich, mir, mich, mich

159C

accusative, dative, dative, accusative, accusative

160A

1. Dieses Dampfbügeleisen ist mir viel zu teuer.
2. Jene gesellschaftlichen Probleme, die die Politiker diskutiert haben, sind noch ungelöst.
3. Wie komme ich am schnellsten dorthin?
4. Er muß von daher/dorther gekommen sein.
5. Diejenigen, die schwarzfahren, werden bestraft.
6. Hat jemand etwas dagegen?
7. Dieser Computer arbeitet viel schneller als jener.
8. Bisher ist alles gut gegangen.

9. Derjenige, der meinen Schlüssel findet, bekommt eine Belohnung.
10. Hierdurch teilen wir Ihnen mit, daß Ihre Kamera beim Fundbüro abgegeben worden ist.
11. Bis dahin kannst du fahren, dann mußt du zu Fuß (gehen).
12. Es war eine jener / von jenen der Telefonnummern, die immer besetzt sind.
13. Hiermit bestätige ich den Empfang / den Eingang Ihres Briefes.
14. Ich werde noch darauf zurückkommen.
15. Was verstehen Sie darunter?
16. Er hatte dadurch große Verluste.
17. Ich habe mir nichts dabei gedacht.
18. Jene Bücher können/dürfen Sie (sich) bei der Bibliothek nicht ausleihen.
19. Hierüber sprechen wir noch.
20. Darüber läßt sich streiten.

160B

dies, dieser, diesem, dieses

160C

denjenigen, denjenigen, denjenigen, derjenige

160D

darüber, dabei, dagegen, davon, dabei

161A

1. Ich suche einen Rechner, den man mit Netzstrom betreiben kann.
2. Ein Staubsauger ist eine Maschine, mit der man Teppiche säubert.
3. Das Haus, das wir kaufen wollen, liegt weit vom Bahnhof entfernt.
4. Das Mädchen, an das du denkst, ist gerade in den Bus (ein)gestiegen.
5. Der Roman, den ich lese, ist aus dem Russischen übersetzt worden.
6. Das Baby hat die ganze Nacht durchgeschlafen, was wir nicht erwartet haben.
7. Die Studenten, deren Examen vorbei waren, tranken im Garten Champagner.
8. Alles, was er mir erzählt hat, habe ich auf Tonband aufgenommen.
9. Die Möbel, die dir gefallen, wurden aus Schweden eingeführt.
10. Es gibt eine Karte für Busse und Bahnen, die die ganze Familie benutzen kann.

11. Die BRD zählt glücklicherweise zu den Ländern, in denen es nicht an Wasser mangelt / fehlt.
12. Im Sommer badeten wir in einem See, dessen Wasser kalt und klar war.
13. Der Ingenieur, dem wir gestern begegneten, ist gerade befördert worden.
14. Das, was am meisten Spaß macht, ist hier verboten.

161B

den, dem, dem, die, dem, der

161C

die, der, denen, denen

162A

1. Keine Eile! Jeder kommt d(a)ran / an die Reihe.
2. Sämtliche Veranstaltungen des Festspiels waren schon letzte Woche ausverkauft.
3. (Im Jahre) 1789 hat man mit dem Bau des Brandenburger Tor begonnen.
4. Das kann jeder sagen.
5. Jeder dritte Erwachsene in diesem Land hat Übergewicht.
6. Blickt man sich um / Wenn man sich um blickt, erkennt man, wie schön die Landschaft ist.
7. Man muß sich damit nicht abfinden.
8. Alle haben / Jeder hat nur eins im Sinn.
9. Dieses Blatt gibt einem nicht genügend Informationen.
10. Er hat sich schon um mehrere Stellen beworben.
11. 'Alles Gute,' sagte er und stieg in den Wagen ein.
12. Niemand konnte vorhersagen, daß Deutschland 1990 vereinigt wäre.
13. Als wir alle tanzten, hat (irgend)jemand die Polizei angerufen.
14. Wer zu spät ankommt, den bestraft das Leben.
15. Wer als erster keine Steine mehr hat, ist Sieger.
16. Wasser ist die Quelle allen Lebens.
17. Haben Sie (irgend)jemanden in der Botschaft erreichen können?
18. Sämtliche Produkte werden in diesem Jahr FCKW-frei hergestellt.
19. Einige (Leute) haben ihre Karten im voraus gekauft.

162B

alles, alle, allen

162C
jeder, man, irgendwo, allen, keiner, jeder, jeder, kein, jedem, jemand

163A
1. Welcher Roman hat Ihnen am besten gefallen?
2. Wen hast du gefragt?
3. Woran denkst du eigentlich?
4. Er fragte, ob es eine Busverbindung nach Schwandorf gibt.
5. Wessen Büro ist im obersten Stock?
6. Welchen Film möchten Sie lieber sehen?
7. Wer hat den Paß bei der Polizei abgegeben?
8. In welchem Labor hat man dieses Experiment gemacht?
9. Warum springt denn der Motor nicht an?
10. Um wieviel Uhr hat die Bank zugemacht?
11. Was für einen Geschäftswagen fahren Sie?
12. Wo und wann treffen wir uns?
13. Worüber und mit wem haben Sie im Hotel gesprochen?
14. Worauf legen Sie viel Wert?
15. Auf wen kann ich mich verlassen?
16. Worauf warten Sie?
17. Wem haben Sie geraten, diese Aktien zu kaufen?
18. Worum geht es?

163B
1. Was für ein Mensch war Heinz?
2. Wo wohnte Klöpfgeißel?
3. Was war Heinz von Beruf?
4. Wessen Tochter war Bärbel?
5. Warum konnte Klöpfgeißel (die) Bärbel nicht heiraten?
6. Wann ging der Vater aus dem Haus?
7. Wen traf Klöpfgeißel abends?
8. Wie oft besuchte Heinz Bärbel?

164A
1. Ich habe die richtige Stelle schließlich gefunden.
2. Sie haben das alte Bauernhaus verkauft.
3. Hast du die französische Villa gemietet, die du gesehen hast?
4. Die breiten Straßen der Hauptstadt waren voller Autos.
5. Die erschöpften Flüchtlinge sind endlich in Sicherheit gelangt.
6. Die zwei Männer hatten dieselbe glänzende Idee.
7. An der nächsten Haltestelle ist sie aus dem Bus ausgestiegen.
8. Das Feuer bedrohte Häuser und eines der bekanntesten Hotels.

9. Die ergriffenen Maßnahmen haben schneller als erwartet gewirkt.
10. Züge verkehren jetzt durch den neu eröffneten Tunnel.
11. Tu die geschälten Kartoffeln in das kochende Wasser.
12. Der neue Mercedes ist jetzt lieferbar.
13. Stell das Buch bitte ins oberste Regal!
14. Sie übernachten in einem der teuersten Hotels der Stadt.
15. Der Fahrer hat die rote Ampel nicht gesehen.

164B

italienischen, junge, begabte, schönen, launischen, lieben, treuen, hochintelligenten, tüchtigen, attraktiven, Richtigen

164C

langen, romantischen, bunten, ungezählten, andere, unbekannte, verschlafenen, weiten, fruchtbaren, bizarren, ideale

165A

1. Meine Frau schenkte mir eine teure Uhr zum Geburtstag.
2. Dein brauner Lederkoffer ist abhanden gekommen.
3. Sie durchblätterte eine deutsche Zeitschrift.
4. Ich fahre einen umweltfreundlichen Wagen.
5. Eine japanische Fabrik steht jetzt da, wo einst/früher seine alte Schule stand.
6. Wann besuchst du unser Berliner Büro?
7. Sie wurden mit einem versteckten Fotoapparat / mit einer versteckten Kamera fotografiert.
8. In Spanien haben wir einen Mann mit einem komischen Hut gesehen.
9. Gehen Sie an einer alten Kirche vorbei und biegen Sie rechts ab.
10. Der Makler trug ein blaues Hemd und einen grauen Anzug.
11. Die Firma wird einen neuen Vertrag aushandeln müssen.
12. Ein weiterer Anstieg der Zinsen ist zu erwarten.
13. Das ist ein kleiner Schritt für den Menschen und ein großer Sprung für die Menschheit.
14. Diese Entwicklung ist Teil eines neuen Investitions-Planes.
15. Nach dem Abendessen saßen die Gäste vor einem offenen Kamin.
16. Heute habe ich einen sehr hektischen Tag gehabt.
17. Brauchst du heute nacht eine Wolldecke?
18. Er sucht ein bequemes Hotel.
19. Haben Sie ein scharfes Messer mit(gebracht)?

165B

herben, tiefen, kleinen, alte, schwarzes, schlohweißes, massives, lange, dunkle, dichten, lichtdurchfluteten

166A

1. Er hatte noch drei italienische Briefmarken in seine Brieftasche.
2. Dieser Film ist für kleine Kinder geeignet.
3. Wir kauften frisches Obst im hiesigen Markt.
4. Alte Medikamente sollte man wegwerfen.
5. Das Fleisch sollte auf heißen Tellern serviert werden.
6. Trotz starken Nebels beschlossen sie, nach Schottland zu fahren.
7. Diese Firma baut Häuser mit Materialen von hoher Qualität.
8. Nach Ansicht deutscher Ärzte verursacht Ozon keine dauerhaften Gesundheitsschäden.
9. Man sieht immer mehr ausländische LKWs Lastwagen auf den Straßen.
10. Der Manager sprach mit streikenden Arbeitern.
11. Die Regierung hat günstige Voraussetzungen für den Konjunkturaufschwung geschaffen.
12. Er hat eine Leidenschaft / Er schwärmt für schnelle Autos.
13. Die Sitzung findet hinter geschlossenen Türen statt.
14. Grüne/Unreife Bananen sind ungesund.
15. Streuen Sie gehackte Petersilie darüber!
16. Die Finanzberater wurden wegen gewisser Versäumnisse getadelt/kritisiert.
17. Diese Firma hat eine schöne Auswahl guter Spiele.
18. Alle Produkte werden nach strengen Qualitätsnormen hergestellt.

166B

(i) zwanzigjährigen, alleinlebender, alleinlebender, männlicher
(ii) limitierter, metallisierter, folgender, abgedunkelte, getönte, gepolsterte, spezielle
(iii) industrielles, spannendes, erholsame, lebendiges, regionalen

167A

1. Ich möchte gern den neuesten Film sehen.
2. In Bayern befindet sich / ist der höchste Berg in Deutschland / Deutschlands.
3. Einen besseren Schläger finden Sie da drüben.
4. Die nächste U-Bahn-Station ist 500m entfernt.

5. Der Analphabetismus ist in den ärmsten Ländern weit verbreitet.
6. Der Kaffee könnte stärker sein.
7. Hier ist der Fluß am tiefsten.
8. Die längsten Tage im Jahr sind normalerweise auch die wärmsten (Tage).
9. Könnten Sie bitte langsamer fahren?
10. Die teuersten Autos sind am bequemsten / die bequemsten.
11. Das Telefon ist eine der nützlichsten Erfindungen des 20. Jahrhunderts.
12. Haben Sie etwas Preiswerteres / Billigeres?
13. Spieglein, Spieglein an der Wand, wer ist die Schönste im ganzen Land?
14. In welcher Stadt regnet es am häufigsten?
15. Ich brauche einen schnelleren Computer.
16. Russisch ist viel einfacher zu lernen als Japanisch.
17. Ist unser neuer Mitarbeiter ehrgeiziger als der Abteilungsleiter?
18. Im Augenblick ist Edinburg kälter als Moskau.
19. Je größer die Mengen, die Sie bestellen, desto niedriger / billiger die Preise (,die Sie bezahlen).
20. Herr Schwarz arbeitet am zuverlässigsten / ist der zuverlässigste Arbeiter.

167B

immer weniger, immer häufiger, immer mehr, am ehesten, am deutlichsten, weniger

167C

längsten, tiefsten, nächsten, interessantesten, modernste

168A

1. Ich sammle Briefmarken aus aller Welt.
2. Kaufst du noch den/jenen Gebrauchtwagen?
3. Er weiß, was er tut/macht.
4. Diese Quellen beweisen/zeigen, daß sein Ziel klar war.
5. Der Vortrag endet gegen 22 Uhr.
6. Sie vergißt immer ihren Paß .
7. Der Weltmeister tritt in den Ring.
8. Sprichst du fließend Griechisch?
9. Ich angle gern im Ammersee.
10. Wohin läufst du?
11. Der Arzt mißt den Blutdruck des Patienten regelmäßig.

12. Paß auf, daß du dich nicht daran stößt!
13. Die Familie Schmidt lädt uns jedes Jahr ein.
14. Diese Woche wechsle ich £500.
15. Atme(n Sie) durch die Nase [formal]!
16. Es wird dunkel.
17. Werner hilft ihm bei der Arbeit.
18. Wie heißt du?
19. Hans ißt kein Fleisch – er ist Vegetarier.
20. Mutti! Franz bindet die Lotte an einen Baum!

168B

ist, errichtet, ausstrahlt, gibt, gewährt, läßt, ist, entwickelt, engagieren, hat, beginnt, tragen, können, sind, darf, gilt, gebärden, kann, engagieren, läßt . . . zu

168C

ist, steht, benötigt, entspricht, ist, fahre, befördern, haben, müssen, rächen sich, rumpelt, schließt sich . . . an, bringt, weigert sich, annimmt, gilt, muß, benutzt, fällt, sind, ablegt, fahren, nimmt, liegt, weiß, wird, dauert

169A

1. Letzten Herbst kaufte er einen japanischen Wagen.
2. Sie wartete im strömenden Regen auf den Bus.
3. Er nickte und öffnete sein Tagebuch.
4. Er reichte der Prinzessin eine Schachtel Zigaretten.
5. Die Maschine startete pünktlich von Hannover.
6. Der Klempner reparierte das Rohr innerhalb einer Stunde.
7. Der Brand verursachte einen Sachschaden, der auf 500.000 DM geschätzt wird.
8. Der Oberst eröffnete ein Konto bei der Dresdner Bank.
9. Sie fürchtete, daß ihr Mobiltelefon nicht funktionierte.
10. Am Dienstag beobachtete ein Spion ihr Treffen.
11. Es hagelte gestern überall in der Stadt.
12. Die Mädchen lächelten und winkten, bis die Fähre losfuhr / abfuhr.
13. Von der Bundesstraße zweigte ein kleiner Pfad / Weg zum Wald ab.
14. Der Koch setzte sich an den Schreibtisch und stützte den Kopf in die Hände.
15. Sie überlegte, ob sie ihren Freund / ihre Freundin um ein Darlehen bitten solle.
16. Plötzlich richtetest du deinen Blick auf mich.

17. Der Bauunternehmer kritzelte ein paar Zahlen auf ein Stück(chen) Papier.
18. Wir verhandelten monatelang mit den Arabern über diesen Vertrag.
19. Die Politiker beglückwünschten die Fußballspieler zu ihrem Erfolg.
20. Wir sparten (Geld) auf / für einen Mercedes.

169B

bäumte, zerrten, feuchtete . . . an, spritzte, legte, hörte, klopfte, mochte / mag, hockte, öffnete, lallte

170A

1. Hat dir sein neuer Film gefallen?
2. Er verlor seine Notizen immer vor den Sitzungen.
3. Die Messe fand letztes Jahr in Leipzig statt.
4. Der Kellner empfahl diesen australischen Wein.
5. Der Geschäftsmann flog nach München und kam um drei Uhr im Büro an.
6. Er sprang von seinem Pferd, lief bis zur Theke und trank zwei Whisky.
7. Das Hündchen fiel vom Stuhl.
8. Meyers blieben im Wartesaal.
9. Die Finnen schossen innerhalb von achtzehn Minuten sieben Tore im Eishockeyspiel.
10. Wir vergaßen, Zwiebeln und Knoblauch zu kaufen.
11. Sie versprach, ihn zur Ausstellung zu begleiten.
12. Soldaten rissen 1989 die Berliner Mauer ab.
13. Sie fuhren mit der U-Bahn zu seinem Onkel.
14. Am Bahnhof aß er eine Wurst und trank ein Glas Sprudel / Wasser.
15. An der Grenze gerieten / kamen wir in Schwierigkeiten.
16. Am Samstag schien die Sonne den ganzen Tag.
17. Der Chirurg befand sich in einer schwierigen Lage.
18. Vor der Operation wog der Patient 85 Kilo.
19. Der Vertreter verließ das Hotel um halb sieben.
20. Mein Vetter besaß mehrere wertvolle Ölgemälde.

170B

hatte, hatte, bevorzugten, griffen, erhoben, erstritten, stieß, gelang, ließen, scherten, führten, wollten, wurde, hatte

170C

verlor, spürte, gab, raste, prallte, teilte . . . mit, überschlug, schleuderte, landete

171A

1. Bevor wir auf die Fähre fuhren, hatten wir vollgetankt.
2. Wollen wir gehen? Ich habe schon bezahlt.
3. Bevor die Witwe das Haus verließ hat, hatte sie ihren Koffer gepackt.
4. Weißt du, ob er aus Siberien hat anrufen können?
5. Man hatte ursprünglich eine Tankstelle auf diesem Grundstück bauen wollen.
6. Haben Sie je das Bedürfnis verspürt / Lust gehabt, alles aufzugeben und ins Kloster zu gehen?
7. Habt ihr euch als Kinder für Briefmarken interessiert?
8. Die Waschmaschine war kaputt, also habe ich sie selber / selbst repariert.
9. Ich habe dir ein riesiges Essen vorbereitet. Hoffentlich hast du Hunger.
10. Man ist den Geschäftsleuten überall hingefolgt.
11. Den ganzen Tag (lang) habe ich nur / lauter Sirenen gehört.
12. Der Vorsitzende hat gerade einen Bericht über die Verhandlungen erstattet.
13. Mein Freund hat mir seinen Wagen zur Verfügung gestellt.
14. Ödipus war sein ganzes Leben vom Schicksal verfolgt.
15. Die Polizei hatte den Täter schon mehrmals verhaftet.
16. Die Mannschaft hat bis zum Ende des Spiels zäh gekämpft.
17. Herr Dr Schneider hat sich (bei der Arbeit) für die Firma kaputtgemacht.
18. Der neue Professor hat die Neugier der Studenten geweckt.
19. Der Direktor hat den Beschluß gefaßt, fünfzehn Mitarbeiter zu entlassen.
20. Der Passagier hat auf den roten Knopf gedrückt.

171B

hat . . . verkündet, hat . . . angekündigt, hat . . . angeordnet, hatte . . . eingeführt, hatte . . . vorbereitet

172A

1. Der Autoverkehr hat in den letzten Jahren erheblich zugenommen.
2. Er hatte ein Versprechen abgelegt, nie darüber zu sprechen.
3. Ich habe viel Schlimmeres gesehen.
4. Ein 19-jähriger hat eine Rentnerin überfallen.
5. Die Mutter hat vor Wut geschrieen, nachdem ihr Kind Orangensaft auf den Teppich vergossen hatte.

6. Fritz ist mit dem Schäferhund spazierengegangen.
7. Die Umstände hat der Richter natürlich in Betracht gezogen.
8. Bei der Besteigung der Zugspitze ist er in Schwierigkeiten geraten.
9. Dieser berühmte Stürmer hat neun Tore in der Weltmeisterschaft geschossen.
10. Nachdem der letzte Gast gegangen war, spülte der Gastgeber in der Küche.
11. Die Lebenshaltungskosten sind im letzten Jahr um 7% (an) gestiegen.
12. Das Gesetz ist schon in Kraft getreten.
13. Der Eigentümer hat seine Küche ausbauen lassen.
14. Der Elektriker hatte sich in den Finger geschnitten.
15. Es war mir nie gelungen, der Versuchung zu widerstehen.
16. Hat dir die Oper gefallen?
17. Die Entscheidung ist so (aus)gefallen, wie wir es gehofft hatten.
18. Nachdem er den Kühlschrank in die Küche getragen hatte, setzte er sich auf einen Stuhl.
19. Ich war sicher, daß ich seine Anweisungen richtig verstanden hatte.
20. Haben Sie das Ergebnis mit der gestern gehaltenen Umfrage verglichen?

172B

ist . . . zugefallen, war . . . vorbeigegangen, gehalten ist, verstorben waren, waren . . . gewesen, hatte . . . bestiegen

172C

gerichtet war, gesessen hatte, war weggelaufen, gewesen waren, war . . . eingereiht, ausgeschnauft hatte

173A

1. Mercedes wird den neuen 6-Zylinder-Motor von Volkswagen A. G. beziehen / erhalten.
2. Die Gesellschaft wird mehr als 2 Milliarden DM in das Projekt investieren.
3. In der neuen Fabrik werden bis zu 3.000 Arbeitnehmer tätig sein.
4. Das Produkt wird billiger sein als / nicht so viel kosten wie / das Vorgängermodell.
5. Mein Freund wird wohl die Waschmaschine reparieren können.
6. Die Gäste werden schon auf dem Heimweg sein.
7. Der Ministerpräsident wird mit den anderen Parteien verhandeln müssen.

8. Bis Monatsende werden wir eine Lösung gefunden haben.
9. Der letzte Bus wird mittlerweile abgefahren sein.
10. Bis Jahresende wird meine Tochter lesen gelernt haben.
11. Der Wahlkampf wird wahrscheinlich im Oktober stattfinden.
12. Ich werde wahrscheinlich das Haus meines Onkels erben.

173B

(i) wird . . . geben, wird . . . kommen
(ii) wird . . . sein, wird . . . hinweghelfen, wird . . . .gehen

174A

1. Darf ich das Fenster aufmachen?
2. Wir werden nicht zum Empfang gehen dürfen.
3. Sie soll sehr reich sein.
4. Er wird nie Holländisch sprechen können.
5. Sie hat nie pendeln müssen.
6. Er hat immer in die Tschechische Republik fahren wollen.
7. Er durfte nicht ins Labor gehen / das Labor nicht betreten.
8. Das mag wohl wahr sein.
9. Er mußte es wiederholen.
10. Sie sollten am Nachmittag (an)kommen.
11. Er kann Berichte sehr schnell zusammenfassen, nicht wahr?
12. Er konnte die russische Zeitung lesen.
13. Magst du Karrotten / Möhren?
14. Er muß es um 6 Uhr getan haben.
15. Du hattest in einem Schnellimbiß arbeiten wollen.
16. Wirst du es bis nächste Woche fertig machen können?
17. Darf ich hereinkommen?
18. Ich möchte zwei Flaschen Olivenöl und ein Kilo Apfelsinen / Orangen.
19. Wir wollten eine Kristallvase kaufen.
20. Du sollst nicht stehlen.

174B

wollen, dürfen, müssen, wollen, können

174C

müssen, müssen, müssen, könne, solle

175A

1. Leider haben sich ihre Eltern vor kurzem scheiden lassen.
2. Diese Fehler lassen sich schnell mit einem Makro korrigieren.

3. Ich habe mir die Haare schneiden lassen.
4. Richard läßt dich grüßen, fügte er hinzu.
5. Nach dem Unfall mußte sie sich gründlich untersuchen lassen.
6. Der Wasserverbrauch läßt sich mit diesem Gerät erheblich reduzieren.
7. Gewiß läßt sich noch mehr tun.
8. Das läßt sich leicht ändern.
9. Seine Freunde haben ihn im Stich gelassen.
10. Ich wollte meine Genehmigung verlängern lassen.
11. Ich lasse es mich etwas kosten.
12. Der Minister hat seinen Berater zu sich kommen lassen.
13. Sie hatte beim Geschirrspülen eine Untertasse fallen lassen.
14. Wir ließen uns nicht beeindrucken.
15. Der General hat zusätzliche Soldaten in die Stadt verlegen lassen.
16. Eine Menge Müll läßt sich einsparen, wenn man Mehrwegflaschen kauft / benutzt.
17. Ich weiß schon, daß er sein Auto hat reparieren lassen müssen.
18. Der Metzger hat sich einen Bart wachsen / stehen lassen.
19. Ich werde meinen Tennisschläger zu Hause lassen.
20. Laßt euch von niemandem und nichts beirren.

175B

has had to listen to reason, can be read as accounts of dreams, the world can be understood as a dream

176A

1. Was hat der Kellner empfohlen?
2. Wir unterschrieben den Vertrag sofort.
3. Der Zollbeamte fragte, was wir zu verzollen hätten.
4. Er hinterließ seinem Neffen ein ganzes Vermögen.
5. Er hatte nicht das richtige Wort betont.
6. Er fuhr in die Stadt, um Geld von der Bank abzuheben.
7. Er ist bei der Prüfung zum zweiten Mal durchgefallen.
8. Jenes häßliche Hochhaus wird abgerissen (werden).
9. Der Professor unterbrach seinen Vortrag, um einen Schluck Wasser zu trinken.
10. Der Hund lief auf die Straße und verursachte einen Unfall.
11. Die Größe des Doms imponierte ihnen.
12. Bayern München, seine Lieblingsmannschaft, hat eine schwere Niederlage erlitten.
13. Der Diplomat mißtraute dem Frieden im Balkan.

14. Ein Affe griff einen Touristen im Naturschutzgebiet an.
15. Ich wiederhole den Satz noch einmal.
16. Der Glockenturm wurde durch ein Erdbeben zerstört.
17. Die Armee / Das Heer zerschlug allen Widerstand.
18. Entwerten Sie Ihren Fahrschein, bevor Sie in den Zug steigen!
19. Der Student hat sein Konto überzogen / überzog sein Konto.
20. Ich kann allem widerstehen, nur der Versuchung nicht.

176B

dreht sich . . . vorbei, umgeht, verringern sich, schieben sich . . . heraus, bereiten . . . vor, überqueren, ergreifen, packe . . . auf, mache . . . fest, stolpere . . . hinunter, sehe ich mich um, bietet . . . an, wende mich ab, lächelt . . . an

177A

1. Ich habe vor, am Freitag Nachmittag anzukommen.
2. Er hoffte, die Staus auf der Ringstraße zu vermeiden.
3. Ich schlug vor, eine Runde Golf zu spielen.
4. Es ist verboten / untersagt, in der U-Bahn zu rauchen.
5. Der Kellner hatte vergessen, Senf zu bringen.
6. Sie will nichts damit zu tun haben.
7. Es ist (der Firma) Eurotunnel gelungen, einen Tunnel unter dem Kanal zu bauen.
8. Es ist wichtig, die richtigen Akten zur Konferenz mitzubringen.
9. Er hat mehrere Banken überredet, kräftig zu investieren.
10. Die Russen haben versprochen, der chinesischen Industrie zu helfen.
11. Morgen versuchen wir, mit der Botschaft Kontakt aufzunehmen / die Botschaft anzurufen.
12. Haben Sie Zeit, diesen Bericht durchzulesen?
13. Die Polizisten sind hereingekommen, ohne zu klopfen / ohne anzuklopfen.
14. Jeder Form von politischem Extremismus ist zu widerstehen / muß man widerstehen.
15. Ich habe keine Lust, Unkraut zu jäten.
16. Um eine Pizza vorzubereiten, braucht man unter anderem Teig, Tomaten und Käse.
17. Es wird nie möglich sein, die Motive der Täter nachzuweisen.
18. Der Rhein hält den traurigen Rekord, der am stärksten verschmutzte Fluß Mitteleuropas zu sein.
19. Es ist notwendig, Vorsorge zu treffen.

177B

durchzusehen, sinken zu lassen, anzuklopfen, zu verlangen, vorzusprechen, zu gehen, zu lassen, zu reden, zu gehen, bemerken zu können, zu orientieren, einzuwenden, abzuwarten, zu konzentrieren

178A

1. Er sagt, er habe zu viel Arbeit.
2. Die Sekretärin behauptet, der Chef laufe im Park.
3. Der Patient sagte, er sei schon lange krank.
4. Würden/Könnten Sie mir bitte einen Gefallen tun?
5. Könnten Sie mir bitte den Pfeffer reichen?
6. Die Geschäftsfrau erklärte, ihre Kinder besuchten ihren Onkel.
7. Hans sagte, er würde spät nach Hause kommen.
8. Das Ehepaar erklärte, es sei / wäre am Sonntag ins Kino gegangen.
9. Ihr Chef sagt, sie müsse fleißiger / tüchtiger arbeiten.
10. Der Arzt riet dem Patienten, er solle / sollte nicht rauchen.
11. Dürfte ich Sie bitten, diesen Brief (in den Briefkasten) einzuwerfen?
12. Der Journalist berichtet, das Gesetz werde bis Monatsende verabschiedet werden.
13. Ich hätte den Zug beinahe verpaßt / nicht mehr erreicht.
14. Könnten Sie gegen sechs Uhr vorbeikommen?
15. Das hätten wir geschafft!
16. Er sagte, er habe eine gute Nachricht (zu berichten).
17. Der Staatssekretär stimmte damit überein, daß es eine ausgezeichnete Möglichkeit für die Beendigung des Krieges darstelle.

178B

hätten gesehen, gegangen sei, gefangen habe, habe gesehen, zurückgekehrt sei

178C

sei, einnähmen, habe, könne, habe, repräsentiere, angehe, sei, übe, verfüge

178D

habe . . . gehabt wie wir, habe sich . . . bemessen, seien, habe sich . . . ausgedehnt, beginne, habe sich . . . verdreifacht, sei . . . geworden, gebe . . . aus, rangiere . . . an, entfielen, gehöre

179A

1. Wenn ich Zeit habe, werde ich dich in Venedig besuchen.
2. Wenn er das wüßte, würde er nicht fragen.

3. Wäre die Straßenbahn pünktlich am Bahnhof angekommen, so hätten wir den Zug nicht versäumt / verpaßt.
4. Wenn er nach Berlin gefahren wäre, hätte er den Auftrag / die Arbeit erledigt.
5. Wenn das Projekt klappt, könnte es später ausgedehnt werden.
6. Was wäre geschehen, wenn der Strom ausgefallen wäre?
7. Wenn du schneller arbeitetest, könntest du mehr verdienen.
8. Es wäre ratsam, wenn du mich vorher anriefst.
9. Wenn du dir Mühe gegeben hättest, hättest du den Termin einhalten können.
10. Wäre die Europäische Union in einer besseren Lage, wenn Großbritannien früher beigetreten wäre?
11. Wenn die Verschmutzung nicht weiter begrenzt wird, (so) verschlechtert sich der Treibhauseffekt .
12. Wenn wir jenes baufällige Haus kauften, würden wir eine Menge Geld ausgeben müssen, um es zu renovieren / würden wir für die Renovierung eine Menge Geld ausgeben müssen.
13. Wenn er den Vortrag gehört hätte, hätte er viel über Rilkes Gedichte erfahren.
14. Wenn ich Zeit gehabt hätte, hätte ich mir die Haare schneiden lassen.
15. Wenn er in der Sitzung nichts gesagt hätte, hätte er Gewissensbisse bekommen.
16. Auch wenn alle Kassen geöffnet wären, würden sie diesen Menschenandrang nicht bewältigen.
17. Wenn die Alarmglocke ertönt, verlassen Sie sofort das Gebäude.
18. Ihnen würden dieses Thema nicht gleichgültig sein, wenn Sie die Fernsehsendung gesehen hätten.
19. Auch wenn ich die Lotterie gewonnen hätte, hätte ich nicht aufgehört zu arbeiten.
20. Wenn Sie das deutsche Wort nicht kennen, schlagen Sie es im Wörterbuch nach.

179B

hätte sich . . . entschieden, wäre . . . gestoßen, wäre . . . eingefallen, hätte er sich . . . entschlossen, hätte . . . getragen, wäre . . . geworden, wäre . . . geblieben, hätte . . . geendet

180A

1. Fragen Sie / Frag ihn nach dem Weg zum Dorf!
2. Helfen Sie / Hilf der alten Dame!

3. Gehen Sie / Geh um die Ecke!
4. Kaufen Sie / Kauf eine Tageskarte! Sie ist sehr günstig / billig / preiswert.
5. Bleiben Sie / Bleib hier!
6. Geben Sie / Gib ihm deinen / Ihren Kuli / Kugelschreiber / Füller!
7. Ziehen Sie sich / Zieh dich sofort an!
8. Steig (in den Zug) ein! / Steigen Sie ein! / Einsteigen!
9. Seien Sie / Sei artig!
10. Hören Sie / Hör mal / gut zu!
11. Wecken Sie / Weck mich um 6 Uhr auf bitte!
12. Schreiben Sie / Schreib es in dein / Ihr Tagebuch!
13. Machen Sie / Mach das Licht bitte aus!
14. Unterschreiben Sie / Unterschreib das Formular bitte unten!
15. Holen Sie / Hol den Besucher vom Flughafen ab!
16. Heben Sie / Heb jene Kiste hoch!
17. Prüfen Sie / Prüf bitte die / jene Zahlen!
18. Steigen Sie / Steig in Stuttgart um!
19. Raten Sie / Rate mal, was ich gekauft habe!
20. Halten Sie / Halte durch!

180B

zieh, stell, benutze, achte, nutze, achte, benutze, verzichte, bewässere, achte, gieße, gib, zeig, verzichte, verwende

181A

1. Das Rheinwasser wird durch Schadstoffe gefährdet.
2. Die Folgen des sauren Regens wurden zuerst in skandinavischen Ländern beobachtet.
3. Es wurde getanzt und gesungen.
4. Die Bahn wird durch Mineralölsteuererhöhungen finanziert werden.
5. Der Käfer ist seit langem in Deutschland nicht hergestellt worden.
6. Wir hoffen, daß ein Impfstoff entwickelt werden wird.
7. Widerrechtlich abgestellte Fahrzeuge werden abgeschleppt.
8. Sie wurden mitten in der Nacht verhaftet.
9. Der Film ist in Deutschland von mehr als 5 Millionen Zuschauern gesehen worden.
10. Die Angeklagten wurden beschuldigt, Autos gestohlen zu haben.
11. Operationen werden gegen Ende des Jahres aus Kostengründen verschoben.
12. 1883 wurden auf einer Ausstellung in Wien elektrische Staubsauger gezeigt.

13. Alle zwei Minuten wird in Deutschland in eine Wohnung eingebrochen.
14. Dein Anzug kann am nächsten Dienstag von der Reinigung abgeholt werden.
15. Die Antworten dürfen nicht mit Bleistift geschrieben werden.
16. Maßnahmen müssen ergriffen werden, um eine weitere Luftverschmutzung zu verhindern.
17. An der Grenze wurde das Auto von Zollbeamten angehalten.
18. Der Auftrag wird vor deiner Rückkehr erledigt worden sein.
19. Die Zusammenarbeit der beiden Gesellschaften soll auch in der Zukunft fortgesetzt werden.
20. Das europäische Parlament wird auf fünf Jahre gewählt.
21. Der Preis für ein Pfund Kaffee wurde um zwei DM erhöht.

181B

werden . . . zugelassen, gesendet werden, verurteilt wird

181C

berücksichtigt . . . gewichtet werden, verbunden werden, intensiviert wird, wahrgenommen werden, umgesetzt werden

181D

1. Die Menge des von Haushalten beseitigten Abfalls erhöht sich jede Woche.
2. Die vom Arzt verschriebenen Medikamente muß man zweimal pro Tag / täglich / am Tag nehmen.
3. Hat man bei Ihnen eine schwarze Brieftasche abgegeben?
4. Hinter den von Polizisten bewachten Absperrungen waren die Straßen voller Autos.
5. Nachtfahrten sind zu vermeiden, da Sie den Schlafrhythmus der Kinder stören.
6. Der Lernerfolg bei den Japanern ist nicht zu unterschätzen.
7. In der Bibliothek war kein Geräusch / nichts zu hören.
8. Man sollte sich fragen / die Frage stellen, warum die Firma in Südafrika nicht investiert hat.
9. Die Menge des in Deutschland getrunkenen Biers hat sich verringert.
10. Bei Alleinstehenden ist ein Anstieg um 25% registriert worden.
11. Dieses Produkt verkauft sich in allen Filialen.
12. Natürlich haben wir Angst, daß man Betriebsgeheimnisse preisgeben könnte.
13. Man verbraucht zu viel Papier.
14. Man sollte in Betracht ziehen, daß er keine Erfahrung hat.

15. Die Zahl der Unfälle war sich worden.
16. Dieser Streitpunkt kann in unserer nächsten Besprechung geklärt werden.
17. Man sollte sich die Haare alle drei Tage waschen.
18. Busfahrkarten kann man in diesem Geschäft kaufen.

182A

1. In kleinen Lokalen reden die Männer über Fußball und schließen Wetten auf das kommende Italien Spiel ab.
2. Das Wasser ist im Freibad kalt, aber wir gehen trotzdem schwimmen.
3. Er wollte Schriftsteller werden, jedoch hatte er zu wenig Einbildungskraft.
4. Die Stadtverwaltung war nicht mehr im alten Turm sondern war in ein modernes Bürohaus umgezogen.
5. Er setzte seinen Sonnenhut auf und begann, den Rasen zu mähen.
6. Diese Kabel bieten Ihnen nicht nur britisches Fernsehen, sondern auch Sendungen aus ganz Europa.
7. Für die Wanderung bringen Sie einen Anorak, Stiefel sowie eine Landkarte mit.
8. Dieses Auto hat einen Dieselmotor, das heißt man kann / darf kein Normalbenzin tanken.
9. Er ging in die Küche, denn er wollte die Spülmaschine anmachen / anschalten.
10. Er wollte am Samstagnachmittag einkaufen, aber alle Geschäfte waren zu geschlossen.
11. Auf dieser Universität kann man europäische, afrikanische sowie asiatische Sprachen studieren.
12. Ich rief den Steuerberater an, denn ich mußte eine neue Steuererklärung machen / abgeben.
13. Sie hat ihren Geldbeutel stundenlang gesucht, hat ihn aber nicht gefunden.
14. Damals war Salz soviel wert wie Gold, doch heutzutage streut man Salz tonnenweise auf die Straßen.
15. Es wird eine lange Reise. Nehmen Sie einen Roman, Spielkarten sowie etwas zu essen mit.

182B

weder, noch, oder, und, doch, doch, und

182C

dann, denn, sondern, doch, aber, doch

183A

1. Ich freue mich auf meinen Urlaub in Griechenland, zumal ich dort viele Freunde habe.
2. Ich hoffe, daß das Baby bald laufen lernt.
3. Die meisten Leute wollen sich, wenn sie von der Arbeit nach Hause kommen, bloß in einen Sessel plumpsen / fallen lassen.
4. Sie hat mich nicht angerufen, obwohl sie Großbritannien besuchte.
5. Je länger er wartete, desto schlimmer wurden seine Zahnschmerzen.
6. Der Artikel darf nicht veröffentlicht werden, bevor er seine Zustimmung gegeben hat.
7. Die in Zitrusfrüchten enthaltene Säure ist so stark / aggressiv, daß sie den Zahnschmelz schädigen kann.
8. Als sie nach Berlin zogen, hatten sie zwei kleine Kinder.
9. Er las den Bericht des Direktors (durch), damit er besser auf das Interview vorbereitet wäre / war.
10. Sobald er am Ferienziel angekommen war, hat er sich das Fußgelenk verrenkt / sich den Fuß vertreten. Kaum war er am Ferienziel angekommen, da hat . . .
11. Da der Wechselkurs so ungünstig steht / ist, können wir uns nur wenige Andenken leisten.
12. Bevor sie ins Theater ging, schminkte sie sich.
13. Statt daß man etwas Sinnvolles mit ihnen anfängt, wurden sie auf die Deponie geworfen.
14. Seine Frau fragte ihn, ob er Kleingeld bei sich hätte / habe.
15. Das Kind lag im Bett und tat als ob es schliefe.
16. Er öffnete den Brief ohne zu zögern.
17. Seitdem er hier unterrichtet, haben viele Studenten Latein gewählt.
18. Statt seine Hausaufgaben zu machen, hat Franz den ganzen Abend ferngesehen.
19. Soweit ich weiß, werden in diesem Feld keine Häuser gebaut werden.
20. Wir haben ein neues Fenster einbauen lassen, so daß das Zimmer heller wird / mehr Licht ins Zimmer kommt.

183B

daß, als, daß, während, wenn, wenn, damit, als, als, wenn

184A

1. Galilei behauptete, daß die Erde sich um die Sonne dreht / drehe.
2. Das Geschäft ist bis nächsten Montag zu geschlossen.

3. Das Liebespaar schlenderte das / am Flußufer entlang.
4. Wider alles Erwarten hat der Faulpelz das Examen bestanden.
5. Ohne deine/Ihre Hilfe hätte ich das nie machen können.
6. Die Familie sitzt um den Tisch.
7. Als ich in Belgien war, hielt man mich für einen Deutschen/eine Deutsche.
8. Nach dem Spaziergang lehnte er sich gegen eine Eiche.
9. Der Umsatz ist im letzten Jahr um ein Viertel gestiegen.
10. Er schaute durchs Fenster, konnte aber niemand(en) sehen.
11. Wieviel hast du für deine Satellitenschüssel bezahlt?
12. Sie hielt das Dia gegen das Licht.
13. Wir haben das Büro für eine halbe Million DM gemietet.
14. Gehen Sie / Geh um die Ecke und durch die Unterführung!
15. Die Maus lief die Wand/die Mauer entlang.

184B

den, den, Kinderbeauftragte, die

185A

1. Viele Grüße aus der Türkei!
2. Seit meinem Urlaub habe ich nur von Ägypten geträumt.
3. Im Augenblick wohne ich bei meinen Schwiegereltern.
4. Von Anfang an hat das Ehepaar nur gestritten.
5. Außer dem Bürgermeister war niemand zu sehen.
6. Er schaute zum Fenster hinaus. Er schaute aus dem Fenster.
7. Dem Gerücht nach / zufolge bekommen wir alle eine Gehaltserhöhung.
8. Beim letzten Fest saß er mir gegenüber.
9. Der neue Fahrplan ist ab nächster Woche gültig. / Ab nächster Woche gilt der. . . .
10. Man wird nicht aus eigener Kraft mit den Drogenproblemen fertig.
11. Die Partei hat bei den Kommunalwahlen eine schwere Niederlage erlitten.
12. Ihre Eltern kommen aus wohlhabenden Verhältnissen.
13. Zu meiner großen Enttäuschung hat sie meine Einladung abgelehnt.
14. In Karate muß man sowohl mit den Händen als auch mit den Füßen kämpfen.
15. Gegenüber der Tankstelle befindet sich ein wunderschönes Fachwerkhaus.
16. Der Buchhalter arbeitet schon seit drei Jahren bei / in dieser Firma.

17. Mein Vetter macht aus seiner Sorge keinen Hehl kein Geheimnise.
18. Er fuhr mit der Straßenbahn zum Konzert.
19. Die junge Mutter schob den Einkaufswagen aus dem Supermarkt (hinaus).
20. Der Manager fragte nach der Wettbewerbsfähigkeit der deutschen Stahlindustrie.

185B

(i) laut, seit, zu, aus, mit, aus, bei, aus
(ii) nach, bei, von, aus, aus, nach, gegenüber, aus, mit, nach, bei, von, nach, aus

185C

der, der erpreßten, beim, der, der, den, weiteren, dem, der, seinem, der, einer, der

186A

1. Er flüchtete über die Schweiz in die Vereinigten Staaten.
2. Der Dieb verschwand über den Gartenzaun.
3. Der Bauer setzte sich an einen Tisch in der Ecke.
4. Er setzte sich neben die Frau des Vorsitzenden.
5. Wir haben eine halbe Stunde an der Bushaltestelle gewartet.
6. An deiner Stelle würde ich das Risiko eingehen.
7. Über dem Bett hängt ein altes Bärenfell.
8. Meine Nichte wohnt auf dem Land(e).
9. Die Schauspielerin küßte Helmut auf die Backe.
10. Unter keinen Umständen dürfen Sie dieses Zimmer verlassen!
11. Der Metzger kann dich unter den Tisch trinken.
12. Um zu verstehen, was er meint, muß man zwischen den Zeilen lesen.
13. Ich werde vor dem Kino auf dich warten.
14. Dort sehen Sie die neue Brücke über die Themse.
15. Ich arbeite immer noch an meiner Doktorarbeit.
16. Du brauchst nicht auf den Tisch zu schlagen / hauen.
17. Der Hund fiel in den Fluß, dann schwamm er ans Ufer.
18. Der Tiger ging in seinem Käfig auf und ab.
19. Das Nachbarkind hat sich in unserem Kleiderschrank eingeschlossen / eingesperrt.
20. Er klopfte an die Tür und ging ins Büro.

186B

den, der, einem, dem, keinem, den, dem, die, den, soziale, die, die, dieser, der

187A

1. Während seines Aufenthalts sprach er viel Deutsch.
2. Wegen des Staus kamen sie mit drei Stunden Verspätung/drei Stunden zu spät in Mannheim an.
3. Die Prager Altstadt liegt unterhalb des Schlosses.
4. Statt eines Radios haben wir eine Stereoanlage gekauft.
5. Trotz des heftigen Regens spielten die Kinder im Garten Fußball.
6. Die Schafe weiden nicht oberhalb einer gewissen Höhe in den Bergen.
7. Ich muß innerhalb der nächsten zwei Wochen einen Käufer finden.
8. Statt einer Geburtstagskarte hat er eine Gasrechnung bekommen.
9. Außerhalb der Sprechstunden ist Dr. Schmidt zu Hause zu erreichen.
10. Der Flug ist wegen technischer Schwierigkeiten verschoben worden.
11. Wegen versuchten Mordes hat ihn das Gericht zu einer lebenslänglichen Freiheitsstrafe verurteilt.
12. Trotz seiner Ausbildung kann er immer noch keine Sicherung einsetzen.
13. Während der Sitzung mußte er seine Frau anrufen.
14. Die Gastgeberin hat das alles meinetwegen getan / gemacht.

187B

1. Außerhalb Europas ist der Alkoholkonsum auch gestiegen.
2. Die Männer in vielen Entwicklungsländern kaufen viel Bier statt Lebensmittel.
3. Trotz der Gefahr des Alkohols für die Bevölkerung läßt die Regierung den Alkoholkonsum nicht bremsen.
4. Wegen des Trinkens muß Trinidad viel Geld im Gesundheitsbereich ausgeben.
5. Trotz der hohen Preise wird viel Geld für Alkohol ausgegeben.
6. Während der letzten 25 Jahre hat sich der Bierverkauf in der Dritten Welt vervielfacht.
7. Der Alkoholkonsum ist wegen der Werbung gestiegen.

188A

1. Niemand zweifelt an Ihren Fähigkeiten.
2. Der Ingenieur ist sehr stolz auf seine Erfindung.
3. In den Ferien hatte er an einer tropischen Krankheit gelitten.
4. Der Vorsitzende ist mit einer Französin verheiratet.
5. Sie mußte sehr lange auf das nächste Luftkissenboot warten.
6. In der Wirtschaftskrise hat er um seine Stellung gebangt / war er um seine Stellung besorgt.
7. Diese Polizisten sorgen für die Sicherheit der Gäste.
8. Er reagierte sofort / blitzschnell auf die Verbilligung der Produkte seines Konkurrenten.
9. Er pochte auf sein Recht, Er bestand auf seinem Recht, mit einem Anwalt zu sprechen.
10. Der Bürgermeister berichtete über seinen Besuch in der Partnerstadt.
11. Während ihres Aufenthalts in Italien hat Ruth an einer Demonstration teilgenommen.
12. Er lachte über unsere Erfahrungen im Hotel.
13. Wir sind sehr dankbar für Ihre Hilfe.
14. In seiner Rede hat er mehrmals auf die Bibel angespielt.
15. Arbeitest du immer noch an deinem Roman?
16. Trinken wir auf die Zukunft!
17. Die Stadtverwaltung ist für die Müllabfuhr verantwortlich.
18. Ich bin mit dieser Erklärung nicht zufrieden.
19. Hast du dich für deine Unhöflichkeit entschuldigt?
20. Herr Ahrens zweifelte an der Wahrheit jener / der Geschichte.

188B

davor, dafür, darum, über, daran

188C

für, auf, aus, dazu, zu, vom, vom, dafür

189A

1. Vor zehn Jahren gab es hier nur Wiesen. Jetzt läuft eine Straße durch diese Gegend.
2. Damals mußte man (auch) am Wochenende arbeiten.
3. Vorgestern hat sie ihren Führerschein gemacht.
4. Zuerst wollen wir die Einzelheiten dieses Plans besprechen, dann machen wir Feierabend.
5. Der Finanzdirektor bekommt nächsten Monat einen neuen Geschäftswagen.

6. Als wir in Dänemark waren, hat es ständig / dauernd geregnet.
7. Da die Telefonnummer ständig besetzt war, mußte er sie immer wieder wählen.
8. Wenn ich besonders beschäftigt bin, esse ich manchmal an einem Schnellimbiß.
9. Die meisten Aktionäre kommen nie zur Jahreshauptversammlung.
10. Schließlich hat die Gesellschaft / Firma Bankrott / Pleite gemacht.
11. Gehst du morgens oder abends schwimmen?
12. Wo einst das alte Schloß stand, dominiert ein mehrstöckiges Kaufhaus.
13. Die Handelsbilanz ist seit einigen Jahren in den roten Zahlen, seitdem haben wir höhere Steuern zahlen müssen.
14. Meinst du, Ausländer sollten künftig stimmberechtigt sein?
15. *Die Zeit* erscheint wöchentlich.
16. Ich komme gleich.
17. Das neue Gesetz tritt übermorgen in Kraft.

189B

eines Morgens, jeden Tag, diesmal, noch niemals, dann, gleichzeitig, sofort, noch niemals, gleich

190A

1. Er steht / ist zweifellos auf dem Höhepunkt seiner Karriere.
2. Nächstes Jahr werden wir wahrscheinlich nach Spanien fahren.
3. Der Vertreter wartet draußen.
4. Gerade / Ausgerechnet heute muß es regnen!
5. Er wird es bestimmt/gewiß sorgfältig überprüft haben.
6. Stellen Sie das Paket dorthin!
7. Ein Visum ist für die Einreise keinesfalls / sicherlich nicht / ganz bestimmt nicht / erforderlich.
8. Die Kinder gingen in die frische Luft hinaus.
9. Kommen Sie sofort herein!
10. Fahnen hingen aus den Fenstern (heraus).
11. Frau Fisch nahm einen schwarzen Rock aus ihrem Koffer (heraus).
12. Als es klingelte, stürzten die Schülerinnen die Treppe hinunter.
13. Komm hierhin / herüber!
14. Ich spiele besonders gern Federball.
15. Die Akte ist unten im Regal.
16. Darf man in deutsche Busse vorne oder hinten einsteigen?
17. Wie komme ich am besten dorthin?
18. Briefe soll man links unten unterschreiben.

190B

besonders, drastisch, selbst, besonders, daher

190C

rund, darüber, nicht, überall, auch, verzweifelt, her, wiederum, nie, auch

191A

1. Ich gab ihnen unsere neue Telefonnummer.
2. Ich fahre jeden Tag mit dem Bus zur Arbeit.
3. Er hat aus finanziellen Gründen das Land verlassen.
4. Wegen der Hitze arbeiten die Lehrer in der Schule nur bis 12 Uhr.
5. Bring es mir sofort (hierher)!
6. Ich komme mit Vergnügen nächste Woche zu eurer Abendgesellschaft / eurem Abendessen.
7. Jutta ging gestern wegen der Prüfung voller Angst in die Uni(versität).
8. Sie hat ihren Geldbeutel gestern dummerweise im Freibad (liegen) gelassen.
9. Du hast mir gestern schon diese Geschichte erzählt.
10. Der Präsident hat gestern in Berlin seine Antrittsrede gehalten.
11. Die Busse fahren ab morgen wegen der Straßenbauarbeiten an unserer Wohnung vorbei.
12. Der Lehrer hat mir erst vorgestern das Ergebnis des Examens mitgeteilt / gesagt.
13. Die Firma hat gestern nicht dem Kunden die Waren geliefert.
14. Während Hans in der Hauptstadt war, ging er oft ins Theater.
15. Er gab / schenkte der Sekretärin einen Blumenstrauß zum Geburtstag.
16. Hat er es dir bewiesen?
17. Der Polizist hat sie ihm weggenommen.

191B

1. Bringen Sie mir bitte das Brathähnchen!
2. Darf ich es ihr abnehmen?
3. Eigentlich sollte man öfters Blut spenden.
4. Ich fahre jeden Tag mit der U-Bahn zur Arbeit.
5. Reichen Sie mir bitte das Salz!
6. Der Professor hat dir wegen seiner Krankheit noch keinen Brief geschrieben.
7. Ich habe vorgestern dummerweise meinen Regenschirm in der Straßenbahn vergessen.
8. Hast du mit ihr gestern auf der Party gesprochen?
9. Die Tante steckte dem Kind eine Tafel Schokolade zu.
10. Sie kam gegen 20 Uhr nervös ins Zimmer.

192A

1. Wir haben keine Pfirsiche gekauft.
2. Wenn ich dieses Problem nicht anpacke, dann packt es niemand an.
3. Sie müssen sich nicht nehr anstellen, sondern bekommen in der Regel eigene Termine.
4. Die Ergebnisse zeigen, daß kein Gerät frei von umweltbelastenden Stoffen ist.
5. Es wird nicht bekanntgegeben, wer mit wem fliegt.
6. Kinder dürfen nicht wie Maschinen behandelt werden.
7. Der Anwalt sagte, sein Mandant könne nicht von der Justiz / von den Gerichten verurteilt werden.
8. Aufträge gibt es genug, nur können die Abnehmer oft nicht zahlen.
9. Wir haben keine Angst vor Spinnen.
10. Diese Urkunde ist von keiner großen Bedeutung / ist nicht sehr wichtig.
11. Der Patient darf keinen Alkohol / keine alkoholischen Getränke trinken.
12. Obwohl unser Sohn Maschinenbau studiert, wird er nicht Ingenieur.
13. Der Priester fährt nicht Auto.
14. Die Reisekosten des Direktors (allein) betragen 6000 DM.
15. Diese Ausgabe ist so veraltet, daß sie nicht mehr gelesen wird.
16. Wegen der lauten Musik in der Diskothek habe ich letzte Nacht kaum geschlafen.

192B

1. Wie sich mittlerweile abzeichnet, scheint dieses Vorhaben nicht befriedigend lösbar zu sein.
2. Obwohl sich Wissenschaftler in den letzten Monaten intensiv mit diesen Fragen befaßt haben, ist Klarheit nicht in Sicht / ist keine Klarheit in Sicht.
3. Die SPD kann, was beeindruckendes Personal angeht, nicht aus dem Vollen schöpfen.
4. Das ist sein Eingeständnis, daß er die Wahl nicht nach dem Muster des Duells gewinnen kann.
5. Ein Zweikampf findet nicht statt, auch weil der Herausforderte sich nicht darauf einläßt.
6. In dieser Frage macht sich nicht beliebt, wer abseits steht.
7. Es blieb ihm nicht anders übrig.

8. Ich werde diese Diskussion nicht neu vom Zann brechen.
9. Zu mehr Klarheit haben diese Arbeiten nicht beitragen können.
10. Auch für den Verbraucher ist der Umgang mit Abfall nicht einfacher geworden.

Appendix I
Verb-finding table

Some verb forms are difficult to identify because they are very different from the infinitive – which is the form normally found in a dictionary. For example, *lief* in *er lief* (he ran) is very different from the infinitive *laufen* (to run). This table helps you identify verbs by listing the forms you are likely to come across in a text in the left-hand column and the infinitive in the right-hand column. Verbs which consist of a prefix + root verb (e.g. *versprechen, sitzenbleiben*) are not listed separately unless only one or two prefixes are possible, so look up the root verb (e.g. *versprach* under *sprach*).

The forms are classified according to tense or mood and according to person, using the following abbreviations:

pres.	present
imp.	imperfect
sub.	imperfect subjunctive (only the irregular forms are listed)
p.p.	past participle, leaving out the *ge-*
1	first person
2	second person
3	third person
pl.	plural

FORM IN TEXT	TENSE / MOOD / PERSON	INFINITIVE
aß	imp. 1, 3	*essen*
bäckt	pres. 3	*backen*
band	imp. 1, 3	*binden*
gebar	imp. 1, 3	*gebären*
barg	imp. 1, 3	*bergen*
barst	imp. 1, 3	*bersten*
bat	imp. 1, 3	*bitten*
begann	imp. 1, 3	*beginnen*
-beten	p.p.	*bitten*
bewog	imp. 1, 3	*bewegen*
gebiert	pres. 3	*gebären*
bin	pres. 1	*sein*
birgt	pres. 3	*bergen*

FORM IN TEXT	TENSE / MOOD / PERSON	INFINITIVE
birst	pres. 3	*bersten*
biß	imp. 1, 3	*beißen*
-bissen	p.p.	*beißen*
bist	pres. 2	*sein*
bläst	pres. 3	*blasen*
blich	imp. 1, 3	*bleichen*
-blichen	p.p.	*bleichen*
blieb	imp. 1, 3	*bleiben*
-blieben	p.p.	*bleiben*
blies	imp. 1, 3	*blasen*
bog	imp. 1, 3	*biegen*
-bogen	p.p.	*biegen*
-boren	p.p.	*gebären*
-borgen	p.p.	*bergen*
-borsten	p.p.	*bersten*
bot	imp. 1, 3	*bieten*
-boten	p.p.	*bieten*
brach	imp. 1, 3	*brechen*
-bracht	p.p.	*bringen*
brachte	imp. 1, 3	*bringen*
-brannt	p.p.	*brennen*
brannte	imp. 1, 3	*brennen*
brät	pres. 3	*braten*
bricht	pres. 3	*brechen*
briet	imp. 1, 3	*braten*
-brochen	p.p.	*brechen*
buk	imp. 1, 3	*backen*
-bunden	p.p.	*binden*
-dacht	p.p.	*denken*
dachte	imp. 1, 3	*denken*
verdarb	imp. 1, 3	*verderben*
darf	pres. 3	*dürfen*
deucht	pres. 3	*dünken*
deuchte	imp. 1, 3	*dünken*
gedieh	imp. 1, 3	*gedeihen*
-diehen	p.p.	*gedeihen*
verdirbt	pres. 3	*verderben*
verdorben	p.p.	*verderben*
drang	imp. 1, 3	*dringen*
drischt	pres. 3	*dreschen*
drosch	imp. 1, 3	*dreschen*
-droschen	p.p.	*dreschen*
verdroß	imp.1, 3	*verdrießen*
verdrossen	p.p.	*verdrießen*
-drungen	p.p.	*dringen*

FORM IN TEXT	TENSE / MOOD / PERSON	INFINITIVE
-dungen	p.p.	*dingen*
verdürbe	sub.3	*verderben*
-durft	p.p.	*dürfen*
durfte	imp. 1, 3	*dürfen*
befahl	imp. 1, 3	*befehlen*
empfahl	imp. 1, 3	*empfehlen*
fährt	pres. 3	*fahren*
fällt	imp. 1, 3	*fallen*
fand	pres. 3	*finden*
fängt	pres. 3	*fangen*
ficht	pres. 3	*fechten*
befiehlt	pres. 3	*befehlen*
empfiehlt	pres. 3	*empfehlen*
fiel	imp. 1, 3	*fallen*
fing	imp. 1, 3	*fangen*
flicht	pres. 3	*flechten*
flocht	imp. 1, 3	*flechten*
-flochten	p.p.	*flechten*
flog	imp. 1, 3	*fliegen*
-flogen	p.p.	*fliegen*
floh	imp. 1, 3	*fliehen*
-flohen	p.p.	*fliehen*
floß	imp. 1, 3	*fließen*
-flossen	p.p.	*fließen*
focht	imp. 1, 3	*fechten*
-fochten	p.p.	*fechten*
beföhle	sub. 1, 3	*befehlen*
empföhle	sub. 1, 3	*empfehlen*
befohlen	p.p.	*befehlen*
empfohlen	p.p.	*empfehlen*
fraß	imp. 1, 3	*fressen*
frißt	pres. 3	*fressen*
fror	imp. 1, 3	*frieren*
-froren	p.p.	*frieren*
fuhr	imp. 1, 3	*fahren*
-funden	p.p.	*finden*
gab	imp. 1, 3	*geben*
galt	imp. 1, 3	*gelten*
-gangen	p.p.	*gehen*
begann	imp. 1, 3	*beginnen*
vergaß	imp. 1, 3	*vergessen*
-gessen	p.p.	*essen*
gibt	pres. 3	*geben*
gilt	pres. 3	*gelten*
ging	imp. 1, 3	*gehen*

FORM IN TEXT	TENSE / MOOD / PERSON	INFINITIVE
vergißt	pres. 3	*vergessen*
glich	imp. 1, 3	*gleichen*
-glichen	p.p.	*gleichen*
glitt	imp. 1, 3	*gleiten*
-glitten	p.p.	*gleiten*
glomm	imp. 1, 3	*glimmen*
-glommen	p.p.	*glimmen*
-golten	p.p.	*gelten*
begönne	sub. 1, 3	*beginnen*
begonnen	p.p.	*beginnen*
gor	imp. 1, 3	*gären*
-goren	p.p.	*gären*
goß	imp. 1, 3	*gießen*
-gossen	p.p.	*gießen*
gräbt	pres. 3	*graben*
griff	imp. 1, 3	*greifen*
-griffen	p.p.	*greifen*
grub	imp. 1, 3	*graben*
half	imp. 1, 3	*helfen*
hält	pres, 3	*halten*
-hangen	p.p.	*hängen*
hast	pres. 2	*haben*
hat	pres. 3	*haben*
hatte	imp. 1, 3	*haben*
hieb	imp. 1, 3	*hauen*
hielt	imp. 1, 3	*halten*
hieß	imp. 1, 3	*heißen*
hilft	pres. 3	*helfen*
hing	imp. 1, 3	*hängen*
hob	imp. 1, 3	*heben*
-hoben	p.p.	*heben*
-holfen	p.p.	*helfen*
hub	imp. 1, 3	*heben*
hülfe	sub. 1, 3	*helfen*
ißt	pres. 3	*essen*
ist	pres. 3	*sein*
kam	imp. 1, 3	*kommen*
kann	pres. 1, 3	*können*
-kannt	p.p.	*kennen*
kannte	imp. 1, 3	*können*
klang	imp. 1, 3	*klingen*
klomm	imp. 1, 3	*klimmen*
-klommen	p.p.	*klimmen*
-klungen	p.p.	*klingen*
kniff	imp. 1, 3	*kneifen*

FORM IN TEXT	TENSE / MOOD / PERSON	INFINITIVE
-kniffen	p.p.	*kneifen*
-konnt	p.p.	*können*
konnte	imp. 1, 3	*können*
kor	imp. 1, 3	*kiesen / küren*
-kor	p.p.	*kiesen / küren*
kroch	imp. 1, 3	*kriechen*
-krochen	p.p.	*kriechen*
lädt	pres. 3	*laden*
lag	imp. 1, 3	*legen*
gelang	imp. 1, 3	*gelangen*
mißlang	imp. 1, 3	*mißlingen*
las	imp. 1, 3	*lesen*
läßt	pres. 3	*lassen*
läuft	pres. 3	*laufen*
-legen	p.p.	*legen*
lief	imp. 1, 3	*laufen*
lieh	imp. 1, 3	*leihen*
-liehen	p.p.	*leihen*
ließ	imp. 1, 3	*lassen*
liest	pres. 2, 3	*lesen*
erlischt	pres. 3	*erlöschen*
verlischt	pres. 3	*verlöschen*
litt	imp. 1, 3	*leiden*
-litten	p.p.	*leiden*
log	imp. 1, 3	*lügen*
-logen	p.p.	*lügen*
verlor	imp. 1, 3	*verlieren*
verloren	p.p.	*verlieren*
erlosch	imp. 1, 3	*erlöschen*
verlosch	imp. 1, 3	*verlöschen*
lud	imp. 1, 3	*laden*
-lungen	p.p.	*gelingen*
mißlungen	p.p.	*mißlingen*
mag	pres. 3	*mögen*
maß	imp. 1, 3	*messen*
mied	imp. 1, 3	*meiden*
-mieden	p.p.	*meiden*
mißt	pres. 2, 3	*messen*
-mocht	p.p.	*mögen*
muß	pres. 3	*müssen*
-mußt	p.p.	*müssen*
mußte	imp. 1, 3	*müssen*
nahm	imp. 1, 3	*nehmen*
-nannt	p.p.	*nennen*
nannte	imp. 1, 3	*nennen*

FORM IN TEXT	TENSE / MOOD / PERSON	INFINITIVE
-nas	p.p.	*genesen*
nimmt	pres. 3	*nehmen*
-nommen	p.p.	*nehmen*
genoß	imp. 1, 3	*genießen*
-nossen	p.p.	*genießen*
pfiff	imp. 1, 3	*pfeifen*
-pfiffen	p.p.	*pfeifen*
pries	imp. 1, 3	*preisen*
-priesen	p.p.	*preisen*
quillt	pres. 3	*quellen*
-quollen	p.p.	*quellen*
rang	imp. 1, 3	*ringen*
-rannt	p.p.	*rennen*
rannte	imp. 1, 3	*rannen*
rät	pres. 3	*raten*
rieb	imp. 1, 3	*reiben*
-rieben	p.p.	*reiben*
rief	imp. 1, 3	*rufen*
riet	imp. 1, 3	*raten*
riß	imp. 1, 3	*reißen*
-rissen	p.p.	*reißen*
ritt	imp. 1, 3	*reiten*
-ritten	p.p.	*reiten*
roch	imp. 1, 3	*riechen*
-rochen	p.p.	*riechen*
rönne	sub. 1, 3	*rinnen*
-ronnen	p.p.	*rinnen*
-rungen	p.p.	*ringen*
sah	imp. 1, 3	*sehen*
-sandt	p.p.	*senden*
sandte	imp. 1, 3	*senden*
sang	imp. 1, 3	*singen*
sank	imp. 1, 3	*sinken*
sann	imp. 1, 3	*sinnen*
saß	imp. 1, 3	*sitzen*
säuft	pres. 3	*saufen*
geschah	imp. 1, 3	*geschehen*
schalt	imp. 1, 3	*schelten*
schied	imp. 1, 3	*scheiden*
-schieden	p.p.	*scheiden*
geschieht	pres. 3	*geschehen*
schien	imp. 1, 3	*scheinen*
-schienen	p.p.	*scheinen*
schilt	pres. 3	*schelten*
schiß	imp. 1, 3	*scheißen*

FORM IN TEXT	TENSE / MOOD / PERSON	INFINITIVE
-schissen	p.p.	*scheißen*
schläft	pres. 3	*schlafen*
schlägt	pres. 3	*schlagen*
schlang	imp. 1, 3	*schlingen*
schlich	imp. 1, 3	*schleichen*
-schlichen	p.p.	*schleichen*
schlief	imp. 1, 3	*schlafen*
schliff	imp. 1, 3	*schleifen*
-schliffen	p.p.	*schleifen*
schliß	imp. 1, 3	*schleißen*
-schlissen	p.p.	*schleißen*
schloß	imp. 1, 3	*schließen*
-schlossen	p.p.	*schließen*
schlug	imp. 1, 3	*schlagen*
-schlungen	p.p.	*schlingen*
schmilzt	pres. 3	*schmelzen*
schmiß	imp. 1, 3	*schmeißen*
-schmissen	p.p.	*schmeißen*
schmolz	imp. 1, 3	*schmelzen*
-schmolzen	p.p.	*schmelzen*
schnitt	imp. 1, 3	*schneiden*
-schnitten	p.p.	*schneiden*
schnob	imp. 1, 3	*schnauben*
-schnoben	p.p.	*schnauben*
schob	imp. 1, 3	*schieben*
-schoben	p.p.	*schieben*
scholl	imp. 1, 3	*schallen*
-schollen	p.p.	*schallen*
-scholten	p.p.	*schelten*
schor	imp. 1, 3	*scheren*
-schoren	p.p.	*scheren*
schoß	imp. 1, 3	*schießen*
-schossen	p.p.	*schießen*
schrak	imp. 1, 3	*schrecken*
schrickt	pres. 3	*schrecken*
schrie	imp. 1, 3	*schreien*
schrieb	imp. 1, 3	*schreiben*
-schrieben	p.p.	*schreiben*
-schrien	p.p.	*schreien*
schritt	imp. 1, 3	*schreiten*
-schritten	p.p.	*schreiten*
-schrocken	p.p.	*schrecken*
schuf	imp. 1, 3	*schaffen*
-schunden	p.p.	*schinden*
schwamm	imp. 1, 3	*schwimmen*

FORM IN TEXT	TENSE / MOOD / PERSON	INFINITIVE
schwand	imp. 1, 3	*schwinden*
schwang	imp. 1, 3	*schwingen*
schwieg	imp. 1, 3	*schweigen*
-schwiegen	p.p.	*schweigen*
schwillt	pres. 3	*schwellen*
schwiert	pres. 3	*schwären*
schwoll	imp. 1, 3	*schwellen*
-schwollen	p.p.	*schwellen*
schwömme	sub. 1, 3	*schwimmen*
-schwommen	p.p.	*schwimmen*
schwor	imp. 1, 3	*schwören*
-schworen	p.p.	*schwören*
-schwunden	p.p.	*schwinden*
-schwungen	p.p.	*schwingen*
schwur	imp. 1, 3	*schwören*
seid (ihr)	pres. 2pl.	*sein*
-sessen	p.p.	*sitzen*
sieht	pres. 3	*sehen*
sind (wir, sie)	pres. 1pl., 3pl.	*sein*
soff	imp. 1, 3	*saufen*
-soffen	p.p.	*saufen*
sog	imp. 1, 3	*saugen*
-sogen	p.p.	*saugen*
sönne	sub. 1, 3	*sinnen*
-sonnen	p.p.	*sinnen*
sott	imp. 1, 3	*sieden*
-sotten	p.p.	*sieden*
spann	imp. 1, 3	*spinnen*
spie	imp. 1, 3	*speien*
-spien	p.p.	*speien*
spliß	imp. 1, 3	*spleißen*
-splissen	p.p.	*spleißen*
spönne	sub. 1, 3	*spinnen*
-sponnen	p.p.	*spinnen*
sprach	imp. 1, 3	*sprechen*
sprang	imp. 1, 3	*springen*
spricht	pres. 3	*sprechen*
-sprochen	p.p.	*sprechen*
sproß	imp. 1, 3	*sprießen*
-sprossen	p.p.	*sprießen*
-sprungen	p.p.	*springen*
stach	imp. 1, 3	*stechen*
stahl	imp. 1, 3	*stehlen*
stak	imp. 1, 3	*stecken*
stand	imp. 1, 3	*stehen*

FORM IN TEXT	TENSE / MOOD / PERSON	INFINITIVE
-standen	p.p.	*stehen*
stank	imp. 1, 3	*stinken*
starb	imp. 1, 3	*sterben*
sticht	pres. 3	*stechen*
stieg	imp. 1, 3	*steigen*
-stiegen	p.p.	*steigen*
stiehlt	pres. 3	*stehlen*
stieß	imp. 1, 3	*stoßen*
stirbt	pres. 3	*sterben*
stob	imp. 1, 3	*stieben*
-stoben	p.p.	*stieben*
-stochen	p.p.	*stechen*
-stohlen	p.p.	*stehlen*
-storben	p.p.	*sterben*
stößt	pres. 3	*stoßen*
strich	imp. 1, 3	*streichen*
-strichen	p.p.	*streichen*
stritt	imp. 1, 3	*streiten*
-stritten	p.p.	*streiten*
stünde	sub. 1, 3	*stehen*
-stunken	p.p.	*stinken*
stürbe	sub. 1, 3	*sterben*
-sungen	p.p.	*singen*
-sunken	p.p.	*sinken*
-tan	p.p.	*tun*
stak	imp. 1, 3	*stecken*
traf	imp. 1, 3	*treffen*
trieb	imp. 1, 3	*treiben*
-trieben	p.p.	*treiben*
trifft	pres. 3	*treffen*
tritt	pres. 3	*treten*
troff	imp. 1, 3	*triefen*
-troffen	p.p.	*treffen*
trog	imp.1, 3	*trügen*
-trogen	p.p.	*trügen*
trug	imp.1, 3	*tragen*
-trunken	p.p.	*trinken*
wächst	pres. 3	*wachsen*
wand	imp. 1, 3	*winden*
-wandt	p.p.	*wenden*
wandte	imp. 1, 3	*wenden*
gewann	imp. 1, 3	*gewinnen*
war	imp. 1, 3	*sein*
warb	imp. 1, 3	*werben*
ward	imp. 1, 3	*werden*

FORM IN TEXT	TENSE / MOOD / PERSON	INFINITIVE
warf	imp. 1, 3	*werfen*
wäscht	pres. 3	*waschen*
weiß	pres. 1, 3	*wissen*
gewesen	p.p.	*sein*
wich	imp. 1, 3	*weichen*
-wichen	p.p.	*weichen*
wies	imp. 1, 3	*weisen*
-wiesen	p.p.	*weisen*
will	pres. 3	*wollen*
wirbt	pres. 3	*werben*
wird	pres. 3	*werden*
wirft	pres. 3	*werfen*
wirst	pres. 2	*werden*
wob	imp. 1,3	*weben*
-woben	p.p.	*weben*
wog	imp. 1, 3	*wiegen / wägen*
-wogen	p.p.	*wiegen / wägen*
gewönne	sub. 1, 3	*gewinnen*
gewonnen	p.p.	*gewinnen*
-worben	p.p.	*werben*
worden	p.p.	*werden*
-worfen	p.p.	*werfen*
wrang	imp. 1, 3	*wringen*
-wrungen	p.p.	*wringen*
wuchs	imp. 1, 3	*wachsen*
-wunden	p.p.	*winden*
-wunken	p.p.	*winken*
würbe	sub. 1, 3	*werben*
wurde	imp. 1, 3	*werden*
würde	sub. 1, 3	*werden*
würfe	sub. 1, 3	*werfen*
wusch	imp. 1, 3	*waschen*
-wußt	p.p.	*wissen*
wußte	imp. 1, 3	*wissen*
zieh	imp. 1, 3	*ziehen*
-ziehen	p.p.	*ziehen*
zog	imp. 1, 3	*ziehen*
-zogen	p.p.	*ziehen*
zwang	imp. 1, 3	*zwingen*
-zwungen	p.p.	*zwingen*

Appendix II
List of irregular verbs

Listed below are the infinitive, the third person singular in the present tense and the imperfect tense and the past participle of the most common irregular verbs. Compound verbs are not listed separately. So, for example, for *beweisen* or *erweisen* look under *weisen*, for *erheben* look under *heben*, etc.

INFINITIVE	THIRD PERSON SINGULAR, PRESENT TENSE	THIRD PERSON SINGULAR, IMPERFECT TENSE	PAST PARTICIPLE	ENGLISH
backen	*bäckt*	*buk / backte*	*gebacken*	to bake
beginnen	*beginnt*	*begann*	*begonnen*	to begin
beissen	*beißt*	*biß*	*gebissen*	to bite
biegen	*biegt*	*bog*	*gebogen*	to bend
bieten	*bietet*	*bot*	*geboten*	to offer
binden	*bindet*	*band*	*gebunden*	to bind
bitten	*bittet*	*bat*	*gebeten*	to ask
blasen	*bläst*	*blies*	*geblasen*	to blow
bleiben	*bleibt*	*blieb*	*(ist) geblieben*	to stay
brechen	*bricht*	*brach*	*gebrochen*	to break
brennen	*brennt*	*brannte*	*gebrannt*	to burn
bringen	*bringt*	*brachte*	*gebracht*	to bring
denken	*denkt*	*dachte*	*gedacht*	to think
dürfen	*darf*	*durfte*	*gedurft*	to be allowed
essen	*ißt*	*aß*	*gegessen*	to eat
fahren	*fährt*	*fuhr*	*(ist) gefahren*	to go/drive
fallen	*fällt*	*fiel*	*(ist) gefallen*	to fall
fangen	*fängt*	*fing*	*gefangen*	to catch
finden	*findet*	*fand*	*gefunden*	to find
fliegen	*fliegt*	*flog*	*(ist) geflogen*	to fly
fliehen	*flieht*	*floh*	*(ist) geflohen*	to flee
fliessen	*fließt*	*floß*	*(ist) geflossen*	to flow
fressen	*frißt*	*fraß*	*gefressen*	to eat (of animals)

INFINITIVE	THIRD PERSON SINGULAR, PRESENT TENSE	THIRD PERSON SINGULAR, IMPERFECT TENSE	PAST PARTICIPLE	ENGLISH
frieren	*friert*	*fror*	*gefroren*	to freeze
geben	*gibt*	*gab*	*gegeben*	to give
gehen	*geht*	*ging*	*(ist) gegangen*	to go
gelten	*gilt*	*galt*	*gegolten*	to be valid
gewinnen	*gewinnt*	*gewann*	*gewonnen*	to win
graben	*gräbt*	*grub*	*gegraben*	to dig
greifen	*greift*	*griff*	*gegriffen*	to grasp
haben	*hat*	*hatte*	*gehabt*	to have
halten	*hält*	*hielt*	*gehalten*	to hold / stop
hängen	*hängt*	*hing*	*gehangen*	to hang (intransitive)
heißen	*heißt*	*hieß*	*gehießen*	to be called
helfen	*hilft*	*half*	*geholfen*	to help
kennen	*kennt*	*kannte*	*gekannt*	to know
kommen	*kommt*	*kam*	*(ist) gekommen*	to come
können	*kann*	*konnte*	*gekonnt*	can/to be able
lassen	*läßt*	*ließ*	*gelassen*	to let / leave
laufen	*läuft*	*lief*	*(ist) gelaufen*	to run
leiden	*leidet*	*litt*	*gelitten*	to suffer
leihen	*leiht*	*lieh*	*geliehen*	to loan
lesen	*liest*	*las*	*gelesen*	to read
liegen	*liegt*	*lag*	*gelegen*	to lie
messen	*mißt*	*maß*	*gemessen*	to measure
mögen	*mag*	*mochte*	*gemocht*	to like
müssen	*muß*	*mußte*	*gemußt*	must / to have to
nehmen	*nimmt*	*nahm*	*genommen*	to take
nennen	*nennt*	*nannte*	*genannt*	to name / call
raten	*rät*	*riet*	*geraten*	to advise / guess
reiten	*reitet*	*ritt*	*(ist) geritten*	to ride
rennen	*rennt*	*rannte*	*(ist) gerannt*	to run
riechen	*riecht*	*roch*	*gerochen*	to smell
saufenn	*säuft*	*soff*	*gesoffen*	to drink (of animals; also: slang)
scheinen	*scheint*	*schien*	*geschienen*	to shine/seem
schieben	*schiebt*	*schob*	*geschoben*	to push
schießen	*schießt*	*schoß*	*geschossen*	to shoot
schlafen	*schläft*	*schlief*	*geschlafen*	to sleep
schlagen	*schlägt*	*schlug*	*geschlagen*	to hit
schließen	*schließt*	*schloß*	*geschlossen*	to close
schneiden	*schneidet*	*schnitt*	*geschnitten*	to cut

INFINITIVE	THIRD PERSON SINGULAR, PRESENT TENSE	THIRD PERSON SINGULAR, IMPERFECT TENSE	PAST PARTICIPLE	ENGLISH
schreiben	*schreibt*	*schrieb*	*geschrieben*	to write
schreien	*schreit*	*schrie*	*geschrien*	to scream
schwimmen	*schwimmt*	*schwamm*	*(ist) geschwommen*	to swim
sehen	*sieht*	*sah*	*gesehen*	to see
sein	*ist*	*war*	*(ist) gewesen*	to be
senden	*sendet*	*sandte*	*gesandt*	to send
singen	*singt*	*sang*	*gesungen*	to sing
sinken	*sinkt*	*sank*	*(ist) gesunken*	to sink
sitzen	*sitzt*	*saß*	*gesessen*	to sit
sprechen	*spricht*	*sprach*	*gesprochen*	to talk / speak
springen	*springt*	*sprang*	*(ist)gesprungen*	to jump
stechen	*sticht*	*stach*	*gestochen*	to sting
stehen	*steht*	*stand*	*gestanden*	to stand
stehlen	*stiehlt*	*stahl*	*gestohlen*	to steal
steigen	*steigt*	*stieg*	*(ist) gestiegen*	to climb
sterben	*stirbt*	*starb*	*(ist) gestorben*	to die
stinken	*stinkt*	*stank*	*gestunken*	to stink
streichen	*streicht*	*strich*	*gestrichen*	to stroke / spread / paint
tragen	*trägt*	*trug*	*getragen*	to wear / carry
treffen	*trifft*	*traf*	*getroffen*	to meet
treiben	*treibt*	*trieb*	*getrieben*	to drive / push
treten	*tritt*	*trat*	*(ist) getreten*	to step
trinken	*trinkt*	*trank*	*getrunken*	to drink
tun	*tut*	*tat*	*getan*	to do
unterscheiden	*unterscheidet*	*unterschied*	*unterschieden*	to differentiate
verlieren	*verliert*	*verlor*	*verloren*	to lose
wachsen	*wächst*	*wuchs*	*(ist)gewachsen*	to grow
waschen	*wäscht*	*wusch*	*gewaschen*	to wash
weisen	*weist*	*wies*	*gewiesen*	to show/point
wenden	*wendet*	*wandte*	*gewandt*	to turn
werden	*wird*	*wurde*	*(ist) geworden*	to become
werfen	*wirft*	*warf*	*geworfen*	to throw
wiegen	*wiegt*	*wog*	*gewogen*	to weigh
wissen	*weiß*	*wußte*	*gewußt*	to know
wollen	*will*	*wollte*	*gewollt*	to want to
ziehen	*zieht*	*zog*	*gezogen*	to pull

Bibliography

If you want to follow up some of the areas covered in this book you may like to consult the reference works listed below.

Aktuell '95: Das Lexikon der Gegenwart, Harenberg Lexikon Verlag, Dortmund 1991

Anderson, B., and M. North: *Cassell Colloquial Handbook: German*, London 1992

Arnold, Roland, and Klaus Hansen: *Englische Phonetik*, VEB Verlag Enzyklopädie, Leipzig 1975; Lizenzausgabe Max Hueber Verlag, München 1978

Beile, Alice, and Werner Beile: *Sprechintentionen: Modelle 4*, Internationes 1980

Beile, Alice, and Werner Beile: *Themen und Meinungen im Für und Wider: Modelle 6*, Internationes 1983

Blass, Armin, and Wolf Friederich: *Englischer Wortschatz in Sachgruppen*, Hueber, München 1976, 1991

Bock, Ingrid, and Jürgen Kienzler: *Aufsatz: Tips und Techniken*, Schöningh, Paderborn 1983,

Bulitta, Erich, and Hildegard Bulitta: *Deutsche Sprache in Wortfeldern*, Don Bosco Verlag, München 1981

Cassell's German–English: English–German Dictionary, edited by H. T. Betteridge, London 1978

Collins German–English: English–German Dictionary, edited by Peter Terrell *et al.*, Glasgow 1980

Dodd, W. J. D., C. Eckhard-Black, J. M. Klapper, and R. Whittle: *A Modern German Grammar*, Routledge (in press)

Eckhard-Black, Christine: *Aktuelles aus Radio und Presse*, Macmillan Education Ltd, Basingstoke & London 1990

Eppert, Fanz: *Grammatik lernen und verstehen: Ein Grundkurs für Lerner der deutschen Sprache*, Klett, Stuttgart 1988

Everyday German Idioms, edited by J.P. Lupson, Stanley Thorne, Cheltenham 1987. (Parts borrowed for section 139.)

Everyman's English Pronouncing Dictionary, Dent & Sons Ltd, London 1977

Friederich, Wolf: *Moderne Deutsche Idiomatik*, Hueber, Ismaning 1976

Greenbaum, Sidney, and Randolph Quirk: *A Student's Grammar of the English Language*, Longman 1990

Hammer, A E.: *German Grammar and Usage*, Edward Arnold, London 1991, revised edition by Martin Durrell

Häublein, Gernot, and R. Jenkins: *Thematischer Grund- und Aufbauwortschatz Englisch*, Klett, Stuttgart 1991

Helbig, Gerhard, and Joachim Buscha: *Deutsche Grammatik: Ein Handbuch für den Ausländerunterricht*, VEB Verlag Enzyklopädie, Leipzig, 1984

Heringer, Hans Jürgen, *et al.*: *Syntax*, Fink, München 1980

Hueber, Hans-Georg: *Talk One's Head Off: Ein Loch in den Bauch reden und ihre deutschen* 'Opposite numbers', rororo Sprachen, Hamburg 1990

Kars, Jürgen, und Ulrich Häussermann: *Grundgrammatik Deutsch*, Diesterweg, Frankfurt 1989

Kunne, Michael, and Birgit Strube: *Kleines Wörterbuch des DDR Wortschatzes*, Edelmann, Düsseldorf 1981

Langenscheidt Jiffy Phrasebook: German, 1986

Luscher, Renate, and Roland Schäpers: *Deutsch 2000. A Grammer of Contemporary German*, Hueber München 1976

The Oxford Duden German Dictionary: edited by W. Scholze-Stubenknecht and J. B. Sykes, Clarendon Press, Oxford 1990

Pascoe, Graham, and Henriette Pascoe: *Sprachfallen im Englischen. Wörterbuch der falschen Freunde*, Hueber, München 1985.

Rittendorf, Michael, Jochen Schäfer and Heipe Weiss: *angesagt: scene deutsch: Ein Wörterbuch*, Extra Buch Verlag, Frankfurt 1983

Taylor, Ronald, and Walter Gottschalk: *A German–English Dictionary of Idioms*, Max Hueber, München 1973.

Index